THE PHILOSOPHY OF
PARAPSYCHOLOGY

PROCEEDINGS OF AN INTERNATIONAL CONFERENCE

HELD IN COPENHAGEN, DENMARK

AUGUST 25–27, 1976

THE PHILOSOPHY OF
PARAPSYCHOLOGY

PROCEEDINGS OF AN INTERNATIONAL CONFERENCE

HELD IN COPENHAGEN, DENMARK

AUGUST 25–27, 1976

Edited by

Betty Shapin and Lisette Coly

PARAPSYCHOLOGY FOUNDATION, INC.

NEW YORK, N.Y.

ISBN 0-912328-29-0
Library of Congress Catalog Number: 77-75663

Manufactured in the United States of America

The opinions expressed herein are those of the individual participants and do not represent the viewpoints of the editors nor of the Parapsychology Foundation, Inc.

PARTICIPANTS

John Beloff · University of Edinburgh
Scotland, U.K.

Hans Bender · Institut für Grenzgebiete der Psychologie
und Psychohygiene
Freiburg, West Germany

Frederick C. Dommeyer · San Jose State University
San Jose, California, U.S.A.

Hoyt L. Edge · Rollins College
Winter Park, Florida, U.S.A.

Rolf Ejvegaard · Västertorp Junior College
Stockholm, Sweden

Peter A. French · University of Minnesota
Morris, Minnesota, U.S.A.

Renée Haynes · Society for Psychical Research
London, England

Pierre Janin · Epernon, France

Lawrence LeShan · New York, N.Y., U.S.A.

Seymour H. Mauskopf · Duke University
Durham, North Carolina, U.S.A.

J. Fraser Nicol · Lexington, Massachusetts, U.S.A.

Terence Penelhum · University of Calgary
Alberta, Canada

Emilio Servadio · Psychoanalytic Center of Rome, Italy

Rex G. Stanford · Center for Parapsychological Research
Austin, Texas, U.S.A.

Shivesh C. Thakur · University of Surrey
Guildford, England

OBSERVERS

Louis Bélanger	University of Montreal, Canada
Heinz C. Berendt	Israel Parapsychology Society Jerusalem, Israel
Kaare Claubewitz	University of Copenhagen, Denmark
William E. Cox	Foundation for Research on the Nature of Man Durham, North Carolina, U.S.A.
Douglas Dean	Newark College of Engineering New Jersey, U.S.A.
Elmar R. Gruber	Institut fur Grenzgebiete der Psychologie und Psychohygiene Freiburg, West Germany
Scott Hill	H. C. Orsted Institute University of Copenhagen, Denmark
Martin Johnson	Parapsychology Laboratory State University of Utrecht, Holland
Klaus Kornwachs	Institute fur Grenzgebiete der Psychologie und Psychohygiene Freiburg, West Germany
H. Kromann Kristensen	Selskabet for Psykisk Forskning Copenhagen, Denmark
Richard Mattuck	H. C. Orsted Institute University of Copenhagen, Denmark
Peter Niehenke	Institut fur Grenzgebiete der Psychologie und Psychohygiene, Freiburg, West Germany
Poul Nissen	Copenhagen, Denmark

Peter Reinsholm	Copenhagen, Denmark
W. G. Roll	Psychical Research Foundation Durham, NorthCarolina, U.S.A.
Gerald Solfvin	Psychical Research Foundation Durham, North Carolina, U.S.A.
Anna Maria Turi	Rome, Italy
Elle Wesche	Selskabet for Psykisk Forskning Copenhagen, Denmark

PARAPSYCHOLOGY FOUNDATION, INC.

Eileen Coly	President
Allan Angoff	Chairman, Domestic and International Programs
Robert R. Coly	Administrative Secretary

CONTENTS

INTRODUCTION

ALLAN ANGOFF: Good morning, ladies and gentlemen, I am Allan Angoff of the Parapsychology Foundation. For the officers and trustees, I call to order this Twenty-fifth Annual International Conference of the Parapsychology Foundation. For the next three days we shall address ourselves to the theme, "The Philosophy of Parapsychology."

We have assembled in the city of Copenhagen where, fifty-five years ago, this very month—this very day, in fact as it happens—in August, 1921, the first meeting of the International Organization for Psychic Research Congresses was held. The general secretary of this pioneering group was Mr. Carl Vett, a distinguished Danish industrialist of this city, for many years a leading figure in the Danish Society for Psychical Research. Mr. Vett worked closely with the London Society for Psychical Research, and with American organizations in this field. And indeed, during the First World War, when Denmark was a neutral, with psychic researchers on both sides of that conflict, he somehow managed to keep in touch with everyone. He was successful beyond all expectations—so much so that he followed up the Copenhagen Conference with meetings he planned during the next fifteen years in Warsaw, Paris, Athens, and Oslo.

At the Copenhagen Conference, coming so soon after the end of the war, when national tempers even among scientists were tense, some did not even want to attend a meeting with their former enemies in war. Mr. Vett deliberately went to the writings of statesmen and scientists of the former warring nations, to cite them on psychical research. For Britain, he went way back to the Victorian Prime Minister, William Gladstone, who had said of psychic research, "I consider it the most important subject in the world today." Then he noted Pierre Curie of France had, shortly before his death, spoken of psychic research as the most important of the sciences. And from Germany, he presented these words of Arthur Schopenhauer: "Psychic phenomena are, at least from a philosophical standpoint, by far the most important of all facts in human experience. Therefore," continued Schopenhauer, "it is the duty of each scientist to bring himself to a fundamental knowledge of them."

Professor Charles Richet of France, then eighty years old, had been expected to preside at this first congress in Copenhagen fifty-five years ago, but illness did not permit this and he sent the following message: "Courage and energy are needed to oppose difficulties, but also the sarcasm and the disdain of all the enemies of free research. Do not let fear of such things embarrass you. The first duty of the scientist is to brave unpopularity, and to be in advance of an epoch means unpopularity. Do not cling to the clouds; confirm the facts—the facts with inexorable strength." That was Charles Richet of France.

Eileen Garrett, founder of this organization, the Parapsychology Foundation, was a warm friend of Carl Vett. She admired his international activities. When she established the Foundation twenty-five years ago, she continued, under the sponsorship of this new organization, the International Meetings begun by Mr. Vett. Eileen Garrett said, "Scientists were still isolated, and it was still essential to bring them together in international meetings such as this one in the Parapsychology Foundation series, so that, men and women from many lands could advance beyond an easy orthodoxy of thought and technique into the broader aspects of physics, chemistry, and biology, and to relate these fields of research to the human personality and the largely unknown extrasensory capacities it contains."

And so, ladies and gentlemen, we may well say that this meeting, this conference here in Copenhagen, carries on in a great tradition with which are associated Carl Vett, Eileen Garrett and their colleagues of those early pioneering congresses.

I'll pause for a moment now to introduce Mrs. Garrett's successor as president of the Foundation—Mrs. Eileen Coly.

EILEEN COLY: Ladies and gentlemen: It is a pleasure to welcome you all to this conference, and I am happy to also greet the many observers who have joined us this morning. We have a stimulating program ahead of us, so let us proceed without delay.

ARE PARAPSYCHOLOGISTS PARADIGMLESS IN PSILAND?

Rex G. Stanford

It has frequently been alleged that parapsychology, now almost one hundred years old, lacks any basic theory and is characterized by "dust-bowl empiricism." It is sometimes also said that we are at a preparadigmatic stage of our development, in Thomas Kuhn's sense of the term "paradigm."

Recently, however, things have begun to change in this regard, and we have found ourselves with models and theories (e.g., Schmidt, 1975b; Stanford, 1974a, 1974b) which, though they be at a relatively low level, are generating research and helping us to feel that something meaningful can be shaped out of the empirical dust which we find all around us. Perhaps most important, the workers in parapsychology now seem more willing and ready to conceptualize their findings.

Ironically, the very attempts to conceptualize these findings are making it evident that despite the apparent dry empiricism of parapsychology, our thinking and therefore our research have been very strongly guided by and, indeed, constrained by certain *preconceptions* about the nature of psi phenomena, preconceptions which have almost always remained just that, for they have very rarely been conceptually or empirically questioned. It is my intention in this paper to show that such preconceptions have existed and have strongly influenced the directions taken by research. It is also hoped that the specific nature of these preconceptions can be made clear and that we can begin to examine whether they should remain as our guiding precepts.

Parapsychology, as the name itself implies, has operated under a *psychobiological* model or paradigm (perhaps, in almost a Kuhnian sense of the latter word) for much of its existence. For the most part, it continues to do so, although troublesome questions are now being asked from some quarters, especially by the considerable number of physicists who have recently become interested in psi phenomena and who are not always terribly happy to say that what they are doing is "parapsychology." Let me explain why I think the term "psychobiological" appropriately describes our traditional assumptions.

First, consider the events called "extrasensory perception" or "ESP." It would seem that ESP has been assumed to be some particular form of sensitivity on the part of the organism which has appeared during the course of evolution and which may either be developing during the course of that evolution or may be gradually disappearing in its prominence as a survival mechanism. Such a view naturally puts an emphasis upon ESP as basically an information-receiving capacity and would seem to imply that in some sense either a specialized receptor or the brain and nervous system must have the capacity to receive and process such information. (The channel or specific means for the transfer of such information need not be specified in such a model and typically has not been speci-fied.) In such a view, extrasensory information is used like any other (i.e., sensory) information in guiding the activities of the organism. When applied to the problem of PK, such a view assumes that extrasensory information is used, albeit unconsciously, to guide the application of the unexplained PK force to the target system and thus to control the outcome. In other words, there is con-ceived to exist a feedback-control loop for the application of PK to the target system, the feedback being made possible by "unconscious" ESP. Thus, the psychobiological model of psi functions as a cybernetic model when applied to the PK situation.

Such a view of psi function has been largely responsible for the actual guidance of parapsychological research. Its impact is evident in the problems discussed by parapsychologists, by the emphases in the research, and in the actual terminology of the field. All too often one gets the impression that this model is simply accepted without conceptual or empirical question as the appropriate one, though there exist a few notable exceptions in the history of parapsychology.

This psychobiological perspective has led to much discussion of such problems as: How is psi ability spread throughout the phylo-genetic scale? Is psi being fostered, reduced, or eliminated by the processes governing evolution? The question of whether or not it is really doing *any* of these things, but may be something more basic than an evolved ability to handle information present in the environ-ment, seems very rarely considered.

Similarly, though no parapsychologist would claim that an ESP organ has been found, the question still receives discussion even though there is not a shred of evidence to support the claim that such a specialized organ exists. Evidence for such an organ would certainly constitute excellent support for a psychobiological model. The current surge of interest in the possibility that extrasensory function inheres primarily in the right hemisphere of the brain (in right-handed persons) may in part be based upon a felt need to localize the function of ESP within the organism. This need may derive from implicit acceptance of the psychobiological model.

It is probably from implicit acceptance of such a model that we so readily use terms like "ESP ability" in much the same sense that we use terms like "intellectual ability," "musical ability," etc. Perhaps even more germane, we use terms like "sensitive" in reference to a person. This seems to imply that our ESP tests measure basic extrasensory "sensitivity," which, obviously, they do not. In fact, we do not know what it means to speak of psi sensitivity. We do know what this means in the case of vision or hearing, for we know of an organ which responds to a certain form of energy. We can systematically vary the parameters of that form of energy and can measure resultant changes in response—thus, for instance, we measure auditory sensitivity.

In a related vein, we often use expressions such as "extra-sensory response to the target stimulus," terminology clearly borrowed from sensory and behavioristic psychology. This is in spite of the fact that there is no evidence that the analogue implied in such language is a valid one. In what sense does the extrasensory "target object" act as a "stimulus" and thus "stimulate" the subject?

The *Journal of Parapsychology* regularly defines psi (in its glossary) as "a general term to identify a person's *extrasensorimotor* [my emphasis] communication with the environment." In J. B. Rhine's writing he has considered psi as a nonphysical energy which has two "sides" or functions, one (ESP) a perceptive or receptive one, the other (PK) a responsive, active one which performs work on the environment. Thus ESP and PK are nonphysical analogues of sensory perception and motor action, respectively. One may be inclined to ask, "Is there any other way to think of them?" Yes, there is, but it has rarely occurred to parapsychological researchers to do so. Later one such possibility will be considered.

The basic terms of our field reflect this strong psychobiological model. The term "parapsychology" itself we have already noted reflects this bias; "extrasensory perception" means "perception without the aid of the senses"; "clairvoyance" literally means "clear seeing"; "precognition" means "knowledge beforehand"; "telepathy" literally means "feeling at a distance," or, colloquially, "reading a mind"; and "psychokinesis" literally means "motion produced by the mind" or, colloquially, "mind over matter." Thus, some of the terms simply treat "ESP" as analogous to sensory response or to other cognitive functions known to psychologists. The concept of "psychokinesis" clearly suggests the active influence of a "mind," whatever that may be, on matter, and the term "psychokinesis" itself suggests the influence is upon the motion of matter, a rather manipulative concept.

The purpose of the present discussion is not to question the usefulness of such terms, but to point out that they seem to reflect a psychobiological model. This is perfectly understandable, given the history of this field, but, as we shall see below, some of the implications of such terms may be misleading or at least should not be taken for granted. It is important to make explicit what is usually implicit, to question any implicit assumptions, and to ask whether other formulations are at least equally reasonable.

Let us briefly consider in a bit more detail the typical psychobiological view of psychokinesis. That approach considers that the organism involved (the "subject," for instance) in a PK effect is the *cause* of the effect and this concept of cause is not really different from the sense in which a person is said to cause an automobile to turn left when he turns the steering wheel in that direction. This analogue is appropriate because many, and possibly the great majority, of parapsychologists accept the cybernetic view of PK discussed earlier, according to which the PK influence is guided by implicit extrasensory monitoring of the target system.

J. B. Rhine long ago proposed such extrasensory guidance for PK, and I adopted this proposal as a working hypothesis in a recent theoretical paper (Stanford, 1974b). Now I have some second thoughts about the matter. The reasons for these doubts will be given later. Here it is sufficient to note that despite this cybernetic assumption about PK function, PK subjects have not reported any awareness of guiding the PK operation (e.g., guiding the fall of dice or the operation of an electronic random event generator) through extrasensory monitoring. If extrasensory monitoring is the guiding force behind PK, it must be wholly unconscious in character. It must also operate with considerable facility, given that subjects often have no idea of what form of device controls the desired outcome in such tests and given that the device is often complex and beyond the normal comprehension of the subject. Permitting the assumption of extrasensory, cybernetic feedback-loop guidance for psychokinesis requires that we think of "ESP" as something very different from what we are taught about it by our traditional cognitive-perceptual, psychobiological model of extrasensory function.

An excellent example of how the psychobiological model is influencing contemporary psi research is the concept of "remote viewing" invoked by Targ and Puthoff in their studies of extrasensory response to distant targets. The same kind of thinking has deeply influenced much of the research on OBE's, in which the governing idea is a perceptual one. Such thinking is reminiscent of that which seems to underlie the term "extrasensory perception."

Parapsychological researchers and commentators have often tended to interpret anything less than a full-blown perceptual-cognitive ESP experience as a degraded form of ESP in which the psi-mediated information is somehow blocked from fully reaching consciousness. The assumption would seem to be that ESP is perceptual in its basic character and that it somehow struggles for expression in just that form, often, however, finding obstacles to expression in its "true" form. Louisa Rhine's writing on spontaneous cases provides a good example of such a position. Although such a position seems increasingly doubtful on the basis of experimental evidence, the psychobiological model forces us to think of extrasensory function as, if not basically perceptual, at least basically cognitive in function.

All parapsychologists will readily admit that not all ESP takes a perception-like form, for they are well aware that much ESP takes a nonperceptual cognitive form, such as "hunches" and the use of automatisms for the expression of psi-mediated information. In the latter case, although it would be inappropriate to speak of a "conscious cognition," the function is certainly cognitive in the sense that such cases do allow at least a partial reconstruction of the information "at the other end of the line," just as do the cases of perception-like ESP (e.g., a vivid dream of a distant event, a veridical "vision," a veridical auditory hallucination, etc.) and "hunches." This, however, is still not the whole story.

We have both anecdotal and experimental examples of events for which we would wish to use the term "ESP," but which do not really share this cognitive characteristic. (For an early review of such evidence, see Stanford, 1974a; for a more recent review, see Stanford, 1977.) In such instances what happens is that a response is made possible by psi which is instrumental in allowing the person to encounter a favorable event or to avoid an unfavorable one, yet there is nothing in such cases which suggests an actual perception or cognition of the event to which one is responding.

Such cases are thus termed nonperceptual, noncognitive examples of *psi-mediated instrumental response* (PMIR). As a concrete example, in some of the experimental work on nonperceptual-noncognitive PMIR subjects have shown a decreased reaction time in responding to a particular word on a word-association test when, unknown to them, their doing this increased their probability of experiencing a favorable event. Thus, subjects were simply responding in an unselfconscious, appropriate way to contingencies in their environment.

The net result of considerable work along these lines has been to suggest that what we find in *all* extrasensory response is, in very general terms, behavioral, imaginal, mnemonic, or other organismic activity which is *appropriate* in the context of events relevant to the concerns, dispositions, or needs of the organism, but which is happening out of the range of its sensory contact. Such response may take the perception-like or cognitive form only when the circumstances make this appropriate (e.g., the need consciously to experience the target object, as in many ESP experiments; or, in everyday life, in circumstances when only the development of a conscious idea about the target circumstances will have maximal adaptational value, as in preparing the person for a tragic loss of a friend). The circumstances under which the appropriate response (PMIR) might take the conscious, cognitive-perceptual form, as opposed to some other, are discussed at greater length in the paper describing the PMIR theory applied to extrasensory function (Stanford, 1974a).

Even if we adopt the terminology and concepts of the PMIR model, we are still within a psychobiological paradigm, at least as the PMIR model has been enunciated in published form (Stanford, 1974a; Stanford, 1974b). The model was developed from the perspective of the psychologist and/or the biologist. This has been true of almost everything done in parapsychology, empirically or conceptually. Some writers have even implicitly deprived physicists of the opportunity of saying anything about these phenomena by labeling them "nonphysical." Such has been the extent of the influence of psychobiological and dualistic thinking within this field.

Dualistic and psychobiological perspectives have, in fact, been a pretty happily married couple in most parapsychological quarters. This has led to a double dualism in much parapsychological thinking: mind-matter and living-nonliving dichotomies as basic principles. It is generally said, without any evidence, that psi is a function of living (as opposed to nonliving) systems, and one often gets the feeling that the basis of the distinction of living and nonliving is that the former has associated with it some element of "consciousness" (whatever that may be) and thus of that magical ingredient, "psyche," "spirit," or "vital something-or-other." It seems as though that ingredient either magically emerges as a function of evolution or that it is from the start a separate principle which somehow gets united with matter to produce a living being. Apparently because of this strong psychobiologistic and, often, dualistic bias, the question seldom ever gets asked whether "dumb matter" is really so "dumb" after all. Might not some form of responsiveness or "intelligence" exist as part of the very nature of our world? The psychobiologistic bias within parapsychology makes us consider only the possibility that "consciousness" and "intelligence" are the products of, or at least only find expression as a result of, evolution and causes us to ignore the possibility that evolution itself may in part be a function of some very interesting "intelligent" qualities inherent in the nature of the world.

At the level of day-to-day research activity, psychobiological thinking has strongly influenced and circumscribed the types of studies undertaken. This is evident from the strongly psychologistic orientation of almost all the work done in experimental parapsychology, from the reasons given for interest in work with lower species, and from the paucity of studies which examine *basic* questions about psi processes (i.e., about underlying mechanisms or processes as distinguished from purely psychological or biological questions).

It may well be that the prevalence of the psychobiological paradigm, quite stringently adhered to by our small in-group of psychologically- and biologically-oriented psi researchers, has placed empirical and conceptual blinders upon us which have prevented our seeing the possibilities for conceptualizing our phenomena in alternative, more basic fashions and has caused us to ignore certain features of our own data which may call into question that very paradigm.

It is quite remarkable that something resembling a Kuhnian paradigm should exist in a developmentally young science which many claim is "preparadigmatic." Let us not forget, however, that while we are developmentally young, we are in fact quite an old science, having had formal existence now for almost a century. Furthermore, parapsychology has been generally and sometimes systematically ignored by other disciplines such that their inputs and perspectives have had little influence upon us. Until quite recently we have largely been communicating with ourselves. The result has been the development, in this isolation, of something akin to a Kuhnian paradigm, and, true to form, this paradigm has seldom been questioned either empirically or conceptually by the active researchers in the field. We have too often seemed blind to alternative possibilities.

That we can at the moment begin to see some questioning of this psychobiological paradigm, some cracks in our conceptual walls, may be closely related to the fact that for the first time a large number of new scientists are actively becoming involved with this field, including more physical scientists than ever before. It may also be related to the fact that some systematic theorization is now being attempted by the very persons active in parapsychological research (e.g., Schmidt, 1975b; Stanford, 1974a, 1974b). Efforts at theorization require us to assess what we have learned and to consider how it may be understood. This can draw our attention to empirical generalizations which we have seldom sufficiently pondered, generalizations which pose serious questions for our previous implicit or explicit conceptualization. This seems to be what is happening. Permit me to record some of my own experience in this connection.

As noted earlier, when I prepared my paper on ESP as PMIR, I rejected the concept that ESP is intrinsically perceptual-cognitive and substituted the empirically more adequate notion that it is disposition-subserving. While I questioned a particular version of the psychobiological paradigm, I did not question the basic paradigm. The PMIR theory assumed that extrasensory information is obtained through some form of psi-scanning of the environment and that internal neuronal machinations process and integrate the extrasensory information such that PMIR is the ultimate result. It further assumed that extrasensory PMIR occurs through psi-mediated facilitation or release of otherwise ready or available appropriate response patterns in the brain (e.g., the release of memories or habits). The theory did not address itself to how the appropriate state of available brain activity is selected from among the various possibilities. Even though it was not reflected in that paper, I was at that time deeply interested in and concerned by this problem of selectivity.

Then I turned to applying the PMIR model to PK events (Stanford, 1974b). In the case of PK one had to invoke a form of implicit ESP to account for the application of the supposed PK force to the target system. It was precisely here that the psychobiological paradigm with its cybernetic implications became stretched almost to the breaking point. It seemed to require precise, moment-to-moment extrasensory monitoring combined with skillful computer-like computation to allow precise, effective application of the PK force. Perhaps in the case of the die-face experiments it implied an intuitive knowledge of kinetics! In the case of modern, complex electronic or quantum-based random event generators, often running at fast speeds, the cybernetic model seemed, if anything, even more troublesome. It was a hard pill to swallow, but I did so, for years of training in the psychobiological paradigm allowed me, initially, to think of no other possibility. I was just thinking like a good psychologist! I made a few reverential bows before the conceptual image of the Ultimate Integrative Instrument, the Brain, and went about my theory-building business trusting in its Almighty Power.

Nonetheless, in the process of writing the PMIR-PK paper, I had considered a fairly broad range of findings in the PK area, and I privately began to have some serious misgivings about the adequacy of the psychobiological model. But at that time I still did not have fully in focus the extent of the evidence which could bring into question the psychobiological model.

It was months later, while I was completing a very extensive review of the experimental PK literature for the *Handbook of Parapsychology*, that the full extent of that evidence did come into focus. (The aforementioned volume is edited by Benjamin Wolman and is to be published, as I currently understand it, in 1977, by Van Nostrand.) It was evident that PK could operate effectively when the subject was sensorially unaware of the PK target; indeed, results seemed at least as good as when the subject did know the target. Furthermore, considerable data suggested that the efficiency of PK is not reduced by increases in the complexity of the target system, by changes in the speed of target generation, or even by radical and sensorially unknown, moment-to-moment changes in the physical nature of the target system or in what direction this system must be influenced in order to produce success.

The inescapable fact was that deductions from the cybernetic model of PK would have led to opposite predictions about the results of the kinds of manipulations discussed earlier. The necessity of gathering ESP information about PK targets should reduce PK efficiency, even if the *only* problem were integrating this information with the PK effort, which seems unlikely. Similarly, changes in target-system complexity, target generation speed, whether known to the subject or not, should reduce efficiency, but especially so in the case in which the subject has no warning of their occurrence. This should also hold for sensorially unknown, radical, moment-to-moment changes in the nature of the physical target system or in the direction in which it must be influenced in order to produce success. Experimental evidence contradicted all these deductions from the traditional cybernetic model. True, it would not hurt to have more investigation of such findings and more efforts at replication. Nevertheless, what was so impressive here was that *all* the available evidence, evidence of diverse kinds, converged upon the conclusion that the cybernetic model had been falsified.

Many parapsychologists have eschewed theoretical thinking, except in terms of vague generalities which are not examined for their consequences in practice. Thus, even though experimental evidence contradicting the traditional paradigm has been mounting for decades, its theoretical ramifications have not been fully considered. In addition to the evidence from the PK work, there have been results from considerable ESP experimentation which lead toward the same conclusion. Foster, decades ago (1940), obtained ESP results for blind- and open-matching tests which were incompatible with the notion that ESP information, in the blind-matching situation, is separately gathered for key and target cards and then integrated, as would seem to be required by a psychobiological model. Numerous other ESP studies have shown that subjects' ignorance of many aspects of the target situation—including even the time at which targets were to be generated—did not deter success. Such studies seem generally to have had results as good as when subjects do have such information, even though studies have rarely been designed specifically to compare two or more such conditions.

Surely such evidence, derived from both PK and ESP work, provides at least a *prima facie* case for conceptually and empirically reopening the question of the appropriate underlying model for parapsychological research.

To be constructive, one must do more than critically examine past conceptualization. One must suggest new directions for our theorization and research. In a few moments I will outline my own preliminary efforts in this direction.

The awareness of the need to develop some new concepts to understand psi phenomena at the most basic level has been dawning on at least some researchers for some time now. For some time parapsychologists have discussed and wondered at a strange characteristic of psi processes, their "goal-oriented" character, as it is now termed. This term summarizes many of the findings discussed above. It refers to the fact that psi processes (both

ESP and PK) accomplish precisely what is needed in a given situation and do so in a way which seems uninfluenced by the complexities of the target situation or of the task *per se* (although performance may be influenced by subjects' perceptions of the "difficulty" of the task, if they know of the complexities). This goal-oriented character of psi, though still in need of refinement as a concept, must be given essentially a cornerstone status in any effort at building a theoretical edifice for psi phenomena. Helmut Schmidt, a leading PK researcher and psi theorist, has commented on this goal-oriented character by noting that experimental results like those summarized above suggest that "PK may not be properly understood in terms of some mechanism by which the mind interferes with the machine in some cleverly calculated way but that it may be more appropriate to see PK as a goal-oriented principle, one that aims successfully at a final event, no matter how intricate the intermediate steps" (Schmidt, 1974, p. 190).

To fully explore the extent to which such a principle controls psi operation, it is necessary to carefully eliminate contaminating psychological factors when one varies physical parameters in psi tasks. Thus, for instance, Schmidt has recently done many experiments in which subjects are blind as to the precise physical nature of the target system or how it is functioning. Many of Schmidt's contributions from such experiments are among the best evidence forcing a reconceptualization of PK processes and psi processes in general. Accordingly, Schmidt has recently developed his own theory of psi function (1975b). His theorization in some ways parallels my own, but differs on certain key points. (Compare Schmidt, 1975b, with my remarks below and with Stanford, 1977.) The differences of our theories can be resolved by future experimental research, for they make some divergent predictions. It is interesting that Schmidt, a theoretical physicist, should be doing a large part of the work which brings into question our traditional psychobiological paradigm. His recent work on time-displaced PK (Schmidt, 1975a, 1976) can be construed as further threatening our traditional paradigm, and I understand that it has caused considerable distress in certain parapsychological quarters.

What follows represents my own preliminary effort to reconceptualize psi phenomena. This effort is in need of much conceptual and empirical refinement. It is simply one possible starting point.

All psi phenomena are considered within this theoretical perspective as *conformance behavior*. Conformance behavior can, initially, best be understood in relation to the circumstances under which it occurs. For it to occur we need: (1) a *disposed system*, usually (at least in our past experimentation) an organism with a need, wish, or want of some kind; (2) *a source of incompletely determinate alternative states (or events)*, henceforth called for simplicity a random event generator (REG); and (3) circumstances such that outcomes from the REG control the probability that the disposed system will encounter an event favorable to its disposition. It is assumed that the world is built in such a way that under these circumstances the outcomes produced by the REG will be biased to favor the state(s) which will increase the probability of a disposition-favorable event. The name given the proposed phenomenon is *conformance behavior*. It describes the proposed order or biasing which will tend to develop out of randomness (or relative disorder) whenever the latter is contingently linked to the fate of a disposed (and therefore relatively highly ordered) system.

Since, according to this proposal, conformance behavior tends to occur in an REG with respect to the disposition of any system contingently linked to it, at some point in the development of this theory one or more rules will have to be specified as to how the final state of the REG will be determined with respect to all the disposed systems contingently linked to it. Presumably the final state will reflect a net resultant of the several state-related vectors or forces involved. The precise delineation of such a rule or rules must await further developments. With respect to a given disposed system, it is conceivable that the tendency toward conformance behavior in a contingently-linked REG will depend upon the magnitude of the disposition and the magnitude of the consequences, for that disposition, of a given alternative state which could be produced by that REG. Again, precise specification of these matters must await future developments.

It can immediately be seen how the theory of conformance behavior subsumes the events we have traditionally studied in the laboratory as PK. What may be less obvious is how it subsumes extrasensory events, so-called. If we consider, as seems very likely, that the nervous system or the brain, especially, is among other things a complex and sophisticated REG in the sense described above, then what we have traditionally termed "ESP" is precisely analogous to the outcome of a hidden-target PK experiment, i.e., one in which the REG is "willed" to encode hidden target material. (We have seen earlier that studies of the latter kind have been quite successful.) The only difference in the case of "ESP" is that the REG which shows conformance behavior is the brain. It shows such behavior because the fulfillment of the organism's disposition is contingently linked to the outputs of the brain's REG-like processes.

In conformance behavior, whether the precise specification of the desired or favorable event exists in some sense in one's own head (as in traditional PK tasks in which the subject knows the target) or is hidden and unknown to the subject (as in hidden-target PK or an ESP task) is irrelevant *in principle*. What is conceived as the cause of the REG's doing the "right" thing is that a specific REG outcome will bring about the favorable event; its production will actually result in that favorable event because of the contingent linkage of the disposed system and the REG. This concept of contingent linkage resulting in conformance behavior is the crucial one. No biasing of the REG will occur in its absence, but if the contingent linkage is present, then any complexities of the target situation are irrelevant in the sense noted earlier.

Such a perspective has the important advantage of economy, and it unifies the facts we have gathered over decades of experimental research. It fits in neatly with the growing body of evidence that so-called ESP works by biasing the brain (REG) to select favorable states from among those it has available on the basis of its past experience and that when such favorable states are relatively unavailable there is less "ESP." It accords very nicely with the massive amount of work on internal states and ESP performance, since what such studies basically show is that whenever the mentation of the organism is preoccupied with goal-directed or logical thinking or whenever the organism is attending to irrelevent stimuli no ESP is evident. The theory of conformance behavior suggests this is analogous to removing the baffles from a dice-throwing or ball-rolling PK machine, such that the state of the system is a highly determinate or nonrandom one. Experimental PK results, in fact, suggest that when dice have little opportunity to bounce or when balls roll without considerable interruption in their pathway, there is little or no evidence of a PK effect. (For a review of this, see Stanford, 1977.) This conception of psi neatly handles the diverse forms of "extrasensory response," not by assuming that ESP strives for perceptual expression, but that conformance behavior automatically favors the generation of the specific kinds of thoughts, behavior, etc. which will produce a favorable event. Since only on special occasions (as described earlier) is a perception-like mental picture of a target circumstance a favorable event, perception-mimicking

ESP is only a special case of conformance behavior in neural processes. This conceptualization also has no trouble with the growing evidence for the possibility that lower organisms have psi ability, including PK ability. A lower organism is a disposed system, and with the abandonment of the cybernetic view of PK, there is no reason why conformance behavior cannot occur in a REG which is contingently linked to that organism's dispositions. PK effects, if they are conformance behavior, are not mediated through cybernetic loops involving the organism's nervous system, so the complexity of that nervous system is not itself a barrier to the occurrence of PK.

One effect of this conceptualization is that it becomes improper to think of a PK subject as the "source" or "cause" of the effect, in the usual sense of those words, though this is not to say that conformance behavior is acausal in the sense that Carl Jung used that term in connection with the concept of synchronicity. In a parapsychological context the "usual sense" of the words "cause" and "source" is psychobiologically and cybernetically based and implies that the organism is literally *doing something to* the REG. Such language is not meaningful in the conformance behavior context. Causation in this theoretical construction does not arise from something the subject does, but from the relationship between the subject's disposition and a REG, the contingent relationship.

Numerous testable deductions could be derived from the premises of the theory. There is no opportunity to discuss them at this time.

This conceptualization opens up some heretofore unexplored questions. For instance, what limits shall be put upon the term "disposed system" as used in the theory? Are effective disposed systems found only among living organisms, or can dispositions be found among non-living systems which are involved in conformance behavior. The theory does not presently specify whether such dispositions exist among the less complex systems we call "nonliving," but it does encourage the exploration of this possibility. Indeed, it demands it, if we are to systematically explore the basic nature of psi processes. It similarly requires us to explore the possible role of organizational complexity (in the disposed system) in relation to the concept of conformance behavior. One wonders whether organizational complexity determines simply the number of effective dispositions which can be found, or whether it influences the possibility for or magnitude of conformance behavior. Thoughts such as these also open up questions about whether conformance behavior may actually play a role in the development and evolution of living systems.

One also cannot but wonder, if the concept of conformance behavior is valid, whether conformance behavior may play a role within our own brains in such matters as creative problem solving, memory retrieval, and perhaps even the control of internal states. Curiously, the very factors which seem to interfere with these purely internal operations are the ones which appear to interfere with psi function. This new conceptualization also strongly suggests that so-called active agent telepathy is possible under specific circumstances. In that case the REG is the brain of the other person.

This line of reasoning also calls for extensive research to delineate the generalizable characteristics of so-called "random event generators." Such research could tell us much about the fundamental nature of psi processes. It may be that in studying the characteristics of systems capable of conformance behavior (REGs) and of characteristics which make them more or less responsive in this respect, we will for the first time discover physical boundary conditions for psi function and physical lawfulness in its operation. The psycho-biological model may have hindered the discovery of physical lawfulness in psi phenomena by focusing interest upon whether there could be found evidence of an energy by which psi information could be transmitted across space. The assumption was, of course, that since ESP is perceptual in character, we should be able to find some form of energy transmitted to some form of receptive mechanism, just as in the case of the known senses. Then, in the failure of such an effort, it was proclaimed that ESP was "nonphysical." The more reasonable thing to do would have been to abandon the psychobiological model!

Once we break out of the paradigm which has enclosed our thinking for so many years, the vistas of research are considerably broadened. So far we might be said only to have made short excursions along the shores of psiland. It may prove to be a bigger and more surprising place than we have generally dared to imagine.

REFERENCES

[1] Foster, A. A. "Is ESP Diametric?" *Journal of Parapsychology*, 1940, *4*, 325–328.

[2] Schmidt, H. "Psychokinesis." In E. D. Mitchell et al., *Psychic Exploration: A Challenge for Science*. New York: Putnam's 1974. Pp. 179–193.

[3] Schmidt, H. "Observation of Subconscious PK Effects With and Without Time Displacement." In J. D. Morris, W. G. Roll, and R. L. Morris (Eds.), *Research in Parapsychology 1974*. Metuchen, N.J.: Scarecrow Press, 1975. Pp. 116–121. (a)

[4] Schmidt, H. "Toward a Mathematical Theory of Psi." *Journal of the American Society for Psychical Research*, 1975, *69*, 301–319. (b)

[5] Schmidt, H. "PK Experiment With Repeated, Time Displaced Feedback." In J. D. Morris, W. G. Roll, and R. L. Morris (Eds.), *Research in Parapsychology 1975*. Metuchen, N.J.: Scarecrow Press, 1976. Pp. 107–109.

[6] Stanford, R. G. "An Experimentally Testable Model for Spontaneous Psi Events. I. Extrasensory Events." *Journal of the American Society for Psychical Research*, 1974, *68*, 34–57. (a)

[7] Stanford, R. G. "An Experimentally Testable Model for Spontaneous Psi Events. II. Psychokinetic Events." *Journal of the American Society for Psychical Research*, 1974, *68*, 321–356 (b)

[8] Stanford, R. G. "Experimental Psychokinesis: A Review from Diverse Perspectives." In B. Wolman (Ed.), *Handbook of Parapsychology*. New York: Van Nostrand, 1977.

DISCUSSION

EDGE: I'm interested in your paper. I've written a second paper coming out of the one I'm going to give later, coming up with the theory that, I think, is fairly close to what you're saying now. I've had a problem, and I just want to see whether or not you think you have overcome it, in trying to specify what you call the disposed state in terms that themselves are not cybernetically based. That is, if one has a natural disposition to talk about dispositions in terms of one's normal psychological processes, and if we want to get away from the psychobiological model, it seems to me then that we'll have to try to define a state of disposition in some other way than what would be, I think, our normal disposition to do so. I think that perhaps you've gotten farther than I have on this problem.

STANFORD: I don't see it as a problem. Well, this may be somewhat of an oversimplification. One can partially operationalize what one means by disposition in a given situation in terms of the conduct of the system over time under specifiable circumstances, and that hasn't troubled me.

MATTUCK: I am very much interested in the model which you proposed, because it sounds like a qualitative version of the quantitative theory formulated by Evan Harris Walker, a physicist. You have the two basic ingredients which are present in Walker's theory. One is the existence of what you call a random number generator or some random states which the mind of the medium can choose from, and the other is what you call the disposed system, that is, the mind which desires to influence something. In terms of PK, this would be the desire to influence the external system, which is characterized in terms of random states. Now, in Walker's theory, the wish or disposal of the mind to influence this external system is described in terms of hidden variables. In other words, what the mind does is to adjust its hidden variables to express its wish and the hidden variables then select the appropriate random state which is available in the external system. Hence I think there is a one-to-one correspondence between your two points and those in Walker's theory. However, there's one thing which I miss in your presentation and that is the concept of *information,* which is central to Walker's theory; i.e., the selection of random states via hidden variables involves transmission and processing of information. I was wondering if you care to comment on your feelings about information and what sort of role it will play in your theory.

STANFORD: In my paper, in discussing the concept of information, I wasn't referring to the very generalizable concept of information, but referring more to a psychological notion. Specifically, this model does not allow the concept of information transmission in the sense of transmission across space or anything of this sort. But it certainly is construable that this very preliminary concept deals with information in that I referred to changes in the ordering of a relatively unordered system in relationship to a relatively ordered system with the disposition, and if that is information, then that's what we're dealing with. But I don't see that as the crucial construct. Yes, I feel that one can call that information in an abstract kind of way. It seems to me that what is of central importance here is that this is a disposition subserving function and that we need to get away from the notion that ESP is a kind of information processing factor in any fundamental sense.

BELOFF: In view of your rejection of what you call your psychobiological model, I wonder if you could enlarge on how you conceive the ordinary processes of perception. By that, I mean, do you take some sort of epiphenomenal view of perception and simply attribute it to the natural workings of the brain, or do you allow for some kind of psi element in normal perception? In other words, is there something like the mind scanning the processes of the brain and somehow making sense of them and raising them into consciousness, a dualistic model of the mind/brain relationship. So much of what you've been saying accords very well with my views of ESP and PK, but I would like to know how you want to relate psi with normal cognitive processes.

STANFORD: I did state in the paper that we ought to consider the possibility that functions such as memory and creativity may involve some conformance behavior in the neurons connected with them. Indeed, I left out, because of lack of time, the statement that there are some rather curious parallels between the factors that block and facilitate such things as memory retrieval and creativity which parallel some of the things we think we're learning about effective psychological states relating to PK performance. I am certainly very open to the possibility that psi factors may be involved in normal cognition and perhaps perception. How one is to interpret that is another question. Personally, I prefer to stay away from the dualistic interpretation—because I feel it gets us into some other kinds of problems and I would describe this as a non-dualistic interpretation of psi.

PENELHUM: You spoke once or twice about difficulties in the understanding of psychokinetic phenomena as causal processes. You seem to find this difficult. Can you explain again for me how it is that the model you're proposing avoids construing PK phenomena causally?

STANFORD: When I said in the paper that I wasn't applying causation to PK phenomena, I was specifically referring to a particular view of causation, namely, the notion of a kind of cybernetic guidance by means of which some calculated effort was applied to the system under a feedback loop guidance. That's one kind of causation. I consider that my own theory is, in a sense, a causal theory and would not identify it with the synchronistic view, which I think lacks the kind of explanatory value and testability that this kind of model should have.

ON THE POSSIBILITY OF A CAUSAL THEORY OF EXTRASENSORY PERCEPTUAL KNOWLEDGE

PETER A. FRENCH

Philosophers viewing the discoveries of parapsychological research are confronted with a seemingly unending array of intriguing issues. Many of the great concerns of philosophy find reflection in the theoretical aspects of parapsychology. In my book, *Philosophers in Wonderland*, I argue that the very conceptual groundwork of shared certainties on which our scientific researches, not to mention our daily more mundane endeavors, are based is shaken by many of the purported findings of parapsychology. Nevertheless, there are certain areas of concern where neither philosophers nor parapsychologists seem to have provided much help for one another. In fact, popular though faulty philosophical theories have inflicted a distorted vision of their own subject matter on parapsychologists too willing to accept the standard epistemological "line." I am, in particular, concerned with the proper way to treat extrasensory perceptual knowledge claims—claims to know something made by subjects on the basis of ESP experience. I shall suggest that the popular account of what it is to know something is not plausible, nor is the equally popular account of what is known when someone does know something, and I shall provide reasons to support a rather nontraditional view on both issues. My hope is that adoption of the epistemological position of this paper will lead to an avoidance of the predilection of both parapsychologists and their critics to characterize ESP as a variety of guesswork and consequently as no reliable source of knowledge.

One of the truly great problems that is peculiar to the enterprise of philosophy is that of trying to determine what knowledge is. The problem can be traced to the very origins of reflective thought. Plato, for example, gives the question a thorough examination in what is probably his greatest philosophical dialogue, the *Theaetetus*. In that work, he discusses a certain solution to the problem that has, in a new guise, in years since been widely accepted: to know something is to have a justified true belief about that something. Plato, of course, did not recommend this theory. Plato held that knowledge involves no kind of belief at all. The Platonic alternative has been thought, however, to be less than useful by most modern epistemologists. The "knowledge as justified true belief" theory (hereafter "JTB") in this century found clear statement in the words of A. J. Ayer. He writes: "The necessary and sufficient conditions for knowing that something is the case are first that what one is said to know be true, secondly that one be sure of it and thirdly that one should have the right to be sure."[1] Ayer goes on to talk of the ways the "right to be sure" is earned, but that will not be of importance at this time.

Let us, for reasons of clarity, state JTB somewhat schematically as: S knows that P if and only if (1) P is true; (2) S believes or is sure that P (is true); and (3) S is justified in believing (has the right to be sure) that P (is true).

On this interpretation of what knowledge is, the door on ESP as a knowledge source is slammed abruptly shut. Purported ESP cases cannot, it is often argued, satisfy condition (3). It is generally maintained that the holding of a belief that P is true cannot be justified if the only claim the subject can make in support of his having that belief is a feeling that P has to be so. Conceptual analyses of ESP have, by and large, identified it with guesswork and are supported in so doing by the JTB. Antony Flew's[2] masterful criticism of Rhine's accounts of ESP is a clear case in point. Unfortunately, many of those sincerely interested in the possibility that ESP might be a source of knowledge, including Rhine, have adopted some version of the JTB and have thereby fallen into the conceptual quagmire of trying to equate what can only be called guesswork with good reasons to believe that P is true. It is most disappointing that defenders of parapsychology have generally felt so bound to the JTB that a frontal attack could not have been mounted on those critics of parapsychology who have argued that its subject matter is but the phenomenon of lucky guessing. The moral is that as long as one holds JTB, ESP can be treated as nothing but guesswork.

Recent literature in epistemology, however, provides evidence that the death blow has been dealt to the JTB—not, interestingly, by the Platonists who have always told us it was a circular theory—but by American analytic philosophers such as Edmund Gettier,[3] who has showed us that the conditions for knowledge set by JTB can be met when we would not want to say of someone that he knows that P.

I do not want to spend time recreating Gettier's examples. Quite the contrary, I shall grant that Gettier has administered the *coup de grace* to the JTB and will leave it to others to bury it once and for all in that "boot hill" reserved for old and fondly cherished theories. However, something must be offered in its stead. I propose to defend a version of what has been aptly called the "causal theory of knowledge." The stake in doing so, for our purposes, is that, in my view, that theory will accommodate the attempts to treat ESP as a knowledge source without leading us into an endless battle over what conditions are necessary to justify a belief.

The JTB demanded that if S knows that P, S must be able, at the time that "S knows that P" is true, to state his reasons, or his grounds, for believing that P. The causal theory (hereafter C) will make no such strong demand on S. What then will be a reasonable formulation of C? I adopt a version first formulated by Alvin Goldman[4] as a working definition: C = S knows that P if and only if the fact P is causally connected in an "appropriate" way with S's believing P. "Appropriately causal processes" usually are limited to perception, memory, or some demonstrable causal chains[5] or some combination of perception, memory, or a causal chain.

I make no pretense of the fact that this formulation is far from precise. Some might prefer a restatement of C to: C_1 = One cannot know that P (a sentence expressing P) is true, unless P must be used in a causal explanation of anyone's knowing that P is true. (This version admits a Platonic account of mathematical knowledge, but I will not discuss its virtues, etc. *vis à vis* C.) In order to indicate the value of adopting C or C_1 by parapsychologists, I first will have to clarify what it is that is known, what can be substituted for P in C or C_1, and second, I will offer some reasons for believing that the kinds of processes allowable as causally "appropriate" sources of knowledge do not *prima facie* exclude ESP.

Too little attention has been paid by epistemologists to the content, signified by "P," of a standard knowledge claim. Specifying what can stand in place of P in genuine cases provides further though indirect support for a causal account of knowledge. "P" is usually taken to represent a proposition. When we say we know something, what we know has been generally assumed to be propositional. "Proposition" is a technical term—meaning different things to different philosophers. Indeed, there is much dispute in the literature of the philosophies of logic and of language as to what a proposition actually is. A simple way, for our purposes, to understand what a proposition is, will be to hold that whatever a person is asserting

when he utters a declarative sentence is a proposition. Some philosophers are fond of saying that propositions are what such sentences
are about or what they state. P in our statement of C, then,
would be a symbolic replacement for a sentence or a significant
part of a sentence, a sentence token, that is either true or false.
But this traditional view of the content of knowledge obscures a very
important distinction, and hence is misleading in the examination
of knowledge claims.

Suppose that there are two sentence tokens ("a" and "b") that in
different ways express the same proposition, e.g., His cat is on the
mat, John Brown's pet is on the mat. Anyone, it would seem, who
knows "a" must also know "b" and vice versa, because "a" and "b"
express the same proposition (P). There is no limit to the way we
could expand this example. We may suppose that the same proposition can be expressed by 10 or 20 or 1000 different sentence tokens.
The standard theory is committed to the position that if anyone
knows one of those sentence tokens to be true he knows them all to be
true. It might be an entertaining diversion at this stage to set about
the task of providing exemplifications that clearly contradict the
expected results: cases in which someone can truthfully be said only to
know that one or some of the sentence tokens are true while being
quite ignorant of the truth value of the others. I will not embark on
such an enterprise, but I do believe it to be fruitful to do so.
We can expect, however, that the subject of our supposed case would
be regarded by traditional epistemologists as really not knowing
the sentence token he purports to know. This argument would likely
turn on the notion of justification. The subject simply could not be
justified in claiming to know "a," if he could not truthfully make an
equal claim about "b" through "n." This would amount to providing
a necessary condition of knowing: it must be true of the knower
that he knows all sentence tokens of the proposition he knows.

If we use the device of stating the same proposition in what gram-
marians call "cleft sentences," a very important element of what one
can be said to know will be revealed. Consider the sentence Pa,
"John murdered Bill." It can be rendered in cleft sentences: Pa_1 "It was
John who murdered Bill." Pa_2 "It was Bill who was murdered by
John." Pa_3 "What John did to Bill was murder him." We can represent
these cleft sentences similarly as: Pa_4 "*John* murdered Bill." Pa_5 "John
murdered *Bill*." Pa_6 "John *murdered* Bill." (where underlining or italics
is used to show stress or intonation). Pa_1-Pa_3 differ in terms of what
philosophers of language call presupposition. (Pa_4-Pa_6 differ in a like
manner.) In effect, what is asserted in each member of the triads

of cleft sentences is different, and what is presupposed is different. The assertive content of Pa_1 is different from that of Pa_3 even though they both express the same proposition, Pa.

In order to refer to these differences, I shall adopt a technical term originally borrowed from genetics, chemistry and physics by Fred Dretske.[6] I shall refer to Pa_1-Pa_6 as "propositional allomorphs" of Pa. In chemistry an allomorph is any variety of a substance that has more than one crystalline form but always the same chemical constitution. For our purposes here we will define a proposition as allomorphic if it has or can have more than one assertive content even though it has the same propositional content, and we shall refer to the various cleft sentences that express the different assertive contents of a proposition as its allomorphs.

Because its allomorphs all express the same proposition they must have the same logical consequences. If we are concerned about what they entail, whether or not they are true, etc., what is the case for one allomorph must be the case for them all. That is, it cannot be the case that Pa_1 is true and Pa_2 false or that Pa_2 implies P_b and Pa_3 implies not-P_b. Logic is not concerned with assertive content and hence when we deal from the logical point of view with allomorphs their differences are treated as insignificant; indeed, they are transparent. When, however, we put an allomorph of a proposition in a sentence that makes a knowledge claim, the allomorphic differences rise to the fore; they become opaque. It matters greatly whether the subject is claiming to know that it was John who murdered Bill or that it was Bill who was murdered by John. Entirely different sorts of things follow from possession of knowledge in the one case than do in the other. The first case presupposes that Bill has been murdered and makes the claim that John is the villain. The second assumes John to be a murderer and identifies his victim, or one of his victims. In the first case, we all know, let us say, or we will all stipulate that Bill is the victim, but who killed him? John. One of us advances the knowledge claim expressed by Pa_1 (and also incidently by Pa_4). In the second case we are not interested in who did it, we want to know to whom it was done: Bill.

S knows that P or S knows P is an incomplete representation of the content of a knowledge claim. P must be re-interpreted as some allomorph of P. In effect, knowing is sensitive to propositional allomorphic differences. The person that knows Pa_1 (It was John who murdered Bill) knows something different from the person who knows Pa_2 (It was Bill who was murdered by John) in one important respect, even granting that logically they both know the same proposition to be true. The sense of my position rests on the way we would establish that someone did know a certain allomorph to be the case but not another. Surely the evidence a person has for believing that it was John who murdered Bill will usually take for granted that it was Bill who was murdered and that he was *murdered*. In some cases, the evidence in support of the claim to know Pa_1 will be so very good that the knower will be warranted in saying that he also knows Pa_2 and Pa_3. But that need not usually or even often be the case. It may take quite different sorts of evidentiary data to support a knowledge claim in the case of each of the different allomorphs of a proposition. The point is that coming to know other allomorphs is not guaranteed by knowing one, and it certainly is not built into knowing one allomorph.

When we know something, what we know is not a proposition, or, more cautiously, not usually a proposition. It is a propositional allomorph, the sufficient support for which is not necessarily sufficient to support a claim to know another allomorph of the same proposition. Drawing this distinction between allomorphs of the same proposition invites a number of important conclusions. Most obviously, all allomorphically sensitive verbs take causal analyses. It is always appropriate to inquire about the causal path by which the subject came to known an allomorph, and consequently it is likely that the discovery that different causal processes may result in the knowing of different allomorphs of the same proposition will be made. I would not, however, wish to suggest that each allomorph is knowable by one and only one causal process. The same allomorph may be known through different processes. For example, the propositional allomorph "It was John Wilkes Booth who assassinated Lincoln" may be known by me through a combination of memory, perception of words on a page or a drawing, etc., and inference, while a member of the audience at Ford's Theatre on that fateful evening might have come to know the same allomorph primarily by perception of the actual event. More important, however, a failure to see that knowledge is not *per se* propositional but allomorphic tends to force epistemologists into systematic disregard of alternative avenues of coming to know. Researchers must take care to establish what allomorph of what proposition a subject is claiming to know. The fact that he could not have, as far as we are aware, evidence to support a knowledge claim regarding the proposition seen from the logical point of view is not *prima facie* reason to dismiss his claim. The subject of an ESP experiment, if he knows anything at all, knows an allomorph of a proposition. Our first query must be to discover which allomorph and then to examine the possible causal routes by which knowledge of that allomorph may be acquired.

I have not, however, provided adequate argumentation that all allomorphically sensitive contexts are causal. To try to do so would be well beyond the purview of this paper. I do, however, want to indicate a good reason for thinking that they are. Propositional allomorphs must be about something, they must have some worldly counterpart that they describe. When one nominalizes propositional allomorphs, different noun phrases are obtained that refer to them as "allomorphic events."[7] Events, it would seem, may divide into their allomorphs just as propositions do. Dretske writes: "To refer to an event is to refer to something which occurs at a particular time, in a particular place, in a particular manner. A reference to the allomorphs of this event is a reference, not to the event which occurs at that time, in that place, and in that manner, but to its occurring at that time, in that place or in that manner."[8] For example: Lincoln's assassination's occurring at 10:00 p.m. on April 14, 1865 is not identical to Lincoln's assassination occurring in Ford's Theatre, nor are either of those identical to Lincoln's assassination's occurring by gunshot. This is not to say that each of these is a different event. There is the one event of Lincoln's assassination. He obviously was not assassinated more than once. It will matter in significant ways, as already suggested, which propositional allomorph is embedded in a knowledge claim and hence which allomorphic event is the cause of the subject's having a belief. The truth of the sentence "S knows that John murdered Bob" depends on which allomorph of "John murdered Bob" is being used in the sentence and then whether or not the corresponding allomorphic event caused S (in some appropriate way) to believe that propositional allomorph to be the case. The truth, then, of a knowledge claim is dependent on a causal relation between an allomorph event and a subject's belief regarding a propositional allomorph. The question for the researcher is which allomorphic event is causing S to have the belief. The various allomorphs of an event have different causal efficacy. "John's *murdering* Bob" leads to his eventual prosecution and life prison sentence. "John's murdering *Bob*" leads to the widowhood of Bob's wife. The fact that John *murdered* Bob is not what made his wife a widow — she would have been a widow had John accidentally killed Bob or killed him in war. John's murdering *Bob* is what made her a widow, that caused her unhappiness, not John's murdering. If a subject claims to know that John murdered Bob, the researcher has to discover whether it is *John's* murdering Bob or John's *murdering*

Bob or John's murdering *Bob* that is the cause of the subject's belief. Unless he does that he cannot determine not only what the subject claims to know, but whether or not the subject actually could know that. Changing the propositional allomorph in a knowledge claim context is tantamount to changing the causal claim being made about the subject.

I want now to say a few words in an attempt to make somewhat clearer the causal theory of knowledge that I am recommending and have assumed in the above before applying the foregoing to ESP knowledge claims. There are, as many of you are aware, a number of recent philosophical discussions of the notion of "cause." Since Hume so convincingly showed that our notion of cause has no corresponding impression, which meant for Hume that we could not find any cause *per se* in the empirical world, philosophers have sought to provide an acceptable alternative account of the idea of causation. Surely the idea of cause is at the very backbone of our conception of ourselves as persons (agents), let alone of our doing any kind of science. Three theories or definitions of what a cause is have current popularity. I will mention two of them but not discuss them. I will defend a third account. I will not, I hope, overburden you with argumentation for my view because it is not crucial to the argument of this paper. I do think that researchers, however, must settle the issue of what a cause is in order to fully understand knowledge claims.

Very briefly, John Stuart Mill[9] might have argued that X is a cause of E if and only if X and E actually occur and X is sufficient (*ceteris paribus*) for E. Ernest Nagel[10] argues for the competing definition, that X is a cause of E if and only if X and E actually occur and X is (*ceteris paribus*) necessary for E. Ingenious arguments, however, have been put forth to show the inadequacies of both of these definitions. Interestingly, both can be shown to lead to the same unacceptable consequence that "If fire causes some smoke, then Antarctica's being cold also causes some smoke."[11] There are also, as might be suspected, grave difficulties with the parenthetical *ceteris paribus* clause.

The causal view that I am suggesting is adopted in part from J. L. Mackie's analysis of statements that assert a singular causal sequence.[12] If X is a cause of E then X is an insufficient but necessary part of a condition that is unnecessary but sufficient for E at that time. In order to explain this definition let the event in question be Lincoln's assassination. Imagine that A stands for the political beliefs of John Wilkes Booth, that B stands for the play being presented at Ford's Theatre that attracted Lincoln's interest, C the lack of protection extended to Lincoln, D the location of the Presidential box, etc. (represented by F). In a rough fashion, we may say that the conjunction of the conditions A–F is a "minimal sufficient condition" of Lincoln's assassination. There certainly are a number of other conceivable "minimal sufficient conditions" that might have resulted in Lincoln's assassination. G will stand for the disjunction of all other conceivable sets of minimal sufficient conditions; then "ABCDEF or G" is the necessary and sufficient condition of Lincoln's assassination. No conjunct of "ABCDEF" and none of the conjuncts of all of the disjuncts of G is a sufficient condition, but each is what Mackie called an INUS condition[13] of Lincoln's assassination. If any conjunct of "ABCDEF" were also a conjunct of every disjunct of G then that condition itself would be a necessary condition for the assassination. "A was the cause of Lincoln's assassination" we should understand as the conjunctive assertion that: 1) A is at least an INUS condition of the assassination; 2) A was present at the time of the assassination; 3) All conditions other than A in a set containing A that comprise a minimal sufficient condition of the assassination were also present; 4) every disjunct of G that does not contain A as a conjunct was not present at the time of Lincoln's assassination. When we say that for S to know that P it must be the case that the allomorphic event Pa_n caused the belief that P in S, we are saying that the allomorphic event Pa_n is at least an INUS condition of S's having the belief that P, that that allomorphic event was present, etc. (conditions 1–4). In other words, a knowledge claim is an assertion about the existence of certain condition(s) at the time the subject has a belief. If the condition(s) was not present, the subject cannot be truthfully said to know. The program for researchers would then be to clarify what propositional allomorph is the object of the knowledge claim and verify that the corresponding allomorphic event was present and was an insufficient but necessary part of a set of minimal conditions that is unnecessary but sufficient for the presence of the belief that the propositional allomorph is the case.

This may appear a very complicated way of saying that we need to discover that a particular allomorphic event was the cause of a belief by focusing on the conditions present at the time the subject came to have that belief. In large measure that is what I am recommending, but the INUS condition account of "cause" allows us to avoid concern over identifying the allomorphic event as the sole condition for the belief. It need only be a necessary part of a set of conditions which taken as a whole are sufficient for having the belief. Perhaps alone it is not sufficient to generate the belief. I would like to suggest how that might be the case, but I am afraid the example would take us further afield. Instead, let it suffice to say that in many cases the allomorphic event's occurrence will not in itself constitute a minimal condition of the belief, that other conditions will be necessary conjuncts to it, and that producing insufficient evidence that the set was present will lead people to unjustly criticize the subject's knowledge claim.

We need only comment on the idea of "appropriate" causal "ways" used in our original definition of the causal theory of knowledge. Traditionally, as earlier mentioned, perception has been credited as such a "way." Perception is itself a causal notion, in that understanding what it is to say "X sees something" involves identifying the presence of the object as at least an INUS condition of the having of the visual image. Memory is another "way." Our account of what it is to know allows, however, that any other process productive of a minimal set of conditions for a belief to be present can result in a justifiable knowledge claim. The onus on the researcher of a knowledge claim lies not on eliciting from the subject his reasons or grounds for making the claim but on reconstructing the situation in terms of the conditions present at the time the subject claimed to know some propositional allomorph to be the case. I do not exclude the possibility that the knowledge of the propositional allomorph may be derived for the subject inferentially, though I have not discussed such routes. I would, however, insist that some non-inferential causal claim must be discoverable in every true inferential knowledge claim. In other words, some causal process must be identifiable in the path from the occurrence of the allomorphic event to the true claim of the subject to know that the corresponding propositional allomorph is the case.

My conclusion shall be an attempt to apply the foregoing analysis to the problem of whether ESP is a knowledge source. Two points stand out: (1) that nothing in my analysis of a knowledge claim excludes ESP as an appropriate causal process; (2) that my account opens, I hope, important doors to seeing how ESP cases should be treated. I am not a parapsychologist. I do not do research with ESP subjects. I cannot, then, provide data for your consideration. What I hope to do, however, is to suggest what kind of data ought to be collected and how it ought to be collated. The fact that there is a disparity between what I suggest and the famous examples of such data gathering in the past[14] may hopefully indicate why I think the account herein could provide the philosophical basis for further investigation.

In the first place, to my knowledge, no parapsychology researcher has cared much about the content of the ESP claim he is recording. Unless he does have such a concern, however, as I have shown, he is a captive of the misconception that all knowledge is propositional. When attention is paid to propositional allomorphic differences, the researcher will be able to draw distinctions between what the subject is actually claiming to know and what is merely assumed or presuppositional about his claim. The fact that the subject may have poor grounds for his presupposition is irrelevant to an evaluation of his knowledge claim. Secondly, heeding allomorphic distinctions all but forces the researcher to investigate the allomorphic differences in events. This, I suppose, amounts to coming to see the world in many different ways. When we regard events not as one dimensional but as "aspectional" we have a significant clue as to how the belief that Pa can arise despite the fact that the subject would not assent to or would be uncomfortable with ascribing to himself the belief that, e.g., Pa_2. The explanation is the causal one: the allomorph of event P referred to by Pa_1 and not that referred to by Pa_2 was a cause of the subject's belief. Finally, by treating "cause" as "at least an INUS condition that was present" we overcome the difficulty of showing that a single stimulus or condition had to be present for a subject to know something. Parapsychologists ought to concentrate on discerning the contents of the set of conditions sufficient for a knowledge claim to be justified and then investigate whether or not they were actually present. Statistical summaries of hits and misses cannot in the end supplant such an investigation. In fact, the old idea that such statistical data is relevant is a grand illusion that ultimately works against the parapsychologist's goals. At best such data suggests the identification with guesswork. As I have maintained, the notions of guesswork and knowledge are disparate. The best one can get with a guess is a correct one. A correct guess is not knowledge. On the other hand, if there are actual cases of ESP, we want to be able to say that ESP is knowledge. I do not pretend to have the data necessary to establish that ESP is a causal process of the appropriate sort: that it can be identified in actual cases with the presence (perhaps even the creation) of a set of minimal sufficient conditions for a belief that a certain propositional allomorph is the case. My hope in writing this paper is to interest serious parapsychologists in the investigation of "conditions research" in order to broaden the accepted list of "appropriate" ways by which persons come to know things. At the very least such investigations will not be open to the criticism of making a mountain out of a molehill, knowledge out of lucky guessing, justification of knowledge claims out of statistical summary reports. Someone, of course, once remarked that making a mountain of a molehill was no mean task, that it calls for all sorts of inventiveness and sometimes sheer magic. My proposal if taken as a guide will not render research any less of a task, but magic, mystery and the like will be ruled out of order from the start. Magicians know that there is a causal account for each and every trick in their repertoire.

REFERENCES

[1] Ayer, A. J., *The Problem of Knowledge* (Penguin Books, 1956), p. 35.
[2] Flew, Antony, "A New Name for Guesswork," *The Listener*, October 4, 1951.
[3] Gettier, Edmund, "Is Justified True Belief Knowledge?" *Analysis*, No. 23, 1963, p. 121–123.
[4] Goldman, Alvin, "A Causal Theory of Knowing," *The Journal of Philosophy* 64, 12 (June 22, 1967), p. 357–372.
[5] Goldman has carefully constructed a number of causal chains to provide examples. See *Ibid.*
[6] Dretske, Fred I., "Referring to Events," *Midwest Studies in Philosophy* Volume II, February, 1977 and "The Content of Knowledge" to appear in a collection of the papers read to the Philosophy Colloquium, University of Western Ontario, 1972.
[7] I also borrow this term from Dretske. See "Referring to Events."
[8] *Ibid.*
[9] Mill, John Stuart, *System of Logic* Book III, Chapter V, 1879.
[10] Nagel, Ernest, *The Structure of Science* (Harcourt, Brace and World, 1961), pp. 559–560.
[11] See Sosa, Ernest, *Causation and Conditionals* (Oxford University Press, 1975), pp. 2–3.
[12] Mackie, J. L., "Causes and Conditions," *American Philosophical Quarterly* Vol. 2, 1965, pp. 245–264.
[13] *Ibid.*
[14] I have in mind, most obviously, the well-known work of J. B. Rhine and that of S. G. Soal.

DISCUSSION

DOMMEYER: I think I know, Dr. French, what you mean by allomorphs of a proposition, but I wonder, for one thing, why these allomorphs are not themselves propositions; in which case, these propositions would have allomorphs and the resulting propositions more allomorphs, and you'd run off into an infinite regress. Another thing I wondered, too, is how you know, given the truth of the proposition, that the allomorphs are true, unless you have a very logical implication with respect to these allomorphs coming from the original propositions. So I'm really puzzled about the nature of these allomorphs. First, it seems to be they run off into an infinite regress; and second, the question of their truth is raised for me. And, also, I wonder if you would ever get false allomorphs. Could an allomorphic fact cause a false allomorph? In which case, belief in it would clearly not be knowledge. These are some things that have occurred to me in light of your paper. I'm probably confused here, but I need clarification of that confusion.

FRENCH: I'll try to take those one at a time. In regard to the first question: "Why these allomorphs are not themselves propositions," what I'm doing is taking the notion of proposition as that which is expressed by a person when he states something in a standard way. There is no logical difference between allomorphs when one wants to talk about entailment, implication, etc. All the allomorphs of the same proposition will have the same logical outcome. I'm borrowing the term "allomorph" from chemistry; the same crystalline structure will be there but taking different forms. I find it useful for logical reasons to talk about propositions, but then when we're talking about the nature of what somebody is saying, it is useful to make the allomorphic distinctions. No, we're not going to reduce this to an infinite regress, although I would admit there are "N" number of possible allomorphs in a proposition. I'm not attempting to delimit that. I think that the notion of allomorphs would be useful not only in epistemology but in such things as moral philosophies—when one talks about advice. Advice-giving is causal in a sense, and allomorphic differences would arise there. When I tell someone to do something—exactly which allomorphic proposition am I telling him or am I expressing or asserting, etc? But again, the logical consequences are always going to be the same for every allomorphic proposition, so I don't think this gets into an infinite regress. I can't recall the second question.

DOMMEYER: False allomorphs.

FRENCH: Oh, yes. So far as the proposition is false, the allomorph would be false.

DOMMEYER: What about the allomorphic event that causes an allomorph, the causation that one might say is true—hallucinations, false propositions, false beliefs are a cause too.

FRENCH: If you want to talk about false beliefs being causes, there is no problem for my position. Insofar as epistemologists have no problem with that, I don't have any problem with that either. There is a problem—I'm not trying to hide it—the problem of illusion and so on, but I don't want to get into that problem.

THAKUR: I'm in general sympathy with the non-propositional

account of knowledge that you have in mind, because I believe some
such account, if it were found to be a satisfactory one, would be useful.
However, I do have a couple of comments to make. It is important to
make sure that your propositional allomorphs don't in fact happen to
be propositions themselves, because if they turn out to be the same,
you wouldn't achieve the results you're after. You can't have a non-
propositional account of knowledge if your propositional allomorphs
are in fact propositions disguised or initially introduced under some
other guise. I would like to put it to you in this way: if your propositional allomorphs are elements that can be doubted, disputed,
believed, stated, etc., and can be translated, for instance, then since
these are some of the very characteristics which make us adopt the
terminology of propositions they would seem to share those
features, and then your account won't be non-propositional. I would
add just one comment to this: I thought you took a bit of extra
mileage from Gettier's objections to the *Justified True Belief* account.
Now a colleague of mine has read a paper where precisely that same
treatment was given to some of the logical connectives used by
Gettier, either/or, for instance. If you make them context dependent
rather than seeing them as semantically fixed, then Gettier's objections
fall to the ground and knowledge as *Justified True Belief* stands un-
refuted. So, maybe, if you should be allowed to do this, perhaps
that treatment should be allowed, too.

FRENCH: I don't know whether I can comment on the latter point.
I'd be interested in seeing the paper. I find it very useful not to
talk about propositions in terms of knowledge claims and related
issues and to talk about propositions in terms of logic alone, for the
reasons I've already given. I didn't think I was taking Gettier
all that strongly, but perhaps I am. I'll have to give that some thought.

MAUSKOPF: I may return to perhaps a more simple level since I'm
not a philosopher but an historian. I was particularly struck, as an
historian, by your comments towards the end about the set of INUS
conditions, by which we know something happened. I think this is the
way most historians, whether we know it or not, intuitively think. We
really think in terms of sets of conditions, the sum of which, I gather,
you say may add up to the necessary and sufficient conditions but no
one of which can be separated off. How would you apply this? What
is your application of this to ESP knowledge? If I can just introduce
the dirty word "proposition" once again, may I assert the proposition that the symbol on an ESP card (that I cannot see) is a circle.
What would you, then, want to be able to do?

FRENCH: I would want to establish that that was an INUS condition—again, INUS being kind of a shortened way of saying an insufficient but necessary part of an unnecessary but sufficient condition. I'd first establish it was one of those conditions. Then the set of conditions that are minimal sufficient conditions for the occurrence of the belief or the knowledge claim would have to include it in that set. It may not be sufficient. If it's an INUS condition, it isn't in itself a sufficient condition. It's insufficient but a necessary part of a sufficient condition. So, having established that, we have the card as an INUS condition; we have a minimal sufficient set, and then we have to establish that indeed that set existed, was present at the time.

MAUSKOPF: Can I just pursue this for one minute? By the minimal conditions, then, do you mean—what shall I call them—experimental correlations for successful ESP, the guessing that parapsychologists have been searching for all these decades?

FRENCH: Well, if they have been searching, maybe they should continue. I'm not quite sure I understand your question.

MAUSKOPF: In other words, aside from the INUS condition, that is, of the circle on the card, what else do you mean? Do you mean essentially a theoretical framework that every science has, by which one can specify unforeseen conditions?

FRENCH: Specific conditions necessary for the production of that particular piece of information, and, hence, that set of conditions would in some way or other be drawing a causal path into the subject.

STANFORD: Toward the end of your talk, you brought up the topic of statistical methodology in parapsychology. I cannot claim, just from hearing your paper that I fully understood your discussion of that or other aspects, so the first thing for me to do is to try to get a clarification. You seemed to be criticizing the strongly statistical approach that parapsychologists make and, if I understood that correctly, the reason seemed to be that statistics (the way you interpreted it) are not giving us a real knowledge about ESP; that we, in effect, use statistics to put together such things as chance correspondences and genuine knowledge events or ESP, and we really do not stop and look at the event of knowing itself, because of our use of this statistical method. I can't help but feel a fondness for that notion, but it troubles me a great deal, because I think if we could do that, first of all, our research would cost a lot less, we might do away with our computers, we could do away with all error of measurement, etc. What do you do with the problem or error of measurement, which is precisely why we use our statistics? What concrete suggestion do you have as to how we could abandon statistics and make reliable general statements?

FRENCH: I'm not suggesting the total abandonment of statistics. What I am suggesting is that the assumption that statistics somehow replace conditions research leads to having an account not of knowledge, but of guessing. Though there is no equation between guessing and knowledge in my account, I wouldn't want to suggest that one do away totally with it, but I am suggesting alternative methods of research. Again, I'm not a researcher in parapsychology, but we're talking about knowledge claims in general. It seems to me that statistics would play a somewhat minor role, if you wanted to know whether or not someone knew something in history, for example or something of that sort.

LeSHAN: I'd like to differentiate the end of your paper from the main body of it. At the end you say that this program will reduce and remove the mystery and magic from the field. You know, I'd really hate to see that happen more than we've done it already. We have already removed so much of this that, like modern philosophy, I feel it's so dry that the slightest wind is about to blow it away; there's practically nothing left. You go on a little bit more and say, quite rightly: "It's no mean task to make a mountain out of a molehill." But I would point out that we, in this field, have been engaged successfully in a harder task—that since we gave up the name of "psychic researchers," and called ourselves "parapsychologists," we've been very successful in making a molehill out of a mountain, and that's harder!

KORNWACHS: I will give some impressions on your paper. I do not think your theory is too complicated; it's too simple, for its purpose. I have two objections. The contents of propositions depend not only on the possible classes of allomorphic events, but also on the contextual interpretation of the receiver, so the boundary conditions must be considered, because they influence the interpretation of given propositions, such as a wish or a warning, etc. That holds both for normal cognitive processes as for knowledge given by ESP. And my second objection is that the causality definition seems to me a very formal one, so I'm suspecting that you're going on to interchange the formal conditions of causality with the underlying reality of events which are claimed to be connected by causality.

FRENCH: I think what you talk about in your first comment, I subsume under the notion of presupposition. With your latter comment, I would agree, but I don't want to get into that at this point.

PENELHUM: I do have a slightly more radical worry about your argument. It seems to me you share a certain assumption with the philosophers you began by criticizing. You criticize those who adopt the definition of knowledge as *Justified True Belief* by saying that this excludes certain types of explanation of ESP phenomena, because it introduces certain tacit assumptions about what can be a justified mode of believing. And then you go on to refine the notion of knowledge in ways designed to avoid this difficulty, but you still retain a causal definition of knowledge. Now this seems to me to have a very difficult consequence. That is, whatever causal conditions you finally end up by specifying, you cannot know that someone knows that P until you also know that his assertion, his belief, his state of mind, has been appropriately caused. Now this assumption seems to follow both from your view and from the views you criticized, and it seems to me awkward in the case of ESP phenomena. What always interests me about ESP phenomena is that I frequently find myself wanting to say, "Manifestly this person knows that P, or knew that P, and the interesting question is: how on earth did *he come* to know that P?" It seems to me that you are going in a very difficult circle if you want to prevent anyone saying that he knew, until you have some knowledge of *how he came* to know. It seems to me that the interesting investigations often arise from the fact that we recognize knowledge without having any idea of its sources. On your view, it seems to me, we couldn't be sure it was knowledge until we knew what its sources were.

FRENCH: I'm not sure that that follows from my position, Terry, but I would say that indeed we wouldn't begin the research unless we had that belief that we knew. What I'm suggesting is the way we might go about establishing that indeed we do know. I agree with you wholeheartedly that anybody interested in whether somebody knows something, probably already has a pretty good indication that he does or he wouldn't look into it. I won't elaborate on it further at this point. I agree with you also in regard to the reading of the spectacular cases. I'm afraid that's what I do more than the others, as well.

BENDER: I am a practical parapsychologist and somewhat innocent about the problems you were just speaking of. May I just take your example, "John murdered Bill," to draw your attention to practical experiences, not with statistical methods, but with qualitative ones.

Take the case of "John murdered Bill" as a criminal case. Bill is dead, but John is not yet known. The case is submitted to a sensitive—take Croiset, for example. Now Croiset should find John and give statements which help the police to find him. Now what happens is this: Croiset very probably immediately gets impressions. They are noted, they are tape-recorded and the police try to check them. Now, our experience shows that there are different types of statements. The first type is fantasy—unconsciously produced fantasy. Nothing is proven. With the second type, the statements of the sensitive don't help the police, but when John is found some statements are proved to have been paranormal. They had a link with the case, but they did not help. The third type is very rare, but it happens: the statements of the sensitive lead to the finding of John. Full success. Now in the fourth type the statements of Croiset turn out to be a reflection of what other people think of the case—a mixture of everything. Now my practical experience is that the sensitive, this gifted person, has no criterion by which to discern if he has real knowledge or not. It is absolutely impossible to determine. So, even when the sensitive makes statements which are absolutely true, which lead to finding John, the sensitive doesn't know. So my thesis is the sensitive does not know that he knows, and I would very much appreciate it if you could explain this in terms of your position.

FRENCH: My view is entirely consistent with the position that someone may not know that he knows something and it would still be true that he knows it. That is not the case with the *Justified True Belief* theory where one of the requirements of knowing is that you have the belief and the belief be well founded.

BACKWARD CAUSATION

John Beloff

Every paranormal phenomenon must, in the nature of the case, arouse suspicion and skepticism, but the claim to be able to foretell events which have not yet occurred, which is what we mean by *precognition*, is apt to raise doubts as to whether this concept is even coherent. A number of eminent philosophers, including some like the late C. D. Broad (1967) or C. W. K. Mundle (1964) who were known for their interest in and involvement with parapsychology, came reluctantly to the conclusion that precognition, taken in its literal sense as a knowledge of the future, was not just impossible in point of fact but was logically impossible.

I want to start by considering some of these logical objections that have been brought against the concept of precognition. It has been pointed out, for example, that if an event has not yet occurred, then it cannot have any effects and, in particular, it cannot be an object of knowledge. Something which does not exist may be imagined, but it cannot literally be known. Moreover, even if we disregard this obvious point, in order for a future event to become the cause of my present precognition of it, it would have to exert a backward effect in time and this, it has been said, is inadmissible on at least three counts. First, because it is part of the meaning of the word *cause* that a cause should precede its effect, hence a cause which followed its effect would be a contradiction in terms. Secondly, and more seriously, if, forgetting about the semantics of the case, we do posit a backward causation, this would be tantamount to asserting that we could alter the past. But what has been, has been and nothing that anyone can do after the event can change it in any way. Hence, the very idea of backward causation is a radical absurdity. And, thirdly, even if we could somehow overlook the two previous objections and persist with the idea of backward causation, we should find ourselves committed to the following paradox: If it were possible to intervene in the past then, in principle, we could intervene in order to prevent our own birth. But, in that case, who was it that intervened in the first place? We would thereby have negated our own existence!

These are not by any means the only objections that have been raised with respect to precognition and I shall have more to say on the point towards the end of my talk but, in the meanwhile, I want to look very closely at the concept of backward causation which I believe is the real root of the trouble. I hope to show that, contrary to what many philosophers have maintained, there is nothing radically wrong with this concept and hence it cannot be invoked as a reason for rejecting precognition on *a priori* grounds. Furthermore, I shall try to show that, once we have come to terms with this seemingly paradoxical idea, we shall be ready to appreciate an exciting new development in experimental parapsychology, namely the study of backward or retroactive PK. In what follows, I would like to acknowledge my debt to a young American philosopher, Bob Brier, who alerted me to this problem and convinced me that the *a priori* case against precognition could be met. Bob Brier propounded his views in a brief but important monograph entitled *Precognition and the Philosophy of Science*, which was published in 1974 with the subtitle "An Essay on Backward Causation." Brier, in turn, was following the lead of the English philosopher Michael Dummett, whose article "Bringing about the Past" first appeared in the *Philosophical Review* for 1964. But, having acknowledged my intellectual debts, I consider myself free to develop my theme in my own way and draw my own conclusions. Let us return, therefore, to the objections which I have already listed and see whether they are really as cogent as they may at first appear.

The idea that future events do not exist and can, therefore, have no conceivable influence upon the present is a case of begging the question. For, in fact, many if not most contemporary philosophers of science who have written on the problem of time take a realist or objectivist view of the temporal order. I mean by this that they deny that the expressions *past, present, future* have anything more than a subjective or, at least, mind-dependent basis, indicating the relationship between the observer and the event in question, like the expressions *here* and *there*. In a mindless universe, they argue, no particular instant of the time series would have a preferential status over any other instant. Each event would still stand to any other event in the relationship *earlier than* or *later than* but none would stand out from the rest as representing a unique *now*, that is, the instant which the universe had attained on the time series. All events would simply co-exist in the timeless sense in which we talk of facts as existing or *being the case*. Now, I am not saying that the realist view of time is necessarily the correct one or that the concept of *now-ness* or *becoming*, as something extra which an event attains when it actually takes place, is a concept with no clear meaning. I mention this view simply to show that one cannot just assume, without further argument, that future events are any less real than past or present events. And, certainly, those cosmologies which treat the universe as a single four-dimensional continuum, in which every object is represented by a certain determinate world-line, recognize no division of the universe into a past, present and future.

Let us agree, then, that there are no *a priori* objections to our treating future events as sufficiently real to have causal consequences. The question we must then consider is whether the direction of such causation must always extend from earlier to later, never from later to earlier. Let us look again at the reasons that are offered for refusing to admit any sort of backward causation. First, I do not think that the purely verbal objection need detain us for long. It may well be the case that, in ordinary language, a cause is always understood as preceding its effect, since this, after all, is what happens in ordinary experience. But, given new circumstances, linguistic usage tends to become reasonably pliable and if we can show that there are paranormal cases where the cause comes after its effect, I am quite sure we would not be deterred from acknowledging them by the constraints of language. At worst we might have to write the word "cause" in adverted commas, to signal that this was a rather special kind of cause that we were dealing with.

What is much more problematic is whether the admission of backward causation would lead us into a logical impasse. It seems at first that this would indeed commit us to asserting that the past could be altered and this, I would agree, is nonsense. But, although we cannot alter the past in the sense of making something to have happened which did *not* in fact happen or, conversely, preventing something from having happened which *did* in fact happen, it does *not* follow that what *did* happen might never have happened, or might have happened differently, *but for* certain later events. We may find this supposition strange, but it is certainly not illogical. In fact, the case is no different logically when we are considering the future. If what has been, has been, then, equally, what will be, will be and in this sense one can no more alter the future than one can alter the past. But, of course, we quite rightly believe that what will be may depend on what we now do and, in this sense, we can *influence* the

future even if it makes no sense to talk of altering it. The fallacy
which previous philosophers have fallen into arises from the fact
that they failed to observe Brier's distinction between altering the
past and influencing the past. The point to grasp is that the past
might not have been what it was, had it not been for some action in
the present.

We are now in a position to deal with the other paradox of the
man who by dint of backward causation cancelled his own birth.
Given the fact that a person was born on such and such a date,
it follows that nothing thereafter can *alter* this fact. But it does not
follow logically that his having been born might not have been due
to some subsequent action that was taken. For example, a pious
Christian mother might well believe that her child would never have
been born, but for the fact that, at the appointed time, she had it
baptized. Now, we may mock her for her credulity as much as we
please, but we cannot fault her logic. The fact that we cannot use
backward causation to cancel our birth is no more problematic than
the fact that we cannot cancel any event once it has occurred.

Critics of backward causation point out that causation is an essentially pragmatic concept. Thus, we say that A is the cause of B
when we are satisfied that we can bring about B by taking action
involving A. However, if we know that B has already occurred, then
any action we take involving A would be superfluous, since we have
now obtained B whether or not we do A. Conversely, if B has
failed to materialize at a given time t_1, any action we take involving
A is then futile insofar as it was designed to make B occur at time
t_1. Hence, from the pragmatic point of view, every instance of backward causation must be either superfluous or else futile.

Brier offers an amusing example to show, nevertheless, that backward causation need not be devoid of pragmatic import. Suppose a
man were to discover, by sheer trial and error, that whenever he
received a letter through the post he had only to clap his hands
and, when he then opened the envelope, he would invariably find
there a check made out in his favor, while, conversely, if he forgot
or failed to clap his hands there would be no check. In this situation,
Brier asks, would any of us, whatever our philosophical prejudices,
refrain from clapping our hands? And, if so, could any of us honestly
deny that clapping our hands at the right moment was a necessary
condition or cause of the check having been inserted into the
envelope at an earlier time? Now, you may say at this point: well,
supposing the envelope were transparent, what then? The man
would then know as soon as he caught sight of the letter either that

there was a check inside, in which case he would not bother to clap his hands, or that there was no check, in which case no amount of hand-clapping would help him! And yet, surely, a causal connection which depended for its validity on the knowledge or ignorance of the agent would be a very queer sort of cause.

But consider, any causal connection whatsoever is circumscribed by certain boundary conditions. Indeed, as Ducasse (1969) and other philosophers have stressed, causation actually involves a triadic relationship, A causes B under conditions C. Striking a match will cause a flame but not if the match is damp or the surface is too smooth. It is not, therefore, surprising if what we might call the epistemic aspects of the situation should constitute the boundary conditions where human actions are involved. Here, again, a comparison with actions directed towards the future may help to clarify this point. Thus, if I *know* that tomorrow I shall be killed, it follows logically that nothing I can do today can prevent it, since knowing something logically implies that it is the case, but, granted that I do *not* know whether I shall be killed, it is entirely rational for me to takes steps to avoid getting killed.

Similarly, if the letter I receive arrives in a transparent envelope, so that I know that there is no check inside, no magic on my part can conjure one into having been inserted, but, granted that the envelope is opaque and that I do *not* know, it is entirely rational for me to clap my hands. What makes these two cases appear different is that normally we do *not* know what lies in the future, whereas normally we *do* know, or at least we can very easily find out, what has happened in the past. But this is an empirical difference as between past and future and, of course, there are many such empirical differences. The logic of the two situations, however, is entirely symmetrical and it is the logical aspect that now concerns us. From the aforegoing we are, I submit, entitled to conclude that there are no logical objections to saying that A is the cause of B, so long as we believe that B would not have happened but for A, regardless of whether A is earlier than B or B is earlier than A.

Up to this point we have discussed the question of backward causation in purely hypothetical terms, using examples drawn from the realm of fantasy or superstition. I now want to turn to the actualities of parapsychological research and consider its relevance in that context. It has been widely held by parapsychologists that ESP is essentially independent of space, time and matter, so that when we use our extrasensory powers, instead of relying on our sensory channels and their associated brain-mechanisms, there is no inherent reason why we should not become aware of events occurring in the past or the future as much as events occurring contemporaneously, just as there is no inherent reason why we should not become aware of events occurring in remote places or events shielded from us by intervening matter. In the case of PK, however, it has been the practice to use target-systems located in the subject's immediate vicinity and much less has beèn made of the potential time and space transcendence of the phenomenon. And yet it would be very odd if PK behaved any differently in this respect from ESP, considering that the two are so closely linked that it is customary to subsume both phenomena under the generic term *psi*. The trouble is, however, that it would, in the nature of the case, be very difficult, if not impossible, to demonstrate unequivocally the existence of a PK effect directed towards the future that would be the analog of precognitive ESP. For, whereas in a precognition experiment the subject has simply to record his guess at time t_1, and then wait for the target event to occur at time t_2, against which he can compare it, in the case of PK there is no objective way of registering the relevant mental effort at time t_1 that might be responsible for the target event at time t_2. The point is that PK is known only through its effects. It cannot be identified with any sort of conscious effort on the part of the subject. Moreover, even if one went to the extreme of killing the subject between the time t_1 when he is given the instruction to try exerting a PK effect on the future and the time t_2 when the effect is observed, one could still not rule out the possibility that the effect was due to a delayed-action PK or, even, that the deceased subject was exerting a PK effect from the life beyond, as it were.

We may note in passing that the problem of demonstrating forward PK is exactly matched by the problem of demonstrating backward ESP, otherwise known as retrocognition. In the latter case, although the subject's response can be recorded prior to verification, the verification would not be possible but for the existence of certain records in the present. Hence, there can be no unequivocal test of retrocognition. Fortunately, there is no such logical barrier in the way of demonstrating unequivocally the existence of a backward or retroactive PK, which is what I want to talk about now. The way it can be done is as follows: Some physical effect can be automatically recorded at time t_1, but kept secret until later. At time t_2, the subject is instructed to try producing this particular physical effect or outcome on this particular target-system and then, but only then, is the result checked against the original record at time t_1. This, basically, is the method used by Helmut Schmidt in his recent experiments on PK with time displacement, but others, too, have been working independently along similar lines elsewhere (Janin 1974). For a straightforward test of PK, Schmidt uses, as his target-system, a device known as a "random number generator." This usually has a binary output such that, when it is operating in isolation, the two possible outcomes will occur with approximately equal frequency. The PK task is to upset the randomicity of the machine by getting it to generate an excess of the one digit or the other, depending on the arbitrary instruction that is laid down. A prominent feature of the Schmidt set-up is the feedback system. This may take a variety of forms, visual or auditory, for example a recording pen that shifts from side to side or a fluctuating tone etc. The principle, in every case, is that the feedback is controlled by the random number generator in such a way that an excess of hits or successful trials will produce a shift in one direction, while an excess of misses or unsuccessful trials will produce a shift in the opposite direction. This feedback is not just an amenity designed to engage or sustain the interest of the subject; it is, according to Schmidt's (1975) mathematical model of psi, a crucial part of the whole process. It is, indeed, the feedback which is said to activate the psi source. However that may be, the subject is encouraged to concentrate his attention on the feedback and to try getting it to move in the desired direction, and not to bother about the random number generator which actually governs it.

This, as I say, is what happens in the straightforward or contemporaneous type of PK test. To convert this into an experiment on retroactive PK, only one modification is necessary. The output of the randomizer is now determined by a solid state memory on which a sequence of digits has been recorded, based on a previous output from the machine. Hence, instead of generating a fresh sequence of random digits by being triggered from a source of quantum indeterminacy or of electronic noise, it now merely repeats the series recorded at this earlier time. So far as the subject is concerned, however, nothing has changed; he does not need to know that the situation is any different from what it is in the standard case. Nevertheless, if the subject is to succeed in making a significant score under these new conditions, it is necessary for him to influence the behavior of the machine, not as it *is* currently, since it is now strictly determined, but as it *was* when the target sequence was originally recorded. His PK, in other words, is now operating retroactively. Although, so far, very few such experiments have been reported, it is beginning to look as if PK with time displacement may be a fact (Schmidt 1976).

In our department at Edinburgh, Richard Broughton, one of my postgraduate students, has already started work on a project which depends on the retroactive properties of PK. His point of departure is the notorious *experimenter effect*, that is, the idea that the experimenter himself, rather than the ostensible subject, is the real psi source which is responsible for the positive results which are observed. Without some such hypothesis, it is hard to explain why certain parapsychologists obtain positive results time and time again while others hardly ever do so. Indeed, Broughton had begun to wonder whether his own positive results, which he had himself obtained earlier, while working on his thesis project designed to demonstrate a hemispheric lateralization effect in ESP, might not have been the product of such a psi experimenter effect. In this new project, what he does is to generate a certain expectation in his subjects regarding the kind of scores which they may expect, more specifically, that they may expect to do better under one condition in which they perform their ESP task than they will under another condition, on account of certain unspecified artifacts. Actually, there is no objective difference between the two conditions under which they perform, and it is only when they go to the computer to receive a print-out of their scores at the termination of the experiment, that they are told which was the high-scoring condition and which the low-scoring condition, the assignment being arbitrarily determined by the computer. This means that the expectation is generated in the subject, not at the start of the experiment, but only when it is all over. The idea, if you follow me, is that any significant difference that is then found as between these two arbitrary categories must be due to the subject's retroactive PK. In other words, what he expects to find at time t_2 must influence the scoring level recorded at time t_1. A pilot experiment along these lines has already been run which did in fact produce some significant differences and Richard Broughton has been reporting on them to the Parapsychological Association Convention at Utrecht (Broughton 1976). There are further refinements in his experiment which I have not bothered to mention and a much larger experiment is planned for next year, which the Parapsychology Foundation has generously agreed to support, but I have taken it as an illustration of the fact that backward causation is beginning to enter into the current thinking of experimental parapsychologists.

Nor is it only PK that operates retroactively. If we adopt the Schmidt axiom, that all psi interactions depend critically on feedback, then ESP, too, involves backward causation, proceeding from the moment at which feedback is received to the earlier moment in time at which the response was given. Even precognition, on the Schmidt model, is elicited not, in the first instance, by the future event that is precognized, but rather by the subsequent confirmation, whether by the subject himself or the experimenter, that the event in question has come to pass.

Armed with the concept of backward causation let us finally turn back to the problem of precognition which I introduced at the outset of this paper. Undoubtedly, one reason why precognition has engendered so much resistance is that to many people it seems to cut at the root of the belief in free-will. If our future actions could be known, it is feared, this would make a mockery of our claim to be able to determine our actions by a spontaneous act of will. Applying the concept of backward causation, however, this fear would seem to be unfounded. For, when I spontaneously choose or decide upon some course of action, then my choice or decision could just as well have caused you to have had a precognition of it the week before, as it could be the cause of your remembering it a week later. Whether this entirely disposes of the uneasiness we all feel at the thought of the future being already in some sense laid down and knowable, I do not know. Certainly, we like to feel that the future lies open before us waiting to be created, but whether this intuition is philosophically justifiable, I must leave you to judge. I will say, however, that there is one restriction we must impose on the scope of precognition if we are to retain the idea of free-will. We clearly cannot both precognize our own future actions and, at the same time, freely decide upon them when the time comes. For, deciding implies being in a state of uncertainty which is terminated only when the decision is made. But, if we already *know* what we are going to do, it would be absurd to talk of our then *deciding* what to do. Having perfect precognition, which would include knowing all one's future actions, would indeed be incompatible with living one's life in the sort of way that characterizes human existence.

I am not claiming that the concept of backward causation can solve all the problems connected with the idea of precognition— there is, for example, the notorious *intervention paradox* which raises quite different questions—but what I have tried to do in this paper is to show that precognition cannot be dismissed on logical grounds alone, and that the idea of backward causation, so far from being nonsensical, is now being taken seriously by more and more experimentalists as a basis for testing psi in the laboratory.

REFERENCES

[1] Brier, Bob, *Precognition and the Philosophy of Science: An Essay on Backward Causation*. New York: Humanities Press, 1974.

[2] Broad, C. D., "The Notion of Precognition." In J. R. Smythies (Ed.) *Science and ESP*. London: Routledge, 1967.

[3] Broughton, Richard, "An Exploratory Study of Psi-based Experimenter and Subject Expectancy Effects." (Paper at 19th annual convention of the Parapsychological Association) see *Research in Parapsychology 1976*. Metuchen, N.J.: Scarecrow Press.

[4] Ducasse, C. J., *Causation and the Types of Necessity*. New York: Dover, 1969.

[5] Dummett, M. A. E., "Bringing about the Past." *Philosophical Review* 23, 1964, 338–359. (reprinted in R. M. Gale (1967) *op. cit.* below)

[6] Gale, R. M., (Ed.) *The Philosophy of Time: A Collection of Essays*. New York: Macmillan, 1967.

[7] Janin, Pierre, "PK into the Past?: An Exploratory Experiment." Unpubl. 1974.

[8] Mundle, C. W. K., "Does the Concept of Precognition Make Sense?" *Internat. J. Parapsych.* 6, 1964, 179–198.

[9] Schmidt, Helmut, "Towards a Mathematical Theory of Psi." *J. A. S.P.R.* 69, 1975, 301–321.

[10] Schmidt, Helmut, "A Logically Consistent Model of a World with Psi Interaction." In *Quantum Physics and Parapsychology*. Parapsychology Foundation Inc., 1975.

[11] Schmidt, Helmut, "PK Effect on Prerecorded Targets." *J. A. S.P.R.* 70, 1976, 267–293.

DISCUSSION

THAKUR: You did mention that time can be viewed not as something extending out there, but something that minds read into it. Now, this is very interesting and that is what makes a rigid division between past, present and future implausible. But then, given that fact, an important question immediately arises. One can legitimately say that these minds which, if you like, create the past, present and the future, are conceptually determined, and part of the conceptual determination of these minds is that future events aren't supposed to exist. Our minds are made in such a way, apparently, that we don't acknowledge the existence of future events, and that means, from this angle, it does seem to be the case that future events can't exist. To this, it won't be an answer, except a very odd one, to say, "Well normally they don't, but in the case of special people, or under special circumstances, they do." In order to do that one would have to devise a larger theory which will make room for this.

BELOFF: I didn't follow your point about "minds creating past, present and future . . ."

THAKUR: "What I thought I was doing was what you suggested, namely, that it's the context of minds that brings these divisions, and one can take that point and then come up to formulate that particular objection in the way I just stated that minds, one could say, have certain conceptual determinants, certain things they will allow and certain things they won't. And one of the conceptual determinants is that future events aren't supposed to exist. Most people just don't believe that future events exist, so the net result of this objection, put in this way, would be the same.

BELOFF: Of course, I admitted at the outset that both the idea of backward causation and the idea of precognition were paranormal concepts. In other words, in some sense, it violates our common sense assumption about the world, including the fact that the future is nonexistent—a sort of common sense assumption that would be somehow violated by the claim to know the future—that if you claim to know something, it exists in some sense. So, I entirely agree with you that it creates a paradox of a sort, but not a logical difficulty or objection to the concept of backward causation. And I don't thing that you are exactly claiming that it does, are you?

THAKUR: No. I'm not claiming that it's a logical objection, because it is obviously confined to a particular feature of human minds, the way they're constituted—so in that sense it is an empirical one rather than a logical one. But while it is an empirical feature, it's a sufficiently powerful one to exercise as much of constraint as a logical one would do.

FRENCH: First of all, the idea that future events are real or as real as present events and past events, is also a necessary element in prudential thinking, and a number of ethicists have pointed this out recently. But, to the point of your paper, I'm wondering if you would care to talk about what appears to me to be an implicit ontological commitment that you're making, regarding the existence of future events. I take it that the ontology suggested has all events existing contemporaneously in some way or another. If that's the case, then I'm also interested in the sense of the word *backward* that you're using, because it seems to me that that may only be a convenient handle to use for ordinary people to understand what you're talking about. Perhaps it doesn't serve the function of being a technical term.

BELOFF: Well, I haven't used the term *causation* in a very technical way, really. I'm nothing of a professional philosopher. I mean, I wouldn't try to formalize it to that extent, so the notion I'm working with is a very informal one. I mean, I'm satisfied "A" is the cause of "B," if I think "B" wouldn't have occurred but for "A." As informally as that. And this can still hold, even though there is a certain *prima facie* paradox about talking of forward and backward links in a four-dimensional world of events. But I don't think it's an insuperable difficulty; it can be given a special meaning. One would still have causal connections, it seems to me, whether your universe is in the process of becoming, or whether you take it as a kind of block extension of events in four dimensions, or whatever. I would maintain that, though I can't obviously argue it in detail.

SERVADIO: I think that an additional element of evidence about the possibility of the future influencing the past in qualitative parapsychology, is given by what could be called *protective precognitions*. We know that sometimes a person has a certain dream in which he finds himself in a very difficult and perhaps a lethal situation, but then, in what we can call the future, something happens and at the last moment the fatal issue is avoided. So it seems that from what we call the future, a certain warning has come to the person, giving this person the possibility of dreaming something and of avoiding the final ill consequences of what he has dreamt.

BELOFF: Of course, what you've just said raises one very, very crucial difficulty for precognition, which is the intervention paradox. Because, you see, if he avoids this dreaded event, in what sense was his dream a real knowledge of the future? That future never occurred. And this leads one on to all sorts of wild speculations about branching universes as an alternative, ideas about what precognition might be. I cut this out of my discussion because it would lead me too far away from the idea of backward causation which I was concerned to try and defend. But certainly, a precognitive dream is a good example of backward causation, in my sense.

HAYNES: There were two points raised by this talk which I'd like to ask about. One is: Is one thinking of a future event as something caused by the present, or as something as an idea? For instance, I was asked just now what was going to be done about the SPR Centenary. That is an idea of a future event which is going to work backwards and make us take this or that course, but it's not, I think what Professor Beloff has in mind. The other thing is: How far can what looks like backward causation be attributed to a telepathic or clairvoyant acquaintance with the circumstances that look like bringing about the future event itself, so that the event itself is not necessarily determining what is happening now, but we are aware of its present causes?

BELOFF: In the first point you're using backward causation in a some-what different sense. This is not quite relevant to me, because the idea after all, precedes the event in your first example, and therefore this isn't backward causation as I was using the expression. The second point, if I understood you, is that precognition might be a sort of reading into the present tendencies of the universe, what will come about rather than projecting into the future. This way of conceptualizing precognition is one that a number of philosophers, the late Adrian Dobbs, for instance have tried to work out and use. But, to me, it's a more far-fetched and a more complicated way of trying to think about precognition, and I think it was really sold to us, partly, because people have mistakenly thought that precognition was a logical im-possibility, therefore they had to evolve some other theory such as reading the objective probabilities into the present.

MATTUCK: You mentioned the fact of secrecy after the random number generator prepares the tape of trials. If the RNG prepares a tape on Tuesday and everything is held secret so that no observer whatsoever knows what the content of this tape is, then, when it's played on Wednesday for the subject, I can see the possibility of his exerting backwards causation and causing a change to take place on the tape which was made the day before. But, what would you expect if somebody else looks at the tape on Tuesday and it's completely random? Then it should be impossible for the subject to influence the tape on Wednesday, because now it's not secret any more. I.e., some-body knows what the content of the tape is and if the subject then in-fluences on Wednesday the tape that was made on Tuesday, it seems to me there would be a logical contradiction of the sort which you get in your transparent envelope paradox. I would like to know if the ex-periment has been done in these two ways—in the first case, keeping the contents of the tape prepared on Tuesday secret from *everybody* and then playing it on Wednesday; and in the next case, allowing one observer to observe the tape just after it was made on Tuesday, and finding on Wednesday that the subject is unable to influence the tape and shift it in some sort of non-random direction.

BELOFF: So far as I understand, a paradox arises only if the subject himself is allowed to inspect the information, not if some other ob-server does. Although, it is quite true that Schmidt has always taken great care, and so did others who followed him, to keep the tape secret even from himself. But I think that the sort of logical epistemic difficulty arises only when the subject himself knows whether there's an excess or a deficiency of a particular digit, and this makes it, as it were, futile or redundant for him then to try influencing it. It would be, of course, desirable, that the experiment you've outlined should be performed, I mean just as an empirical demonstration, but I foresee only logical difficulties where the subject himself knows what is now the case.

MATTUCK: I think that the logical difficulty would also occur if, for example, Schmidt himself or any other observer observed the tape and wrote down what the content of the tape was. It's not just a matter of logical difficulties with the subject, but logical difficulties which would arise if *any* observer in the universe looked at that tape and noted that it was random, then it should be impossible for the subject to influence it.

BELOFF: There, I'm afraid, we differ. Let's remember what the subject is trying to do. Suppose he's trying to produce an excess of "ones" rather than "zeros" in the output. Now, Schmidt can look at the printout and see that there is an excess of "ones." He doesn't tell the subject this. The subject is instructed to produce an excess of "ones," and he is successful. Now, we, knowing that this experiment has consistently given this kind of effect, will conclude that what produced the original excess of "ones" was the future exertions of the subject towards that end. What happens intermediately does not seem to me to matter very much, only in these very special cases where the subject himself knows, because this, as it were, paralyzes him epistemically.

BERENDT: Coming from the qualitative side in parapsychology, I would like to know the viewpoint of Dr. Beloff about the chair tests by Croiset; that's my first question. The second is this: As our whole development in parapsychology to date seems to tend to changes in our ideas of nature, making a broader aspect possible, it could be that our approach should be changed concerning our predominant causal thinking about nature. I mean, that the cause/effect relationship is certainly for us the basic one, but there are other relationships which may add to it. I only wanted to add one point. There are certainly great difficulties in bringing a happening in the future into a naturalistic explanation. There is one theory which looks upon sayings by a paragnost about the future as though the paragnost sees a framework, as Neuhäusler calls it—a blueprint—but as it is not the original, it must not be taken as reality in every detail. It could also be that paranormal PK or paranormal mental process could change, and then, of course, the prediction is not precise, but still keeps the framework of what was said.

STANFORD: Just for the record, would you, please, specify in more detail the precautions which Schmidt took to rule out contemporaneous experimenter psi mediation of the effects.

BELOFF: I wonder whether Monsieur Janin might care to comment on that, because he's a great expert in precautions.

JANIN: I would say that Schmidt did not methodically take precautions to avoid the effect. At least, I have the impression that in my own experiments, which I undertook quite independently of Schmidt and at about the same time, I was much more concerned than he about the problem. Although the question has somewhat slipped out of my mind at this moment, I do remember that in some of his backward PK tests, the future target side of the random number generator was already known to the experimenter at the time of target recording. In such conditions, an experimenter's effect is at least as likely to explain whatever PK is actually observed as would the future subject's future wish.

STANFORD: I just would like to mention for the record that I do know that, in at least one of his backward PK studies, Schmidt did take the specific precaution of making a number of tapes and only one was a relevant one for a given subject; the others were not and he was totally blind as to which tape was the non-used tape and which one was to be the one that was used.

PHILOSOPHY AND PARAPSYCHOLOGY: IMPOSSIBLE BEDFELLOWS OR THE MARRIAGE OF THE FUTURE?

Lawrence L. LeShan

The data of parapsychology consistently face us with the basic question: "How does the world work?" We cannot look at the report of a single experiment or spontaneous incident without the specter of the question peering at us from between the lines. We parapsychologists are always standing on the edge of the abyss of the unknown as we go about our daily work.

This condition is true of all science. There is, however, a difference. As the history of science has repeatedly shown, there is a consistent and now (since the work of Kuhn[1] at any rate) a well known pattern. Science deals in terms of an accepted and coherent view of the nature of reality and does its work from this base. Standing solidly on it, scientists gradually become aware of problems, discrepancies and contradictions. Facts appear that do not fit the accepted view. These slowly mount up until a new view, a new picture of reality is presented which resolves these new problems. The older generation of scientists, by and large, rejects the new view and remains comfortable resting on the old world picture. A new generation grows up accepting the new one, gradually takes over academic posts and the authorship of textbooks and science moves on, now resting on its new base. The process is presently repeated. No one is ever very uncomfortable as everyone stands solidly on a world picture, on a basis of interpreting reality that their data and most of the professional material they read and write seem to support.

Parapsychologists are in quite a different position. There is no accepted world picture that gives us a base to stand on as we do our work. Our data consistently fly directly in the face of accepted interpretations of reality or else they are not "paranormal" and therefore not of primary interest to us. We are constantly reminded by this data that what we believe are the laws of reality (Broad's

"Basic Limiting Principles"[2]) are being violated and that we have no viable alternatives, no alternative world-picture we can stand on. In a profound psychological sense, we need always to defend ourselves against "culture-shock," against what Kurt Goldstein[3] has called the strongest of all anxieties, "Catastrophic Anxiety." This is the anxiety felt when the perceived foundations of reality on which we have built our egos are crumbling before our eyes and no longer support these egos. Our defenses against this threat are so strong and ingrained that we are hardly aware of them and they only emerge into view when we wonder why we, personally or as a profession, have so rarely followed up the few good leads we have found in the past 80-odd years, why there are so few of us or why so many of us leave the field.

One other symptom of our suppressed anxiety and our defenses against it is probably our theoretical timidity. At first glance there seems to be a large scale paradox in our work. We have the courage to work in the most "far out," the least accepted, of all scientific fields. We face the open or thinly disguised rejection of our scientific colleagues and the lack of understanding of what we are trying to do by the public at large. This intellectual courage, however, seems to have disappeared when we attempt theoretical explanations of our data. The number of our theories is very small and most of them are attempts to reconcile our findings with well-accepted, Newtonian scientific concepts. In spite of the fact that we are all well aware that the data do not fit these concepts, we keep trying to cram them in. We continue to do this in spite of the fact that C. D. Broad in his *Lectures in Psychical Research*[4] and John Beloff in his *The Existence of Mind*[5] have completely and finally disposed of this possibility. Louisa Rhine put in succinctly when she wrote: "The facts of mental ability already discovered in parapsychology no more fit the current idea of a space-time world than such a fact as that ships disappear bottom-first over the horizon fits the model of a flat earth."[6] We all know this and go right on trying to fit the facts into "the current idea of a space-time world." The contradiction between our lack of timidity shown in our choosing to work in this field and our excess of it in devising theories to fit our data can only come from severe psychological stress.

There are various other aspects to this stress than the problem of catastrophic anxiety. Some of these I and others have described elsewhere.[7] Overall, however, these have led us to generally keep away from philosophic exploration of the meaning of our data and to eschew metaphysics as if it were the plague. Our approach has been what William James called "radical empiricism." We have just concentrated on experiments and trying to get facts. In this way we have become trivial. Without the synoptic and synthetic functions of philosophy we have become fact collectors. And if there is one thing that philosophy has learned, it is that facts without a context are meaningless and silly. The context of the *Journal* of the ASPR and the *Journal of Parapsychology* is not enough. Our work is isolated from the mainstream of science and the mainstream of our culture. It is irrelevant and trivial because we have rejected our philosophic roots and the synthetic aspects of philosophy. Without these we stand on chaos. (A theory may be invalid, but it gives us a place to move on from.) About all we can do without them is to do new experiments at about the same rate that we forget old ones. We are so isolated and irrelevant at a time of tremendous cultural interest in the paranormal, parapsychology libraries are deserted, financial support for serious work is terribly low, and the public interest is shunted off to Atlantis and astrology while we sit in our ivory towers and write statistics to each other.

However, parapsychology is not the only field that has become irrelevant and trivial in a time of great cultural need. "Seldom before," wrote Morris Rafael Cohen, "has the general craving for philosophic light seemed so vast and the offerings of professed philosophers so scant and unsubstantial."[8] Before we can understand the strange relationship between parapsychology and philosophy, we must look briefly at the recent development of philosophy.

Since Newton, there has been in the modern world a great quest for simplicity; a belief that development and progress in understanding meant a simplification to straightforward, basic principles. In the present century, philosophy has hoped that "Either language would be reduced to an all inclusive 'logical' system, or essences and principles that would reveal reality in all its marked elegance and simplicity would be revealed."[9] Berkeley and Hume built tables out of squareness and brownness. Pavlov built intellect out of conditioned reflexes. Loeb built life out of tropisms.[10] And parapsychologists continue to try to build ESP out of card-guesses.

The belief, furthermore, was that human life could be ultimately explained in "logical" terms in the ordinary, everyday meaning of the term "logical." Ultimately, it could be broken down to something like: "Either p or q or pq." Freud saw the unconscious as being logically understandable and comprehensible and believed that if unconscious forces are made conscious, then we would logically see where our real pleasures lay and behave rationally. In a curious parallel to Freud, Bertrand Russell believed the same. In John Maynard Keynes words, Russell ". . . sustained simultaneously a pair of opinions ludicrously incompatible. He held that in fact human ideas were carried on after a most irrational fashion, but that the remedy was quite simple and easy since all we had to do was to carry them on rationally."[11] The Logical Positivists believed that there was "a unique model for all real science and that when they had described it they would unify all science and eventually all human experience."[12]

With this basic hope and thrust—of explaining the world and human beings logically and simply, of reducing it to a set of axioms, basic limiting principles—parapsychology was anathema to philosophy. The data of parapsychology show *in each instance* that the usual framework of the world as we perceive it is not consistent. It "slips" and things that could not happen, happen. It is, however, a basic aspect of the models of reality that we have been working towards in the last few centuries that they are completely consistent; they admit of no exceptions, no "miracles."

The input that parapsychology would bring to philosophy is not the usual kind of scientific input. The usual kind (except for relativity theory and quantum mechanics) can be fitted into the usual views about the nature of reality. If the sun moves about the earth or vice versa, is certainly a major difference, but the implied revolution is limited. In both cases you still have two material bodies relating to each other in time and space. The implications from paranormal data are far greater.

Philosophers either implicitly or explicitly understood the problem. Allow in one good case of paranormal activity and you have destroyed the chance for a basic, simple model and opened the door to almost anything. (As Beloff described it,[13] you cannot even reduce the number of things you accept and still be safe. One is enough. You cannot be a little bit pregnant.) The best that can be done after admitting a single case, is to hold the rearguard action that the laws we ascribe to reality *usually* work. This we already knew.

The size of the perceived danger is illustrated by an incident described in Ernest Jones' biography of Freud.[14] Shocked and startled that Freud considered telepathy valid, Jones exclaimed: "If we are prepared to consider the possibility of mental processes floating in the air, what is to stop us from believing in angels?" Freud replied: "Quite so. And even *der Liebe Gott*." Although the data of parapsychology does not necessarily lead us to a belief in angels and a loving God, Freud was not underestimating the size of the problem.

To both philosophers and parapsychologists the danger has been clear; the facts of the paranormal would create immense havoc. To the philosophers, they ran counter to the faith in simplicity, rationality and consistency. For the parapsychologists the danger was that if they explored the meaning of their data with the sharp and terrible clarity of philosophical tools, they would have to face the fact that the world-design (to use Binswanger's term) on which they had built their egos and by which they lived, was not universal and did not fully work. Each saw the other as an impossible bedfellow.

This has been the situation and it is still to a large degree true. There have been, however, major developments in the past decades which are building up pressure on professionals in both fields to perceive that they cannot continue to live without each other. It may be a forced marriage that is developing, but it will be a real one.

From the viewpoint of philosophy, one pressure that is developing is the gradual failure of Cartesian dualism to work any more. (H. H. Price once described this as "a very brilliant theory that had been very useful in the past, but is now a nuisance."[15]). Modern science has been indicating this lack of usefulness for many years. For example, for Descartes the essence of matter was spatial extension; the essence of mind was its cogitations. Today in science, however, matter is seen either as a consistent source of sensations or else as stress points between spatially unbounded fields of energy. The distinction has broken down.

The definition of matter as "real" has also been broken down by developments in particle physics. The basic building blocks are no longer solid. An electron can perhaps be best defined as a region of space that exhibits a certain inertia, repels other electrons and attracts protons. (The best definition of a proton is probably that it is a region of space that exhibits a certain inertia, repels other protons and attracts electrons.) In location it is, in Max Planck's words "smeared all over a probability distribution" and in Heisenberg's words "It has a tendency to exist." As the fundamental building blocks of "real matter," these are insubstantial indeed.

Further there has been a general switch from the search for "reality" to a search for useful ways to construe reality. We have largely given up the hope of knowing what is "out there." In a typical statement, Suzanne Langer defined natural laws as ". . . simply the most general facts we know about the universe."[16] The definition is in terms of knowledge, not eternal verities.

The quest for one, absolute reality has been battered by one event after another in science: the determination of the speed of nerve transmission and of the finite speed of light, the doctrine of the specific energies of nerves and the work of Riemann and Lobachevsky, relativity theory and the principle of complementarity, Gestalt psychology and the work of Boas and Whorf, the Existentialist movement and the production of the movie that made *Rashomon* a household word, to name only a few. It does not stand as useful any more.

These developments have certainly not gone unnoticed in philosophy and the search for a new way of relating to them has been going on for some time. "In every age," wrote Langer[17], "philosophical thinking exploits some dominant concepts and makes its greatest headway in solving problems conceived in terms of them." As the usefulness of Cartesian dualism has faded, the search has developed for the concepts of the next age.

William James once suggested that the universe might not be a consistent system, but ". . . essentially a loose jointed assemblage of odds and ends," a "pluriverse" rather than a "universe." And, from a superficial point of view, science seems to be moving in that direction. We have the viewpoint of relativity theory that the truth about an event is partially determined by the coordinate system from which you are viewing it, the view of quantum physics that the position of the electron is indeterminate, the fact that the "basic, moving agents" on one level seem to be statistical factors, on another cause and effect, field interactions on another. That "organizing forces" exist on biological levels and probably teleogical forces on psychological levels. The four kinds of forces of physics today seem to have little to do with each other except for the fact that the same entities may be involved in more than one of them.

It has become clear from psychology and anthropology that Husserl's "enormous *a priori*" differs considerably with different people and different cultures. The Linguistic Analysts such as Ryle and Wisdon pointed out that the major function of language was not as something to be made perfect so as to absolutely reflect the structure of reality, but rather as a tool whose fundamental use was human communication and the insuring of common experience. V. V. O. Quine, in particular has pointed out that a single proposition is not a specific unit of discourse. It is modified and changed much more by our total "man-made fabric" of experience and expectation than it modifies the fabric.[18]

Overall philosophy has been part of a movement of our culture towards a new paradigm to replace the older, no longer useful one. It is being generally recognized that this will not be a simple, but a complex paradigm, that it must encompass differences involved in different levels and different points of view. In the *Tractatus* of an early

Wittgenstein we see the high organization of the search for the clarity and sharpness of an approach to language that will absolutely relate it to reality. In the Introduction to the *Philosophic Investigations* of his later work, Wittgenstein describes the book not as a coherent answer to the problems, but as a set of sketches from which we may be able to get a picture of a landscape. No one angle of vision would be sufficient.

Life is seen as complex in the new development. It is, as John Austin put it, to come up against many problems you can't anticipate or predict. (Ann Landers once wrote that life is what happens to you when you have other plans!) The function of language is to adjust itself to all sorts of demands and it is its ability to do so that makes it so significant.

It is being slowly realized that no one kind of language can deal with all the types of communication we human beings need. We cannot describe meter-readings and deep feelings of sadness with the same grammatical structure. If we start from *experience* and attempt to describe, clarify and communicate it (and this has been seen as crucial in philosophy in this century—to describe what is felt and experienced) we need different types of language with different grammatical structures.

The story is told[19] that in a conference of English and American philosophers, Gabriel Marcel was trying to explain his ideas about grace and transcendence. The audience continually responded with requests that he clarify his language and say exactly what he meant. Finally he said "Perhaps I can't explain, but if I had a piano here I could play it." We know now that the great effort of the Logical Positivists to build *one* language that would reflect "reality" cannot succeed. Life is simply too complex for this. Being in love and the Kinsey approach to sex are such different kinds of experience that they cannot be communicated in the same *types* of language, any more than what is communicated in meter-readings and Beethoven's Ninth Symphony. We have come past the point of saying "What we cannot speak about we must consign to silence."[20] There are many other ways to speak and Picasso's *Guernica* clearly expresses one type of experience in a way no "logical" language could hope to.

To be modern in European and American philosophy today is to ". . . give up simple explanations of man and the world, to embrace complexity once and for all, and to try, somehow, to manage it."[21]

Through modern developments in science, changes in Western culture, the existentialist philosophers and the Linguistic Analysts, the development of philosophy has arrived at a point where the data of parapsychology are not only acceptable, but necessary.

It is only by incorporating the new knowledge that each age brings forth that philosophy can continue its task. Unless it does this, it becomes trivial or else it becomes a tool for maintaining an outworn status quo. The new knowledge of our age is of the many kinds of reality we are and embody; that things are different from different viewpoints, and that different laws function and different entities exist when we look from different angles and with different purposes. Without the discipline and overview, without the synoptic thrust that only formal philosophy can bring to bear, the knowledge remains a chaos of unrelated fragments and confusing facts that provides no guidelines as to how we can direct and enrich our lives. Without incorporating the new knowledge, philosophy is unrelated to the living human being and desiccates in its academic home.

Further, it must relate the new knowledge to experience. The input from parapsychology and from theoretical physics is of much the same structure, but the paranormal relates directly to our own experience. The cloud chamber photographs and the equations of physics relate only indirectly.

Every survey has shown the high percentage of Western culture individuals who have had experiences that they regard as paranormal. It is only because of the older orientation of philosophy that the world works in a completely consistent way and that therefore they could not have happened, that these almost universal experiences have been ignored.

In a very basic way, the data of parapsychology typify the new understanding, the new conceptualization that is developing for our time. It demonstrates with heavy experiential impact that the usual laws governing reality do not work all the time; that there are exceptions and that—since this is intrinsically forbidden by these laws—there are other sets of laws, other world designs that are also valid.

Once this is accepted, and accepted it must be (the principle of complementarity may have been first enunciated in physics, but it can no longer be restricted to that domain) parapsychological data fill in a gap in philosophy by relating the new conceptualization directly to human experience. And unless this gap is filled, philosophy remains irrelevant and unrelated and cannot fulfill its task.

Both philosophy and parapsychology need each other at the present. Parapsychology needs philosophical orientations and tools so it will not remain a trivial business of collecting unrelated facts and remain outside of our culture. Without an overarching view, without general theory, it is just a hobby at best.

Philosophy needs parapsychology to fill the gap between the new conceptualization it is moving towards and human experience. Further, the paranormal is far too widespread a human experience for philosophy to ignore and still claim to be the field that searches for the deepest possible understanding of man and the cosmos, that seeks for the answer to Kant's three questions: What can I know? What ought I to do? What dare I hope?

Perhaps one of the most interesting things about the new conceptualization of reality that is emerging is that it automatically brings in its wake a theory of the paranormal. This may seem surprising, but perhaps, from a wider view it should not be. Each basic definition of reality accepts certain questions and provides a path to answers to them. It regards other questions as unreal and makes them unanswerable. The previous reality definition of our culture legislated the paranormal out of existence by definition. The new one indicates a basic and workable theoretical understanding of it.

In a brilliant paper in 1964, Gardner Murphy[22] suggested that we had been looking in the wrong way and the wrong place for laws of psychic phenomena. He suggested that "the paranormal presents not a system of laws, but a very different kind of reality; namely a sort of vehicle or modality in which reality may express itself."[23] He said that ESP events appear "when we tear loose from the ordinary framework of our space-time organization of knowledge."[24] "The medium through which such [paranormal] is conveyed may be a medium alien to the ordinary concepts of time and space."[25] There is, said Murphy, no new knowledge gained in ESP, only access to knowledge inaccessible through ordinary sensory channels. The different modalities, our everyday one, the dream one, the one in which ESP occurs, Murphy compares to "the different notation which in some respects can be translated back and forth and in some respects cannot."[26] It is in this paper that the first hint—of which I am aware—of the new theoretical understanding of ESP occurs. (I recently read this paper for the first time after I had just completed a new book *Alternate Realities*. To my surprise I found that the book carried out a suggestion and a program of research suggested by Murphy twelve years before.)

A basic aspect of the new conceptualization of reality is that how-the-world-works is, to some degree, up to us. There are a number of ways in which the world can be construed and when we construe it in one of these ways, that is the way it works. Whether matter is continuous or discontinuous, whether light travels in particles or waves, is determined by the purpose and world-design with which we approach the problem. I am not suggesting that any schizophrenic fantasy is valid and that if there are 432 inmates of a mental hospital, there are 432 different valid ways of organizing reality. Rather there is a limited number of basically different world-organizations valid for human beings. These are coherent, highly organized metaphysical systems. Certain things occur or can be done in each of them—they are "normal"; certain other things cannot occur or be done—they are "paranormal." In a somewhat overstated account of this, A. S. Eddington wrote: "In my observatory there is a telescope which condenses the light of a star on a film of sodium in a photoelectric cell. I rely on the classical theory to conduct the light through the lenses and focus it on the cell: I switch on to the quantum theory to make the light fetch out electrons from the sodium film to be collected in an electrometer. If I happen to transpose the two theories, the quantum theory convinces me that the light will never get concentrated in the cell, and the classical theory shows that it is powerless to extract the electrons if it does get in. I have no logical reason for not using the theories in this way, only experience teaches me that I must not. Sir William Brigg said that we use the Classical Theory on Mondays, Wednesdays and Fridays and the Quantum Theory on Tuesdays, Thursdays and Saturdays."[27]

The essence of this statement—and of the knowledge emerging in a dozen different scientific fields—in that when we use one of various different valid organizations of reality, when we really perceive-react to the world in this way, then that is the way the world works; that is how reality is organized. There is no "way-the-world-works," there are, at least, a number of different ways that we can choose. "There is, in fact,'" wrote Suzanne Langer, "no such thing as *the* form of the 'real' world; physics is one pattern which may be found in it, and 'appearance,' or the pattern of *things* with their qualities and characters is another.[28]

What is legitimate in one metaphysical system is not in another; one system's "normal" is another's "paranormal." From this viewpoint, ESP occurs when we have shifted (consciously or not) from the everyday, sensory organization of reality in which it can *not* occur (and no twisting of logic will remedy this fact) to another system in which it occurs "normally."

I have elsewhere described some of the valid systems of construing reality which are presently known.[29] In one of them (which I have called, for various reasons, the "Clairvoyant Reality" or "Clairvoyant Mode of Being," ESP is the normal way information is communicated. I first came across this concept when I questioned Mrs. Eileen Garrett for many hundreds of hours on the subject "What was going on?" "How did the world look?" at the moment when she was attaining "paranormal" information. Slowly there emerged from her answers the picture of a full-fledged, organized metaphysical system with which she was—at that moment—organizing reality. Investigation showed that other psychics such as Rosalind Heywood and Douglas Johnson agreed enthusiastically that this was indeed their experience. Further work showed that this particular organization of reality was the same one used by serious mystics of both East and West and by relativity theory.

It is neither feasible nor desirable to repeat here the analyses of the different organizations of reality valid for human beings that I have done elsewhere. My purpose in this paper has been to point out that there have been good psychological reasons in the past for philosophy and parapsychology to keep away from each other; that developments in each have now reversed the situation to the point where they deeply need each other. Further that these developments have led to a theoretical model which provides a solution to the "impossible paradox" of ESP.

Our deepest anxiety today lies in the fact that the diversity of human beings has become too close to us, the complexity of the world too much for us, and we realize we can no longer deal with it with the concepts and words we have from the past. Attempting to deal with this through the study of semantic issues is more an attack on the symptoms of the problem than on the problem itself. We need to accept the complexity, the different valid approaches to reality, in order to make sense out of our modern experience. With its clear and unequivocal statement that the laws about reality which generally apply do not always apply to our experience (and therefore to the world we live in), parapsychology brings us face to face not only with the complexity, but also with a potential set of guidelines for exploring and defining that experience from different viewpoints. It brings us face to face with the principle of complementarity which may be for our age what Cartesian dualism was for the past one.

REFERENCES

[1] Kuhn, T., *The Structure of Scientific Revolutions*. Chicago: Univ. of Chicago Press. 1962.

[2] Broad, C. D., *Lectures on Psychical Research*, London: Routledge, Kegan Paul, 1962.

[3] Goldstein, K., *Human Nature in the Light of Psychopathology*. Cambridge, Harvard Univ. Press, 1940.

[4] Ref. # 2.

[5] Beloff, J., *The Existence of Mind*. N.Y., Citadel, 1964.

[6] Rhine, L., Parapsychology Then and Now. *J. Parap.* 31, 1967, p. 242.

[7] LeShan, L., On the Non-Acceptance of Parapsychology. *In'tl J. Parap.* 1966, Vol. 8, No. 3. pp 367–386.

[8] Cohen, M. R., *Reason and Nature*. N.Y. Harcourt Brace, 1931, p. viii

[9] Kohl, H., *The Age of Complexity*. N.Y., Mentor, 1965.

[10] Langer, S., *Philosophical Sketches*. N.Y. Mentor, 1962, p. 53.

[11] Keynes, J. M., *Two Memoirs*, London, Rupert Hart Davis, Ltd. 1949.

[12] Ref. #9, p. 36.

[13] Ref. #5, p. 219.

[14] Jones, E., *The Life and Work of Sigmund Freud*. London, Hogarth, 1957 Vol. 3, p. 408.

[15] Heywood, R., *The Sixth Sense*, London, Pan, 1959, p. 224.

[16] Ref. #10, p. 124. Langer quotes (p. 15) Whitehead that Metaphysics is " . . the most general statement we can make about reality."

[17] Ref. #10, p. 53.

[18] Quine, V.V.O, *From a Logical Point of View*. Cambridge, Harvard University Press, 1953, p. 42.

[19] Ref. #9, p. 17.

[20] Wittgenstein, L. J. J., *Tractatus Logico-philosophicus*, 6.7.

[21] Ref. #9, p. 15.

[22] Murphy, G., "Lawfulness versus Caprice: Is there a Law of Psychic Phenomena?" *J.A.S.P.R.*, Oct. 1954, No. 4, Vol. LVIII pp. 237–249.

[23] Ref. #22, p. 240.

[24] Ref. #22, p. 242.

[25] Ref. #22, p. 244.

[26] Ref. #22, p. 245.

[27] Quoted in Tyrrell, G.N.M., *Grades of Significance*. London, Ryder and Co. 1930, p. 54.

[28] Ref. #10.

[29] LeShan, L., *The Medium, The Mystic and The Physicist*. N. Y., Viking, 1973. *Alternate Realities*. N.Y., Evans Publ. Co. 1976.

DISCUSSION

DEAN: The papers today have brought very well to our minds the problem facing philosophy and especially so in the last paper by Dr. LeShan, who has shown very forcefully what the problems are. I would like to take an example from some of our work to show that when we tested presidents of business companies or chairmen of the boards of directors, these people told us that they very definitely do know what's going to happen and make the decisions for their companies in accordance with what they know. And there is a very heavy dollar sign or pound sterling sign on their being right in knowing. Now you can be cynical and say that when a company gets big, it can't go wrong no matter what it decides. But there is the experience of Lockheed, despite the enormous bribes that it gave, nearly going bankrupt and saved only by one vote of the U.S. Senate, and Rolls Royce nearly going bankrupt with it also, except that it was bailed out by the British government. If I may take one example, there is the experience of Conrad Hilton, the man who built up the enormous hotel empire. In his biography, *Be My Guest*, he explains very well that he knew which hotel to start out with — the Stevens Hotel in

Chicago. He knew which one to go for next. He knew which man to put in as a director for each of his hotels, so that they would be financially solvent. He knew all these things and, of course, has become very, very wealthy on account of it.

Now, I would like to put in a plea for philosophy to change as physics had to do. If you ask me how can philosophy do it, then I say go back to the father of western philosophy, Descartes, because he put forward the idea, though it wasn't understood, of a two-headed animal. Well, that's just what we are. Our brains are split into two hemispheres—a left hemisphere and a right hemisphere. The left one is very good at logical, analytical, deductive, mathematical problem-solving, counting, time estimation, and verbal description. When philosophers use words, they're doing it with their left hemispheres. But I would put in a plea for there to be a philosophy of the right hemisphere; a non-logical philosophy along holistic, Gestalt, non-logical lines using the data from parapsychology, and I think that the example which Dr. LeShan gave of Mrs. Eileen Garrett was a very good one. She could be common sense using her left hemisphere, her logical part, but she could also switch over to the other clairvoyant sense (as Dr. LeShan called it) for this new type of philosophy.

MATTUCK: I would like to comment on your statement that what parapsychology seems to lack is bold theories. I disagree with that because there has been at least one bold theory which has been put forth, and this is the theory which I mentioned before—the theory of the physicist, Evan Harris Walker. It's extremely bold. Perhaps it's too bold, but if I may quote you, quoting somebody else, " . . . you make more progress from error than from chaos," and certainly one thing which is not present in Walker's theory is chaos. That is absent! Now it may be in error, but at least it makes quantitative predictions. It gives support for a view of the universe which should be extremely interesting to philosophers, i.e. a *dualistic* view in which there is matter, described by wave functions, and mind, described by hidden variables, and a mind-matter interaction in which the hidden variables cause collapse of the wave functions. Unfortunately, Walker's presentation of his theory in the book *Quantum Physics and Parapsychology* is fairly incomprehensible. However, there is another more pedagogical presentation of the ideas involved in a new book by Stanley Krippner and Alberto Villoldo, *Realms of Healing*. In the appendix of this book there is a ten-page description of Walker's theory which is, I think, capable of giving the man in the street or the non-physicist, a qualitative idea of what it's all about. The theory makes predictions. It leads to experiments which can be performed in the laboratory, both in extrasensory perception and in psychokinesis, and I think philosophers especially should spend some time trying to find out what Walker's theory is about. The theory may be in error, but I think just the fact that it gives us an extremely well organized picture of the universe which can be either confirmed or falsified, is an important step forward. I think it's the first time in the history of this field that such a step has been made.

BELOFF: Since Dr. LeShan has done me the honor of citing me in his talk, I would just like to make it clear that I don't entirely go along with all the things he says subsequently. In particular, you see, I've never really abandoned the realist position. There, I'm much more Popperean, I suppose, than he would like me to be. His thinking, it seems to me, shows a dangerous sort of subjectivist/relativist tendency that I find has to be viewed with very considerable care. He puts it all so charmingly that we're almost seduced into admitting all sorts of things that I think, upon reflection, we ought to be very careful about. I agree with him that there are multiple possible descriptions of reality—that an artist will describe things in one way in one mood and in another way in another mood as with Douglas Dean's two halves of the brain—there are all kinds of ways of communicating and describing things. But I still abide by the old fashioned idea that there is a single series of events, a single reality, and that reality isn't just a creation of the mind.

MEANINGFUL COINCIDENCES IN THE LIGHT OF THE JUNG-PAULI THEORY OF SYNCHRONICITY AND PARAPSYCHOLOGY

Hans Bender

Let me begin with an anecdotal case of the encounter type of meaningful coincidences which I have observed myself. At the age of 14, Mrs. G., her parents and her younger brother visited Mont Saint-Michel in Brittany. I drove their car. While we visited the abbey, she and her brother examined the parked cars and she climbed into one of them which was particularly attractive. Its driver—so she reported with indignation—snapped at her in a foreign language and threw her out. Eight years later she met her future husband, a Scandinavian engineer, in Munich. Once, when she was married, turning over the pages of his photograph album, she found a picture of Mont Saint-Michel with the same car and driver. She had climbed into her future husband's car. The significant point, however, was to follow years later. In the same way as she had been thrown out of the car, she would be thrown out of this marriage, years later. For years the divorce hung like a shadow over her and hindered her children's development. Just a coincidence, but a meaningful one. One cannot help considering this event an omen for her future fate. By the way—the very moment I was writing this a letter from Mrs. G. was handed to me. She had not written for a long time and told me that she was struggling with depression caused by the sad fate of her son.

When we try to locate this case in the frame of normal experience or of parapsychology, we are at a loss. It resists explanation, not only in terms of physical causality, but also in terms of the categories of classical extrasensory perception, telepathy, clairvoyance or precognition. One can speculate. If Mrs. G. had dreamt of the car and had perhaps made a sketch of the dream scene, one might have thought it was a precognitive dream. In dreams, vehicles often appear as symbols for libido and it would have been plausible to interpret the throwing out as a clearly allegorical presentation of the divorce. But Mrs. G. did not dream the scene but experienced it in reality.

I talked about this, and other cases, with Carl Gustav Jung who, throughout his whole life, paid the utmost attention to paranormal experiences as an explorer of the unconscious psyche. He told me if it was a dream or real life, it is all the same thing. It is an expression of the same cryptic acausal relationship between psyche and nature. The extraordinary aspect does not lie in the paranormal qualities of our perception but in the event itself. That is why he did not speak of telepathy, clairvoyance or precognition, but of synchronistic events.

I can now define the subject of my paper: The main purpose of my contribution to this symposium on "The Philosophy of Parapsychology" is to draw the attention of the participants to the importance meaningful coincidences, outside the framework of parapsychology, might have for our understanding of psi.

Allow me—at the risk of telling you something you all know—to give a brief account of the theory of synchronicity which Jung worked out in collaboration with or under the tutorship of the eminent physicist Wolfgang Pauli, discoverer of the "Pauli Exclusion Principle," one of the cornerstones of modern physics. The essay: "Synchronicity. An Acausal Connection Principle," first appeared in German in the volume *Naturerklärung und Psyche* (1952) together with a paper by Wolfgang Pauli on "The Influence of Archetypical Ideas on the Formation of Kepler's Scientific Theories." Jung had formulated the concept of synchronicity as early as 1930, and applied it for the first time when he attempted to explain the Chinese oracular practice of the I Ching, as an unexpected parallelism of psychic and physical events which is experienced as a "relative simultaneity." Later on, he tried to include with this concept extrasensory perception and psychokineses (meaningful coincidences in the strict sense adopted in this paper), omens, fateful encounters, oracles and, even, astrology. Jung defines synchronicity as "the simultaneous occurrence of two meaningfully but not causally connected events"[1] or alternatively as "a coincidence in time of two or more causally unrelated events which have the same or similar meaning."[2] Widely cited is the example Jung gives in his essay of the case of the scarab: "A young woman I was treating had, at a critical moment, a dream in which she was given a golden scarab. While she was telling me this dream I sat with my back to the closed window. Suddenly, I heard a noise behind me, like a gentle tapping. I turned round and saw a flying insect knocking against the windowpane from outside. I opened the window and caught the creature in the air as it flew in. It was the nearest analogy to a golden scarab that one finds in our latitudes, a scarabaeid beetle, the common rose-chafer (Cetonia aurata) which contrary to its usual habits, had evidently felt an urge to get into a dark room at this particular moment."[3]

For the patient, this meaningful coincidence unlocked her hitherto completely blocked conscious and analysis proceeded rapidly. The scarab is a classical symbol of rebirth, interpreted by Jung as the expression of an archetypal condition of the patient's psyche, aimed at change. The cardinal point of Jung's theory is the affirmation that the "archetypes"—dispositions of the "collective unconscious" with a strong charge of psychic energy—constitute the procedures of instincts and impulses, but also the "true elements of the spirit," acting as "organizers" beyond the unity of personality and transcending the dimensions of space and time, inducing the parallelism of psychic and physical events. In such events, the paradoxical schizoid nature of the archetype is split and appears here as an image (psychic) and there as an exterior event, occasionally also as an object (physical, material)—dream and scarabaeid beetle in Jung's example. "The archetype," writes Aniela Jaffé, Jung's close collaborator, in her essay "C. G. Jung and Parapsychology," arranges or manifests itself in the facets of the synchronistic event. In other words, we are dealing here with an unusual manifestation of its "emergence into consciousness" by means of a split. Such a split, as we know, underlies the process whenever something comes into consciousness. We recognize one thing because we distinguish it from another. Under normal circumstances, the split leading to consciousness takes place within the individual's psychic world—in his thoughts, dreams, intuitions and experiences. In synchronistic phenomena, however, the various aspects of the archetype are torn apart. They present themselves at different times and at different places. This strange "behavior" may be explained by the fact that synchronistic phenomena are as much connected with consciousness as with the unconscious. The underlying or "organizing" archetype is not yet fully conscious; it is still partly in the unconscious—hence the relativity of space and time. But it has partly penetrated into consciousness, hence the split of its psychoid nature into two or more distinct and perceivable facets.[4]

This makes evident that the somewhat misleading term "synchronicity" does not mean "happening at the same time." In his book *Roots of Coincidence*, Arthur Koestler criticizes the term which implies simultaneity but does not mean what it says. It includes, for instance, precognitive dreams or cases of the Mont-Saint-Michel type. "He tried to get around the time paradox," writes Koestler, "by saying that the unconscious mind functions outside of the physical framework of space-time; so, precognitive experiences in Jung's words are— evidently not synchronous but are synchronistic since they are experienced as psychic images in the present as though the objective event already existed!"[5]

In the summary of his essay (Chapter 4), Jung presents a fourfold conceptual scheme of world events which should serve as the basis for a comprehensive understanding of the totality of human experience: a cross with "space" and "time" vertically opposed, "causality" and "synchronicity" horizontally opposed. Following a suggestion of Wolfgang Pauli, he added an elaboration of this diagram with the view of adapting his theory with data derived from modern quantum mechanics. We find "indestructible energy" opposed to "time-space-continuum" and, horizontally, "constant connection owing to the operation of causality" to "inconstant connection based on meaningful relationships, synchronicity, or so-called contingency." "The modern discovery of discontinuity," Jung comments (e.g., the disposition of energy quantums, of radium decomposition, etc.), "has put an end to the undivided sovereignty of causality and, therefore, to the trinity of principles. The territory the latter lost belonged in olden times to the realm of *correspondentia* and *sympathia*, concepts which reached their utmost deployment in the preestablished harmony of Leibniz."[6] Synchronicity figures as a principle of nature equal in rank to causality—a concept which Pauli did not contradict. Yet he maintained reserve toward the "organizing" archetype in the sense of the Jaffé citation. In a conversation I had with him in 1957 and which I recorded on tape, he said with regard to the split of an archetype in a dream and therefore to the corresponding reality: "Jung would say so, but he would have to characterize this archetype. I am a physicist; I cannot do so." He had no sooner said this, when he remembered, with regard to the Mont Saint-Michel case which we were discussing, that the driver is an old archetypal image like Krishna in the Indian mythology. He gave an interpretation in this sense but cut off remarking: "I could go astray." He was well acquainted with archetypal symbols.

As a precursor of the idea of synchronicity, Jung cites the Tao perception in "entire" (*ganzheitlich*) Chinese thinking, the antique idea of the sympathy of all things and the medieval philosophy of correspondentia with its characteristic example in Pico della Mirandola's doctrine: "Firstly there is the unity of things whereby each thing is one with itself, it consists of itself, and coheres with itself. Secondly, there is the unity whereby one creature is united with the others, and all parts of the world constitute one world. The third and main unity is that one by which the whole world is one with its creator like an army with its leader."[7] Passing through Agrippa of Nettesheim, godfather to the concept of "occultism," the line goes through Kepler, looking for the formative potencies at the base of correspondence in an "Anima telluris," a terrestrial soul, to the preestablished harmony of Leibniz. In the eighteenth century, in the wake of the Newtonian revolution, causality became the unique principle that explained matter and mind, to be questioned early in the twentieth as a consequence of the revolution in physics. In the middle of the materialistic nineteenth century, Arthur Schopenhauer, in his famous essay "Über die anscheinende Absichtlichkeit im Schicksale des Einzelnen" ("About the Apparent Premeditation in the Fate of the Individual"), stated that everything is interrelated and mutually attuned defining coincidence (in the sense of meaningful coincidence) as the simultaneous occurrence of causally unconnected events. In his view of causality, these events are based on a *causa prima*: "If we visualize each causal chain progressing in time as a meridian on the globe, then we may represent simultaneous events . . . by the parallel circles of latitude."[8]

Near relations to the concept of synchronicity are to be found in Paul Kammerer's *Gesetz der Serie* (*The Law of the Series*) (1919). This Austrian zoologist defines a series as "a lawful recurrence of the same or similar things and events—a recurrence, or clustering in time or space whereby the individual members in the sequence—as far as can be ascertained by careful analysis—are not connected by the same active cause."[9] The typology of non-causal concurrence related to numbers, names, situations etc., which he gives in the first part of his book, was enlarged some years later by a collection of meaningful coincidences which the writer Wilhelm von Scholz published under the title: *Der Zufall und das Schicksal* (*Coincidence and Fate*), first edition 1924. The collection contains many examples of remarkable coincidences which do not fit into ESP. He discusses them in detail and illustrates a gradation reaching from "mere chance" to "strange coincidence," and from "remarkable coincidence" to "fate" or "destiny." Dr. von Scholz finds that he can best describe the nature of such improbable events as a force: "The attractive force of the relevant" ("Anziehungskraft des Bezüglichen"). He likens the "attractive force of the relevant" to the forces of association of ideas in the mind and ventures the speculation of regarding the external world as the mental world of a greater being whose associated ideas constitute our material reality. Here is an example out of the material of this book, which has been enlarged from one edition to the next by new cases reported to the author: Shortly before the outbreak of World War I, a lady then living in Strasbourg in Alsace photographed her first baby in the Black Forest. She had the film developed in Strasbourg but forgot to collect it when she moved to Frankfurt soon after. She regretted the loss. Two years later she wanted to photograph her second baby. She bought a film, but when developed, it proved to have been exposed twice. The first exposure showed her first baby in the Black Forest. "Attraction of the relevant": A lost property returns to its owner by tortuous paths. As in a magic world— the author says—the sorrow felt at the loss of the film seems to have attracted the same.[10]

Frederick W. Knowles, who reviewed the fifth edition (1950) of *Coincidence and Fate* in the *Journal of Parapsychology*, recognizes the bearing of meaningful coincidences irreducible to ESP—the problem we are dealing with here—when he writes: "This work suggests that the spontaneous phenomena heretofore studied by parapsychologists may be only a fraction of a very much larger field of coincidence phenomena awaiting exploration and experimental demonstration. The other phenomena may be more common than those which parapsychology has covered so far."[11]

C. G. Jung discusses in his essay on synchronicity the well known vision which Swedenborg, the Swedish statesman, scientist and seer, had in Göteborg of a fire which was ravaging Stockholm: "We must assume that there was a lowering of the threshold of consciousness which gave him access to absolute knowledge. The fire in Stockholm was in a sense burning in him, too. For the unconscious psyche space and time seem to be relative; this is to say, knowledge finds itself in a space-time-continuum in which space is no longer space, nor time time. If, therefore, the unconscious should develop or maintain a potential in the direction of consciousness, it is then possible for parallel events to be perceived as 'known.' "[12]

"We are, however, urged to some such assumption unless we prefer to regress to a magical causality, and to attribute to psyche a power that far exceeds the empirical range of action. In that case we should have to suppose, if we don't want to let causality go, either that Swedenborg's unconscious staged the Stockholm fire, or conversely that the objective event activated in a quite unconceivable manner the corresponding images in Swedenborg's brain. In either case we come up against the unanswerable question of transmission discussed earlier. It is of course entirely a matter of subjective opinion which hypothesis makes more sense . . . I prefer the latter because it does not, like the first, conflict with the empiric concept of causality and can count as a principle sui generis."[13]

I have cited Jung at such length to illustrate his point: paranormal events such as Swedenborg's "true" vision are not "perceptions" stemming from paranormal capacities and induced by some sort of "magic causality" but corresponding events based on the relativity of space, time and causality. They manifest an "absolute knowledge of the unconscious" which mostly emerges into consciousness in an archetypical condition of the psyche.[14]

Dr. Peter Ringger referred, in an article "C. G. Jung's Concept of Synchronicity" in the journal *Neue Wissenschaft*[15] to a precursor of the idea of synchronicity who had escaped Jung: Max Dessoir, who proposed, in 1889, the term "parapsychology," said with regard to Swedenborg's vision and in order to avoid admitting extrasensory perception: "If the encounter is no coincidence, one should, at the utmost, be entitled to think that there can be meaningful relations between simultaneous, but differently originating events which point to a hidden structure of the order of universe. Such a secret correlation would be referred to the meaning of processes and not at all to their mechanical or psychological formation." Such are Max Dessoir's suggestions in his book *Vom jenseits der Seele* (*About the Beyond of the Psyche*).[16] If Dessoir had passed over the obstacle of "simultaneity" by making space and time relative, the idea of synchronicity had been formulated.

In a letter addressed to H. Rossteutscher[17] in 1958, Jung characterized synchronicity as a "makeshift model" and as "a proposed name which takes into account the fact that causality is a statistical truth which, by necessity, presupposes exemptions." Let us now discuss if this "makeshift model" proves to be a plausible theoretical frame for the diverse manifestations of psi.

As for *spontaneous phenomena*, experience teaches that they arise almost regularly in emotional situations. The statistical evaluation of several thousands of cases gathered in the archives of the Freiburg

Institute for Border Areas of Psychology and Mental Hygiene show the
following distribution (cf. *Unser sechster Sinn*:[18]

Kind of Psi		Kind of Experience		Topics		Contents	
Telepathy and clairvoyance	50%	Dream	43%	Death	44%	negative affects	82%
precognition	39%	Presentiment	24%	Illness injuries risk of death	19%		
		hallucination and vision	18%	Important events	26%		
						positive affects	10%
		physical affects	7%				
Mixed forms	4%	other forms of experience	8%	events without importance	11%	ambivalent	2%
Psychokinesis	7%	(illusions, inner voices etc.)				indifferent banal	4%
						insecure	2%

It is clear that these experiences are predominantly situations
of existential importance. It is striking that these situations are of a
threatening character in most cases: danger-to-life and death, risk,
fatal developments, etc., in 40 percent of the reports. International
research shows the same results. Jung's concept that in such emotionally charged existential situations a disposition of the "collective
unconscious"—an archetype, identical with "objective nature"—is
activated, constitutes a plausible mythology. It acts like an "organizer,"
inducing corresponding events. In her lecture "Synchronicity and
Causality in Parapsychology," *Eranos* 1973, Aniela Jaffé mentions
that Jung pointed out explicitly "that the supposition of a paradoxical
background reality is at bottom only an explaining myth or a model
for something essentially unimaginable."[19]

The meaningful coincidence which cannot be reduced to the ESP
hypothesis constitutes a special case among spontaneous phenomena.
Their numbers as percentage of extraordinary events are not yet
registered statistically. This type of unexpected event corroborates
strongly Jung's concept that it is not perception which is paranormal

but the event itself. The problem is, as Knowles remarked, either the spontaneous phenomena which fit into the ESP hypothesis are only a fraction of a larger field of coincidence phenomena, perhaps modified by the possible interference of what parapsychologists call telepathy, clairvoyance and precognition, or they are phenomena *sui generis*, having perhaps to do with some form of causally inexplicable interaction between two or more organisms in the case of possible telepathy. I shall come back to this fundamental problem later on.

As to the interpretation of success obtained with intent in psi experiments, I must admit that the theory of synchronicity does not seem satisfactory to me. Jung counted even Rhine's card experiments among synchronistic phenomena. The archetype which comes into existence in such experiments is, in his mind, "the miracle," the emotionally exciting expectation of something that is impossible in the sense of our familiar concept of the world. It is a fact of repeated observation that with routine and becoming accustomed to the tension, expectation subsides and the rate of positive results declines or disappears completely. There is no doubt about the essential part that the "field of affection" plays in this state of tension, but we cannot decide whether it is originated in the archetype as Jung thinks. In the ordinary card experiments intended to prove the existence of psi and realized without variables, a synchronistic interpretation may seem more or less plausible. In my opinion, however, it must be rejected as soon as intentionally introduced variables show induced correlations of positive results. Here is an example from the files of the Freiburg Institute reported in my book *Our Sixth Sense*.[20] A technical assistant, Michael W., obtained significant scores of an astronomical height in the following experimental situation: He had before him a pack of 250 ESP cards containing five times fifty randomized symbols. He looked at a card, named the symbol, using a tape recorder and pressed a button to give a signal using an electrical device, which secured an equal length, to a subject separated from him by two rooms. The subject tried to recognize the symbol Michael was looking at, and called her guess over a microphone. This went on for the 250 symbols. Michael heard the subject's call— this possibility of a feedback proved to be encouraging—but had of course no direct speech-communication with the subject. Agent and percipients (five) often achieved 70–75 hits instead of the chance expectation of 50. In a total of 3575 calls 985 hits were obtained, 270 above chance expectation, which corresponded to a critical ratio of 11.25 or to a probability of $1:10^{-29}$.

This general ESP situation did not allow us to differentiate between telepathy and clairvoyance. A variable was therefore introduced. At random intervals, Michael did not look at the cards and the subject did not know of this change. In this clairvoyance situation he could not, of course, call the symbol on the microphone. A number of calls equal to the GESP situation gave mere chance results whilst in the same series "telepathy" was functioning. This inductive correlation demonstrates clearly that the subject's calls corresponded to Michael's mental representation of the symbol. Thus it appears reasonable to call him "the agent."

I need not discuss in detail that in such an obvious causation the fundamental concept of synchronicity does not become effective, at least not without most remarkable modifications. In the same way— to cite another example from a lot of similar material—Vasiliev's experiments with the "hypnogene method" cannot be interpreted by the theory of synchronicity. At a given moment, the hypnotist causes, as a telepathic agent, by means of mental suggestion, the beginning of hypnosis in the subject as well as his or her return to a waking state. In the same way, experimentally induced out-of-the-body experiences or paranormal influences on the healing of wounds, all intentional psi-effects, resist interpretation by the concept of synchronicity, which lays stress on the phenomena of "unexpected meaningful coincidences." These considerations are not a plea for the term "extrasensory perception." Indeed, we do not know if psi-information stems from a perceptive faculty of the psyche. I should prefer to use the term "extrasensory experience," but I still keep using the traditional one, as I use the term "parapsychology," which badly needs to be replaced by another one covering the whole field of scientific approaches to the paranormal.

With regard to experimental psychokinesis, Aniela Jaffé, the administrator of Jung's spiritual heritage, expresses her doubts that the concept of synchronicity can be applied here. In *Synchronicity and Causality in Parapsychology* she writes as follows: "For an explanation of psychokinesis, synchronicity seems scarcely convincing. Jung's hint at the psychical relativity of time and space, 'then the moving body must possess, or be subject to, corresponding relativity', does not lead us much further. He did not mention the question of psychokinesis with more than this short remark. But in his work as well as in his letters he does hint at a possibility that the psyche can influence non-psychical things in some way and that, therefore, there may exist some so-to-speak causal relation."[21]

Such a "would-be causal" relationship which does not fit into synchronicity is obvious, as a matter of fact, in all PK experiments, especially in qualitative ones. There are, the "metal-bending experiments"—induced by Uri Geller's genuine or trick demonstrations—which are actually widely discussed and examined by parapsychologists as well as by physicists like John Taylor, J. B. Hasted, H. D. Betz and others. At the P.A. Convention of Utrecht, in August 1976, I reported, with film recordings, successful experiments with the technical designer and graphic artist Silvio from Berne, who deforms pieces of cutlery of metal and plastic material, with or without touching, and partly breaks them. An "optimistic group of physicists" (as John Beloff described them at the Parascience Conference of London in September 1975)—among them John Taylor—are trying to ascribe the phenomena to effects of electromagnetism, but others remain cautious and reserved and do not reject connections as yet physically inexplicable. Among others, the following hypothesis develops: the subject transmits, by unknown means, information to the material object, influencing in such a way the "behavior" of the molecules; the energy needed for such modifications stems from the object itself (Puthoff and Targ, 1974).[22] Von Lucadou and K. Kornwachs introduce, for the PK organization of the thermal energy of the object, a hypothetical macroscopic function of probability ψ.[23] It is evident, that the concept of synchronicity does not lead any further in this connection.

I should like to devote some consideration to the book by Alister Hardy, Robert Harvie and Arthur Koestler, *The Challenge of Chance* (1973), which I came to know only after having chosen the topic for my contribution to the present symposium. Just as is my intention, the authors treat the long neglected problem of "meaningful coincidences outside the framework of parapsychology;" especially Koestler in "Speculations on Problems Beyond our Present Understanding." As many of you will know, Koestler contributes a collection of anecdotal cases based—like the material of Dr. von Scholz—on readers' letters to the author, personal communications from friends and answers to a questionnaire sent out by the Religious Experience Research Unit (RERU). The guiding principle of selection was emphasis on the "coincidental" nature of the experience.[24] However, he could not present a rigid categorical distinction because "coincidental" and "ESP type" phenomena overlap sometimes. The categories range from the "library angel"—coincidental events of a verbal nature—to cases involving mechanics and engineering, poltergeists (where, to my astonishment, I found the Rosenheim case which I do not regard as overlapping but as spontaneous recurrent PK bound to an "agent"), practical joke types of stories, places or dwellings involved with people and serial phenomena, in Kammerer's sense, which show a "clustering" or "converging" of events which are meaningfully related but causally unrelated. In this context, Koestler remarks that "some people become coincidence-prone, as others become accident-prone."[25]

This is very true and leads me to report on an observation of my own regarding a complex of "coincidental events," where Mrs. E., a friend of mine, was the "catalyst." This lady proved to be not only "coincidence-prone" but also "psi-prone": precognitive statements from sensitives came true for her with astonishing precision. The same sensitive persons gave barely telepathic statements with regard to myself. My case was as follows: At the end of World War II, I was occupied, as physician and interpreter, in a prison camp near Marseille. I often had arguments with a colleague, Prof. W., on behalf of a young friend of mine whose progressive political ideas he rejected whilst I agreed with them. Mrs. I. was a girl friend of this young man. Back home, I made her acquaintance through him. In 1953, Mrs. Eileen Garrett invited me to take part in a symposium on "Unorthodox Healing" in Saint-Paul-de-Vence. Flying back via Marseille, I realized suddenly, beneath the plane, that the prison camp must be there. In a sort of uncontrolled excitement, I said to an unknown neighbor, without any rational connection: "We are just crossing the location of a prison camp where I spent months with Prof. W." My neighbor replied, deeply astounded: "I know him well and shall see him in the next few days." Some time later, I met Mrs. E. in Stuttgart. When dining with her in a restaurant, I told her this story. At that very moment, the door opened, and in came a man and a woman. I could not trust my eyes; the man seemed to be Prof. W. I was so flabbergasted that I did not ask him directly if he really was my colleague in Marseille. Later I asked the receptionist to call him to the telephone. He promptly answered—it was he!

This encounter type of synchronistic event emerges from a manifold intense affective field. Jung could most probably reduce it to an archetypical condition of the psyche. But what about the trivial cases —those serial events with names that Koestler defines with the question: "What unknown agency plays the clustering games with names"?[26] This poses the question which type of acausal relationships can legitimately claim to be of a meaningful nature, and which has to be dismissed as neither causal nor acausal, but merely arbitrary?

In an unpublished interview with C. G. Jung in December, 1960, eight months before his death, the problem of the trivial cases was discussed. Jung acknowledged that he himself had trivial precognitive dreams and commented: "There are evidently such phenomena where we see the future but where we cannot speak of synchronicity, because we do not see any possibility of participation mystique, because there is no archetype to which we could refer . . . The fact that we can see such nonsense [trivial things] leads us to consider that, obviously, one may see 'beside the peep-hole of time' . . . That is, of course, quite another explanation, another hypothesis. That's why I do not make theories, I keep saying these cases must be treated separately." As this remark shows, Jung was far from applying the theory of synchronicity as a doctrine. In the same way, his idea that the extraordinary moment lies in the event itself and not in a perceptive process, must not be considered as absolutely valid for him.

In the first part of *The Challenge of Chance*, the well known zoologist, Alister Hardy, compares the positive results of experiments in telepathy of a qualitative kind to somewhat comparable "hits" in pure coincidental situations—the Spencer-Brown problem. Koestler suggests the category of "para-randomness" as a special form of different categories of coincidences which all show what he tentatively calls "the convergent effect." In this context, he introduces the term "order from disorder," an integrative tendency in Nature in which the converging or clustering effects—synchronicity—would appear as the highest manifestation "although their modus operandi is at present unknown and may not be beyond the faculty of comprehension in our species." Koestler cites a number of tentative formulations of this principle: the formal or formative cause of Aristotle as distinct from the "effective" cause which corresponds to mechanical causation, Galen's and after him Kepler's "facultas formatrix," its reflection in Spinoza's pantheism and its echo in Goethe's "Gestaltung" and Bergson's "élan vital." He mentions the German biologist Woltereck, who coined the term "anamorphosis" for nature's tendency to create higher forms of life, and von Bertalanffy who adopted the term as a contrast to "morpholysis"—the disintegration of inorganic matter. One could add Driesch's entelechy and many others. It is related to Schrödinger's concept of "negative entropy," the reversal of the Second Law of Thermodynamics. "What all these tentative formulations have in common," Koestler concludes," is that they regard the morphic, or formative, or integrative tendency, Nature's striving towards creating order out of disorder, cosmos out of chaos, as an ultimate and irreducible principle, to be considered as equal in importance to mechanical causation, and complementary in quantum theory."[27]

I have neither the time nor the competence to comment on the relationship of the theory of synchronicity with modern physics, which

Koestler exposes in relation to parapsychology in his book, *The Roots of Coincidence*. I am eager for information and would like to become enlightened, if there are physicists here, on the paradox that a solid world arises from the unpredictable behavior of particles in microphysics or on the problem that the half-life period of any grain of radioactive substance is precisely fixed but—as Bohm points out— "it does not have any causes." Maybe the much discussed "hidden variables" may one day appear as a factor of convergence between physics and psi.

As you have noticed, my contribution is a mainly pragmatic one, the chief purpose of which is to provide material for a philosophical discussion. Let me conclude with a case which involved me very personally: the "coincidence" of events which led to my marriage. It made me think of Schopenhauer's already mentioned essay "Über die anscheinende Absichtlichkeit im Schicksal des Einzelnen" ("About the Apparent Intentionality in the Destiny of the Individual") where he writes of the "simultaneity of not causally connected things which we call coincidence." By means of the already mentioned image of meridians and transverse lines, Schopenhauer illustrates meaningful coincidences in the field of partnership relations: "All events in the life of a human being would then underlie two fundamentally diverse kinds of connection: firstly, the objective, causal connection of natural processes; secondly, the subjective connection which exists only with regard to the individual who is experiencing this connection and which is as subjective as this individual's dream . . . These two kinds of connection exist at the same time, and the same destiny is notwithstanding integrated as a link of two quite different chains so that the destiny of one corresponds each time to the destiny of the other; everyone is therefore at the same time, the hero of his or her own drama and a figure of a foreign drama; all this defies our comprehension and seems only possible by way of the most miraculous harmonia praestabilita."[28]

When one brings to mind, retrospectively, the ways which led us to know our life partner, tiny "coincidences" often prove to have been instrumental for an encounter, a type of encounter-synchronicity which gives rise to a feeling of numinosity. Here is my case: When I was 19 years old, I left my gloves—in general use in those times—after a visit; when I went to fetch them, the intelligent lady of the house recommended my visiting a university lecturer in Heidelberg, a friend of hers, with my study problems. This conversation induced me to choose a university teacher from Heidelberg as my tutor, and I moved with him from Heidelberg to Bonn where he had been called. There

I made the acquaintance of a girl student. It was love at first sight. A little later I showed her photo to my mother, whom I met in Zürich. She became very thoughtful and reluctantly told me that this girl very much resembled a man to whom she nearly got engaged. This man was my girl friend's father. He happened to be in Zürich at the same time, and my mother met him for the first time after 25 years. He recognized me at once for my resemblance to my mother and was very perplexed. Besides, it turned out that the lady who had recommended me to go to Heidelberg was a friend of his. The girl became my wife much later. A meaningful coincidence, indeed, the implications of which—as Schopenhauer puts it—defy our powers of comprehension.

While Schopenhauer still tries to bridge, with concepts of causal thinking, the Cartesian gap between spirit and matter, for which a connection of objective aspects in natural processes with psychical aspects seems to make no sense, Jung attempts, as a metaphysical background to synchronicity, a hypothesis of a *mundus unus*, a unitary aspect of being. After a careful evaluation of present-day science, especially of physics and the psychology of the unconscious, he concluded that the two background realities were possibly one and the same thing. This would be, he writes, "as much physical as psychic and therefore neither, but rather a third thing, a neutral nature which can at most be grasped in hints since in essence it is transcendental."[29]

REFERENCES

[1] Jung, C. G., "Synchronizität als ein Prinzip akausaler Zusammenhänge" in: C. G. Jung, W. Pauli: *Naturerklärung und Psyche* Zurich. 1952, p. 26. See also C. G. Jung: "The Structure and Dynamics of the Psyche," Collected Works, Vol. VIII, London 1960, p. 441.

[2] Ibid., p. 26.

[3] Ibid., p. 22.

[4] Jaffé, Aniela, "C. G. Jung and Parapsychology." in: *Int. J. of Parapsychology 10* (1968) p. 37–55.

[5] Koestler, A., *The Roots of Coincidence* London 1972, p. 95.

[6] Jung, C. G., op. cit., p. 104.

[7] Pico della Mirandola, *Opera Omnia*, Basel 1557, p. 40.

[8] "Versinnlichen wir uns jetzt jene einzelnen Kausalketten durch Meridiane, die in der Richtung der Zeit lägen; so kann überall das Gleichzeitige und eben deshalb nicht in directem Kausalzusammenhange Stehende, durch Paralellkreise angedeutet werden." Artur Schopenhauer, *Parerga und Paralipomena*, original edition Vol. VIII Stuttgart 1851, p. 204; compare the citation in: A. Koestler: op. cit., p. 107.

[9] Kammerer, Paul, *Das Gesetz der Serie* Stuttgart, Berlin 1919, p. 36.

[10] von Scholz, Wilhelm, *Zufall und Schicksal* Leipzig 1942 (4. ed.), p. 60 ff.

[11] Knowles, Frederick W., Book Review in: *J. of Parapsychology 17* (1953) p. 155–157.

[12] Jung, C. G., op. cit., p. 67.

[13] Ibid., p. 68.

[14] Ibid., p. 68.

[15] Ringger, Peter, "C. G. Jungs Synchronizitätsbegriff" in *Neue Wissenschaft 3* (1952) p. 12–18.

[16] Dessoir, Max, *Vom Jenseits der Seele* Stuttgart 1931 (6. ed.), p. 190.
[17] in: C. G. Jung: Briefe III (1956–1961), ed. by A. Jaffé Freiburg-Olten 1973, p. 179 f.
[18] Bender, Hans, *Unser sechster Sinn* Stuttgart 1971, p. 8.
[19] Jaffé, A., "Synchronizität und Kausalität in der Parapsychologie." in: *Eranos 42* (1973) p. 2–42.
[20] Bender, Hans op. cit., p. 65 ff.
[21] Jaffé, A., op. cit., p. 2–42.
[22] Puthoff, H., and Targ, R., "Physics, Entropy and Psychokinesis," in: *Quantum Physics and Parapsychology* Proceedings of an International Conference New York: Parapsychology Foundation, 1975.
[23] von Lucadou, W., Kornwachs, K., "Grundzüge zu einer Theorie paranormaler Phänomene," in: *Zeitschrift für Parapsychologie und Grenzgebiete der Psychologie 17* (1975) p. 73–87.
[24] Hardy, Alister, Harvie, Robert, Koestler, A., *The Challenge of Chance*, London 1973, p. 160.
[25] Ibid., p. 194.
[26] Ibid., p. 197.
[27] Ibid. p., 238.
[28] Schopenhauer, A., op. cit., p. 208 f.
[29] Jung, C. G., *Mysterium Coniunctionis*, Vol. II, Freiburg Olten 1971, p. 318.

DISCUSSION

THAKUR: I'll leave the substantive questions to the others and will only ask what might be just a simple terminological one, but in asking it, I don't mean to be difficult. At one stage you say something about reality itself being paranormal. I found this a bit strange because I would have thought that reality is something that just is. Reality itself isn't either normal or paranormal.

MAUSKOPF: Your summary of the Jung-Pauli Synchronicity Principle sounded very similar (to what I understood, at least) to Rex Stanford's remarks this morning. I would be interested in any dialogue between the two of you. Is this the sort of thing you were driving at in your concept of disposition as opposed to psychological/biological causality?

STANFORD: Well, I'm not really sure because I still don't feel that I have an understanding of the concept of synchronicity. It seems to me that Professor Bender was in many ways, commenting on and perhaps even expanding that concept and trying to clarify it, but as the concept stands, at least to the best of my understanding, it would not match my own concepts. It would attempt to deal with the many facts that I attempt to deal with in my theory and indeed in my earlier theory, but I have attempted to develop a theory that I feel has clearly testable implications. I have long felt that synchronicity doesn't have testable implications because, being an acausal theory, it has taken a form where there are no clearly antecedent conditions to anything, and therefore I don't think we're talking about the same kind of theory.

BENDER: Well, I quite accept what you're saying and understand your point of view.

SERVADIO: Of course, I quite accept that there can be meaningful events which are linked by mechanisms, or whatever we may call them, that cannot be traced back to causality, time, or space. But let us not forget that Jung started making his observations in a clinical frame of reference and his case of the scarab which you quoted at the beginning, has become famous. Now I think there can be a danger in using the term *synchronicity* as a sort of label for many events that we *prima facie* just cannot explain. In my clinical experience I have had many cases, of course, of extrasensory perception—psi events between analyst and patient—and have seen in several cases that it would have been skipping the issue to label the case as synchronicity and nothing else; whereas, in many cases it was quite possible to assess the very subtle conditioning of an interpersonal relationship on conscious levels, which were really prominent in producing this psi effect between analyst and patient. So I would warn people who are interested in this particular area against the temptation of just putting on a label of synchronicity and stopping at that.

BENDER: I would point out that while the main point of my contribution was to draw your attention to spontaneous cases which imposed themselves as meaningful coincidences but do not fit into ESP and PK, the matter can be discussed without the theory of synchronicity. That's empirical work which has to be done to give statistics as to how often these cases are reported. Take, as a type, the Mont Saint-Michel case which I have observed myself. If you accept my impression that it has a precognitive bearing but cannot be reduced to ESP—well, this is a big problem, which we can discuss without synchronicity.

FRENCH: This is probably only a semantic question, but I'm a little bit puzzled about the use of the word *meaningful*, and I wondered if you could tell me if it would make sense to talk about a *non-meaningful* coincidence or if *meaningful* here is perhaps what I think it may be.

BENDER: The term *meaningful coincidences* is what we call anthropomorphic, because the meaning relates to a human being. I don't know if there are meaningful coincidences in this sense—for instance, in animal behavior, maybe—so, of course it's very difficult to define what *meaningful* means. It makes sense for someone. This Mont Saint-Michel event—well, it makes sense for the woman who experienced it. For her, it was an oracle for her future life and there are thousands of cases like that.

FRENCH: It just seemed to me that perhaps labeling them as *meaningful* is something that comes rather after analysis than before. It seemed to me perhaps question-begging to call them such before serious research has gone on. That was the only problem I had with understanding what you were talking about. If they are coincidences, then the question of whether they are or they are not *meaningful* would seem to me more to the point.

BENDER: We'll let it go at that.

JOHNSON: Well, it certainly was a very interesting lecture and I think one should allow oneself to speculate, but at the same time I see a great number of problems and, as a matter of fact, some of these problems have already been touched upon. For one thing, the use of labeling events which we can't make sense of. Secondly, how to assess the degree of meaningfulness. It certainly is a very subjective matter and I'm not entirely denying the use of subjectiveness, but at the same time I'm honoring the concept of intersubjectiveness. Do you see what I see? And we need some way of assessing that, I'm quite sure. And then the use of Jung's concept of archetypes. What worries me a bit is, what kind of test implication does it have and, also being a bit of a Popperean, could we ever think of putting the concept of archetypes to the critical test of refutation just as the concept of synchronicity?

BENDER: Of course, synchronicity is a sort of mythology, but I daresay in regard to parapsychology, we are living with mythologies.

MATTUCK: This is a continuation of Professor Servadio's comment. You said that you were going to restrict yourself to meaningful coincidences which could not be put under the category of psychokinesis or extrasensory perception, yet I feel that at least two of the examples which you gave can very easily be put into these categories. For instance, the case of the lady whose baby appeared on a photo as a sort of extra picture—this seems to fit perfectly into the category of psychic photography of the type which Ted Serios makes. There you can clearly see the wish in the lady's subconscious to see the picture of that first baby and it could have been produced by psychokinesis. In the case of the scarab, there are at least two ways in which that could be described, using just ordinary psychokinesis or precognition, namely, either that the lady saw precognitively that the scarab was going to crawl into the window while she was talking to Jung the next day, or that because of her or Jung's wish to confirm the dream of the scarab, they had a psychokinetic influence on one of the beetles crawling around outside. I imagine if you thought hard about it, most of the other cases which you gave as examples of meaningful coincidences, which could not be put into the category of PK and ESP, *could* be put in these categories nevertheless, and there would be only a little residue left of meaningful coincidences which could not be described either as examples of PK or ESP.

BENDER: I think you'll probably agree with me that the case of Mont Saint-Michel can't be reduced to ESP and psychokinesis.

AN ACAUSAL THEORY OF EXTRASENSORY PERCEPTION AND PSYCHOKINESIS

Frederick C. Dommeyer

One of the major difficulties with parapsychology has been that it seems not to accord with the framework of scientific law. C. D. Broad has noted this by pointing out that psi violates "the basic limiting principles of science." J. B. Rhine and J. Gaither Pratt have directed attention to this same incompatibility of parapsychology with orthodox science by calling for a scientific revolution, such that the data of parapsychology can be subsumed under a more comprehensive theoretical structure than science now provides.

This seeming incompatibility creates a number of anomalies in parapsychology which make it impossible for large numbers of orthodox scientists and common-sense persons to accept its claims. It is absurd to believe, they would say, that what is in one person's mind can influence another mind except through a sensory route, e.g., by means of language. They would hold that it is nonsensical to suppose that a person can "see" an object or event except by means of his eyes. They would regard it as ridiculous to believe that one can know a future event will occur except on the basis of present, available data, rules of sequence, and reasoning by means of these. They would regard it as impossible that objects outside a person's own body could be caused to move or change other than by means of his muscular efforts or by some other physical means. These beliefs respectively place telepathy, clairvoyance, precognition and psychokinesis into the category of the absurd.

The "revolution" in science wanted by J. B. Rhine and J. Gaither Pratt has not occurred, nor are there any signs heralding its coming. A more pedestrian solution for these anomalies may therefore be ventured, namely, an acausal theory of ESP and PK. It is sometimes claimed that an acausal theory in psi is "metaphysical" in the bad sense of that term, meaning that it is capable neither of verification nor of disproof. This is, however, not so. The acausal theory could be disproved by verifying empirically a causal theory of ESP-PK. And proof of the theory is possible, as will be observed later, by empirically establishing that the physical entity and its verifying referent are each causally explained without the necessity of citing any causal dependence of one on the other.

Let it be noted first that parapsychology makes use of such mentalistic elements as visions, images, dreams, hunches, and premonitions. I shall refer to these as *psychical entities*, simply to make it possible to discuss them in a general way. These psychical entities are not self-verifying; an hallucinatory premonition, for example, is not *intrinsically* different from a veridical one. If they were different intrinsically, one could tell by an examination of the psychical entity itself whether it was veridical or non-veridical, and this cannot be done. Whether veridical or not, however, psychical entities have an *intentional* aspect, meaning by this that they *intend* an object or event outside of themselves. Almost always, this intentionality is immediate and conjoined with the experience of the psychical entity. There are, however, instances where this characteristic is delayed in that it becomes apparent only sometime after the psychical entity has been experienced. The first case to be cited under precognition will be an example of this "delayed intentionality."

If psychical entities are not self-verifying, as is claimed above, how are they verified or, on the other hand, seen to be hallucinatory? It might be claimed that the psychical entity of Person A can be verified by those of Persons B, C, etc. That is, one might argue, say, that if five sensitives all claim to "see" clairvoyantly the same event E, that this congruence of ESP experience verifies A's belief that E occurred. It is conceivable, however, that this congruence is a result of one purported clairvoyant act and four telepathic ones, with the epistemic status of the belief in the event's occurrence thereby dependent entirely on the purported original clairvoyant act. It is the case, moreover, that parapsychologists depend for verification or disproof on ordinary experiences of the "intended object or event" or the lack of such experiences, e.g., in checking the score on an ESP card test, the experimenter uses ordinary perception in the reporting of his findings. If psychical entities are verified to any degree, it is because ordinary experiences and reports about them corroborate the intentionality of the psychical entities in question, thereby marking them off as special kinds of mental events, which are then called telepathic, clairvoyant, precognitive or psychokinetic. These verifying experiences are of events outside of the subject's mind, i.e., events in another person's mind or in the so-called external world. It is these outside events that are generally believed to be causally related to their relevant psychical entities, though parapsychologists, harboring this belief tenaciously, have never been able to provide satisfactory empirical grounds for it.

What has been called "objects or events outside the mind of the subject" will now be designated as "verifying referents," i.e., of the relevant psychical entities. It is necessary to distinguish between a "minimal verifying referent" and a "maximal" one. Let us imagine that a clairvoyant "saw" a snake dying in an impenetrable jungle. On this assumption, the dying of the snake would be a "minimal verifying referent" because we would admittedly *have* a clairvoyant act, even though it was incapable of verification except possibly by an omniscient God. Parapsychologists holding to a causal theory of ESP, would say that there must be some causal connection between the clairvoyant's psychical entity and the event in the impenetrable jungle. For a verifying referent to be "maximal," there must be a minimal situation and, in addition, an ordinary experience of the object or event intended by the psychical entity, along with a relevant relating of the two.

The desirability of a causal theory of ESP-PK is obvious. If one knew how to cause an instance of ESP or PK, and could repeat similar instances at will, then ESP-PK would have scientific status in the best sense of that term. Before excluding a causal theory with the introduction of an acausal one, some consideration of causal theories of ESP-PK will therefore be in order.

Telepathy is defined as the "extrasensory perception of the mental state or activity of another person."[1] What this means essentially is that Person A can know what is experienced by Person B *without* B conveying that to A by use of language or by any other method of sensory signaling, or by B's facial or bodily movements as they are observed by A, or by any other conceivable sensory channel of information between B and A. Telepathy thus falls completely outside the pattern of ordinary ways whereby A can become aware of B's ideas, images, percepts, emotions, willings. Telepathy is therefore categorically declared by many scientists to be impossible.

Telepathy has so far defied understanding, and one can at best philosophize about various explanations of it. Viewing the problem speculatively, one can imagine certain avenues of approach. One can suppose, say, that an image in B's mind is correlated with a certain physicochemical event in his brain and that electrical activity in his brain activates the brain of A and thereby produces a similar image in A's mind. The difficulty with this theory is well known. The electrical activity in B's brain, though present, is known to be insufficient to produce a change in A's brain. Moreover, there is evidence from

Faraday cage experiments that telepathy is not a result of electromagnetic waves passing from Person B outside the cage to Person A within it. Though the experimental work of those who produced this conclusion is questioned by some parapsychologists, those who question it have not been able to prove the electromagnetic theory of ESP.

But other hypotheses of a speculative sort suggest themselves. It has been noted earlier that there are psychophysical causal relations, which seem to be limited however to one's mind as it affects *its* body. If one extends the idea of psychophysical causation from one's mind to things *outside* of its own body, there comes into focus the notion of a psychokinetic explanation. Telepathy could be explained through this concept, i.e., a mental event in B's mind psychokinetically affects A's brain, producing in it a physicochemical event such that A experiences a state or activity of mind similar to B's. This explanation has the advantage over the previous one in providing a "force" sufficient to produce a physical change in A's brain. There are, in any case, accounts of psychokinetic activities in which heavy objects have been moved by psychokinetic "energy." A difficulty with this explanatory hypothesis, however, is that it "explains" telepathy by means of an even more incredible notion, namely, psychokinesis. It is also the case that established science finds no place for psychophysical causal relations between a mind and a body not that mind's own.

One might however try a psychopsychical causal hypothesis for telepathy, i.e., that the mental event in B's mind can directly affect A's mind in such a way as to produce a similar event in A's mind. If discarnate minds in the next world communicate with one another, as has been claimed by spiritists, it would have to be in such a fashion.

The view presupposed in this explanation of telepathy between embodied human beings would substantially argue for the complete independence of mind from brain so far as causal influence between two minds goes. This position has the handicap of being disbelieved by most scientists, for it violates their basic conviction that one mind can influence another mind only through sensory channels, e.g., by use of language. Another difficulty in the way of this explanation is that, even when there exists in *one* person a psychopsychical causal relation, say, the idea of "man" causing by association the idea "woman," it is highly doubtful that such association is a purely psychopsychical matter; it probably involves intermediary brain-state changes.

Another explanation of telepathy is perhaps even less plausible. There exists in dreams "spatial" relations such that dream-chairs may be in front of dream-tables. Such a situation entails the being of "mental" space in distinction from physical space. There are no spatial relations between these two kinds of space; one is either in one space or the other. It follows that objects in a dream are not therefore spatially locatable in a brain, for a brain is in physical space. This line of thought suggests that things of the mind subsist in a separate realm, i.e., separate from physical things. Is it possible for the contents of the mental world of B to become one occasionally and partially with the mental world of A, in which case a telepathic relationship would occur reciprocally between B and A? This would involve a sharing of identical images, ideas or memories by B and A. If the sharing were complete, there would not be two minds, but only one. When incomplete, however, a telepathic relationship would exist, as was noted. Such a view could be, though it need not be, extended to include the notion of a "world mind." To these hypotheses, an objection can be offered. Both forms, the nonmetaphysical and the metaphysical versions, destroy the commonly accepted "privacy of mind" principle. It is generally maintained that one's experiences are egocentric and not immediately shareable. All sharing of human experiences, it is contended, must be *indirect*; one person cannot have another person's experiences, i.e., in the sense of having *identical* experiences. Also, the assumption, in this view, that things of the mind are in mental space is questionable. Pain, for example, seems to be locatable in a toe or tooth.

There are, of course, other explanations of telepathy that have not been included here. But none of them has resolved the problem of how telepathy occurs, i.e., of what relationship exists between a psychical entity in the telepath's mind and the minimal verifying referent in another's mind.

In the light of these facts, an acausal theory of telepathy (and other forms of ESP and PK) is not unreasonable. It has moreover marked advantages: 1) It makes the revolution that Rhine and Pratt desire unnecessary, for an acausal theory is entirely compatible with ordinary science; 2) it eliminates the anomalies that cause both many scientists and commonsense persons to regard the claims of parapsychologists as absurd; 3) it takes away all bases for such linguistic criticisms as Peter A. French presents in his Introduction to *Philosophers in Wonderland*;[2] 4) it is in complete harmony with the state of affairs in parapsychology, for parapsychologists have been unable to provide a satisfactory (empirically verifiable) causal account of telepathy and other ESP-PK phenomena; and 5) it also fits in with the well-known "elusiveness" of psi phenomena and their rarity in the laboratory (when they are not pseudo-phenomena created by tricksters).

There are acausal events and uniformities in the world, some of

them artifactitious and others of them, natural. As an illustration, two
clocks, one of them mechanical and in the United States and the other,
electrical, and in Switzerland—let us postulate that they have nothing
in common in their respective causal backgrounds in order to save a
lot of additional description—will, if accurate time-keepers, show
12 N. together, or if set differently in a random way, show uniform
differences in their readings. Each clock's time-keeping has its own
separate and independent causal past, but neither clock is related
causally such that one can correctly say that the 12 N. on the one
clock is caused by the 12 N. on the other, or the other way around.
The instances thus displayed are acausal and the uniformity is acausal.
We may call this a Type I kind of acausality.

Such acausal instances and uniformities differ from causal ones. If
a lighted match C, in situation S, is followed by explosion E, and the
existence of E cannot be explained without reference to C and S, we
have an instance of causation. Associated with causation is the principle
that "similar causes in similar situations are followed by similar effects."
It is causal explanation and uniformity of these kinds, and the ability
to control and repeat work in a laboratory situation, that parapsychologists seek and which, up to this time, they have not achieved. By contrast, in an instance of acausality or in an acausal uniformity, we do
not explain A's existence by reference to B, or B's by reference to A,
nor is either a controlling factor over the other in the sense that one
causally influences the other.

There are some acausal relationships (designated as Type II) where
two events are causally independent but where they have some common causal antecedent or antecedents. A case in point—to put it in
terms of a uniformity—would be the blooming of two apricot trees
in a backyard each year, over a period of years and over the same
intervals of time. The bloomings of tree A and tree B are thus a uniform occurrence, but obviously the blooming of A is not caused by
the blooming of B, or the other way around. The two bloomings do
have, however, the common causal antecedent each time they occur,
say, of warm weather or the spring rains.

A third kind of acausality (Type III) is called here "intermittent
acausal uniformity." In this sort, the uniform occurrence of the kinds
of events that A and B are is not constant. It can be sufficiently present,
howver, to be statistically significant. For example, consider AB, CB,
AD, AB, DB, AB, AE, AB, etc., where A is any veridical psychical entity
when it is conjoined with its verifying referent B, and other combina-
tions are neither of these. In CB, for example, B *would be* a verifying
referent if C were veridical, but it is not. Or, in AE, A would be a veridi-

cal psychical entity if E were the verifying referent for it, but it is not. A is therefore in that case a non-epistemic psychical event. Such cases of synchronous or temporally off-set conjunctions of AB may sometimes be of the sort where A and B are causally independent in their respective causal backgrounds or A and B may have a common causal antecedent(s) in their respective causal pasts. An example of a Type III form of acausality might be a series of purported precognitions a person had, which were sometimes hallucinatory, but veridical often enough to produce statistical significance.

We know that the uniform time-keeping of the two clocks is acausal because we know enough of the causal background of each clock to understand that the uniformity can be accounted for fully without the requirement that one clock's time be a cause or a causal condition of the other clock's time. Analogously, in extrasensory perception—for an acausal theory to be plausible—one would have to make it reasonable at least that the psychical entity (dream, image, hunch, etc.) was not causally related to the verifying referent, and that two separate and complete causal explanations would be available for the psychical entity and the verifying referent respectively. This possibility is of course suggested by our inability to find a causal relationship between these two elements in an ESP situation. It would certainly not be difficult to ascertain the causal past of a great many verifying referents, for they are often nothing more than ordinary physical occurrences, e.g., physical events that have been predicted in a precognition. And, so far as the correlative psychical entity goes in ESP, there is no reason for supposing that it, too, could not have a causal past independent of its minimal verifying referent. The existence of hallucinatory psychical entities, which are *intrinsically* indistinguishable from veridical ones, is strongly suggestive of this possibility.

An acausal theory of telepathy would be something of the following sort. It would hold that when B is experiencing X in his mind, telepath A is experiencing X' (something similar to X) in his mind. If this happened only once, as might be the case in a spontaneous instance of telepathy, it would be viewed as such, though the percipient's assurance of that would no doubt depend on the degree of similarity between X and X', an assurance that would come, of course, by normal introspection on the part of the non-telepath and by normal communication between the two participants. Some parapsychologists do not give much credence to single spontaneous cases. If conjunctions of individually different X's and X''s occurred in a series, even intermittently in such a way as to provide statistical significance, there would be a situation analogous to a successful laboratory experiment in telepathy, even though it is held on this acausal view that there is no causal connection between X and X′.

Extrasensory perception is a term that subsumes under it telepathy, clairvoyance and precognition. Of these three kinds of ESP, clairvoyance *prima facie* most closely resembles a form of ordinary perception, i.e., seeing. In ordinary vision, the percipient is affected by light waves reflected from a physical object or event such that these waves produce changes in his retina which, in turn, cause a complicated sequence of changes in the optic nerve and then in the visual centers of the brain, finally resulting in his "seeing a table." There are many mysteries associated with this final effect, "seeing a table," but the general view of veridical vision is a *causal* one, i.e, by which physical objects or events outside of the percipient are causal conditions of the percept he experiences. There are, of course, visual hallucinations, in which the experience is ordinarily non-veridical precisely because an external physical object or event did not function causally as it does in veridical seeing.

Clairvoyance is defined as the "extrasensory perception of objects or objective events."[3] It is, therefore, much like ordinary seeing in its end result. On the other hand, it is a more wondrous phenomenon in that one "sees" clairvoyantly objects or events without the use of one's visual apparatus, with these objects or events often at a great distance from the percipient. Yet, just as the ordinary percipient, when he sees with his eyes, does so through a percept, so also the clairvoyant has an image or some other psychical entity as the vehicle of his special kind of "seeing." The psychical entity, i.e., the vision, dream, etc., that "pictures" (more or less adequately) the verifying referent, doubtless has a causal past without which it would not occur. The immediate causal past would probably be the brain event with which it is correlated. But, in clairvoyance, this causal past of the psychical entity does not lead back to the verifying referent. It is for this reason that some scientists have refused to view clairvoyance as fitting within a scientific framework. Many of them would ask: Is it not absurd to say that one "sees" an object or event without the use of eyes, or in some cases without being anywhere near the object or event, and with no ascertainable causal relationship between the extrasensory cognizer and the verifying referent? (These are some of the anomalies that arise when a causal theory of psi is assumed.)

If one thinks speculatively about clairvoyance, he can hypothesize that, even though it has not been discovered as yet, there *must* be a physicopsychical causal relation between the verifying referent and the image or vision that the clairvoyant experiences and which is the vehicle of his clairvoyance. But this is only a form of *a priori* reasoning. The facts are that there has been a study of clairvoyance by scholarly and scientific investigators in England and elsewhere from the middle of the last century. Yet, there has been no empirically grounded causal linkage established between the verifying referent and the psychical entity, by means of which the clairvoyant experience could be said to have occurred.

An acausal theory of clairvoyance is therefore not implausible. A Type III acausal uniformity between the psychical entities involved and their verifying referents can be postulated. There are no *a priori* reasons for excluding from nature that sort of acausal uniformity. Nor are there any facts of parapsychology that confute it, since no causal theory of clairvoyance has been empirically established. The empirical facts of parapsychology, indeed, support the acausal theory of clairvoyance.

The prediction and anticipation of future events are commonplace in ordinary experience and in science. From available data and rules of sequence, an inference (prediction) can be made. Such predictions vary in their probable truth. Some are true and some, false. The Glossary of *The Journal of Parapsychology* defines precognition as the "prediction of random future events the occurrence of which cannot be inferred from present knowledge." Ordinary predictions and precognitions are thus markedly different, the latter having no basis in ordinary available data or on inferences from them.

Looking at the matter parapsychologically, one can say that there seem to be different forms of precognition, not only in regard to degree of similarity of what the precognitive psychical entity "pictures" and the object or event "pictured," but also in certain other respects. A dreaming man, for example, had an experience of great anxiety as he stood at the side of a very wide walkway over which hundreds of people were rapidly passing in one direction, while he frustratedly sought out a particular person among them. The dream had no immediate intentional quality in that it had no future reference during the dream or upon the dreamer's awakening. Yet, three weeks later, on the University of California campus at Berkeley, this same man found himself in waking life in a precisely similar situation to that experienced in the dream. Only in this campus experience, three weeks after the dream had occurred, was the precognitive and intentional character of it recognized. This was in fact an experience of the writer.

A second example of precognition, cited by Milan Ryzl,[4] represents another degree of it. In this instance, a man employed at a railway terminal had a dream that two trains had collided at his place of work, with much loss of life. The dream was vivid and had alarmed him, but nothing occurred relevant to the dream at his place of work on the next day. But, on the day following, an overdue train got on the same track on which an express was arriving. Remembering his dream, he waved a red flag and succeeded in stopping both trains when they were only a few yards apart. A collision would have occurred except for his action. In this case, Ryzl contends that the precognized parts are those that occurred and that the remaining parts of the dream can be viewed as hallucinatory.

A third example[5] of precognition has neither of the limitations noted in the foregoing instances. It is the case of a woman who, over a period of years, had dreams at irregular intervals of time. A constant in these psi dreams was the appearance of animal or human feces. Such dreams were invariably followed by her receiving or finding money, usually in small amounts (one cent to $10.00), with no signs of such events other than the feces in the dreams. The money usually came to her several hours after awakening, with the longest period being four days. The predictive character of these dreams was based simply on this woman's generalization that, whenever such a dream occurred, she thereafter came into otherwise unexpected money. The puzzling aspect of the dreams is, of course, the presence of the dream-feces as an invariable antecedent of the monies.

Additionally, there are, of course, many reports of non-symbolic precognitions where the verifying referent is "pictured" literally and where there is also a future reference associated with the experience, i.e., an immediate intentional quality.

The puzzling aspect of all precognitions is that there is a totally different kind of ground for the foreknowledge involved, from that in cases of ordinary commonsense and scientific predictions. In precognitive cases, there are impulses, hunches, premonitions, dreams, visions, etc., that serve as the precognitive psychical entities. The epistemic element in these mental occurrences is inexplicable by any ordinary means, i.e., by reference to existing data and inference from them by means of rules of sequence. Because of an inability to give any explanation for the epistemic element in these precognitive mental events (i.e., the dreams, etc.) in terms of antecedent causal or other factors, some parapsychologists have theorized that there can be only one sort of cause for such psi awareness of a future event, namely, the future event itself. This is suggested by analogy with ordinary sense perception, where the physical object or event perceived is an originating causal condition of the perceptual experience. In the case of precognition, however, this would entail that a future event can be a cause of a present precognition. This view violates the generally accepted principle that "a cause must always temporally precede its effect." Douglas Dean, in a brave gesture, asserts: "Thus, instead of a cause preceding the effect, it seems that the effect precedes the cause. Logic has broken down . . . Effects coming before causes are not forbidden in nature; they are only forbidden in our brains, which work with logic circuits composed of neurons like computer logic circuits. Thus, we should not flinch . . . to use breakdowns of logic if they explain precognition."

Despite the extremity of Dean's problem, one does not have to suppose a breakdown in logic to accept his position. The logician can, in fact, offer Dean the needed tools to say what he wishes. The logician can point out that the meaning of the word *cause* in our languages entails that a cause necessarily comes before its effect. "A cause always precedes its effect in time" is therefore a tautology, an analytic truth: It says something about how language is used. But, as Morris Lazerowitz has often said,[7] a tautology is trivial in that it says nothing about the world of fact. "All red things are colored" is analytically true, even though there might be a universe in which there were neither red nor colored things. These comments hold also for the tautology "Causes precede their effects in time." This is a proposition about the meanings ingredient in language, not a statement about anything in the factual world. One can go along with Dean to that extent.

I do not however regard Dean's view of backward causation as satisfactory. It appears to imply a peculiar view of time which, in fact, makes precognition, as that term is ordinarily conceived, into an impossibility. I shall only indicate here, however, that his view of causation is anomalous. An acausal theory of precognition eliminates this anomaly and returns us to a world in which causes always do temporally precede their effects.

Do these considerations suggest an acausal theory of precognition? Is it possible that a precognitive psychical entity is acausally related to its verifying referent, and even that a series of such psychical entities is acausally related to another series of verifying referents? If no intelligible sort of causal relation can be found between a precognitive psychical entity and its verifying referent, this may be a result of the fact that there is none. And if there is none, an acausal theory is the only possible outcome.

The history of psychical research is replete with reports of the strange movements of physical bodies. Reports of numerous spontaneous levitations and poltergeist cases testify, even if not scientifically, to the plausibility of such happenings. J. B. Rhine in 1934 began laboratory work on psychokinesis. It was slow in being replicated elsewhere and some psychologists, e.g., Edward Girden,[8] wrote discrediting articles.

In a philosophical discussion of psychokinesis, it is rather the concept of it that is of interest and, in light of that concept, the raising of questions about possible explanations of such phenomena as it subsumes. Often PK is described as "mind over matter." Louisa E. Rhine's book[9] refers to psychokinesis as resulting from the *will* of subjects. In the Glossary of *The Journal of Parapsychology*, PK is described as "the extramotor aspect of psi; a direct (i.e., mental but nonmuscular) influence exerted by the subject on an external physical process, condition, or object." On a commonsense view of nature, or on an orthodox scientist's conception of it, a causal relation between some aspect of one's mind and a physical occurrence *outside* of its body would be generally viewed as impossible. An occasional exception would be the gambler (with dice), the pinball player or the bowler; some of them act in ways that suggest they believe they can exert control over physical objects in the game *after* they no longer control them muscularly. On the other hand, there were Chicagoans who played "the 26 game" in bars for decades with ten dice, with the players trying for a specific number that they hoped would appear at least 26 times in thirteen rolls. The player was obviously willing—"trying"—to achieve his game objective, but the tally sheets, year in and out, showed the house-take to be what would have been expected on the laws of chance.[10] It would hardly seem that willing for some objective change outside one's body is the key to producing that event. If PK occurs, certainly no one has given a satisfactory account of its causal conditions, though it is often suggested, as with ESP, that there are psychological factors in both subject and experimenter—likes, dislikes, frustrations, etc.—that affect the success of the results. Yet, no one can specify these psychological factors in such a way that strict scientific repeatability can be achieved.

The idea of psychokinesis suggests philosophically some possible explanations of it. A review of a few different kinds of psychokinetic occurrences will be useful in stating them. Bishop Pike and two friends (David Barr and Maren Bergrud), who were staying with him in Cambridge (England), noticed in their apartment inexplicable changes in the location and placement of physical objects upon returning from a weekend spent miles away.[11] None of the three had consciously willed these changes, for they were surprised by them. Many poltergeist cases certainly have no conscious antecedents. The result is that parapsychologists sometimes appeal to the "unconscious" as the causal factor, but this seems unconvincing in the absence of any specification of what precisely it is in the "unconscious" that brings about the outside physical effects in question. Indeed, even explicit willings or wishings to move objects outside of one's body usually have no effect, as "the 26 game" in Chicago so well revealed. There are reports, however, that are based not only on noticed inexplicable dislocations of objects, but on the claim that objects have been seen in motion, with no normal explanation available. Were such "observations" hallucinatory or based on some abnormal state of mind? Was the inexplicable change in the physical object the result of trickery? After careful investigation of Uri Geller for some six weeks at the Stanford Research Institute, Targ and Puthoff were unable to have him achieve a single instance of psychokinesis when the objects were kept out of his hands.[12] Kulagina and Vinogradova have presented puzzling phenomena that suggest a psychokinetic interpretation. Those of Vinogradova, however, seem to be in line with electrostatic operations. Kulagina's phenomena, however, whatever their nature, cannot apparently be explained in that manner, but careful observers, e.g., J. G. Pratt, are hesitant to designate them as psychokinetic.[13]

If one takes the definition of PK, quoted earlier from the Glossary of the *Journal* or L. E. Rhine's notion of willing as the psychic entity preceding movement of physical objects or even the notion that "unconscious" psychic entities are antecedent to psychokinetic occurrences, or just the meaning of the word "psychokinesis," one can fit the laboratory work of Rhine, Cox and others into an acausal theory (Type III). Such acausal uniformities as are discovered can be statistically significant and noted as evidence for this acausal form of PK.

To summarize, the bases for attacking the credibility of belief in telepathy, clairvoyance, precognition and psychokinesis are the following: 1) That it is not possible for one person to know what another is experiencing except by sensory means (excludes telepathy); 2) that physical objects or events can be perceived only through the senses (excludes clairvoyance); 3) that one cannot know the future except through present data and inferences from them (excludes precognition); and 4) that it is not possible for an event in one's mind directly to cause any physical event other than in his own brain (excludes psychokinesis). All of these objections, which have been crucial in causing scientists and others to regard ESP and PK as impossible, if not nonsensical, are eliminated by the acausal theory.

But perhaps the most important consequence of the acausal theory of ESP-PK is the realization that the anomalies in present-day parapsychology are not a result of the facts that parapsychologists are discovering but of the interpretative framework into which they are placed. Change that interpretative framework, as was done in this paper, and the anomalies disappear.

REFERENCES

[1] See Glossary of *The Journal of Parapsychology*.

[2] See his Introduction to *Philosophers in Wonderland*, edited by P. A. French. Saint Paul: Llewellyn Publications, 1975.

[3] See Glossary of *The Journal of Parapsychology*.

[4] *Parapsychology, A Scientific Approach* by Milan Ryzl. New York: Hawthorn Books, Inc., 1970. p. 173.

[5] See *Some Ostensibly Precognition Dreams* by F. C. Dommeyer, *JASPR*, Vol. XLIX, No. 3, July, 1955. Also, *Another Veridically Significant Dream* by same author, *JASPR*, Vol. L., No. 4, Oct., 1956.

[6] *Psychic Explorations, A Challenge for Science*, edited by John White. New York: G. P. Putnam's Sons, 1974, p. 171.

[7] See *Logical Necessity in the Structure of Metaphysics* by Morris Lazerowitz. London: Routledge and Kegan Paul, 1955. pp. 254–256.

[8] Girden, E., *A Review of Psychokinesis* Psychological Bulletin, Vol. 59, No. 5, Sept., 1962.

[9] Rhine, L. E. *Mind Over Matter* London: The Macmillan Co., 1970, p. 359.

[10] Gardner, Martin. *Fads and Fallacies* New York: Ballantine Books, Inc. 1957. p. 212.

[11] Pike, James A. with Diane Kennedy, *The Other Side* Garden City: Doubleday & Co., 1968. p. 81.

[12] From a conversation the writer had with Russell Targ, April, 1976.

[13] In a letter of April 14, 1976, to the writer.

DISCUSSION

EDGE: It seems to me that the names that we have in parapsychology —telepathy, PK, etc.,—really are not explanatory concepts at all. Rather, they are concepts which merely designate, for the time being, a kind of uniformity. Now, it seems to me that what you have been doing is to point out the problem that there does *not* seem to be any causal connection, but from that I would draw the conclusion that these are not explanatory concepts and therefore the putting together of the words, as you have, of an acausal explanation, seemed to me somewhat odd, because I'm not sure then what the nature of the explanation would be, if it is not connected in any way with a causal connection.

DOMMEYER: I grant your point that the terms, telepathy, clair-voyance, etc., carry with them certain connotations, but I thought I had to start somewhere and I started with the definitions that one finds in the Glossary of the *Journal of Parapsychology*, feeling that that was as good a place as I could go for such definitions. Of course, starting out with those definitions, I then proceeded by my acausal theory. Now, when you ask for an explanation of telepathy on my view, I would say that I am making an assumption about nature. Of course, Leibniz, as you may recall, postulated a preestablished harmony, that nature operates in a preestablished way. Well, I don't have to go that far, but I am saying that in nature there are acausal uniformities, and, if you asked me what a clairvoyant act was, I would say, "Well, nature is just working in such a way that if I, the clairvoyant, have an image and then nature reveals the verifying referent, that's clairvoyance." That would be my explanation.

THAKUR: "I'm not convinced that the examples you gave of acausal uniformities can in fact be taken as such. For example, the case of the clocks. It is true that the two clocks are in vastly different places and are not causally related, but then the uniformity is displayed because of certain laws operating about springs and pendulums and balances.

DOMMEYER: Each clock has a causal background.

THAKUR: I'm not quite sure whether it remains acausal, because there is a cause as to why each one of these clocks is behaving or will behave in the future.

DOMMEYER: The acausal relation is between the 12 o'clock on one clock and the 12 o'clock on the other. These are acausally related. I grant fully that the 12 o'clock on clock I is based upon a lengthy causal past and also on clock II, but nonetheless a uniformity of clock I and II cannot be explained as a causal relation between the two clocks.

THAKUR: If I were to say that in the situations where, when it strikes 12 o'clock in New York, it also happens to do so in London—if I were to say that's simply a convention and nothing else?

DOMMEYER: Oh, I don't say it's a convention, that isn't so at all. I simply say that the clock's striking in New York doesn't cause the clock to strike in London.

THAKUR: Assuming that there is ground to talk about acausal uniformities, my question is how does this concept of acausal uniformity explain anything beyond sort of pointing out or drawing attention to the fact that something like this does occur?

DOMMEYER: Well, I think that's about all one can do. For example, this happened to me. I had a dream in which I dreamed of a wide walkway with crowds of people going by and I was very frustrated in my dream, looking for someone. When I awakened, it didn't have any future significance at all and neither did the dream have future significance when I experienced it. But three weeks later I was on the

Berkeley campus. I had taken my son over there to take an English test, to see whether he'd have to take "bonehead" English and he did have to take it, I might say. Well, he came out much later than I had expected after the English exam and I was uneasy waiting there. Here were all these people passing, and it was an exact duplication of the dream, and then I thought to myself, "My goodness, that's exactly what I dreamt." Now, I would say that this would be an acausal kind of case of a precognitive dream, and my explanation of it is simply that nature operated that way. There are acausal instances and uniformities in nature.

FRENCH: What you've done is taken the causal problem and turned it into a uniformity problem and I wonder if after I've said a few words, you might comment on them. It seems to me some of us are still worrying about how we determine cause for some of these extra-sensory events or psychic events. Now, our problem is one of finding out whether or not an event is uniform with another. It seems to me in your I and II types of acausal uniformities, that the problem of uniformity is more or less taken care of by a theory of some kind that accounts for the uniformity. In the case of the clocks, I assume that's a theory of chronometry or something of that sort, but what will count as uniformity in precognitive cases? I'm particularly concerned here where obviously there is no general awareness or knowledge of the one event, that is, the psychic event, other than on the part of the experiencer or individual.

DOMMEYER: Well, I would explain the background of the psychical event in broad terms just as I did the background of the clock. The psychical event might be a dream, and some physiologists or neurologists, I suppose, might give the background of that dream in synaptic connections in my brain, etc., etc. I don't deny that the psychical entity has its causal past just as the clock does, nor do I deny that what I precognized, the events over in Berkeley that I viewed there, also have a causal past. You can explain why those people happened to be walking along there at the time that I was standing there; you can explain why I was standing there frustrated, looking for my son. So I would say the situations are analogous, in that the psychical entity has its causal past and so does the verifying referent have its causal past, and I would simply say that nature operated this way. Obviously it did or the events wouldn't have happened. But the dream was not the cause of the Berkeley event, or that event the cause of the dream.

BELOFF: I have somewhat of a problem in expressing my objections, because in point of fact I think I can say I disagree with practically everything Professor Dommeyer has said in his paper. Perhaps I could start by saying that I'm still terribly unclear as to how Dommeyer's acausal theory would differ from the position of, say, a radical skeptic about parapsychology, who would simply assert that everything which isn't explainable by trickery, which, of course, is a causal theory of its own kind, is explainable by chance. And it would seem to me that adopting Professor Dommeyer's position would, if I have not misunderstood him, be equivalent logically to an explanation as coincidence. Now, perhaps the crucial point of disagreement between myself and Professor Dommeyer is that he seems to imply that a causal relationship must also involve a causal mechanism of the kind that traditional classical mechanics have made us familiar with. Now this, I quite agree, is absolutely absent in all parapsychological evidence, but this is why, for example, Rex Stanford and myself and many others, while not abandoning a causal theory, believe that the kind of causation that operates in psi transactions is of a very different nature. It's much more teleological and it doesn't operate by the sort of pushes and pulls that we so ordinarily, in common sense, associate with causing something to fall over or something of that kind.

DOMMEYER: Well, I would grant that I do introduce an open skepticism here, because I am holding that parapsychologists have not established any causal relation between what I call the psychical entity and the verifying referent. But I would not want to put it on just a chance basis. That, I think, would misconstrue my theory, because I am quite willing to say that nature can operate in this way to produce statistical significance and the fact that it does this is evidence that I'm not postulating very much. Nature does operate in that way. We see it happening, so I'm not really going beyond anything that we can't ascertain empirically.

PENELHUM: I came away about ten days ago from a conference commemorating the bicentennial of the death of Hume, and this may color some of these comments. It does seem to me, however, in view of this morning's discussion, that he might very well never have existed. I was struck by the fact that everyone from Professor Dommeyer onwards seemed entirely clear about what the difference was between causal uniformity and acausal uniformity, and were merely disagreeing about whether the kinds of uniformities involved in psi transactions were of one kind or the other. But, I'm not sure I do understand what the difference is, and I think that when Professor Dommeyer recommends us to think of psi phenomena as involving acausal uniformities, he really ought to say what *he* thinks this difference is. I'm reminded of the classical debates about the difference between inter- actionism and parallelism, the nasty criticism of parallelism, which tells us these things always go together but don't just happen to be causally related, is that it's not discernably different from interac- tionism. What else does the interactionist tell us, but that when one occurs, you can be sure the other has and if that also goes for parallel- ism, are these theories really different? If the sorts of acausal uni- formities that Professor Dommeyer thinks may be operative in the case of psi phenomena, are the kind that might enable one to know that one phenomenon has occurred when the other does, then how is this not a causal uniformity? If they don't enable us to know that one occurs when the other has, then in what sense is it an explanation he is offering?

DOMMEYER: I certainly would agree with you that, if I were to write a book on the topic, I would certainly try to distinguish more ade- quately what I mean by a causal uniformity as distinguished from, say, an acausal uniformity. I would still maintain that I think I can state that distinction and I think there is a difference. For one thing, I believe that a causal condition is an event that has to be present, let us say, in producing a given effect, and one clock doesn't have to be present to produce 12 o'clock on the other clock. I'm thinking here of laboratory control and strict repeatability. And I do think there's a lot of difference between my taking a pill for high blood pressure and having my high blood pressure go down, and one clock, say, being at 12 o'clock and the other clock being at 12 o'clock—there's a big difference there, and that's the difference I'm trying to get at.

STANFORD: I felt a good bit of sympathy with Dr. Beloff's remarks and I think there are a couple of points in which I feel there were factual errors in Dr. Dommeyer's presentation. I see no basis except the most trivial one, for instance, in saying clairvoyance most closely re- sembles ordinary perception, unless he wants to fall back, despite his own ideas, on some kind of causal notion. But most particularly with regard to PK, to suggest that we haven't found any kind of indications of causation, I think ignores a large mass of PK literature. There have been dozens of instances in which persons have run random number or event generators of one type or another, with no kind of contingent linkage to the subject's dispositions where they have got chance re- sults. And then when they're linked with those dispositions they have found a biasing of the generators. It's been repeated again and again. Furthermore, if we talk about machines in general, we find a boundary condition on this relationship because we don't typically find computers being biased in this way. It looks as though you have to have some special characteristic for the machine to function as a PK-influenced random event generator. We don't yet understand what this characteristic is. These findings certainly seem to me a basis for strongly suspecting a kind of lawfulness. Now, you may not accept the evidence in this case as strong enough to establish that kind of a point— that's your right. But now what kind of boundary conditions, if any, does your so-called explanation propose? Does it propose any, even, in principle? And if it doesn't, how is it conceivable that we can differentiate these kinds of acausal connections from accidents? You said a few minutes ago that you're not willing to put this on a chance basis.

DOMMEYER: I think you can't always distinguish between accidents. It's perfectly possible that I might wish to move that glass and then it goes up and it might be a complete accident. My general view of PK is certainly one that's not as comprehensive and detailed as yours. I'm no experimentalist and I would certainly respect anything that you would say there in regard to this, but it's my understanding that no one can indicate the causal conditions that are involved in PK, as my paper tended to suggest all too briefly. You get all kinds of wild differences. In the Chicago bar, these fellows were trying to will certain numbers to come up on the dice for years. And yet it came out in accordance with the laws of chance. One would suppose that if there were some causal explanation, that something other than that would have happened. In other words, I find the area of PK such a difficult area because of the diverse currents running through it, that I would personally, as a philosopher, hate to draw any solid kind of conclusion about it. But I would say, until you can come up with a causal explanation, that I'm going to stand by my acausal theory.

KORNWACHS: I think to speak about uniformity means to state that there is a possibility of correlations, and to make correlations means to bring order into the chance, avoiding the term necessity. The idea of conformity leads me to the idea of a conformal mapping, as it is known in functional analysis. By analogy I try to understand precognition. If one could understand it in the way that a hologram works, that means one could transform the spatial frequencies of a picture by a Fourier transformation in the temporal frequency of these pictures. So for a sensitive person, only a short reception of an interval of these temporal frequencies would be sufficient to re-transform the spatial frequencies of a picture, and so, to get all information of this picture. And in this way I could imagine that I can prevent the difficulties with time, and my question is now: is that a specific sort of correlation which is an acausal one in the sense of your type Number Three you've mentioned?

DOMMEYER: Yes. It's the Number Three type of acausality that I would think would characterize ESP and PK occurrences because that is intermittent and as I see it, parapsychology, so far as its data go, is very intermittent.

MATTUCK: First, I think that the most striking indication of some sort of causal connection is found in the phenomenon of PK, which I think you dismissed much too lightly. There are now a large number of experiments which have been done under what I consider to be adequate control. I am thinking, for example, about psychic children who have been investigated by Hasted in England, and also about the French medium, John Pierre Girard, who has been investigated now by about three or four different scientists. Many examples are coming in every day, of psychokinesis performed under controlled conditions, where the medium for example, bends an object, but has absolutely no means of producing this bending by use of physical methods. That's number one. And number two, I disagree with your statement that there are no theories being proposed now which show a causal connection. I myself am working on such a theory . . .

DOMMEYER: No, I didn't say that.

MATTUCK: I don't see how it is possible for any scientist to work using an acausal model for PK because, as far as I can see, an acausal model is no model at all. The motivating force behind science is finding seemingly unrelated events and trying to find a causal connection between them. This is the life blood of science. We'd all have to stop doing our work in paraphysics and parapsychology if we subscribe to your model.

DOMMEYER: On the point of the bending of objects, I don't believe that a precise causation is known in those cases at all. For instance, when someone strokes a spoon and it bends, how do I know that that is a psychokinetical event. This may be because of the stroking. It may be a purely physical occurrence for all I know. It's completely gratuitous to say that the mind is doing it.

MATTUCK: But the bending occurs without contact with the metal object in some cases!

DOMMEYER: In any event, it's in physical space, and something may be happening to it physically. Why do you pick on the mind as the cause? It might be anything in the world that's doing it.

MATTUCK: But nobody has been able to find any physical cause for the bending.

MAUSKOPF: Briefly, I'll make a statement rather than ask any questions, a statement which now is serving as something of a summary. I got the distinct impression, Fred, that you were suggesting—especially at the beginning and end of your paper—that you would, by this theory, be able to reconcile parapsychology and parapsychological phenomena with more orthodox science and scientific beliefs. In the discussion that ensued since, the point I wanted to make has perhaps been borne out. I see no way whereby your particular proposal would get that reconciliation a bit farther than it presently is. The reaction, I think, seems to bear that out.

DOMMEYER: I have, on my view, simply eliminated all these reasons for the ordinary scientists to say this is nonsense, or for people to say that the sentences are semantically nonsensical. On this view, any scientist could say, "O.K., I agree with parapsychology and the results if that's the interpretation you're going to give to it." So in that sense I bring parapsychology back into orthodox science.

JANIN: Practically speaking, how does an acausal theory allow one to predict parapsychological events?

DOMMEYER: Well, you can't predict them on your view either, so maybe we have an equality there.

LESHAN: We've been offered a challenge to a tremendous tendency we have to always think in terms of actual causal connections, in billiard ball models, and that we've all shown how strongly we defend this instinctively without even thought. Finally, I would like to remind you of Law #3 of "Science as She is Done" by J. R. Vandercrank, in *The Journal of Spurious Diseases*, Vol. 27, 1933, page 144. Law #3 is that it's been scientifically proven by centuries of empirical research that the beating of tomtoms during an eclipse is always followed by the reappearance of the sun.

THE PLACE OF PARADIGMS IN PARAPSYCHOLOGY

HOYT EDGE

Over the past decade, there has been an upsurge in the popularity and use of the concept "paradigm." One can hardly turn to any field of knowledge without confronting the concept. Thomas Kuhn, in his *The Structure of Scientific Revolutions*,[1] employed it in relation to the natural sciences, particularly to physics. Now it is widely used in sociology, anthropology and history, to name but a few areas to which it has been applied in the Social Sciences and the Humanities. It has also grown in popularity in parapsychology with articles discussing paradigms or using the concept in many of the major journals. Yet, it is still not totally clear what paradigms are and the extent to which they can be employed. Margaret Masterman points out at least twenty-one different uses of the term in *The Structure of Scientific Revolutions*.[2] The term has been used in the literature in a variety of ways. To help clarify its proper use, particularly in parapsychology, I propose to put the term in its correct philosophical space. I will outline the philosophical underpinnings of the concept and briefly discuss the limits of the use of the concept. I wish to relate the use of paradigms to the use of language, and finally I will apply my findings to parapsychology in several ways.

For Kuhn, all scientific knowledge is paradigm based. A mature science is cyclic in that it goes through the three phases of normal science with a paradigm, anomalies arising which result in a crisis, and then a revolution, which results in the exchange of paradigms. After the paradigm switch, we are not only dealing with a new theory about the world but, in a real sense, we literally find ourselves in a new world. Kuhn expresses it this way: " . . . during revolutions scientists see new and different things when looking with familiar instruments in places they have looked before. It is rather as if the professional community had been suddenly transported to another planet [for] . . . paradigm changes do cause scientists to see the world of their research engagement differently. In so far as their only recourse to that world is through what they see and do, we may want to say that after a revolution scientists are responding to a different world."[3] From this quote, several questions arise: What is a paradigm? How is it that we are in a different world after a paradigm switch? How does a paradigm-based view of science differ from a traditional view?

Viewed in general terms, paradigms are models of explanation based on specific experimental evidence which guide our understanding, research, observation and explanation. More specifically, there are two senses in which Kuhn uses the term: (1) a paradigm is a disciplinary matrix, which is "the entire constellation of beliefs, values, techniques, and so on shared by the members of a given community,"[4] and (2) a paradigm is an exemplar, which is "one sort of element in that constellation, the concrete puzzle-solutions which employed as models or examples, can replace explicit rules as a basis for the solution of the remaining puzzles of normal science."[5] Using these senses of paradigm, how does a paradigm-based view of science differ from the traditional view of science and how is one viewing a different world after a paradigm switch?

The traditional view of science is based upon traditional empiricism, which argues that all knowledge must be ultimately reducible to sense impressions. John Locke and David Hume are historical examples of this empiricism. Hume argued that all knowledge about the world was the result of information received through the senses. He went so far as to assert: "When we run over libraries, persuaded on these principles, what havoc must we make? If we take in our hand any volume; of divinity or school metaphysics, for instance; let us ask, *Does it contain any abstract reasoning concerning quantity or number? No. Does it contain any experimental reasoning concerning matter of fact and existence?* No. Commit it then to the flames, for it can contain nothing but sophistry and illusion."[6]

In this way, he was instituting a criterion for knowledge about the world. Direct sense experience formed a foundation for all synthetic knowledge. To locate the source of one's knowledge, one had merely to trace the complex ideas down to their simple ideas, which in turn could be traced to sense impressions. All knowledge was reducible to what was given in sense experience. This Given, sense experience, performed several functions. For one, it supplied the criterion of what was admissible as possible knowledge of the world, as we saw in the above quote. The Given also supplied the basis for a solution to disputes. All disputes were ultimately reducible to and theoretically solvable by consulting the Given. For the empiricist, anyone in the proper conditions could receive an uninterpreted, unbiased, undiluted pure perception. Differences of opinion and problems arose only when these pure sense impressions were interpreted, when they were used as the basis for a theory. Man could be wrong about how he interpreted the perception, but he could not be mistaken about the perceptions themselves.

The traditional empiricist view of perception has been held through many detours to form a part of the contemporary empiricist ideal of scientific explanation—the Hypothetical-deductive model of explanation. Very simple stated, this theory asserts that there is a distinction between theoretical and observation statements. Our theoretical statements contain non-observable concepts, postulates, etc. They are used to explain our observation statements. To connect the theoretical statements with observation statements, there exists a set of correspondence rules through which we can attain partial interpretations of some of our theoretical concepts and statements in terms of observation sentences. Using Hypothetical-deductive theories and the correspondence rules, we can derive and predict observation statements. These observation statements are relatively free from theoretical language. Stated perceptually, our observations are free from theoretical assumptions. The observation statements are fixed data which remain, even when we are changing our theory. All that changes is our interpretation of them. Our theories may change; our correspondence rules may change; but the Given (the observations) remains the unalterable and immutable foundation of our knowledge.

This classical view of science contains two assumptions vis-à-vis the progress of science. The first is the consistency condition: "Only such theories are . . . admissible in a given domain which either *contain* the theories already used in this domain, or which are at least *consistent* with them inside the domain."[7] When a theory change takes place, the new theory is at least consistent with the old theory, if not containing it as a special case of the new theory. Einsteinian relativity is not inconsistent with Newtonian mechanics; rather, the latter is contained as a special case of the former, true in its own sphere. The second assumption is the condition of meaning invariance: "Meanings will have to be invariant with respect to scientific progress; that is, all future theories will have to be framed in such a manner that their use in explanations does not affect what is said by the theories, or factual reports to be explained."[8] Insofar as the meanings of the key concepts in the theory have remained constant, the old and new theories can be compared. The upshot of these two assumptions is the view that science progresses by setting up new models for explaining the observable facts. When observations arise that the old theory cannot account for, new models of explanation are offered—ones in which all of the facts explained by the old theory are also explained by the new one, and in addition the anomalous observations are taken into account and explained. Science progresses like an ever hungry animal, devouring not only the old "facts" but the anomalous observations as well. The goal of science is to develop a theory in which all actual and possible observations are explicable in terms of a theoretical framework. This theory will be both an interpretation and a description of the basic sense observations.

As I understand the epistemological foundations of the paradigm approach, it challenges both the consistency condition and the condition of meaning invariance, although Kuhn does not bring this out as clearly as does Feyerabend. In other words, after a paradigm change, the new theory of the nature of reality is not consistent with the old view nor is the old view considered a subset of the new theory, merely a limiting case of it. Nor can one say that the terms used in the new theory mean the same thing that the same terms meant when used in the former theory. The denial of these two conditions is responsible, I think, for the assertion that we live in a different world after a paradigm change. The foundation, I think, for the inadequacy of these two conditions and for the subsequent odd ontological statement about the world changing is a pragmatic approach to knowledge. The difference in Kuhn's view of science and the traditional view results mainly from the acceptance of a pragmatic view of truth and meaning. It is to this that I now turn.

American pragmatism began with the publication of C. S. Peirce's "How to Make Our Ideas Clear" in 1878, in which he is concerned with a theory of meaning. Reacting against the traditional definition of clear and distinct ideas as being much too unclear and indistinct, he proposes the following method for attaining a clear idea of the meaning of an object: "Consider what effects, which might conceivably have practical bearings, we conceive the object of our conception to have. Then, our conception of these effects is the whole of our conception of the object."[9] James puts it: "To attain perfect clearness in our thoughts of an object, then, we need only consider what conceivable effects of a practical kind the object may involve—what sensations we are to expect from it, and what reactions we must prepare."[10] The pragmatic method, following from this, is based on finding what sensible effects an object can have. Stated in another way, if there is disagreement over two theories, we must first become clear as to what practical difference one theory would have as opposed to the other—if none, there is actually no difference in the theories. Derived from the theory of meaning is the pragmatic theory of truth. James defines a true idea as follows: "Any idea upon which we can ride, so to speak; any idea that will carry us prosperously from any one part of our experience to any other part, linking things satisfactorily, working securely, simplifying, saving labor; is true for just so much, true in so far forth, true *instrumentally*."[11] A true idea, then, is one that enables us to accomplish what we set out to accomplish. If that object is, for example, to sail across the Atlantic Ocean, any idea which enables us to do so would be pragmatically true. In fact, pragmatism is very problem oriented. Its metaphysics is a very dynamically oriented one. Man is a product of evolution, and as its highest product, must be understood as the prime example of something having survived through adaptation. James argues, for instance, that consciousness could not be merely an epiphenomenon because, as a product of evolution, it must have a dynamically useful function. Its use must be in its ability to survive, to adapt, to solve problems. As we see, then, man for James is a very dynamic creature as opposed to Hume's traditional empiricist notion of the mind being a *tabula rasa*, a blank tablet on which sense impressions are imprinted. Rather than having a passive view of the mind, pragmatism views man in constant interaction with his environment and overcoming it. Concomitantly, experience is not a matter of a subject being affected by the objective world but rather of one part of the environment, a person, affecting and being affected by other parts of the environment in a mutual interaction. In Peirce, for example, man has certain beliefs, certain habits of action, which he uses in his interaction with the environment. If these habits of action are not successful in achieving the desired results, doubt arises, which in turn forces one to develop a new belief. If this new belief is effective in accomplishing the goal, it is incorporated into one's system until a new doubt arises in relation to it. Then the process is repeated. Any belief which works—that is, any habit of action—is accepted as true.

It is not difficult to see the connection of this outline of pragmatism to Kuhn's theory. Indeed, the description of experience given above is pretty much the outline of the description of the process of science. One merely has to substitute several key words. Let me do this: "For Kuhn, man has certain paradigms, certain theories, which he uses in his interaction with the environment. If these theories are not successful in achieving the desired results, anomalies arise, which in turn force one to develop a new paradigm. If this new paradigm is effective in accomplishing the goal, it is incorporated into one's system until a new anomaly arises. Then the process is repeated. Any paradigm which works is accepted as true."

This last point, one dealing with truth, may need some expansion.

The traditional view of truth is the correspondence theory. In essence, it asserts that a statement is true if and only if the statement refers to a fact. The statement "snow is white" is true if and only if snow is indeed white. The truth of the statement, therefore, is independent of our belief about it. We may believe that snow is blue, but that would not affect the fact that snow is really white and thus the statement is true. It is true that we have certain criteria for determining the truth of any statement, and these turn out to be mainly pragmatic. For instance, if I say that there is water in a swimming pool, I can test this in several ways. I can look at the pool as well as diving into it. Normally, we want to say that if there is water in the pool, then when I jump into it, I will not crash into the bottom, breaking my neck. In other words, if it fulfills my expectations, I take this as justifying the truth of my statement, but this is a pragmatic justification. The *definition* of truth, however, is based on correspondence even if the *criterion* for determining the truth of any individual statement happens to be pragmatic.

The pragmatist will not allow for this separation of the definition of truth from the criterion of establishing the truth. The correspondence theory of truth can mean nothing more pragmatically than what is found in its pragmatic criteria. Put in another way, there is no pragmatic gain in defining truth in terms of correspondence. Any statement that has met the pragmatic criteria for being accepted as true is believed as corresponding to the facts, and in the only way that correspondence makes sense, it does. What this boils down to is the assertion that correspondence with some external, objective world is useless apart from its pragmatic basis. The only notion of truth we have is one that is pragmatically based, which includes coherence with other beliefs. Correspondence is, strictly speaking, useless.

In the same sort of way, I do not believe that we can say that one paradigm corresponds to or describes an external, objective reality. Rather paradigms are accepted for what they can accomplish, for their usefulness. That we cannot talk of a reality external to the paradigm will become evident later.

I can now return to a discussion of the differences between a paradigm-based conception of science and a traditional view. All of the differences I will mention can be traced to the pragmatist rejection of the Given, the uninterpreted sense experience. As opposed to the traditional notion, man is not a *tabula rasa*, a passive receiver of uninterpreted sense data. Rather, he is an active participant. For Kuhn all knowledge is paradigm based. There is no such thing as trans-paradigm knowledge. The reception of data through the senses is also a product of the paradigm. One's conceptual framework affects and molds his perceptual experience. Numerous perceptual experiments have shown this to be the case. For instance, one in which the colors of playing cards were switched produced strange perceptual results. Rather than recognizing the cards flashed on a screen, for instance a black heart rather than a red one, the subjects did not perceive them until long past when they should have recognized them purely physiologically. It is not the case that we have pure, uninterpreted sense data, which we bring together in a theory and against which we can check our theories. There is no perceptual foundation for knowledge in this sense. What we see is dependent on what our paradigm is. It is not possible to get out of our paradigm to have an uninterpreted perceptual experience. To leave one paradigm is to accept another. As Kuhn writes: "The alternative is not some hypothetical 'fixed' vision, but vision through another paradigm."[12] If there is no pure observation, there can be no pure observation language, so there is no ultimate perception or language that is not paradigm-infested. In a sense, then, what we see is what our paradigm dictates is what is there.

With this in mind, the statement by Kuhn quoted earlier, that when there is a paradigm change, we are in a different world, becomes intelligible. When our paradigm changes, what we see literally changes. With a change of paradigms, we are in a different world because the meaning of objects and what we see is dependent on what our paradigm is.

A confusion arises here, though, and it is one that Kuhn is guilty of. Although Kuhn asserts that the scientist is in a different world after a paradigm switch, he turns around and makes statements such as: "Whatever he may then see, the scientist after a revolution is still looking at the same world."[13] Can Kuhn make such statements consistent with his general view about paradigms? I do not think so, and I think that Richard Rorty[14] has pointed this out. As Kuhn brings out in his "Reflections on My Critics," his basic fear is solipsism. If what one sees is paradigm dependent and there is no knowledge that is not paradigm dependent, there does not seem to be any absolute foundation for knowledge, which is disconcerting. Would this not lead to an extreme view that each person has his own paradigm and therefore that each person has his own world? Thus he asserts, " . . . there must be a recourse. Though they have no direct access to it, the stimuli to which the participants in a communication breakdown respond are, under pain of solipsism, the same."[15] As Rorty has pointed out, this sort of view seems to be playing off of the old Kantian distinction between receptivity and spontaneity. The mind receives the stimuli and they are processed through the filters of the mind, or categories of the understanding, as Kant calls them. If this is the way-the mind works, is it not logical to ask why there could not be different categories? What if a paradigm is analogous to the categories of the understanding? On this view, the mind would receive the stimuli and process them to yield the world of experience (the phenomenal world). The problem with this view is the notion of the *Ding-an-sich*, the thing-in-itself, which supposedly supplies the stimuli to be received by the mind. Yet, by definition, this is not something that can be experienced nor is it something that can be intelligible. It is condemned eternally to the unknown. There is no pragmatic justification for such a "world." Once we have dismissed the uninterpreted sense data as the Given in perception, as we have asserted earlier, we can dismiss the function of the thing-in-itself, and with it, the notion of stimuli which are the same through a succession of paradigms. Rather, as Rorty points out, the anti-solipsist burden is borne by a shared programming that is the result of a shared history and a shared language. Paradigm switches are never universal. Kuhn has used the term in its paradigmatic way in referring to changes in science, and these changes, no matter how revolutionary they are, never change the whole of science. In fact, Rorty has shown that the notion of a total change of world view is unintelligible essentially because there would be no way of knowing whether a person we confronted had a totally different world that we could not understand or whether he was simply talking gibberish. This can be understood in the pragmatist notion of experience discussed earlier. We noticed that it progressed in a dialectical fashion from belief to doubt and to resolution, which was another belief. What is doubted for the pragmatist is never the whole world. Whenever something is doubted, there is always a residue of experience that is left unchallenged. It is true that after problem one is resolved, what was unchallenged in that problem may be challenged in the next period of doubt, but something is always left unchallenged. Our world then is not some *Ding-an-sich*, an unknowable thing-in-itself, but rather it is in normal times what is the object of our belief with which our habits of action have intercourse. It is in Dewey's phrase, our "funded experience."

To try to cap off this discussion, let me come back for a moment to the central question of what a paradigm is in light of the preceding. Since English is a language that lends itself so nicely to alliteration and an analogy may help, let me discuss in a rather whimsical, but useful way the notion of a paradigm as a paramour. I will try to not get carried away with this analogy as I don't want an X-rated paper, but the analogy may be helpful. I will list five characteristics which paradigms share with paramours: 1) paradigms seduce. As Kuhn has pointed out, the exchange of paradigms occurs in something like a gestalt switch. Not only does it seem to be all or nothing, but there is no rational reason for the switch. Just as I may switch from the duck to the rabbit and back without any logical reason, the reasons for my choosing another paradigm seem to be more psychological than logical. This seems to follow from characteristic 2) paradigms cannot be done without. All knowledge is paradigm based. If that is the case, there is no such thing as trans-paradigm knowledge or deduction. There is no way to judge two paradigms from the point of view of an absolute, non-paradigm based standard; 3) paradigms satisfy. We understand the world through paradigms. Paradigms work in that they satisfy doubt and accomplish goals that we want to accomplish. It is only when they fail to do this, when anomalies arise, that we put paradigms into doubt and struggle with developing new ones; 4) paradigms work their wiles on you without your recognizing it. Paradigms, as Kuhn has pointed out, for the most part work unconsciously. Their status is more that of tacit knowledge than of rules of action to be followed. This is one reason why the existence and power of paradigms have not been readily admitted previously; 5) paradigms are costly. It is true that paradigms allow us to accomplish certain things, but at the same time they are constraints. If paradigms define what the world is like, they also define what it is not like. Paradigms set the standards as to what good evidence is and as to where one should look for evidence. By implication, other sources are unacceptable. Paradigms allow one to find some things, but force one to ignore others. It is fairly obvious, I think, that a mechanistic paradigm does not allow the existence of psi phenomena, which seem unable to be explained mechanistically. Hansel's book is an example of this kind of thinking. Mass fraud is a better explanation of what seem to be examples of psi than their acceptance, which are not allowed under his paradigm. There are times when one's cosmic egg must be cracked, and this is a terribly difficult thing to accept. Well, lest I be caught up in this analogy and go too far, I shall stop and proceed to consider Kuhn's view in relation to parapsychology.

What we seemingly have in parapsychology are anomalies. As Broad has suggested in his Basic Limiting Principles, parapsychology deals with those phenomena which seem to go against our understanding of the world. Now, there are two approaches that one can take to anomalies, as Kuhn has pointed out. The first is to say that what the anomalies are are merely problems to be solved within the current paradigm. The second approach is to argue that we need a new paradigm. There is much to be said for the first approach. Generally speaking our current paradigm or paradigms have worked very well in solving many problems, and there is no logical reason why they cannot solve the ones posed by psychical research. Indeed, there are indications that we will be able to solve some of the problems. In his study of the poltergeist, Roll has not only found that the phenomena revolve around one individual, but that the objects seem to move in a way described by the exponential decay function, a theory comprising part of the current paradigm. Further, Sister Justa Smith, in her healing experiment, found that the same healing effect on the trypsin occurred when the vial of trypsin was put into a magnetic field as when it was held by the healer. This indicates that at least some kinds of paranormal healing may be a function of controlling electromagnetic fields, again a phenomenon well within the current paradigm. Finally, LeShan has argued that the description of reality as given by a clairvoyant when practicing her ability, is the same as that of the contemporary theoretical physicist. If so, this is another indication that paranormal phenomena may be explicable in terms of the current paradigm. Not only are there these indications that we may be successful, but our cognitive dissonance would be greatly reduced if we could understand what we are studying in terms of the basic paradigms accepted now.

The above reasons have been given to support the view that our current paradigms are adequate to deal with psi. What can be said for the opposite view? For one, the first two reasons above come from the field of the parapsychical, which seems the most likely to be explicable in terms of what we know, but even here there are many cases of PK taking place in shielded cages, and PK, like ESP, does not seem to be attenuated by space or time. Further, I do not think that the description of reality given by the clairvoyant and the physicist is exactly the same. Otherwise, by LeShan's principles, the paranormal would be accepted as normal, and the physicist would be a mystic. I see no indication of either.

Which set of reasons is more compelling, the one for saying that psi is understandable under the current paradigms or the opposite? As Kuhn has pointed out, the decision is not altogether a logical one. Rather, there seems to come a time when the practitioner of a paradigm accepts the problems as true anomalies for psychological reasons, although he may think that he has been persuaded by the logic of the arguments. So the question of whether parapsychology demands a new paradigm in physics is not strictly a logical one and the proponents of each view are essentially talking at cross purposes. I must admit what my psychological biases are. I think parapsychology calls for a new paradigm. What we have to keep in mind is that with a new paradigm comes a new language or at least new meanings for old words, in keeping with the rejection of the condition of meaning invariance. Therefore one thing I am, in effect, saying is that parapsychology must develop a new language.

Language is closely related to paradigms because both are related to action. I have discussed how a paradigm in science guides experimentation and our expectations in experiments. If we relate it back to pragmatism, a paradigm is that model which allows us to solve problems and accomplish what we want to accomplish. On the other hand, the meaning of a word is tied to its sensible effects. A paradigm says what objects there are and language describes these objects in terms of their place in the paradigm. When we learn a language, then, we are at the same time learning a paradigm. It is our inheritance from the culture. Paradigms are shared and they are implicitly embedded in the language. In this sense, language is not purely descriptive. The job of language is not to describe adequately an experience of uninterpreted sense-data. Language may be prescriptive or formative. That is, through learning the language our world may be prescribed to us. The world may be formed in an entirely different way. The Australian aborigines with their Dream Time and the Hopi Indians without a concept of past and future as we know it, are two prime examples.

What this means is that there are no set categories of language, since there is no paradigm that is absolute. I fear that we have come to view language almost in a Darwinistic fashion as the product of survival, and as such, it is the highest and truest description of reality. In one sense, of course, it is. It describes the nature of the world that is a product of the paradigm, but paradigms change. That means language changes and worlds change. The world is not static and language is not either. One of the assumptions of the traditional science that Kuhn's theory rejects was the condition of meaning invariance, which asserted that the meaning of words is invariant vis-à-vis the progress of science. If there is no absolute trans-paradigm world that is set and absolute, there is no trans-paradigm language. Nothing is sacred in language. There may be ideas and concepts that are more resistant to change than others, but they are not immutable. This is true for science, for philosophy, and for our everyday language.

Now my proposal for a new paradigm and concomitant language is in keeping with much of philosophy over the past several decades. Pragmatism viewed itself as an empiricism, but of a new variety. James called it a "radical empiricism" and proposed an approach to experience, along with Dewey, which foreshadowed phenomenology, especially with its rejection of all dualisms, including the dualism of mind and body. Existentialism was an attempt to give a new paradigm, a new language. Witness the difficult prose of Sartre and Heidegger. Jaspers lamented that any language objectified reality, which results in the dualism of subject and object. To skirt this problem, many existentialists turned to art forms, such as drama or novels, where language does not have to be used in an explicatory way. This option is not open to parapsychologists, I feel, but a grappling with the problem of language may be just as severe in an attempt to develop a language adequate to render paranormal phenomena intelligible in a new paradigm.

As I stated earlier, a new paradigm may mediate much of the dualisms that we now find in our everyday *Weltanschauung*, particularly the dualism of mind and body. Paranormal phenomena are now defined in terms of this dualism. Psychokinesis is, loosely, the action of mind over matter. Telepathy is understood as the communication of one mind to another, and because of this Rhine has argued that telepathy is not an experimental concept, because there is no experimental difference between an example of telepathy and what is in fact an example of clairvoyance, where the subject reads the sender's brain rather than his mind. So if dualism is rejected, a new way of decribing paranormal phenomena will have to be developed.

The dualism of mind and body seems inadequate for several reasons. First, it seems that the progress of science has been a history of closing the gap between mind and body since Descartes. This is not to say, as many contemporary philosophers have argued, that mind is nothing but body, at least in terms of what we normally think of as the characteristics of body in our Cartesian fashion. Matter seems to be becoming less material, even to the point that the physicist Jeans could say, perhaps in somewhat of a poetic fit, that the universe resembles a big thought. Nevertheless, as our understanding of mind is becoming more materialized, so our understanding of matter is becoming more "spiritual." This, of course, complicates the problem of survival of human personality, because we normally think of a soul as surviving, but a soul is usually understood in the traditional Cartesian sense as something able to survive apart from the body. The theory of the astral body is usually thought of as an alternative. The astral body is something that is material enough to be body, but spiritual enough to continue without physiological underpinnings. If one takes the theory of the astral body in this sense, it is as doomed as Descartes' theory of animal spirits, which mediated mind and body through the pineal gland. One simply cannot combine these opposite characteristics and solve the problem, because the dualism is still there. In like manner, one cannot mediate the survival problem by stating that there is a third entity, which conveniently has the characteristics of the other two. The way the astral body theory has to be understood is that it is a suggestion for a new language, where the old dualisms are dispensed with. To those in the old paradigm, this may be an ineffable thing, but that is how paradigms work. It may be that the introduction of the new language will create the experience for us because we have seen that language is formative as well as descriptive.

My other reasons for rejecting the dualism of mind and body revolve around the rejection of the mind as being as isolated and unitary as Descartes thought. The evidence from abnormal psychology, particularly from split personalities, shows us that minds are not so unitary, and telepathy shows us that they are not so isolated as once thought. Further, I think there is evidence (from the work of Houston and Masters, as well as others) that there is a level of the mind that is rich in mythic symbolism. It is a level where archetypes reign, and it is as if, as Jung stated, they rise up from a collective unconscious.

Finally, I think we need to take seriously the mystical experience of so many people throughout the ages, that there is a fundamental unity to all things, what we think of as animate and inanimate. Bergson has already pointed out how acceptance of such a theory would facilitate our understanding of telepathy. With this in mind, it is interesting to note the relationship between mysticism and the process of paradigm switch. Deikman[16] has pointed out that the mystical experience is a state of total deautomization, one where the concepts we have built up in categorizing the world break down. Meditation can be understood as a method of deautomizing, of consciously breaking down the conceptual framework that we have built up to deal with the world. The process of creativity also seems to involve this deautomization, and when we break down the old conceptual models, new connections become apparent. This is essentially what happens in a paradigm switch. Old conceptual frameworks are dismissed or broken down and new ones are substituted. A new way of viewing the world is created. If the process of switching paradigms could be understood as a case of deautomization and reautomization, it becomes an intriguing question what the mystical experience is if it is a case of complete deautomization. We had previously said that there is no knowledge without a paradigm, but would the mystical experience be an example? I guess the question would resolve itself into whether or not one would call such non-conceptual knowing a valid case of knowledge.

Finally, a rejection of dualism by-passes some of the most severe problems of the experimenter effect. The dualism between subject and object, a reflection of the mind-body dualism, has been thought to be necessary for objectivity in science. In order to have objectivity, the experimenter had to be apart from the action of the experiment, a disinterested observer of nature. The experimenter effect in parapsychology has brought all of this into question, however. It looks as if the beliefs and expectations of the experimenter (and perhaps even of the statistician who analyzes the results) have a paranormal effect on the outcome of the experiment. The experimenter can no longer be apart from the experiment, but he becomes part of it. Once again the dualism between subject and object seems to be faltering. Now the reason that scientists wanted this split between the subject and object is that they had an ideal of knowledge being completely objective. The subjectivity of the experimenter, his desires and feelings should not enter in to the analysis of the problem. The analysis should be rational and logical, just as choice between theories should be objective, unbiased, and logical. We have seen, however, that paradigms are not accepted on strictly logical grounds. To be sure, there are certain shared values, such as simplicity, that will be used in deciding between paradigms, but there are no logical rules for such a decision. The old ideal of rationality and objectivity is inadequate. This is not to dispense with rationality but only to show its limits. With the rejection of the old notion of objectivity we can accept a more intimate role of the experimenter in the process, as Tart has suggested in his "States of Consciousness and State-Specific Sciences."[17] Another example of this is LeShan's[18] working out a theory and training himself to see if the theory worked, then after doing this, expanding his theory to account for his own "subjective" experiences. LeShan's work also points to what may be an inadequacy in Kuhn's analysis. LeShan has argued that there are three kinds of "reality," three kinds of relations one can have with his environment—the sensory, the clairvoyant, and the transpsychic. According to LeShan, it is possible for one to move in and out of these realities. I think that it is reasonable to refer to these three realities as paradigms, but if so, it looks as if it is possible to switch back and forth from one paradigm to the next at will, something that Kuhn does not seem to think is possible. Firewalking and trance dancers are two other examples of the same thing. Finally, although I don't think that LeShan has fully succeeded in showing that the description of reality of the clairvoyant and the contemporary physicist are the same, one must concede that there are striking similarities. If this is so, we may be very surprised at the small degree of change that is necessary to bring paranormal phenomena into contemporary science.

REFERENCES

[1] Kuhn, Thomas, *The Structure of Scientific Revolution* (Chicago: The University of Chicago Press, 1970).

[2] Masterman, Margaret, "The Nature of a Paradigm" in *Criticism and the Growth of Knowledge*, ed. by Imre Lakatos and Alan Musgrave (London: The Cambridge University Press, 1970).

[3] Kuhn, p. 111.

[4] Kuhn, p. 175.

[5] Kuhn, p. 175.

[6] Hume, David, *An Enquiry Concerning Human Understanding* (LaSalle, Illinois: Open Court, 1966), p. 184.

[7] Feyerabend, P. K., "Problems of Empiricism," in *Beyond the Edge of Certainty*, ed. R. Colodny (Englewood Cliffs, N.J.: Prentice-Hall, 1965), p. 164.

[8] Feyerabend, p. 164.

[9] Peirce, Charles Sanders, "How to Make Our Ideas Clear," in *Charles S. Peirce: Selected Writings*, ed. Philip P. Wiener (New York: Dover Publications, 1966), p. 78.

[10] James, William, "What Pragmatism Means," in *The Writings of William James*, ed. John J. McDermott (New York: The Modern Library, 1968), p. 378.

[11] James, P. 382.

[12] Kuhn, p. 128.

[13] Kuhn, p. 129.

[14] Rorty, Richard, "The World Well Lost," *The Journal of Philosophy, Vol. LXIX (October 26, 1972), pp. 649–665.*

[15] Kuhn, Thomas, "Reflections on my Critics," in *Criticism and the Growth of Knowledge*, p. 276.

[16] Deikman, Arthur J., "Deautomatization and the Mystic Experience," in *Altered States of Consciousness*, ed. by Charles T. Tart (New York: John Wiley & Sons, Inc., 1969), pp. 23–43.

[17] Tart, Charles "States of Consciousness and State-Specific Sciences," *Science*, Vol. 176 (June 12, 1972), pp. 1203–1210.

[18] LeShan, Lawrence, *The Medium, the Mystic and the Physicist* (New York: The Viking Press, 1975).

DISCUSSION

THAKUR: I'll just make two brief comments on what I thought were criticisms of Kuhn, which you seem to approve of. One was the charge of solipsism against Kuhn, on the suggestion that there is nothing to prevent every individual from having his own paradigm. I find this charge particularly unfair to Kuhn, because the significant thing about his account of science is that science has its respectability simply because it is a community activity and a community agrees on a paradigm. So, of course, in principle, anyone can have a paradigm of his own, a private world, but if you want to share it with your community, you just don't do it. There's no point. So I don't think it is a charge that will stick against Kuhn because of this emphasis on science being a community activity.

EDGE: I would agree. I don't think Kuhn in general wants to subscribe to a private paradigm but what I am pointing out is a temptation for Kuhn, and I was responding to where he admits that, I think, the notion of a paradigm could be taken to a level of solipsism. Of course, he wants to reject this, and for very good reasons. For the very reasons just mentioned. And because of this, I think he makes contradictory statements. The two I pointed out. In one part of the book he says, "scientists are looking at a different world," and then he turns around and says "scientists are not looking at a different world." On the surface, the statements look contradictory, and I was responding to this—from this paradox he derives the notion of a stimulus. This was really what I was arguing against. He derives the notion of a neutral stimulus and I think the philosophical basis for his arguments undercuts the possibility of using the notion of a neutral stimulus—a stimulus that is neutral to all paradigms. That's what I was really arguing against. His notion of this neutral stimulus. Not what he, in general, wants. I would agree with you on that.

THAKUR: I have a feeling that this conflict that you find between two different kinds of statements of Kuhn is, in fact, only on the surface, because the two statements are at completely different levels. Now, when you talk about these absolute foundations of knowledge, I'm absolutely flabbergasted because I haven't the foggiest clue as to what you mean. Are there absolute foundations of knowledge? If so, I'd like to know them.

EDGE: I would too. My argument was essentially that there are none, but I think if you look at traditional philosophy, traditional empiricism—both rationalism and empiricism—you have a foundation approach to knowledge. You have in empiricism, the absolute foundation of knowledge being pure, uninterpreted sense data. You have in rationalism, particularly in Descartes, an absolute foundation for knowledge. These are something that any interpretation of the world has to go back to. I'm denying that there are these absolute foundations of knowledge.

MAUSKOPF. A lot of what you said, Hoyt, aroused the *déjà vu* in me, because the call for a new world view or a phrase like that goes all the way back. We're perhaps in the centenary of the call for that in psychical research. The millenium of a new world view has always been at hand in this field, and it still is obviously here. Now, one of the things that perhaps Kuhn is a bit vague about and some of his critics have pointed out, is that scientific revolutions are not quite the process of becoming that he seems to imply, but rather, the revolution itself really only occurs *when* a new paradigm has come into existence.

Chemists—Lavoisier, for example—were quite happy, Priestley was quite happy working with the Phlogiston theory, including oxygen and all the other new gases in terms of the Phlogiston theory, and it was only really when Lavoisier had constructed something new that the generation of new chemists took it up. So, one thing for parapsychology is we're not going to see the revolution you talk about until somebody has actually come up with this new world.

Now, let me just extend this a bit farther. Then the question in reference to Dr. Thakur's comments arises, namely, paradigms for Kuhn are things held in common by a community of scientists—an identifiable, professional group. Now the problem with parapsychology is, I think, rather special here, because parapsychology, as we well know, does not fit into traditional communities of scientists. And I'd be interested in your comments on what sort of paradigm you would need here, specifically with reference to the fact that parapsychologists must of necessity always look out beyond themselves to neighboring scientific disciplines. You can come up with any theory you want for the parapsychologists, but there still is always the problem of integrating it with other sciences. One final comment here. You're asking for a new world view, but new world views since the 17th century have really come from the physical sciences—not even from the psychological sciences, much less from parapsychology, and I'd be interested in your answer.

EDGE: I don't think I would disagree at all, and I didn't think what I was saying would be in any disagreement with what you are suggesting here. What I am suggesting is not a paradigm for parapsychology, which is only for itself to the exclusion of other scientists. What I am suggesting is essentially this: for whatever psychological reasons, I think that the anomalies that parapsychology has shown seem to be in fact real anomalies, and they're not simply puzzle cases. If that is the case, my call for a new paradigm is in terms of the scientific community in general; so that what I'm calling for is a new theory and one that probably will come from physics. I see no problem with that. The only thing I would suggest is more discretion, in the notion of "world" that you use, in the sense of the world view. I am using it in a particular kind of way, but I don't think in what we've said it's necessary to make the distinctions.

MAUSKOPF: Basically, what it seemed to me you were doing was evading the social context of paradigms being shared by professional, identifiable communities. Parapsychology traditionally, in calling for new world views, has done so, I think, at its peril, by evading the fact that it's not really an accepted professional community of scientists.

EDGE: Pragmatism is not uniform in its consideration of the importance of the community. For instance, James is individualistic and he might have some problems with your criticisms, but if we take John Dewey, he argues quite vehemently for the notion of knowledge being a community thing. And so I don't see any necessary conflict with this.

FRENCH: I have two questions. First, I'm wondering whether a paradigm shift, as you understand it, necessarily entails some ontological shift or a new ontological commitment. That is, I understand that you take the notion of different worlds as not metaphoric. And secondly, you seem to want to treat the verb "to see," as an epistemic term and it seems to me in doing so you confuse "seeing" with "observing." It certainly may be true that, for example, someone saw Lawrence Olivier playing the part of Richard III, and yet be false that he knew Lawrence Olivier was playing Richard III. Or, to use the example of Hanson, who I take it is someone you might agree with—it certainly seems to me to be true that a child might see an X-ray tube and yet it might not be true that he knew that what he was seeing was an X-ray tube.

EDGE: Yes, I take the notion of different worlds quite literally and I am saying a change in paradigms would be a change in ontological commitments. This would be apparent in a follow-up paper to this in which I do propose a theory, a metaphysical theory, which makes to most of us, some strange ontological commitments. About the question of perception being epistemic, this is a problem, and I'm not sure how much we can go into it here. I think that perception is more epistemic than we have traditionally thought, but there are obviously cases where (e.g., from Hanson) you still have to leave room for this sort of distinction, of seeing a particular kind of scientific instrument, and not know that it is that instrument.

BELOFF: I hope when I've had a chance to look at Professor Edge's paper in full I will get a better idea as to what underlies his rejection of dualism, because, of course, this was very far from clear from the delivered paper. But in the meanwhile, perhaps I can ask him to clarify his position by putting the following point to him: It seems to me that the initial case for dualism arises simply out of the question of whether it makes sense to talk of matter in material bodies and systems as being conscious. This has, I think, always been at the bottom of philosophers's worries about mind and body. What sort of reply does he want to give? Because I got the impression that he doesn't go along with the central state materialists and other mind/brain identity type theories, and therefore I am left just a little bit in the air as to where he stands vis-à-vis materialism, etc. Perhaps if we concentrate on that side rather than whether parapsychologists are justified in invoking dualism or not, maybe we can get right to the root there; perhaps I will be better able to understand his position then.

EDGE: I think that there are two things that follow from the paper, one that I have worked on fairly extensively, and one that I have not. The one that I have not worked on extensively is a solution to the mind/body problem. But let me tell you at least the direction I am going in. In a part of the paper that I did not read,* dealing more with the question of survival, I said traditionally the survival problem has been viewed where a Cartesian soul is what survives and you have a kind of dualism. And then I have suggested that some people have argued (in the part of the paper I didn't read) an astral body view and I argued that the astral body view is inadequate because it seems to me it is very analogous to Descartes' animal spirits. It seems to me that Descartes just made up these things and said there are animal spirits and they have two kinds of functions. They have body functions and mind functions, and it was fairly *ad hoc*. Well, I think the astral body view taken in the normal setting is viewed as a third kind of entity. You have minds, you have bodies, and you have astral bodies. And I think the view is inadequate because it still keeps this dualism. You've really not solved anything by going to the astral body view. If I reject dualism, according to traditional philosophy, the direction I go in should be materialism. But I do reject materialism, and the direction I would go in is some kind of monism. I don't want to say neutral monism or double aspect, because you get into the problem of what seems to be a neutral *Ding-an-sich*, a thing-in-itself, and I want to reject that. Monism is an astral body kind of thing, and derivative from astral body is what we take to be matter and take to be minds, but these are only aspects of that which is the monistic aspect. Now, as I said, I have not really worked through this completely and so I don't know whether I'm ultimately going to make sense of it or not, but that's the direction I would go in.

EJVEGAARD: You mentioned that the notion paradigm has twenty-one different meanings. Now, it seems to me that you came up with a twenty-second, using the word, the notion more or less synonymous with expectations. It is well known in psychology that expectations have an impact on perception and furthermore, if expectations are a

---

* Dr. Edge did not read parts of pp. 113–114, 118–119 at the Conference because of time limitations.

part of the world, changing expectations is changing the world. So I agree with you on those points, but why do you call it a paradigm?

EDGE: I call it a paradigm because I was trying to understand the epistemological foundation of Kuhn, which it seems to me to be in pragmatism. What is basic for Kuhn is the epistemological cycle described by Peirce of the doubt or need, and in coming up with the belief that in turn becomes an expectation. That is where I see the connection.

STANFORD: I believe you remarked that in developing an appropriate world view for parapsychology, mysticism should be considered. I was wondering if you could further explicate how you thought that would be helpful in a specifically scientific sense, and secondly, if you have an opportunity, please explain further your remark that the experimenter depends on dualism.

EDGE: Where I mentioned mysticism was not directly in connection with parapsychology, but it was one of the points I was using to show dualism inadequate. In addition, I think there are some interesting connections betwen mysticism and parapsychology, but I did not get into that question at all.

To answer your second question, it seems to me that traditionally we've had the view in science that the experimenter is a subject as opposed to the objective world, and the subject/experimenter has to be, even if he feigns it, a disinterested observer of nature out there. So the paradigm of how one gains knowledge in normal science has used the subject/object dichotomy, which I think is really just a shadow of mind/body dichotomy, and has used this then to put the experimenter apart from the world. Now, if that kind of separation is impossible, then we can no longer have the ideal of the experimenter not being intimately involved in the processes in the world; rather it becomes altogether natural, I think, for us to accept the experimenter effect because we no longer have even the possibility of the subject/object dichotomy.

DOMMEYER: I would just like to ask a question: why with all the paradigm changes we've had, say, since western thinking began back in Greece, do certain problems still persist? We've had changes from the Platonic paradigm, say to a medievalistic paradigm, to a scientific paradigm. Yet the same problems that Plato wrestled with, we're wrestling with today. So how do these paradigms get rid of these difficulties?

EDGE: There are many different kinds of paradigms. In other words, I argued in the paper against there being a notion of one big paradigm. In any given generation there are several different levels of paradigms. It seems to me it is *not* the case that science is dealing with the same problems that Plato dealt with. Philosophers may be, but scientists are not. It seems to me that philosophers may be dealing with the same paradigm, but scientists have changed their paradigm.

DOMMEYER: Why cannot scientists now provide a new paradigm such that parapsychology will find inclusion in it?

EDGE: Well, if I'm a Kuhnian, I certainly couldn't think that the persuasiveness of my argument, the logic of my argument, would persuade you. He excludes that. We have all been trained. The one difference is that scientists are not trained, really, in the history of philosophy and we are told that the questions the Greeks wrestled with are still relevant and important. No scientist is ever told this.

PHILOSOPHY AND THE UNPREDICTABLE

RENÉE HAYNES

It seems to be inherent in the nature of human beings to try to make sense of what goes on; what goes on in their own lives and deaths, what goes on in the collective life of the group to which they belong, what goes on in the world at large. In these attempts to understand what is happening lie the roots of philosophy.

I shall be using the word in two ways, general and particular. In general, it will indicate a view of the world held in this or that time or place or culture pattern, an accepted interpretation of the nature of things. In this interpretation many factors will interact; experience, tradition; symbolism; some degree of science; beliefs about law, honor, loyalty and custom and about what they imply in codes of conduct, permitted or tabooed; observations of natural phenomena; and neat, satisfying, often unarguable theories as to how such phenomena are brought about; for instance, that the sun rises because Phoebus Apollo has begun to drive his golden chariot over the sky, or because the sun itself is a great ball of fire that daily encircles the earth.

In a particular sense, I shall use the word philosophy to indicate the carefully linked intellectual structures set up by the founders and followers of various schools of thought from classical times onwards, incorporating in their data the scientific concepts of their own epochs, and all too often taking it for granted that those concepts are immutably valid, will not, cannot, must not be modified, let alone changed. (Yet change they did, sometimes to disappear as completely as the elegant Pythagorean universe of "circling planets singing on their way," Joseph Priestley's theory of phlogiston, and the 19th century belief in "the ether.")

I shall hope to make clear as I go along, in which sense I am using the key word. Of course, its meanings tend to overlap, so that a world-view may crystallize into a philosophy, or a philosophy decay into an assumption whence grows a view of the world. And, equally of course, a mythology—inherited or developed as need arises—will interlock with both; witness the results over the last 150 years or so, of the powerful different mythologies that have proliferated from the ideas of Rousseau, Darwin, Marx, John B. Watson the behaviorist, and Freud (most ingenious of all, this last, in its exploitation of the great principle known to coin-tossers as "Heads I win, Tails you lose").

Parapsychological phenomena fit fairly easily into the intellectual patterns of most pre-literate cultures, where *all* events that cannot otherwise be explained are ascribed to the wills of a myriad gods or spirits, discarnate or embodied; whether from the ultimate Godhead, or from human spirits alive or dead, the spirits of animals, totemic or individual, the spirits of trees or rivers—like "Tiber-Father Tiber to whom the Romans pray"—the spirits of whirlwinds and singing sands and most terrifying of all the spirits benevolent or evil, which are at once everywhere and nowhere.

Ill-luck, sickness, death itself are attributed to their activities. The parapsychologist can sometimes trace in incidents ascribed to them the workings of the unconscious mind. Thus, a branch may fall on your head in the forest because suggestion has made you accident prone, liable to wander in places where they often fall. You may develop rheumatism, or a high temperature, or eczema, because some psychological stress—a curse, an ill-wishing, a sense of guilt—is finding expression in bodily terms.

Even odder things may happen to those who do not *automatically* dismiss them as impossible. Witness the curious case of levitation reported by the late Mr. E. A. Smythies C.I.E. while working as Forest Adviser to the Government of Nepal.[1] Briefly, what happened was that a young Hindu orderly, named Krishna, who had failed to carry out his annual sacrifice to the tutelary spirit of his home village, was observed by Mr. Smythies himself, by a Mahomedan bearer, and by several frightened Nepalis, to be raised some two feet from the ground while in a cross-legged sitting position (from which jumping is physically impossible) and repeatedly bumped up and down on the hard floor of his hut. The light was good, the room was bare, the explanation given by his fellow-workers was that he was being punished for his negligence. I can see no reason to reject the report, but intellectual reluctance to accept disconcerting facts. Whether this curious instance of psychophysical interaction arose from an intolerable sense of guilt on Krishna's part, or just possibly from some telepathic impression received from the village priest remains open to question.

Worst of all, you may even die as the result of a curse; and this, of course, can happen to suggestible people everywhere, even in industrial cultures, as has been shown by the work of Dr. J. C. Barker[2] in my own country, and in the United States by W. B. Cannon[3] and by investigations of "hexing" carried out by Joan Halifax Grof.[4]

Dr. Barker's study, *Scared to Death*,[5] arose from a long corre-

spondence on the subject in the *British Medical Journal*. He cited a
large number of cases from all over the world in which sheer fear
brought about by suggestion seemed to have killed people. He carefully examined instances resulting not only from the direct suggestion
inherent in a curse, or in the discovery that a powerful tabu had
inadvertently been broken, but from the irresponsible remarks of
fortune tellers, and even from a patient's overhearing and misinter-
preting medical observations. The description he gives of the physiological processes at work may be summed up, very roughly, as the
effects of acute fear on the sympathetico-adrenal system. Fear triggers
off the secretion of adrenalin, which supplies extra strength for "fight
or flight." But you can neither fight a curse, nor fly from it, and the
"continuous outpouring of adrenalin" leads to "a disastrous reduction
in blood pressure resulting in death."

Now primitive interpretations of such phenomena do at any rate
recognize that they occur (a recognition often withheld by 18th century
philosophers and 19th century scientists, because they could not
fit events of this kind into their neat working models of the universe).
These early interpretations moreover sometimes provided right, if
inadequate, reasons for what had been observed. A curse, an overt
and terrifying expression of malevolence, *can*, as has been shown,
bring misfortune upon its object, if he or she believes that it will do
so. This is true, irrespective of the *way* in which it works, the complex
interactions between psyche and body that are involved. What we do
not yet know is whether such malevolence can be telepathically transmitted. Evidence either way is difficult to find and if found to establish.

Right or wrong, however, the belief that every inexplicable event
must result directly from mental causes, from the exertion of some
will, does at any rate provide simple and plausible explanations for
all that goes on. Such a belief may both produce and interpret what
look like paranormal phenomena, and it will seem reasonable, and
strengthening to minds awakening to our strange, spontaneous and
often unpredictable world. However grotesque or terrible that belief
may be in itself and its results, it will give some psychological shelter
from the unexpectedness of winds and lightnings and comets, death
and the unplumbed deep.

Because beliefs of this kind give a measure of security, it feels
unsafe to depart from them. If you have always taken it for granted,
as the Aztecs did, that tomorrow's sunrise depends on your tearing
the hearts out of the proper quota of living human sacrifices today,
you will be running a great risk if you stop doing so. The whole
world may be dark, night may last for ever, and it will be your

fault. Better be safe than sorry, so you go on capturing and killing prisoners, and the sun continues to rise. Q.E.D. This particular closed circuit of theory and practice was broken down by a conquering nation which maintained that murder was wrong and human sacrifices were diabolical. And the sun continued to rise.

This grotesque, horrible, backward-rationalized piece of human ingenuity grew up in one fairly sophisticated culture, and was deliberately abolished by men of another. What has, rather too suddenly, been destroying much simpler beliefs and assumptions among primitive communities over the last 70 years or so has been the impact of scientific technology, with a mode of thought based on experiment and buttressed by statistics. Yet in many instances, the old working philosophy, with its curious symbolic imagery, may survive for a while in odd, thought-provoking juxtaposition with the new. In our own culture I have known an educated woman, a university lecturer in literature, to be exact, to whom unpleasant precognitions usually presented themselves in auditory fashion as the hooting of owls or the croaking of carrion crows. She therefore proposed that these two species of birds should be exterminated because they "brought bad luck." The premonition was identified with the symbol through which it was formulated. This is exemplified in a rather less surprising context by a curious incident reported by Ronald Rose, whose study of psi among Australian[6] aborigines was made with the help of grants from this very Foundation. Crisis telepathy, among these people, is often mediated by an image, seen or heard, of some tribal totem. It was in this way that Earl Ferguson, an aboriginal who worked as an engine driver on Australian Railways, received a message. During a rest period, he was sitting with two white fellow workers on the veranda of a small hotel when he saw his totem, a rooster, come onto that veranda, whence it was shooed off by the waitress on her way indoors. He told his companions that it was his totem (*Djurabeels*) and that he was going to get some bad news. They of course poohpoohed this as "blackfellow talk." The waitress then came out again saying there was a long distance telephone call for "a dark fellow called Ferguson." Answering it, he was told of his grandmother's sudden and unexpected death. Here primitive imagery jostles modern technology; the brain trained in railway engineering, the ancient tribal symbol, the long distance telephone, and the telepathic hallucination of the waitress and the two white railway employees. Rose mentions in this connection, that his informant told him it was not uncommon on such occasions for other people to "see" a totem creature, and to believe it an actual animal.

The practical function of imagery in spontaneous ESP needs to be examined in very much more detail than I can give it here. I shall deal more fully later with its role in working out theoretical explanations. Imagery plays a very large part in determining the average human's view of the world in general, and of his own particular experience in it, normal or paranormal. You have only to look at such metaphorical expressions as light and darkness, high and low, cool reason and stifling emotion, to realize this fact. To some extent, moreover, everyone *has* to think in accordance with the imagery of his own time and place, and to communicate his experience in these terms. Thus "breaking the ice" is only valid in a climate where it freezes, and "he's not on my wave length" is only comprehensible in an age familiar with radio.

Was it for this reason that the most learned and acute thinker, Augustine of Hippo, could only conceive of paranormal cognition in terms of a message delivered by some supernatural agency? "It is by the operation of angels", he wrote,[7] "that one who is dead says where his body lies, and where he wants to be buried. God allows this for the consolation of the living." He also attributed to an angelic messenger what happened when a young man he knew in Milan dreamed that his dead father told him where to find the receipt for a debt already paid, for which a claim was being made on the estate. He duly found it. St. Augustine noted, too,[8] the case of a monk who sent word to a lady who wished to consult him "that the following night she would see him in a dream; and so she did, and he gave her the information she wanted. The apparition was not a bodily presence but an image caused in the mind of the lady *by an angel* [my italics] and the monk could only have known it was going to happen by his gift of prophecy." He observed in general, by the way, that "the images of friends seen in sleep are rarely the souls themselves, but phantasms seen because of our previous associations of thought," instancing the fact that "not I, but my image, appeared to Eulogius the rhetorician in Africa, and expounded to him an obscure passage from Cicero."[9]

Some 1300 years later, Daniel Defoe, writing under the pseudonym of Andrew Moreton, was still preoccupied with the idea that extra-sensory perception was brought about by messenger spirits. In his *Secrets of the Invisible World Disclos'd*,[10] he remarked that "some people are for reviving all into Fancy, Whimsy or the Vapours" while others "will have it that every Apparition comes from the Devil." He suggested that precognitions arise because "some intelligent Being who can see into Futurity" conveys "Apprehensions into the mind" by way of "a certain Correspondence between our Spirits, embodied and cased up in Flesh and Spirits unembodied," but he would not have it that these messengers were "the spirits of the dead come to revisit," since his view of the nature of things was that of the Puritan, for whom the belief in Purgatory, a postmortem state of purification and growth, had been abolished, and the souls of the dead were either in heaven, whence they would not wish to return, or in hell, whence they could not get out. No, such messengers were not the dead (though they might choose to put on their likeness) and not necessarily either angels or devils, but perhaps "a fourth class of Spirits," possibly "inhabitants of the planets with bodies made to suit conditions there," whose business it was to transmit information. Here we are not far from the modern concept of benevolent beings from outer space descending from unidentified flying objects to give us arcane knowledge and rather platitudinous advice.

It may seem odd, incidentally, that what is called "ufology" should have arisen now, in spite of the fact that over a hundred years of development in telecommunication has provided us with such useful (though sometimes dangerously misleading) analogies in which to think of psi phenomena. Already in the 19th century people were talking of "the bush telegraph," and, more personally, of receiving messages by "inner telegrams"; and the invention of radio, and even more of television, has made it possible for the mind to accept, without boggling, the fact that a man's voice can be heard and his image can be seen far away from his actual body, which remains at a single spot in time and space.

It may well be, however, that the analogy of the messenger-boy system is attractive because it is so much easier to *visualize*. True, Laurens van der Post's Kalahari Bushman[11] can accept quite simply the idea of a mind-to-mind communication, when he says he is making puffs of smoke from his fire not as a code of signals but to attract the attention of his friend miles away, who, seeing them is alerted to "think my thoughts." More sophisticated groups, however, anxious to discover *how* the process worked, might interpret such activities as rituals undertaken to compel spirits to convey messages. Again the idea of a "world soul" was well known to many educated people, both at the time of St. Augustine and at the time of the Renaissance and after, and the possibility that information might be conveyed through it to individual selves was probably as familiar then as the modern notion of the collective unconscious whence paranormal cognition may well up, is today. But these concepts are rather abstract, whereas the messenger hypothesis explains phenomena in a concrete, satisfying, common sense way; and to many people, in the short view, simple, satisfying, common sense explanations are much more welcome than complex ones, as Voltaire found when he laughed to scorn the proposition that the marine fossils in the Pyrenees showed they had once been under the ocean. Any sea shells found there, he said, were obviously cockle shell badges dropped from the hats of pilgrims on their way from France to the shrine of St. James at Compostella.

The contrast between abstract concepts and concrete imagery as a way of receiving, patterning, and expressing experience, and as a way of thinking and reasoning about it appears in philosophy in both senses of the word, that is, as an intellectual structure and as a world view. This contrast occurs not only at different times and places and levels of sophistication, but in different cultures. Thus, for instance, English speaking people, trained to accumulate facts before making inferences or formulating hypothesis, trained to argue from cases to generalizations, from concrete to abstract, often find it difficult to adapt themselves and their methods of thought to the French and German systems of arguing from abstract principles to concrete instances. And *vice-versa*.

As a result of his study of the electrical activities of the brain, Dr. W. Grey Walter, of the Burden Neurological Institute of Bristol, has suggested[12] that these differences also occur in individuals, and are to some extent genetically transmitted, though they can be modified by upbringing and schooling. Plainly, visualizers do in fact approach experience in different ways from abstract thinkers. This holds good in specialized, as well as in more general groups. Thus, even among "sensitives" it is possible to distinguish between those chiefly aware of apparitions and those chiefly aware of a "sense of presence," between those who perceive symbolic or veridical hallucinations, and those with formless intuitions. Vivid examples of this occurred in experiments conducted by the late Mr. Whately Carington,[13] in which subjects were asked to guess, sketch, and send in a copy of a drawing being shown in his study on one particular night of a series. Some of them would reproduce the actual lines and curves of a drawing, a geometrical diagram as it were, without realizing what the object portrayed was. Others reproduced the *idea* of that object (and in some cases further ideas associated with the original one) without much detailed correspondence with the drawing itself.

Differences of the same kind occur, Dr. Grey Walter maintains, among scientists. Experimental scientists tend (like himself) to think in visual terms; theoretical scientists do not. What is more, the two

groups often find one another incomprehensible, cannot understand the workings of one another's minds. It is interesting that Sir
Francis Galton, as early as 1880, noted not only that "mental imagery
was unknown to the scientists of his acquaintance" but also that "they
didn't believe other people experienced it." Presumably they were all
of the theoretical sort, more interested in classification than in the
data classified.

It looks then, as if every one of us were born, not so much, in the
words of Gilbert and Sullivan, "a little Liberal or else a little Con-
servative," as a little Platonist or else a little Aristotelean: a little
Platonist, for whom reality consists primarily in abstract ideas, particularly those involved in mathematics, or a little Aristotelian, for
whom reality consists in what we can see and hear and measure,
and in what we can deduce from our findings.

This divergence can be traced in different schools of thought in
every age and all over the world, Taoist and Confucian, Hindu and
Islamic, Thomist and Scotist, Realist and Nominalist, Idealist and
Materialist. The variety is endless, the field so enormous that I can
only hop about in it like an observant parrot. What does have to be
remembered continually though, is that whatever the tenets of a
school, the very fact of its existence means that a pattern of inter-
locking ideas has been set up (whether those ideas are generalizations or theoretical concepts). This pattern will appeal, *as such*, to
abstract thinkers, who will incline to defend the system (because it
is a system) against the intrusion of new facts, or new interpretations,
that seem to spoil its perfect polished symmetry. Thus Hume, convinced that miracles could not happen because they were "against
the laws of nature," refused to believe that the psychosomatic cures
at the cemetery of St. Médard had taken place, because he thought
them miracles. He refused to admit any evidence for them, however
trustworthy, because of this *a priori* decision. Again, in a rather milder
way in our own time, I have heard Bertrand Russell maintain, against
the argument of Aldous Huxley just returned from one of the
early conferences at Le Piol, that if extrasensory perception ever did
occur, of which he was extremely doubtful, it happened so rarely and
so unpredictably that no scientific law could be formulated about its
manifestations, and that *therefore* it was unworthy of scientific attention.

Despite their divergences though, there is one way in which philosophies worked out before the rise of industrialism seem to me to
differ from their successors (at any rate until fairly recent times).
Setting aside those few thinkers who conceived the whole universe
as "a fortuitous concourse of atoms," these older philosophies for

the most part assumed the existence of a First Cause, a living invisible source of the changing world and the immortal stars, whose quiet will was working everywhere. Thus, though the old gods were discarded as such—far shooting Apollo, Athene young and virginal and wise, ox-eyed Hera, lustful Zeus transforming himself into a bull, a shower of gold, a swan—the idea of *consciousness* was never ruled out, consciousness which could affect the behavior of men, of animals and of objects. Although the image of the automaton had come into being with Daedalus' bronze robot figure that fought the Argonauts, and the Colossus defender of Rhodes, no one had begun to use it as an image, a working model, or a preconceived idea either of the universe or of the nature of man. That did not happen until the industrial revolution had got well under way. Even Robert Boyle writing in the 18th century of the body as "an hydraulical-mechanical engine" did not include the mind in this definition. And so long as the *fact* of consciousness was recognized, and with it the existence of selves perceiving both the world and their own being, there was room to admit the fact of paranormal cognition; even though no mechanism had been discovered to account for its workings, no physical organ seemed to be involved in its transmission or reception, however much people all over the world tried to attribute the psi function to the pineal gland, the "third eye." This is, in fact, sensitive to light, indirectly in mammals, directly in some other species, and appears to control the processes of reproduction. Insofar as voluntary chastity seems to conduce to ESP, and frustration—including sexual frustration—to psychokinesis, the "third eye" may be relevant to the physiological side of psychical research; but the connection does not seem to be very close.

In the heyday of European classical civilization then, mechanomorphism, the image of the machine as a philosophical model, had not yet come into being. Both Plato and Aristotle recognized, without any painful exercises in mind-boggling, the fact of consciousness and the existence of paranormal cognition. This was thought to occur most frequently and vividly in "fools, idiots and melancholy persons" —"fools" by the way, indicated the illiterate and "melancholy persons" introverts or "people with the power of recalling the soul from outer objects into itself." (Incidentally, though extroverts appear to do better in the experimental field, I have long had a suspicion that introverts may, in fact, produce the greater proportion of spontaneous psi-phenomena; it would be interesting to know if this is, in fact, the case.)

The ancient University of Alexandria, founded in 323 B.C. and closed down in A.D. 529 by the Emperor Justinian because its teaching had become not only Gnostic but definitely anti-Christian, formulated some fascinating ideas about ESP within the framework of Platonism and Neo-Platonism. It was here that Philo the Jew wrote in the first century of our era of three sorts of significant dreams, those that came direct from God, those in which the individual mind was "linked with the world soul" and those in which that mind used its own system of symbols (like the dreams of Pharaoh's butler and baker). It was here that Plotinus, two hundred years later, discussed the world soul indwelling nature, and the "sympathy" it induced in all things, and it was probably from this tradition that the Islamic thinkers Alkindi, Avicenna and Averroes drew some of their ideas. Before the barbarian invasions overran the great civilization of Rome, educated men of different religions and philosophical affiliations could examine without panic the phenomena of extrasensory perception. Among Christians were the great bishop Synesius, who regarded divination as "a noble pursuit," and Augustine, who has already been quoted. Cicero distinguished between what he called intuitive and deductive divination (spontaneous phenomena and those deliberately induced by psychosomatic techniques). Plutarch hazarded that all divination was a natural power, at its lowest ebb in the autumn. Pliny, in his natural history, maintained the existence of such things as a "healing touch" and a "magical force" which could act at a distance. Galen, the doctor, believed in precognition—and had precognitions himself. It is worth noting that all these observations sprang from men who had to deal with the objective world. Synesius and Augustine were bishops, and so administrators; Cicero, a lawyer and a statesman; Plutarch, a biographer-historian; Pliny a man so passionately concerned with natural science that he sailed into the doomed Italian coast to investigate that eruption of Vesuvius which buried Herculaneum and Pompeii; Galen, a physician involved in treating sick people (he had a part time job as doctor to a team of gladiators, as well as his ordinary practice). They were not blindfolded against day-to-day happenings by too closely woven a network of theory.

It was long before Europe was settled enough to think again at leisure. The ideas, as well as the power, of the barbarians came flooding in, and men's minds stood to the defence of what had already been achieved, rather than to the examination of fresh data. In the newly established empire of Islam, however, philosophers were looking again at mathematics, metaphysics, and extrasensory perception. As early as the ninth century, Alkindi was writing a treatise on clairvoyance and divination in dreams, in which he firmly believed, remarking that what we should call paranormal cognition "came through" most easily when attention was withdrawn by sleep from the outer world. This was translated into Latin some time after 1085, when Christian scholars made their way to Toledo, newly recaptured from the Moors, to study their intellectual achievements. Also translated were the work of Averroes, who formulated in his own terminology, something like Jung's idea of the collective unconscious; some long lost Aristotelean writings; and the work of Avicenna.

The Italian Thomas Aquinas, founder of the school of philosophy so powerfully revived by Maritain and others in our own era, was enormously stimulated by the new impact of Aristotle's argument, and, in spite of much opposition, set about integrating its findings with those of Catholic theology, with its insistence on the importance of created things and the significance of matter both in itself and as a means to the knowledge and adoration of God.

As has been seen, the Platonic tradition had been transmitted by the University of Alexandria through the work of Plotinus and later thinkers; and it had proved very easy to slip from the theory that abstract ideas were more significant than material things into the gnostic theory that all abstractions, seen as "spiritual realities," were good, and *all* material objects evil; and further, that the whole process of creation was a fall from spirit into matter, from which the soul must struggle to be free. (This idea, which has been presented in a contemporary context by Dr. Arthur Guirdham, is also implicit in much Eastern philosophy, ancient and modern.) As the psi-function belonged to the spiritual world, then logically a man in whom it appeared must surely have an "intense purity of soul," as Avicenna argued[14] in connection with prophecy.

Thomas Aquinas had worked closely with Albert the Great, one of the earliest mediaeval observers of nature in itself, and he agreed with him that "a certain disposition and physical temperament are needed for natural prophecy," which existed, he maintained, in various animals as well as in humans. It could, moreover, arise in men who had neither sanctity, nor charity, nor even a good moral character.

Although he taught that "there is nothing in the mind that was not previously in the senses" (a statement that could only have been made by someone who thought primarily in sensory images) he did not —indeed, as a Christian, he could not—deny the existence of the mind itself, and his work is a most useful background for psychical research. Invaluable are its emphasis on fact, its power to reserve judgment, and its sturdy refusal to accept such neat oversimplified theories as Avicenna's doctorine of the Two Truths. This asserted that philosophy and theology (or as it might be nowadays, quantity and quality, reason and intuition, thought and feeling) were intrinsically different from one another and independent of one another, and could never be reconciled, each remaining supreme in its own sphere. If this were applied to parapsychology, of course, it might mean that the experimentalist and the student of spontaneous phenomena could never have anything to do with one another, or interrelate their conclusions.

Thomist philosophy was the basis of the great 18th century work[15] in which parapsychological observations were related to scientific findings on the one hand and to theology on the other. This was written by Prospero Lambertini (later Pope Benedict XIV), a genial and brilliant polymath of great scholarly integrity. Born and bred in Bologna, long a lively university center of science and medicine, he became an ecclesiastical lawyer, worked for some years as Devil's Advocate, and published in the 1730s a very close and detailed study of what went on in the legal processes for the beatification and canonization of saints. These processes involved a most punctilious evaluation of the evidence for what were claimed to be miracles. In this connection, he examined very closely what was then known—which was a good deal more than you might think—about psychosomatic disease, the effect of suggestion, and the existence of psi, then called "the preternatural." He accepted this as a fact, to be taken into consideration without fuss, observing that it seemed to happen in mammals and even in fish; that in humans it welled up more often in sleep than in waking life, more often in the illiterate than in the scholarly (because, he said, the sleeping self is not distracted by external events, and the illiterate are not distracted by many ideas). He noted too that minds not wholly taken up with "internal passions or external occupations" were more likely than others to receive preternatural impressions. It is a great pity that the section of his book dealing with such subjects has never been translated into English. He wrote of course in Latin, which was still in his time an international language. His work was the last for many years in which parapsychology was studied as a part of general knowledge, as something clearly recognizable in itself which could be both distinguished from, and related to other subjects.

For much of Europe, though, philosophical development was proceeding along very different lines. After the glowing revival of neo-Platonist ideas at the Renaissance there arose Descartes, for whom mathematics was the primary mode of thought, the supreme discipline; Descartes, whose theory cut the living self into two parts, the ghost and the machine. The ghost was of course an eminently rational one, founded on the proposition that "I *think*, therefore I am"; "I *think*" not "I perceive," or even "I feel." There was little room for the psi function here. And in England it was squeezed out altogether by Locke and Hume. Berkeley might have considered it, had it been formulated in appropriate philosophical or theological terms. In the intellectual climate of his time and place however, the subject fell under such headings as Superstition, or Old Wives Tales, with which the Age of Reason could have no truck. As thinkers began to compare the created universe to a clock Divinely made, wound up and set going in the remote past, the image of mechanism surfaced yet again. In the course of time, the ghost was exercised from the machine, the Creator was dissociated from the clock as an unnecessary hypothesis, and the totality of things was conceived as a vast automaton, framed and modified and changed by the bludgeoning of aeons of chance. Thought, perception and feeling, all alike, were seen as "epiphenomena," byproducts of physiological activity.

The Romantic Movement, with its ghosts and werewolves and doppelgangers, its violence and its terrifying mystery, redressed the balance to some extent in the general literate public, whose craving for the "occult" is paralleled in our own time, also, perhaps, as a reaction against too much purely mental activity, self insulated on the one hand from the raw material of experience, and on the other from value judgments of any kind.

The Romantic Movement could not, however, be called a philosophy in either of the senses in which I have used the word. It was, like contemporary occultism, more concerned with exploiting some of the subject matter of psychical research than with psychical research itself. In many learned circles, the idea of consciousness as an epiphenomenon persisted, and it is not quite dead even today. It was taken for granted in the work of Pavlov and in the doctrines of behaviorism, it is alive in the arguments of Professor Hansel and Professor Skinner (of "rato-morphic" fame) and it is implicit in all reductionism. There is no room to consider psi in such connections unless it is envisaged—as Professor John Taylor[16] sometimes seems to envisage it—as a form of electromagnetic energy, as yet unidentified, which provokes reactions as automatically as a tap just above a crossed knee provokes a jerk.

Other currents of thought, however, have long been running, other thinkers have arisen, both inside and outside the scientific field. The

patterns they have originated are all on the whole less rigid, less inclined either to ignore or to exclude the data of parapsychology.
Bergsen's *L'Evolution Créatrice*, with its concept of an *Elan Vital*,
originating, indwelling, and urging onward the development of life
and consciousness revived in an unfamiliar form the belief in a nonphysical First Cause, and, in consequence, the possibility of nonphysical secondary causes. Significantly, Bergson became a President
of the Society for Psychical Research. *Elan Vital* can of course look
to Christians like a new name for the Holy Spirit, The Giver of life;
and *L'Evolution Créatrice* seems to have played a part in inspiring
Bergson's compatriot, Teilhard de Chardin, in his great attempt to
construct a modern synthesis of knowledge. In the course of this
he broke down Descartes' curious teaching—logical, of course, in
terms of his limited premises—that animals could not feel, because
having no *thinking* souls they *could* be nothing but automata. He believed in "a psyche running through all matter," and ascribed to
all living creatures some degree of awareness (and here his biologist
friend Julian Huxley agreed with him.) In man, who has language
as a stimulant and a tool of thought, consciousness is reflexive, and
concerns his own identity as well as the world. He knows that he
is, and he knows that he knows it. Paranormal cognition can bring
him data to be examined and understood, as well as impressions to
be registered and impulses to take action. He, the perceiving self, is
both involved in and detached from what he perceives. He can think
about it. He can try to interpret it. He can use his free will to decide
what to do.

Once this is realized, it is hard to maintain the idea of consciousness as an epiphenomenon, though the habit of taking it for granted
may be hard to dispel. In 1920, Frederick Pollock,[17] the great international lawyer, was writing to Oliver Wendell Holmes saying that "he
had no patience with the idea;" that "experience in consciousness is
the only thing we know at first hand"; and that "to regard thought
or consciousness as a by product abstracted out of its own content is
a ludicrous muddle." In 1929, Sir Arthur Eddington[18] maintained that
"Mind is the first and most direct thing in our experience; all else
is inference." In 1940, Sir Charles Sherrington[19] wrote of "the 'I' as
a cause within our body. The I . . . is directly experienced. It is the
self." In 1962, Sir Cyril Burt[20] affirmed the truth that "there can
be no observation without an observer," acknowledged that this meant
"reverting to a frankly dualist theory" of mind and body, and asked
why not, if it fitted the facts. In 1965, Sir John Eccles, the brain
specialist,[21] (who had earlier observed that the brain is just such a

machine as a ghost might operate) "faced a fundamental mystery" in disbelieving that "my conscious experiences are *nothing but* the operation of the physical mechanisms of my brain." In that same year, Sir Cyril Hinshelwood[22] noted that "what remains utterly incomprehensible is how and why the brain becomes the vehicle of consciousness." The eminent neurologist Lord Brain, Sir Alister Hardy, and many others agreed. In fact:

> Brain, Bergson, Sherrington, Eccles and Burt
> Rescued poor Psyche from out of the dirt
> Removed all the traces of past inebriety
> Capped her and gowned her with proper sobriety
> And presented her thus to the Royal Society.

In spite of all this, however, a fundamental confusion of thought recurs in our time, as in all times, like a decimal in a sum with threes in it. Consciousness *may* no longer be conceived as an "epiphenomenon", but it is over and over again identified with energy. Although it is easier now for those who frame philosophical systems to admit that parapsychological data exist, this seems to be largely because modern discoveries in quantum physics provide an analogy for them. Now, as has already been noted, analogies are extremely useful in enabling the mind to accept unfamiliar facts, but extremely dangerous in causing confusion between the simile and the reality. It is possible that electromagnetic activities subserve some paranormal processes (particularly, perhaps, that of psychokinesis) just as waves of light and sound subserve the processes of sensory perception. But sensory perception is not identical with light or sound waves, and extrasensory perception is not identical with electromagnetic activities. Both modes of perception have to be received and realized by the perceiver.

I may seem to be overstressing this matter of the perceiving self, but there is so much confusion in this field that the point has to be reiterated up to the edge of boredom. Thought about it tends to be so muddled that I have even heard a speaker adduce Heisenberg's uncertainty principle as a proof of human free will.

This paper is in the main a retrospective sketch of past interaction—or lack of it—between philosophy and parapsychology in the widest sense of each word. I am sure that others will be dealing in detail with the fascinating hypotheses worked out over the last thirty years or so by, for instance, Arthur Koestler, C. D. Broad, John Beloff, H. H. Price, Lawrence Le Shan—and many more for whom psi phenomena seem to emerge from a deeply and delicately interrelated universe, a quivering web of synchronicity.

REFERENCES

[1] *Journal of the Society for Psychical Research* Vol. 36, No. 664, May, 1951.
[2] Barker, J. C., *Scared to Death*. London, 1968.
[3] Canon, W. B., "Voodoo Death." *Psychosomatic Medicine*, 1957. 19. 182.
[4] Halifax Grof, Joan, "Hex Death." *Parapsychology and Anthropology, Proceedings of an International Conference*. New York, 1973.
[5] op. cit.
[6] Rose, Ronald, *Living Magic*. London, 1957.
[7] Quoted by Prospero Lambertini in *De Beatificatione Servorum Dei et Canonizatione Beatorum*, Bologna, 1734–38.
[8] Quoted by Prospero Lambertini in *De Beatificatione Servorum Dei et Canonizatione Beatorum*, Bologna, 1734–38.
[9] Quoted by Prospero Lambertini in *De Beatificatione Servorum Dei et Canonizatione Beatorum*, Bologna, 1734–38.
[10] Defoe, Daniel, *Secrets of the Invisible World Disclos'd*. London, 1735.
[11] van der Post, L., *The Lost World of the Kalahari*. London, 1958.
[12] Walter, W. Grey, "Observations on Man, his Frame, his Duty and his Expectations." Eddington Memorial Lecture. Cambridge, 1969.
[13] "Experiments in the Paranormal Cognition of Drawings." Whately Carington, with an introduction by C. D. Broad. *Proceedings*, Society for Psychical Research, Vol. XLVI, Part 162, June, 1940.
[14] *S. F. Afrian Avicenna, his Life and Works*, London, 1958.
[15] Prospero Lambertini, op. cit.
[16] Taylor, John, *Superminds, An Enquiry into the Paranormal*. London, 1975.
[17] Letters between Frederick Pollock and Oliver Wendell Holmes.
[18] in his Swarthmore Lecture, 1929.
[19] in his Gifford Lectures, 1940.
[20] Burt, Cyril, Paper on "Mind and Consciousness," in *The Scientist Speculates*, London, 1962.
[21] Eccles, John, "The Brain and the Unity of Conscious Experience." Eddington Memorial Lecture, Cambridge, 1965.
[22] Presidential Address to the British Association 1965.

DISCUSSION

NICOL: I understood you to mention early on the cases of Dr. Barker in The Welsh Disaster. Is that right?

HAYNES: I mentioned the cases of Dr. Barker, but I didn't mention specifically the case of the Aberfan Disaster. But I think it's extraordinarily interesting.

NICOL: Barker's cases are impressive, but these collective experiences, when people tell us they have dreams or other impressions of what is going to happen, very often they concern some major disaster such as the sinking of the Titanic. I wondered recently, how many people have dreamt of disaster to the new airplane "Concorde." We haven't heard anything about them and there's been no disaster so far. If one of them has a bad landing, will there be a flood of stories about people who have had these prophetic dreams? Some of the cases we hear about are probably genuine, but there are other instances we don't hear about. If I may mention your very distinguished ancestor, Thomas Henry Huxley, he was once traveling on the continent when he woke up apparently one night to hear a voice saying, "Don't go to Nuremberg." He went to Nuremberg. Nothing happened.

HAYNES: Regarding the points you made, one by one, first of all, in both New York and London, there exist Bureaux of Premonitions to which people with premonitions are asked to write. I don't know whether either has reported on its results. I should very much like to know if it has. That is point one. As to disasters to the Concorde, don't you think there might be a little wishful thinking about it by those of us who don't like noise? As to my great grandfather, these things can come in any kind of way. Perhaps he thought somebody was going to take him around Nuremberg and show him all the tortures including the Iron Maiden, and he wouldn't have liked that one little bit.

BERENDT: I can report a case where a person had a premonition about an airplane accident which would happen through hijacking a plane from Lebanon to London. In the same phone call he told something about a group of children and when I asked him what he meant by "a group of children," he said "this is always something bad when I see it ahead." And he continued about another flight accident. I asked him, "Is this a hijacking too"? He waited for a moment and then said, "No, this is no hijacking. This is something else." This was in February, 1974. In the beginning of March there was a hijacking of a plane going from Beirut to London, which was stopped at Amsterdam airport; people got out and the plane was exploded on the ground. On the very same day—and this was the reason that these things weren't mentioned so much in the press—there was a terrible airplane disaster near Paris, where a DC 10 came down with the loss of more than three hundred people and it came out finally that it was not an explosion, but it was a technical hitch with a door which opened during the flight. So this man was correct in both cases on the same day it happened. There was one other point in it, that he mentioned a name to me about a place in Sinai, Kantarrah. I thought that would be the place where the accident would happen. Actually, what happened was that the second plane was a Turkish plane and the name of the plane was "Ankara," so you have here some symbolism or some likeness in the acoustical area. This is only to make clear that these happenings were reported all at the same time, when I got the phone call from the paragnost Mr. D.

Chen. Directly afterwards I phoned Professor Rothschild and he put it down in writing too. The accidents were actually one week ahead. The paragnost usually is not able to say when things have happened, do happen, or will happen, so the time lapse may sometimes be very great, even up to six months, a year or more, as shown in cases we have from the Society for Psychical Research, about six and seven years even. In this special case, nothing happened within about two months time or more, but in the third month, in the month of May, there was a case in Israel where about twenty children, who had been hostages, were killed in a school.

BENDER: Just allow me to tell you about an extraordinary case of prediction the Freiburg Institute is just checking. It was published in 1951, but we did not notice it. Now it came to our attention, and we checked the authenticity of the material. In August, 1914, a Bavarian soldier wrote two letters to his family in Bavaria, from Alsatia, and he told his family that his unit captured a French civilian and this French civilian was an extraordinary man, somewhat crazy. He told them that Germany will lose the war. It will last four years. Italy will declare war on Germany in one year. We have the letters. The first letter was written the 24th of August and the second letter, the 30th of August. Then he continued, this unknown civilian, "after the war, revolution will break out in Germany and everyone will become a millionaire, but they throw the money out of the window." Then, the French visionary continues, "In '32, a man will emerge from the lower levels of the population. This man will become a dictator. There will be no law, no justice, and he has an extremely terrible strict regime and many people must die." Please note the exact years. In '38, one prepares for war and a war breaks out. This war will last five years. Italy, in this war, will be on the side of Germany, but many German soldiers will lose their lives in Italy. Then it continues, in '45, the war is lost. The man—the symbol, the swastika, will disappear and terrible judgment will break out. Then Germany will be split into two parts. The occupational armies will rob it but they conflict with each other. It's an extraordinary prediction and our work is to make sure that the letters are genuine—and they are!

PHILOSOPHERS AS PSYCHIC INVESTIGATORS

J. Fraser Nicol

The philosopher Henry Sidgwick used to say with regret that he never had the opportunity to meet and talk with "the bald-headed man on the bus." The descriptive expression was in common use by Victorians and means the same as what we call "the man in the street." If Sidgwick on one of his visits to London had got on a bus at King's Cross Station—instead of calling a horse-cab as he probably did —and found himself in conversation with that bald-headed man, I think he would have found the experience intensely interesting. But what would the bald-headed man have thought of Sidgwick? He would have learned that Sidgwick was very sociable and certainly no intellectual snob. (If I may interpolate an anecdote, Sidgwick was once visited by a foreign professor who complained that the English language did not have a word for *savant* or *Gelehrte*. Sidgwick, who had a stutter, replied, "But we do—we call them p-p-p-prigs!")

If Sidgwick had tried to explain the meaning of such words as analysis, synthesis, metaphysics, utilitarianism, and others, his bald-headed companion might have thought that philosophers might be very wise and kindly men, but surely too remote in their mental processes to be of any practical utility in the affairs of this life.

The purpose of this paper is to show that, throughout the ages, philosophers engaged in psychical investigations have shown themselves to be men of sound practical ability unsurpassed, I should estimate, by any other profession. Some of them, it is true, have occasionally fallen into errors of investigation, but rather less so, I believe than members of other professions.

For reasons of space, philosophers of classical times must be excluded from this account, and for the same reason the investigations of a few philosophers happily still in practice will also be passed over. So we are left in this paper with a sort of episodic account of a dozen or twenty philosophers who, through many centuries, have contributed with ability and distinction to the progress of psychical research.

The earliest philosopher deserving of remembrance is Augustine of Hippo. He was born in Numidia (North Africa) in A.D. 354, and died there in A.D. 430. Of him, E. R. Dodds has said that he "deserves a more honorable place in the history of psychical research than any thinker between Aristotle and Kant."

Augustine personally investigated, or collected reports from friends of telepathic dreams, waking visions, precognition and paranormal healing. There was even a case of apparent experimental telepathy. In Carthage, there was a well-known thought reader named Albicerius. When a visitor asked him to say what he was thinking about, Albicerius replied correctly, "A line of Virgil." When invited to say which line, he quoted the line correctly. Augustine, always a cautious inquirer, was at pains to point out that, besides his successes, Albicerius had had many failures.

In a case quoted by Augustine, a man named Curma, a member of the local council, during an illness fell into a trance-like state. On recovering consciousness he said that another man, also named Curma, a blacksmith, was dying. Inquiries showed that the blacksmith Curma had died at the time the percipient was returning to consciousness. When, two years later, Augustine heard the story, he questioned Curma and witnesses. Though some modern writers have accepted the case, Professor Dodds has felt that it may have been a hoax, for reasons which he gives. It seems to me unlikely that so hard-headed a psychical researcher as Augustine would be fooled. And to bring the matter up to our own time, it may be noted that the similarity of names of the presumed agent and percipient would fit in very well with the late Whately Carington's Association Theory of paranormal cognition.

Augustine in his early career was Professor of Rhetoric at Milan. A citizen of that place received a legacy from his father, but was shocked to receive from a creditor a demand for settlement of an allegedly unpaid bill. But the father appeared to the son in a dream, told him the debt had been paid and where he could find the receipt. So it proved.

Those narratives and many others reported by the same philosopher form one of the most illuminating collections in the history of our subject; and, so far as I am aware, nothing of Augustinian quality would be heard of again for more than a thousand years.

Emanuel Swedenborg (1688–1772) was a scientist, inventor and philosopher who is best remembered in psychical research as an investigator of his own phenomena. These included a vast amount of automatic writing, clairvoyant visions and claimed contacts with the Other World. Yet his psychic gifts did not develop until he was 55 years old. His experiences occurred either spontaneously or experimentally.

Of the spontaneous experiences, the most famous happened when he was attending a party in a house in Göthenburg in 1759. Suddenly becoming alarmed, he told the guests that a great fire was raging in Stockholm 300 miles away, and was rapidly approaching his house. Two hours later he joyfully exclaimed, "Thank God! the fire is extinguished; the third door from my house." Within hours, Swedenborg's vision became widely known in Göthenburg; and it was not until two days later that a messenger arriving from Stockholm brought news of the conflagration. It was found that Swedenborg's account agreed in all respects with the facts.

On the experimental side, when Swedenborg was living in Amsterdam, he was visited by a stranger, a German acquaintance of Jung-Stilling. The visitor told him of a friend who had died. During the last conversation, he said, "We conversed together on an important topic. Could you learn from him what was the subject of our discourse?" Swedenborg asked the stranger to return in a few days. When he did so Swedenborg said, "I have spoken with your friend; the subject of your discourse was, *the restitution of all things*." This was true, as was further information given by Swedenborg.

On another occasion, apparently July 18, 1762, Swedenborg, when in the company of some other persons, seems to have fallen into a trance. On recovering he said, "This very hour the emperor Peter III has died in his prison." In fact, that afternoon the Tsar Peter had been murdered in Ropsha Castle.

In 1776, Immanuel Kant published anonymously his small book about Swedenborg, entitled *Dreams of a Spirit Seer*, in which he professed to ridicule Swedenborg. But in places, Kant seemed unable to make up his own mind; and more than one subsequent writer has suspected that Kant's future philosophy was influenced by Swedenborg's writings.

Before the scientific period of our subject began a hundred years ago, there had been quite a number of philosophers who regarded paranormal phenomena as deserving of serious study—men like Schopenhauer, Sir William Hamilton, and, much earlier, Francis Bacon. It may be noted that Francis Bacon was an ancestor, on a side line, of four Presidents of the Society for Psychical Research. They were Arthur Balfour, Gerald Balfour, Eleanor Sidgwick and the fourth Lord Rayleigh. Bacon was their great-great-etc.-grand uncle. As we shall see later, two of those Presidents were themselves philosophers.

The advent of modern spiritualism in the middle of the nineteenth century attracted the interest of a few philosophers, who, however, formed very varied opinions. Immanuel Fichte, philosopher son of a more famous philosopher, was convinced of the reality of mediumistic communications and also of their spiritualistic interpretation.

John Stuart Mill did not share Fichte's sanguine views. Mill seems to have investigated at least one medium, the American Charles Foster, billet-reader and producer of dubious marvels. Afterward, when a rumor got around that Mill was "a believer in spiritualism," he replied "I not only have never seen any evidence that I think of the slightest weight in favour of spiritualism, but I should also find it very difficult to believe any of it on any evidence whatever, and I am in the habit of expressing my opinion to that effect very freely whenever the subject is mentioned in my presence."

Viscount Amberley, though now forgotten, had strong philosophical interests and was the author of a massive two-volume work on the *Analysis of Religious Belief*. He investigated paranormal physical phenomena, but in view of the type of medium he visited in the 1860's it is hardly surprising that he was disillusioned. He is of interest to us because of his two sons. The elder, Frank Russell, was an early member of the Society for Psychical Research and also an officer of the Oxford University SPR. The younger son, Bertrand Russell, was a pupil of Henry Sidgwick; but he seems to have had no knowledge of psychical research. He made occasional jokes about it, which, as W. S. Gilbert might have said, were "funny, without being vulgar." A cousin of his by marriage was Gilbert Murray, twice President of the SPR. They were great friends; but what Russell thought of Murray's telepathic experiments is not known. Russell would have been of little use as an investigator. In spite of his great intellectual powers, his practical abilities were approximately nil. Late in his life he still could not learn how to make a pot of tea.

Of all modern philosophers, the man who has had the greatest impact on the progress of our subject is Henry Sidgwick. Not as an experimenter, nor as a thinker, but as one endowed with matchless gifts of leadership. He was the most distinguished intellectual in Cambridge. On any subject, he was as nearly free of prejudice as mortal men can be. Someone described him as "the sanest man in England." When still a young man at Cambridge, he had been a member of the Cambridge Association for Spiritual Inquiry, familiarly known as the Ghost Society.

When the Society for Psychical Research was founded in 1882, he was elected President, an office he held in two spells for eight years. In fact, though, he was the effective leader for 18 years until his death in 1900. He advised and guided all the time, choosing the right people for the historic investigations—Edmund Gurney for *Phantasms of the Living*, the physicist William Barrett for a great dowsing survey, Richard Hodgson for the prolonged Theosophy investigation, and his own gifted wife Eleanor for the world-wide *Census of Hallucinations*. The Society rapidly increased in numbers; scientists of international reputation flowed in, and psychical research was recognized by the International Congress of Experimental Psychology in 1889.

Sidgwick in the early 1870s investigated a number of physical mediums. His collaborators included his wife, also Gurney, Myers, A. J. Balfour and others. The outcome of these extensive researches was disappointing, not to say suspicious.

As an investigator Sidgwick had his limitations, his powers of observation being imperfect, as he acknowledged. He inquired into and published about a score of spontaneous experiences of varied quality. When the Danish psychologists Alfred Lehmann and Carl Hansen tried by experiment to show that certain SPR telepathy experiments could be explained by "involuntary whispering" by the agents, Henry Sidgwick re-examined the old data and also conducted some new experiments, which showed that whispering could not account for the results.

To diverge for a moment, since I have mentioned Alfred Lehmann and we are here in Copenhagen, we may recall that Lehmann was a founder of the Danish Society for Psychical Research, and another founder was Severin Lauritzen, who, some years later, completed the monumental task of translating Frederic Myer's *Human Personality* into Danish. The Danish SPR was founded in 1905, and so is now one of the oldest psychical organizations in the world. Lastly, it was the Danish SPR, in 1921, that organized the first European international conference on psychical research. The Secretary-General was the devoted and hard-working Carl Vett.

In America, the most notable philosopher to engage in psychical investigation was William James. He is chiefly remembered for bringing to public notice the first great mental medium of the English-speaking world, Leonore Piper. The story of how James first heard of her has often been told, but usually in garbled fashion. The facts appear to be as follows. Mrs. Piper and her husband lived in Boston with his parents, who had in their service an old Irish servant Mary. Now Mary had a sister Bridget who was a maid in another Boston home; and, as a daughter of Mrs. Piper recalled "many and marvelous were the tales with which Mary regaled her sister concerning" the strange doings of young Mrs. Piper. It happened that the home in which this second maid, Bridget, worked was frequently visited by a Mrs. Gibbens, who was William James's mother-in-law. Mrs. Gibbens, having a séance with Mrs. Piper, was enormously impressed and so, soon afterward, was her son-in-law, who was told things by the entranced Mrs. Piper which she could not have known by normal means. James published two reports in the *Proceedings* of the first ASPR. We may look back and reflect with Miss Alta Piper that but for those two talkative Irish maids, "an interesting and baffling psychological phenomenon might have been forever lost to the world."

In the next twenty years, James attended many Piper séances, including those at which his deceased friend Richard Hodgson ostensibly communicated. But on the question of Hodgson's survival after death, though a great deal of talk characteristic of Hodgson came through, he had been a personal friend of Mrs. Piper for many years, and so James found it hard to distinguish quasi-paranormal knowledge from what the medium might have heard from Hodgson in his lifetime.

As an investigator of mediums, James could hardly be called an ideal sitter. He tended to be too restless. In the middle of a séance he would get off his chair and walk about the room, while the deeply entranced Mrs. Piper was speaking or writing automatically. Once, at a sitting with another gifted trance medium, Mrs. Soule, when he was accompanied by his wife, he is reported to have become so tired of it that he left the room and walked the porch outside.

He and Alfred Russel Wallace attended séances with the Boston materialization medium, Mrs. H. V. Ross. While Wallace was deeply impressed, James suspected a certain "roguery" in the appearance of solid ghosts parading about the room.

Nevertheless, James believed that some physical phenomena were genuine, as, for example, when he attended a certain private circle. The observers sat round a table on which was loosely erected a large ring of brass wire. Among other incidents, the brass ring repeatedly rotated a distance of several inches which James was unable to explain on any normal hypothesis.

An out-of-the-body case reported by James concerned a Harvard professor who one evening about 10 o'clock tried to project his double into the home of a woman friend half a mile away. Next day, and apparently without prompting, the woman told him that she was having supper about 10 p.m. when she saw the professor "looking thru the crack of the door." She got up and looked for him but he wasn't there.

James had very little experience of telepathy research on quantitative lines, but on a visit to England in 1889 he spent a day participating in Mrs. Sidgwick's famous telepathy experiments with numbers at Brighton. The results that day were unremarkable, but James found no fault with the experimental conditions.

Richard Hodgson was an Australian. He was educated at Melbourne University where, according to one who knew him well, he was the most brilliant student that university had ever known. He graduated in arts at the age of 19, then proceeded to concentrate on law, in which he obtained another baccalaureate and, at the age of 23, a doctorate. But his greatest interest lay in philosophy; and to deepen his studies in that field he moved to Cambridge, England, to become a pupil and life-long friend of Henry Sidgwick. Sidgwick quickly recognized the young man's intellectual qualities and also his single-minded devotion to truth in any task he undertook. It was not surprising that when the young SPR felt called upon to investigate the extraordinary psychic marvels claimed by the theosophical leader Mme. H. P. Blavatsky, Sidgwick chose Hodgson to go out to India to investigate the lady's claims on the spot. Hodgson did an extensive investigation and, in a report of 80,000 words, demolished Mme. Blavatsky's pretensions for ever. He was appointed an extra-mural lecturer in philosophy at Cambridge, but in 1887 the new American Society for Psychical Research in Boston invited him to become their chief executive officer. For a large part of 20 years he investigated the mediumship of Mrs. Piper. Being suspicious of all mediums, he employed detectives to spy on the young lady and her husband. Nothing detrimental was found. And the séance reports of Hodgson shed new light on paranormal phenomena. They also put mental mediumship on a sound basis for the first time in the English-speaking world. Moreover, his reports led to further developments in mediumship in Britain and indirectly to the historic cross-correspondence investigation that continued for a quarter of a century. The young philosopher had started a revolution in psychical research.

Hodgson also took part in séances with physical mediums, but was apparently unimpressed by any of them. On the other hand, he inquired into and published numerous spontaneous cases of good quality.

In spite of Hodgson's historic work, the American SPR was doing poorly and in 1890 it collapsed for lack of funds. Its assets were taken over by the SPR, which formed a branch of the Society in Boston with William James as Chairman, while Sidgwick and Frederic Myers in Britain subsidized it by helping to pay Hodgson's wages.

In the 1890s, another American philosopher appeared on the psychic scene. James Hervey Hyslop was educated at Wooster College in Ohio. After graduation and a visit to Germany, he lost his religious faith. On returning to America, he eventually became Professor of Logic and Ethics at Columbia University, where, incidentally, the President, Nicholas Murray Butler, was also a philosopher who happened to be seriously interested in psychical research, but took little part in investigative work.

Hyslop met Hodgson sometime in the 1890s. The occasion may have been one of Hodgson's lectures in New York. Hodgson took Hyslop in hand and trained him in the rigors of psychical investigation. Hyslop had a sitting with Mrs. Piper. Some years later, with the approval of Hodgson, who supervised all Mrs. Piper's work, he decided to have a series of sittings. There was an amusing incident before the first sitting. The two friends took the train out to Arlington Heights, where Mrs. Piper then lived in a handsome house. Arriving at Arlington Heights station, they hired a cab to take them up the long steep hill to the house. But Hyslop had been concerned that the medium should not recognize him as a former sitter. So, before getting out of the cab at the home, he pulled a mask over his head and face. Mrs. Piper, however, happening to be standing at an upper window, instantly recognized the man behind the mask and was much amused.

The sittings were very successful. More than that, Hyslop introduced a new principle in the reporting of mediumistic sittings. Hitherto, only items of what was called "evidence" were published. Hyslop held that everything happening at a seance ought to be printed; if that was not done, readers would get a biased picture of the facts. And if it was suggested that it might be sufficient to publish a brief report of the so-called "evidence," and preserve the complete transcript in a society's archives for the use of future students—well, Hyslop was too skeptical a man to swallow that plea. He knew that archives are eminently destructible. Were he alive today, he would find in various parapsychological organizations that the local trash-collector has been kept busy.

Hyslop also realized that seance incidents which seemed trivial at the time, might, for future students in our developing field, be discerned as revelations concerning the psychic process.

I may add that to ensure the complete publication of his verbatim report—650 pages—Hyslop contributed over $1000 to the printing bill, and the estate of Frederic Myers contributed £92. All this was three-quarters of a century ago; and to this hour it remains unequalled for its thoroughness and reliability.

Hyslop's precautions before and during sittings were unique. Someone in a distant part of America might write to him in New York asking if it would be possible to have a sitting with a medium. He would instruct the sitter to meet him at some place in Boston. Then, he would conduct the sitter by a devious route to the address of the medium—perhaps Mrs. Soule—approaching the house from such a direction that even if the medium were watching from a window she could not see them. Before entering the house, the sitter was sworn to total silence. Inside the house, the sitter was not allowed into the séance room until the medium was in trance and seated with her back to the door. The sitter on being admitted was directed by Hyslop's pointing finger to a chair behind the medium. From start to finish the medium neither saw nor heard the sitter. Any speaking was done by Hyslop, who usually knew nothing about the sitter. Under these forbidding circumstances, the evidence collected from the medium was sometimes very remarkable.

After Hodgson's death in 1905, Hyslop founded a new society, but, being a practical-minded man, he would not initiate it until he had collected a sufficiency of funds to ensure its survival. When this had been achieved, he brought it to birth. He called it the American Institute for Scientific Research, which had two sections: the first was to study abnormal psychology; the second had to deal with psychical research, for which, indeed, Hyslop revived the long dead name of the American Society for Psychical Research. The first section never really came to life, and eventually the whole organization became known simply as the American Society for Psychical Research.

In the 14 years of life that remained to him, James Hyslop investigated virtually every type of paranormal phenomena—spontaneous cases, psychic healing, obsession, experimental telepathy and precognition, psychic photography, poltergeists, physical mediumship; but above all the phenomena of mental mediumship, especially as evinced by Mrs. Piper and the other distinguished Boston medium, Mrs. Charles Soule. The evidence convinced him of the reality of postmortem survival. In terms of the amount of published reports, he is by far the most productive psychical researcher in all history. His printed works amount to some 8 million words, the equivalent of about 80 to 100 volumes. For 14 years he carried the ASPR on his back, and except for the last year or so, when he was a sick man, he never accepted a penny payment.

A philosopher-researcher who is almost forgotten now, was William Romaine Newbold (1865–1926), professor of philosophy at the University of Pennsylvania. He was described as "diminutive of body but powerful of intellect." He developed an intense interest in our subject by studying one of the long reports on Mrs. Piper's mediumship. He then contacted Hodgson and they became firm friends. Newbold had many sittings with Mrs. Piper, some of them highly evidential, but it was during one of them that the famous, but seemingly absurd, incident occurred in which the supposed spirit of Sir Walter Scott said there were monkeys living in caves in the sun; but suddenly Sir Walter added, "Oh! I lost my grasp on the light," meaning the medium. In the published report that curious remark was not printed, no doubt because it was of no interest.

But step forward to the present day, 80 years after that incident. We are hearing and reading a great deal about what are called "altered states of consciousness." These include sleep, hypnosis, meditation, trance, out-of-body experiences and other phenomena. In the Piper mediumship, it will be found that there were several variations of altered states of consciousness. The same is true of some other mediums. Unfortunately, 80 years ago investigators, with rare exceptions, confined their interest to paranormal evidence. Other odd things that happened at séances were not reported. But one researcher, James Hyslop, had the vision to realize that what seemed irrelevant at the time of writing might prove of prime importance to future students. So he unearthed the revealing fact of the ostensible communicator losing touch with the medium. That explained the confusion.

It has been reported somewhere that, after Hodgson's death, the SPR in London offered Newbold the vacant post in Boston. Perhaps he realized that being a professional psychical researcher was too risky an occupation. So the American branch was closed down and the philosopher Hyslop founded the second American SPR in New York. A few years after Hyslop's death in 1920, that organization got into dire troubles over the Margery mediumship, and a new and very sane society was started in Boston. Its chief founder was Elwood Worcester, then one of the leading clergymen in New England. But previously he had been professor of philosophy in Lehigh

University. His chief interest was in paranormal healing; but he had experience of mediums, and he published spontaneous experiences which he had thoroughly investigated.

Another psychically-disposed American philosopher, though he is never mentioned in print nowadays, was Hartley Alexander, who was for many years professor of philosophy in Nebraska University. In 1919, he was President of the American Philosophical Association.

In the summer of 1909 he carried out a long series of telepathic experiments with drawings. He was the agent, and the percipient was his wife. Though Alexander's research methods were not ideal by our standards, the results are worth looking at, especially as Alexander published all his target drawings and his wife's responses. They did not see each other's drawings until the end of each series. One historically interesting discovery was that Mrs. Alexander sometimes drew a picture one or more trials *before* her husband drew the same picture as a target—precognition apparently; and on several occasions she drew a picture several trials *after* it had been used as a target—retrocognition. This of course is the so-called displacement effect that Whately Carington discovered nearly 30 years later. Carington's researches, of course, were better conducted; nevertheless, it is certainly interesting that the same effect had been noticed three decades earlier.

Alexander made a study of many hypnagogic experiences of his own in which he reported numerous instances of "pictures in the dark" in the moments before falling asleep. Lastly, in 1926, he attended a seance with the physical medium Mrs. Crandon in Boston; but no account from his pen was ever published apparently.

In summary, and remembering in particular William James, Richard Hodgson and James Hyslop, we can say that, for forty years, the chief leaders of psychical research in America were philosophers. What American psychical research owes to them is beyond estimation.

Arthur James Balfour I can most easily introduce on a personal note. In my salad days in Edinburgh, I attended a meeting in the city (the Usher) Hall at which the speaker was the middle-aged Winston Churchill, a future prime minister. The chairman was a former Prime Minister A. J. Balfour, a past president of the Society for Psychical Research. I did not know until years later that two other people whom I saw on the platform were also former Presidents of the SPR—Balfour's brother Gerald and his sister Eleanor Sidgwick.

At Cambridge, Arthur Balfour was a pupil of Henry Sidgwick. He became a polymath studying all sorts of subjects, reading everything—except newspapers. In later life, he delivered the Gifford Lectures at Glasgow University, subsequently published in two volumes. He did not read them from a manuscript, but from a page or two of notes. This method gave his listeners the impression of hesitancy as if he were uncertain of what he was saying.

Balfour's activities in psychical research began in the early 1870s, when, with members of his family, also Sidgwick, Gurney and others, he had sittings at his home in Carlton Gardens with the physical mediums Catherine Wood, Annie Fairlamb, and Kate Fox (Mrs. Jencken). His sister Mrs. Sidgwick later published an account of these séances, which were uniformly disappointing.

Balfour seems to have had a psychic gift of his own. Andrew Lang, a future President of the SPR, lent Miss Balfour a crystal ball. Balfour took the ball into another room. He came out looking "somewhat perplexed," saying he had seen in the crystal a lady whom he knew. Two days later he met the lady and told her what he had seen of her surroundings and actions in Edinburgh, 50 miles away. She confirmed all his visions.

"On another occasion, after talking to Mr. Lang about Miss Goodrich-Freer [herself a crystal gazer], Mr. Balfour said that he had had a vision, in a glass bowl of water, of that lady's house, and he described its interior to Mr. Lang, which neither of the gentlemen had ever seen. On visiting it afterwards Mr. Lang found that 'Mr. Balfour's description of what he saw in the picture was absolutely correct.'"

While still in his twenties, Balfour fell deeply in love with a girl named May Lyttelton, a few years younger than himself. She, it was evident, was deeply devoted to him. But in a year or two, she died of typhus at the age of 24. Being a very reserved man, Arthur Balfour carried his grief in silence. Thirty years later, when the famous cross-correspondences developed through a number of amateur automatists, there appeared among these writings some incomprehensible allusions to a candle, to "Palm Maiden," and to the Hair of Berenice. Years later when another automatist, Winifred Coombe Tennant (known as "Mrs. Willett"), appeared on the scene with further information, it gradually emerged that the veiled references all pointed to May Lyttelton. The candle represented an old photograph of her carrying a candle; Berenice's hair referred of course to the legend in which Berenice's hair had been cut off, and May Lyttelton's hair had been cut off in her last illness for the relief of pain; the hair was preserved in a silver case. And Palm Maiden pointed to the fact that she died on Palm Sunday.

When Balfour's sister Mrs. Sidgwick and his brother Gerald told him about the evidence he was incredulous. But during the Great War, he had sittings with Mrs. Willett at his London home. When May Lyttelton communicated, Arthur Balfour was deeply moved and he clutched Mrs. Willett's arm so tightly, he feared he must have hurt her. Some time later he expressed his conviction in writing that "Death is not the end," and that May Lyttelton still lived.

Gerald Balfour, younger brother of Arthur, also had strong philosophical interests. After a spell as a Fellow of Trinity College, Cambridge, he entered politics, in which he spent twenty years, part of the time as a Cabinet Minister. Though during most of the same period he was a member of the Council of the Society for Psychical Research, he never attended Council meetings. Nevertheless, in 1906 he was elected President of the Society. The circumstances leading to this surprise appointment are unique, and have not previously been printed. (Part of the following information (concerning Frank Podmore and Gerald Balfour) comes from the Council's private Minute Book, and I am indebted to the President and Council for permission to publish it).

Opponents of our subject have sometimes held it against the Society that, though it claimed to be a critical organization, it never elected the most famous critic in its ranks to the Presidency—Frank Podmore. The historic truth, however, turns out to be rather different. In December, 1905, a movement, led by influential members, was afoot in the Council to elect Podmore to the Presidential office. On learning of this project, however, the physicist William Barrett, who disliked Podmore's critical methods, sought to bring in another candidate— Alfred Russel Wallace. For this purpose, Barrett managed to enlist the support of Sir William Crookes and Sir Oliver Lodge (Letter from Barrett to Wallace, in J. Marchant, *Alfred Russel Wallace*, New York and London, 1916, pp. 437–8). Nothing more is known of Barrett's proposal. It seems likely that Wallace declined, for he was 83 years of age and lived far from London.

Then, at the Council's meeting on December 11, 1905, Mrs. Eleanor Sidgwick proposed and Mr. J. G. Piddington seconded a motion that Mr. Frank Podmore should be elected President of the Society for the year 1906. The motion was carried unanimously. Podmore, on being informed, at first accepted the invitation but soon afterwards regretfully declined on the ground that a change in his professional duties (as a senior civil servant) would take him out of London and occupy all his time.

Finally, Gerald Balfour was unexpectedly drawn into the Presidential picture. At the famous "cataclysmic" General Election of

January, 1906, he lost his seat in the House of Commons. Less than two weeks later, the SPR Council elected him President of the Society. He filled the office with distinction, and psychical research became the dominating interest of his life.

Balfour's Presidential address was mainly philosophical, indicating no great knowledge of the psychical world. This deficiency, however, he soon remedied by engaging himself in the cross-correspondence phenomena, those strange occurrences in which some piece of meaningful quotation from ancient or modern literature would be given in part through one medium and the remainder through one or more other mediums, so that when put together they made sense. There were about a dozen of those cross-correspondence automatists, mostly living in Britain, but there was one in India and another in the United States. All were nonprofessionals, except Mrs. Piper. The one in whom Gerald Balfour was most interested was Mrs. Willett, with whom he had scores, perhaps hundreds of sittings. The leading communicator was an old friend of Balfour, Edmund Gurney, whose discourses were often marked by his characteristic wit. He also showed a considerable knowledge of psychology, philosophy and the classical languages which were outside the range of Mrs. Willett. After 25 years, Balfour was able to create a picture of human personality and its internal telepathic gifts (as he conceived it) which eventuated in a paper 275 pages in length. In this, he described in great detail the three states of consciousness through which Mrs. Willett's gifts functioned. It seems hardly necessary to say that Balfour's discoveries and teachings are highly relevant to our contemporary interest in altered states of consciousness.

F.C.S. Schiller, a philosopher of German origin, is remembered as "the British Pragmatist." Long before he adopted that philosophy, and while still only a young graduate of Balliol College, Oxford, he and his brother and sister experimented with the planchette. Communications came from nine "spirits" (though Schiller did not accept this claim). Schiller's brother was the most successful operator, and for him the planchette would write even when he was engaged in conversation or reading an interesting novel. Once the planchette wrote two sentences in Hindustani. Now Schiller's brother—the planchette operator—had lived in India in his babyhood, but left it at the age of 8 months. Nevertheless, Schiller believed the message might be an example of "unconscious memory."

On an occasion when Frederic Myers was present, there were brief passages in old Norman French and Provencal. The brother had no knowledge of old French, but Schiller evidently realized that he might at some time have glanced at something printed in those languages, which the phenomena of cryptomnesia had brought back via the planchette.

Schiller's brother was much the most successful psychic. Sometimes he used two planchettes, having one hand on each. The right hand wrote in the usual way, but simultaneously the left hand produced mirror writing. Schiller could find nothing in these quasi-spirit communications requiring a paranormal explanation. He attributed them to "unconscious cerebration."

Schiller once silently asked a question and received through his brother's writing an appropriate answer. Schiller had reason to believe that this brother possessed a telepathic gift. To test this, card guessing via planchette was tried. Sometimes the target playing card was seen by an agent, at other times no one saw the card. There were, in this way, 11 trials for telepathy in which of course the expected score would be less than one success. There were actually four hits. For clairvoyance, the number of trials was 116, for which the expected chance score would be about 2; there were actually 9 hits. Those results of guessing by planchette are highly significant.

As for Schiller's reports, one would like to have seen more detail as to the precise experimental conditions — but, of course, the experiments took place in the primitive days of 90 years ago, so perhaps it is pointless to complain. But it is a matter for regret that we hear no more of Schiller's apparently gifted brother.

Many years elapsed before we hear again of Schiller as an investigator. In the 1920s, he had two sittings with Mrs. Crandon in London and six in Boston. From what he had witnessed he concluded that the phenomena had to be classed as supernormal; he could not explain them in any other way. In 1929, in London, he attended a sitting with another physical medium Rudi Schneider, in which he witnessed telekinetic movements of curtains.

Schiller taught philosophy at Oxford for many years, but in 1929 moved to the University of Southern California where he was professor. Looking back through his life, one would say that his psychical inquiries were spasmodic and the most interesting was his early work in planchette writing with his brother and sister. They are still well deserving of our attention.

Turning now to the philosophers of Germany, as in other countries only a few have come to the fore in psychical research, but those few, it is safe to say, have brought distinction to our subject.

In December, 1886, Edmund Gurney, the editor of the SPR *Proceedings*, received in the mail from Berlin a letter bearing the signature of a man he could never have heard of—Max Dessoir. I call him a man, but this is somewhat of an exaggeration, for he was only 18 years of age. Presumably, he had only just left school and begun his freshman studies in philosophy and psychology at the University of Berlin. He had already got deep into psychical investigation, for with his letter to Gurney he enclosed reports of experiments in telepathy. He had also studied the willing game or muscle-reading and observed how easy it was, by muscle reading, to create the appearance of telepathy without telepathy. Dessoir slipped into one or two experimental flaws which Gurney politely corrected in footnotes when the report was published; but it is impressive to notice that before his telepathy experiments with drawings were completed, Dessoir realized that if the percipient was within earshot, it was possible to guess the design of the drawings from the sound of the agent's pencil. Consequently when, later on, the Baroness von Regensburg was percipient, the target drawings were made in another room.

Dessoir's paper being printed when he was only 19, it is safe to say that he is the youngest person who has ever contributed to the *Proceedings* of the SPR in nearly 100 years. It appears also that he must have visited Britain soon afterward. Certainly he came to know Gurney, Myers, and Sidgwick personally, and the respect that seemed to develop was mutual. In 1887, on the motion of Gurney, seconded by Frank Podmore, the Council of the SPR elected him a Corresponding Member—that is an Honorary Foreign Member—when Dessoir was only 20. It is, therefore, an easy guess that he is probably the youngest person elected to that rank in the Society's history. He was still a Corresponding Member when he died 60 years later.

About this time the notorious American slate-writer Henry Slade was touring Europe. Max Dessoir had sittings with him but detected no trickery in his performance, which need not surprise us, for Henry Sidgwick, the physicist Lord Rayleigh, the famous conjuror Hermann, and another conjuror were also baffled by Slade.

In 1889, Dessoir invented the word *parapsychology*, which he first printed and defined in the periodical *Sphinx*. He was fond of coining new words. The American professor and psychical researcher J. Rodes Buchanan introduced the word *psychometry*. Max Dessoir proposed to drop it and substitute *palaeoaesthetic clairvoyance*.

Of the physical phenomena of spiritualism, he became increasingly disheartened. He attended five séances with the Italian medium Eusapia Palladino and concluded that the phenomena were entirely fraudulent. Not everyone, however, would have agreed with his views.

A German apport medium of international fame in those days was

Frau Anna Rothe. Her specialty was flowers and plants which miraculously appeared in her presence. The Berlin police arrested her; and one of the witnesses against her was Dessoir, who said her performance was "sorry trickery that a common juggler would have been ashamed of." Frau Rothe was found guilty and sent to prison.

In the first third of the present century there was in Germany an intense activity in the investigation of physical mediums. The most enthusiastic leader was the neurologist Baron von Schrenck-Notzing, whose standards of reporting séances were often criticized by other psychical researchers. One of his most skeptical opponents was Professor Dessoir, who had a considerable knowledge of methods of deception.

Dessoir found mental mediumship much more impressive and spoke with warm appreciation of Mrs. Piper's mediumship. On the other hand, visiting the SPR in 1900, he had a sitting with the amateur trance medium, Mrs. Rosalie Thompson, of whose psychic powers Frederic Myers held a high opinion. But with Dessoir the evidence was poor.

When he and his wife visited the United States in 1929, he did not meet Mrs. Piper, so far as I am aware, but he did attend three dark séances with Mrs. Crandon in Boston. As so often in the Margery experiments, fingerprints were obtained on dental wax. (It was not until a later time that Crandon fingerprints were found to be bogus.)

Mrs. Crandon's control also tried number guessing. Prior to one sitting, Dessoir had been asked to write four numbers on four pieces of paper. He brought them to the dark sitting and placed them one by one on the séance table, as requested. The control Walter identified each number correctly. What Dessoir thought of this (as well as other "phenomena") is not mentioned in the report; and I don't know whether he ever published his opinion. But it is impossible to believe that so exacting a philosopher would be convinced by such dubious demonstrations. For, if Walter could read numbers placed on the table, couldn't he have read them if they had remained in the experimenter's hands or even in his pocket? Once they were out of Dessoir's control, Mrs. Crandon, perhaps with the help of a confederate, might have read them by means of a concealed luminous plaque no larger than a button. Nevertheless, considering the demonstrations of some other physical mediums, Dessoir felt that not all the phenomena could be explained away as fraud.

Another German philosopher who commands respect is Hans Driesch, who, beginning his professional life as a biologist, gained world-wide renown. But his researches and studies taught him that the facts of life could not be explained by any mechanistic hypothesis. So he turned to vitalism and then to a new career as a professional philosopher, and eventually to the professorship of philosophy in Leipzig University. In 1907–8, he was Gifford Lecturer in Aberdeen University; in 1926–27, he was president of the SPR; and, in 1930, he presided over the Fourth International Congress in Athens.

Driesch's experience of psychical investigations was not extensive, but the standards of evidence which he demanded were extremely high. He required that not only mediums should be open to suspicion, but the investigators also. That doctrine may have seemed startling in the 1930s, but recently Dr. J. B. Rhine, in the most sensational article of his career, has recounted a dozen or more frauds by experimenters which he has personally encountered.

In the field of physical phenomena, Driesch attended séances with Willy and Rudi Schneider at Schrenck-Notzing's home in Munich. From what he observed, he concluded that telekinesis was a genuine fact.

On the phenomena of the direct voice—that is, voices not issuing from the medium's mouth, but at a distance—Driesch expressed doubts, especially after an experience with the American performer George Valiantine. "What I saw of Valiantine in Berlin," said Driesch, "was a lamentable farce." Valiantine, in his later career, was repeatedly exposed in cheating.

At the time of an International Conference on Philosophy at Harvard University in 1926, Driesch attended two séances with Mrs. Crandon in Boston. He was apparently not satisfied and made "certain proposals for the improvement of the conditions." Judging from later reports, it seemed that some improvements had been made; but, remarked Driesch, "darkness still reigns."

In the summer of 1928, Driesch, accompanied by his wife, was on his way to Buenos Aires where he was to deliver a course of lectures at the University. Breaking their journey in Brazil, they managed to get a sitting with the famous, but elusive, medium, Mirabelli. The séance took place in the home of a banker and his wife in São Paulo. Though the séance seems to have been in normal artificial light, it was all a most informal affair. The medium was accompanied by his girl friend. Though it was high summer and no great distance from the equator, Mirabelli wore an overcoat, which, as Driesch observed with surprise, was fitted with "enormous pockets." He was evidently never searched, and when apports began to appear, Driesch was not surprised. Mirabelli had a reputation for xenoglossy—that is (or so it was reported), the spirits spoke through him in his trance in a dozen languages not normally known to him. Driesch judged Mirabelli's trance to be not genuine. The spirits spoke in Italian and Esthonian, which didn't impress Driesch, because Mirabelli's father was Italian born, and his girl friend in the room was an Esthonian from Reval. The medium seems to have moved from the drawing-room to the kitchen and to other rooms, and in the process objects were seen to move without explanation. During an interval in the drawing-room, Mirabelli, Driesch, and the banker's wife strolled through a doorway into a closed veranda. The others remained together in the room. Suddenly the folding doors slowly closed. "It was rather impressive, and no mechanical arrangements could be found," Driesch afterwards reported. Summing up, he thought the telekinesis incidents were genuine, but seemed to feel some doubt because the control of the medium was deficient.

In a Dresden criminal court in 1931, Professor Driesch and another leading German psychical researcher, Dr. Rudolf Tischner, were important witnesses in the trial for psychic frauds of the platform clairvoyant Fred Marion (Josef Kraus) and his impresario and confederate. The jury found them guilty and they were fined, with the alternative of imprisonment. Marion moved to England where he was eventually tested over long periods by various psychical researchers who were apparently unaware that he was a convicted criminal.

A dramatic spontaneous experience happened in Driesch's home. One night his wife dreamed of a fire in the servant's bedroom, and in her dream called out to the cook, "Clara, water! water! put water on the fire—more water still more!—oh, Clara!" The two bedrooms were separated by three doors. In the morning, she asked the cook if anything had happened during the night. "Yes," said Clara, "I read a book by candle light and fell asleep without putting it out. Suddenly, I felt that you, Madam, were awakening me, I opened my eyes, and saw beside me on the little table close to my pillow and to the window curtain a huge fire that seemed to reach the ceiling. In reality it was only the candle that had burnt down and set off a lot of matches. I took the candlestick and threw it into the water in the wash stand. In my hurry, some of the hot wax dropped on my hand and arm!!" Clara showed Mrs. Driesch the inside of her arm, which was covered with red spots up to the elbow. When asked if she was frightened upon opening her eyes and seeing the fire, Clara said, "No, that is the strangest part, I had the feeling that I was awakened expressly and knew exactly what to do, as if I had been told in my sleep."

To add to the strange experiences of the night, it seems that the little maid Ottilie waking during the night had seen a ghost, the fire and smoke. But she seems to have promptly returned to sleep. At what time of night Ottilie saw the apparition is not known. Mrs. Driesch thought the phantom might have been a projection of herself. Anyhow, Professor Hans Driesch slept through it all.

Professor Traugott Oesterreich of Tübingen University seems to have done very little investigative work, but deserves to be remembered for the wonderful accuracy of scholarship he showed in several books he wrote about our subject, the most memorable of which was his large volume on *Possession.*

In conclusion, I would add that those three German philosophers, Dessoir, Driesch and Oesterreich, had at least one very nonparanormal experience in common, and almost simultaneously. When the Nazis came to power in 1933, all three of them were quickly removed from their professional posts.

Further east, in Poland, lived and worked the philosopher and psychologist Julian Ochorowicz (1850–1917), who held professorial posts successively in the universities of Lemberg and Warsaw. He is remembered for his part in the investigation of the hypnotic subject Léonie B., and his investigation of the telekinetic demonstrator Stanislawa Tomczyk.

Mme. Leonie B. was a middle aged woman who at some time, having been the recipient of some great kindness by Dr. Gibert of Le Havre, agreed to be the subject of hypnotic experiments by him. Many famous psychical researchers took part in the investigations and in 1886, Ochorowicz was a member of the group of observers who included Pierre Janet, Frederic Myers, Arthur Myers and others. One spring evening, when Léonie was a guest in a certain house, Dr. Gibert, in his home two-thirds of a mile away, attempted at a certain time agreed to by his colleagues to hypnotize her at that distance and try to bring her to his home by an act of will. Ochorowicz and his colleagues waited in the street outside Leonie's abode, but not visible from it. Soon after the appointed time she emerged from the house, plainly in a somnambulic state, wandering and muttering. She passed two of the watchers without noticing them, then made for Gibert's house by an unusual route, Ochorowicz and the others following. "She avoided lamp-posts, vehicles, etc., but crossed and recrossed the street repeatedly." She arrived outside Gibert's residence, passed him without noting his presence and entered the house.

Ochorowicz is even better remembered for his discovery of the Polish teenage girl Stanislawa Tomczyk. Her unusual telekinetic gift was demonstrated either in broad daylight or good artificial light.

Watched by Ochorowicz, she rolled her sleeves to the elbows and placed her hands palms down about a foot apart on a table. The philosopher then laid some object between them — a cigarette, a match box, a pair of scissors. When she raised her hands, the object rose simultaneously between them. Ochorowicz watched the process from every angle. Sometimes he saw a fine filament stretching from her fingers to the object. It did not resemble a hair, for there were bulges in it. Sometimes there was no filament. Many photographs were taken either by Ochorowicz or by other psychical researchers who investigated Stanislawa's phenomena in different parts of Europe. An independent committee of Polish scientists tested her at length and published a report entirely favorable to her and Ochorowicz. As Stanislawa's fame grew, she tried to improve on the phenomena by occasional tricks — which that fair-minded psychologist Theodore Flournoy of Geneva dismissed with disdain. Nevertheless, Flournoy believed that her telekinetic demonstrations were genuine.

Her powers underwent a slow decline and an investigation by SPR members in London was almost destitute of results. One thing did happen — she fell in love with one of the distinguished investigators — the Hon. Everard Feilding, who married her.

Sixty years after Ochorowicz's death, one wishes that some other philosopher would discover another Stanislawa so that we might solve the mystery of that ectoplasmic filament.

Frederic Myers was not only a scholar of encyclopedic erudition, he had the gift of realizing that something he was reading was of first rate importance even though other readers passed it by unnoticed. It was thus that he was the first person in the English-speaking world to call attention to the writings of Sigmund Freud. Similarly, it was Myers who first drew to the notice of psychical researchers the name of a youthful and unknown Frenchman, Henri Bergson. A report by Bergson on his hypnotic experiments, published in the *Revue Philosophique*, was not epoch-making, but Myers saw its significance.

Bergson and a colleague "found that a boy, who was supposed to be clairvoyant, or a telepathic percipient, could read figures and words under the following conditions. One of the observers hypnotised the boy, stood with his back nearly against the light, opened a book at random, held it nearly vertically facing himself, at about four inches from his own eyes, but below [them], and looked sometimes at the page and sometimes into the boy's eyes." In those conditions, the boy could generally give the number of the page correctly. Questioned, the boy said, and apparently quite honestly, that he "saw" the numbers on the back of the book. It occurred to Bergson, however, that the boy might be reading the figures "as reflected on the cornea of the hypnotiser." Various tests gave support to this view. The printed letters were 3 mm in height and Bergson computed that their corneal image would be about one-tenth of a millimeter.

Myers was so taken by Bergson's discovery that he sought the assistance of H. E. Wingfield (who became well known as a medical hypnotist) and J. N. Langley in repeating Bergson's findings. They reported that they could read on each other's corneas the image of printed letters about 10 mm in height.

Myers, entering into correspondence with Bergson, obtained further information about other experiments with the boy. Bergson had shown the boy a microscopic photograph whose maximum diameter was only 2 mm. It was a picture of twelve men, and the boy faithfully described and imitated the attitude of each man. Reflecting on these incidents, Myers concluded that the hypnotic suggestion which had been administered to the boy had induced "some change in the shape of the crystalline lens which made the eye a microscope for the time being."

Bergson took part in the prolonged investigation of Eusapia Palladino at the General Psychological Institute in Paris in 1905–1908. As usual in her history, Eusapia was not averse to helping the phenomena by normal means. In the end the committee was hesitant to express a positively favorable opinion; but it is evident from the report that there were incidents involving the complete levitation of the table and other objects, which Bergson sometimes witnessed and which could not be explained except in terms of the paranormal.

Though Bergson, during his long life, engaged only infrequently in active research, what he did was and is worthy of study.

The last of our departed philosophers is Charlie Dunbar Broad, who lived and died fifteen centuries after Augustine of Hippo. His interest in our subject probably began in adolescence, when he read about it in a magazine to which his father was a subscriber—the *Review of Reviews*, edited by that redoubtable journalist and spiritualist W. T. Stead. Old numbers of the *Review* that I have seen contained regular articles on psychical research. Going up to Trinity College, Cambridge, as an undergraduate in 1906, he became a member of the Cambridge University Society for Psychical Research, a society that was born in 1885 and still continues 90 years later. Young Broad was in the right atmosphere, for Trinity has had a link with psychical research since the opening of the College by Henry VIII four centuries ago, when one of the first Fellows was the celebrated Dr. John Dee, whose mediumistic investigations are well-known.

Broad did not join the SPR until 1920 when he was 32. Either before that time or soon afterwards he had sittings with various sensitives, including the trance mental medium Mrs. Osborne Leonard. Though he published no formal report, he did state that in those sittings "I have met with clear cases of telepathy between myself and the medium when entranced. But I have noticed that these almost invariably involved past events of which I was not consciously thinking at the time. Thus the telepathic influence must have been due to mere 'traces,' or at most to processes of thought going on in my mind without my being aware of them."

Broad's first name was Charlie; but, in 1935, when he attended a sitting with the medium Frances Campbell, the latter said "Were you very nearly called JOHN?" In a note written later, Broad gave the surprising information, "My father always called me John, though it is not my name."

Broad was a witness in one of G.N.M. Tyrrell's "pointer experiments" with the percipient Miss Gertrude Johnson. This young lady had a remarkable gift for finding lost or mislaid objects. Tyrrell sought to test her skill scientifically by using very simple apparatus. Five boxes placed in a row on a table were open at the agent's side, and on the percipient's side closed by five lids. A large wooden board screened agent and percipient from each other. The agent, usually Tyrrell, would silently put a pointer into one of the five boxes, which were lined with sponge rubber, and it was Miss Johnson's job to open the box into which she thought it had been placed.

When Broad was watching the experiments, there were 500 trials. The expected chance score was 100; Miss Johnson's score was 132 which was very significant. Those early experiments were somewhat primitive, but Tyrrell later greatly improved them by using highly sophisticated electronic apparatus.

On physical phenomena Broad was skeptical. Referring to dice-throwing experiments, he said bluntly he didn't believe in PK. In his distinguished book *Lectures on Psychical Research*, he devoted only one paragraph to physical phenomena, and his attitude can be seen in the Index where the entry for "Ectoplasm" reads "see Butter-muslin." His great interest lay in the mental phenomena of our subject, on which he wrote extensively; and in nothing that he wrote did he fail to clarify and illuminate, for his gift of exposition was masterly.

And now that Broad is gone it is fitting to recall his life-long interest in the survival question. After examining it repeatedly over a period of close on half a century, he concluded in the last words of his last book: "I think I may say that for my part I should be slightly more annoyed than surprised if I should find myself in some sense persisting immediately after the death of my present body. One can only wait and see, or alternately (which is no less likely) wait and not see."

So we come to the end of this rapid survey of philosophers practicing as psychical researchers. Others among the departed might have been mentioned, such as Eduard von Hartmann, Carl du Prel and C. J. Ducasse.

If we consider the mere quantity of work published by philosophers, we need to realize that philosophy is a very small profession—compare its numbers with those of doctors, lawyers, physicists, chemists, psychologists and others; it is safe to say that philosophers have produced more research than other professions.

As for the *quality* of research done by philosophers, well, it is hard to say which profession has provided the ablest psychic investigators, but I believe we can say with confidence that philosophers come very near the top.

DISCUSSION

EDGE: I think it's interesting to take note that there were no real contemporary philosophers who were listed, and I suppose my queries revolve around that. First, just a general kind of question. Do you think philosophers bring anything of particular value to the investigation of psychic phenomena? And secondly, more directly related to my previous comment, all of the philosophers that you mentioned were doing investigations at a time when investigation of mediumship was essentially the important thing. Is it the case now? Would you agree? Do you think that philosophers are of somewhat less value now, since sophistication in the investigation of psychic phenomena probably has gone beyond their normal competence? If you're taking psychic investigation in the sense of empirical investigation. . .

NICOL: On Dr. Edge's first question I would say that the history of psychical research shows that competence in science or philosophy or any other subject is unfortunately no guarantee of competence in paranormal investigations. Some scientists have done valuable work in our subject, but I should estimate that philosophers in proportion to their tiny numbers have done better. They have brought to psychical investigation a degree of open-mindedness and investigative acuity that is rare in any field.

As for the possibility that some of the current research methods might be beyond the competence of philosophers, it is worth noting that some philosophers have had scientific backgrounds—

Swedenborg, James, Bergson, Hyslop and Broad, to name a few. I should estimate that members of a profession who have shown extraordinary skill in controlling mediums in dark rooms would not find it beyond their capacity to control electronic instruments in daylight. Briefly, however, on the general question of competence, we shouldn't ask, Is Jones a good scientist, or Smith a good philosopher, but, rather, Is either of them a good psychical researcher?

Finally, I would add that respect for the abilities of philosophers is so widely shared that the SPR has elected more of them to its Presidency than from any other profession.

HAYNES: I was rather sad to see two earlier omissions, but I know you've had to cut your paper as we all did. One was Thomas Aquinas, who spoke with interest of the fact, not well known in his time, that ESP and other things of the kind could appear in men neither clever nor of good moral character, and that it appeared in animals as well as in humans. The other omission, if you don't mind my saying so, was that of the eighteenth century philosopher-theologian, Lambertini, who did an immense amount of work on this subject, initiated experiments on the liquefactions of the blood of St. Januarius, and made a number of extremely relevant observations on psi which he called the "preternatural," or "natural prophecy." He again observed that it appeared more in the illiterate, of whom there were many then, than in the learned, and he said he thought it came through mostly in people's minds which were not too preoccupied with learning.

NICOL: I agree with you about Lambertini. Did you also mention Ducasse?

HAYNES: Gilbert Murray.

NICOL: I would hardly call Gilbert Murray a philosopher, though certainly a great classical scholar. When I discussed modern philosophers, I was thinking mainly of those who had held philosophical appointments. Thus Gerald Balfour taught philosophy at Cambridge; and Arthur Balfour was a Gifford lecturer; but there is nothing like that about Gilbert Murray. He could have been mentioned, but one has to come to a stop somewhere, of course.

Cox: I wondered what Mr. Nicol thought of the efforts of Frederick Marion to illustrate his self-discovered on-stage ESP ability formally. I saw a magician in Utrecht a few nights ago. At the end of his entertainment for the Parapsychological Association members, he proceeded to do an illustrious ESP effect—but not by trickery, so far as I was able to detect as a magician myself. He did a good job of it. Now, the case for Marion, an entertainer who appeared often to have used fraud, is that he too could attain that mental state where it seems psi actually was of aid, as I recall from his book *In My Mind's Eye*. Thouless and Wiesner felt that he had an inordinate amount of psi, so he was studied later for it successfully. Is that in error?

NICOL: I think the evidence against Marion is too strong. In the 1930s, S. G. Soal published a report in which he described how he and his colleagues sought to prevent Marion from getting information by normal sensory methods. Near the end they had him in what was virtually a closed box. In that situation Marion got nothing at all. At his trial in Germany he was given the opportunity to demonstrate telepathy. He completely failed. More than one psychical organization has been invited to publish reports of Marion's alleged psychic gifts, and they have cautiously preferred not to do so.

Once on a social occasion which I attended in London, Marion shuffled a deck of cards—which he could do with the dexterity of a conjuror—and gave them to me to reshuffle. Then he asked me to draw a card. I did so. He tried to guess it. He was wrong. On a second occasion he was right. The cards were shuffled again and spread face down on a table. Marion said, "Would you like me to pick out the black cards or the red cards?" I told him which color to select. He was right twenty-six times. But this is an old conjuring trick. In some decks the backs of the black and red cards, though seemingly identical, have a slightly different shade, which can be detected with a little study.

SURVIVAL AND IDENTITY: SOME RECENT DISCUSSIONS

TERENCE PENELHUM

My intention in this paper is to explore some recent philosophical discussions of personal identity that have a bearing on the problem of survival. Before beginning, I should say what I mean by "the problem of survival."

Most people assume that we understand well enough what the belief in survival of death means, and that the only problem about it is whether it is true. A great deal of public interest in parapsychology is the result of the awareness that the parapsychologist includes among his studies the investigation of phenomena, especially the phenomena of mediumship, which suggest that the belief in survival *is* true. Such an attitude assumes the correctness of Bishop Butler's famous remark that: "Whether we are to live in a future state, as it is the most important question which can possibly be asked, so it is the most intelligible one which can be expressed in language."[1] But this assumption has been repeatedly questioned by philosophers, some of whom have argued that the difficulty about the belief in survival is not that the evidence is inadequate to establish it, but that it is incoherent, or unintelligible. What they have meant, roughly,[2] is that although the notion of survival readily calls up mental pictures, and is used by millions of people, it nevertheless cannot be spelled out without catastrophic confusions and contradictions—rather as the popular science-fiction fantasy of time-travel cannot withstand even slight critical examination. Such a view requires argument, of course. But if it can be shown to be true, it appears to undercut any appeal to the evidence of parapsychology, by proving beforehand that whatever this evidence shows us, it cannot show us that we survive our deaths, since that proposition cannot be coherently formulated, and consequently cannot be used to explain *any* phenomena, however well-authenticated the phenomena themselves might be.[3]

I

Before looking at some of the arguments, I should first recognize the existence of a very natural retort to what I have said. It would go like this: "Philosophy is full of arguments which are supposed to show that propositions we all know perfectly well to be true are either doubtful or impossible. Philosophers have tried to suggest that there is reason to doubt whether they are sitting on chairs, or whether the future will resemble the past; but everyone knows that there is no alternative but to accept that these things are so. Zeno tried to prove that Achilles could not overtake the tortoise, or the arrow could not fly through the air, yet everyone knows they would. All that such arguments show to us is that we have not fully thought out *how* these things can be. They cannot show us that these things are not so. So we know that there *must* be something wrong with these sceptical arguments, even though we cannot at present see what it is. The same is surely true about survival. Religion apart, we might find ourselves in a position in which the evidence just *forced* us to resort to explanations that involved the postulation of postmortem agency. If that happened, we would just live with the difficulties until we resolved them; or leave them to the philosophers to worry about on their own."

I freely admit to a great deal of sympathy with this kind of response, especially since much of my own work is in philosophy of religion, where it often seems that philosophers are prepared to assume the insuperability of logical objections, which they would try much harder to refute if the beliefs threatened by them were beliefs of secular commonsense. But someone concerned with the evidence of parapsychology cannot rest his case on such a response too complacently. For parapsychologists have a fundamental concern with following scientific procedure as far as the data themselves will permit; and it is clearly necessary for scientific procedure that the explanatory hypotheses that one offers do not embody contradictions or absurdities. For the scientific understanding of motion it was necessary to expose the fallacies in Zeno's paradoxes, and *not* rest content with a commonsense assertion that all is well whatever Zeno said. The discussions of the implications of mediumistic phenomena with which I am familiar[4] are mostly attempts to decide how far it would be unreasonable to persist in explanations of them that avoid postulating survival. It is unfortunate that so few of these discussions recognize that this has to be assessed, not only in terms of the demands of the evidence, but also in terms of the stringency of the difficulties that stand in the way of formulating the propositions about survival with which other hypotheses have to compete.

I shall begin by indicating briefly the nature of the difficulties which the belief in survival appeared to me to have, when I published a small volume on this theme in 1970 called *Survival and Disembodied Existence* (hereafter *SDE*). I shall then comment on some philosophical discussions of recent years which suggest some modification of the views that I expressed at that time.

II

I distinguished, first, between two versions of traditional Western beliefs in survival: the belief in disembodied personal survival (sometimes referred to as belief in the immortality of the soul), and the belief in bodily resurrection. I think there are the strongest historical reasons for holding that the former expectation has Greek origins, and that the Judaeo-Christian-Islamic traditions teach, or at any rate originally taught, the latter doctrine.[5] In connection with each belief, I suggested that two questions could be raised: first, is the mode of life envisaged for post-mortem persons in that doctrine, a mode of life which can be coherently described? Second, can those beings whose existence is predicted in the doctrine be intelligibly identified with pre-mortem persons? If the answer to the first question is negative, then it follows that there cannot be beings of the sort predicted. If the answer to the second question is negative, then even if there could be such beings, they could not turn out to be ourselves—so *survival* would not have been provided for.

In the case of the doctrine of bodily resurrection, the first question does not seem to be serious. If the doctrine teaches that people will survive death in bodily form, it seems to teach that they will exist in a manner essentially similar to their pre-mortem existence.[6] But the case is otherwise with the doctrine of disembodied survival; for this seems to teach that persons will survive, yet in saying that they will have no bodies it seems to make it impossible to apply to them the predicates that it seems essential to apply to any being said to be a person. To illustrate: it is obviously contradictory to say that a disembodied person could talk or walk or blink or sleep or have indigestion, because all these things require bodily organs. But philosophers have suggested that bodilessness also rules out a great many more predicates than this, including mental ones: that a being without eyes or ears or nose could not be said without contradition to see, or hear, or smell; or that a being without hands and limbs and muscles could not be said without contradiction to act; and that the doctrine of disembodied survival is widespread merely because these contradictions are concealed by the improper intrusion of mental pictures (of human bodies, of course) which come to the minds of those asserting it.

My suggestion in *SDE* (for which I cannot repeat detailed arguments here) is that personal predicates that were applied to disembodied persons would have much of their original sense attenuated, but that enough of it would remain for it to be possible still to use them. In particular, I suggested that the language of perception and the language of agency could both still be used. The attenuation must be emphasised: for example, even if a disembodied person can see (by having suitably described visual images) he or she cannot *look*, for looking entails the direction of the eyes; even if a disembodied person can move objects in space, it is not at all clear how, if at all, we can understand the related notion of *trying* to move them, since this is understood in ordinary cases to have reference to the prior movement of one's limbs, and disembodied persons have no limbs to move. But I was, and am, of the opinion that it is logically possible to ascribe predicates to disembodied beings without attenuating those predicates out of existence.

There has been little or nothing in recent philosophical literature that has been directed to this problem. Discussions of the book, and other discussions of survival, have all been directed to the other problem, that of identity. But there is a large recent literature concerning a theory which seems to have a direct bearing upon it. This is the Mind-Body Identity theory, sometimes called Central State Materialism. It has many versions, and even a scanty summary will not fit all of them. But, in general, I understand the theory to be the following. Mental events (such as sensations or after-images) are logically distinct from the neural or brain states that are commonly thought to give rise to them. To say that they are logically distinct is to say that it is not formally self-contradictory to state that the brain-state occurs but the sensation does not, or vice versa. The same, however, is true of certain events or objects that we have no hesitation in identifying. Lightning, we are happy to say, is a motion of electric charges.[7] The Morning Star is the Evening Star, since each is the planet Venus. In these cases we know that the one phenomenon is identical with the other as a result of empirical investigation. Before that investigation, it might very well have turned out that lightning was not a motion of electric charges, and that the Morning and Evening Stars were two different planets. What might very well have turned out in this way to be otherwise, cannot be something which it is self-contradictory to deny, in the way it is self-contradictory to say that bachelors may be married men. So these phenomena, though identical, are not *necessarily* identical, but *contingently* identical. If we admit this, we can (the theory goes) reconsider a common objection against the materialist tradition. The materialist tradition has always told us that mental states are identical with brain states. The objection has been that one cannot identify two things when it is obvious that they are logically distinct. Now it seems that we can and do, identify logically distinct things, like the lightning and the motion of electric charges, or the Morning and Evening Stars. So materialism returns in a new guise, supported as it should be by all the sophisticated development of neural physiology. Its new form is the assertion that mental states are *contingently identical with* brain states. Such a theory avoids, it is said, all the traditional difficulties about the ways in which one kind of state causes another, or why they mysteriously run parallel to each other. Such questions do not have to be asked, if one asserts the identity of the two sorts of state.

It is not hard to see how such a theory could be deployed against the view that one could apply mental predicates to disembodied beings. The sorts of argument that those, myself included, have used to defend this view, have depended upon assuming that even though there is a great deal of evidence to support the belief that mental events depend upon brain states, this dependence is merely causal and not logical, so that it is not self-contradictory to suggest that a being might continue to have mental states when his brain states had ceased. Even if improbable, this suggestion would not be self-contradictory, since mental states and brain states are logically distinct. What Central State Materialism suggests is that this defence is inadequate: that even though mental states and brain states are logically distinct, they are nevertheless contingently identical. If they are identical, then, it seems, the one cannot continue without the other, because even though they might in logic be two, they in fact are merely one.

I think this threat is an empty one; so clearly empty in fact that it makes one wonder what the advantages of this form of materialism could be. The notion of contingent identity is itself problematic, as one can see superficially from the fact that even the traditional stipulation that two identical things must have all their properties in common, does not apply to things which are contingently identical—mental states and brain states do not, for example.[8] But, if the concept of contingent identity is free of *this* restriction, what restrictions do apply to it? What standard is one to use to answer this question? To be brief and specific: if it is agreed that although mental states are brain states, it is logically possible that they might not have been, and the only reason we have for insisting they are is that they are never in fact found separately,[9] what logical barrier stands in the way of someone who wants to suggest that the identity supposed to obtain between them only does so *sometimes*? Why should someone not hold one of the following?

(1) that some kinds of mental states are identical with brain states

and other kinds are not—e.g. after-images are, but daydream images are not;

(2) that some mental states of a particular kind are identical with brain states but other states of that kind are not—e.g. some of my dream-images are brain states but others of my dream-images are not;

(3) that some of the mental states of a given person are identical with brain states and other mental states of that person are not—e.g. my mental life is more closely related to my brain than yours is to your brain;

(4) finally, that even though all the mental states of a particular person during a period (say before physical death) are identical with brain states, none of that person's mental states after that period (say after physical death) are identical with brain states.

The point I am making has nothing to do with the evidence there might be for holding this last proposition. Insofar as the evidence of physiology is against the theory that mental events do not all depend on brain states, it is equally against this theory. What I am asserting is that the key notion of contingent identity is not well-enough defined to preclude the statement of a prediction of disembodied existence *within* Central State Materialism itself. So whatever the theoretical advantages of this doctrine, they do not include a veto on the possibility of disembodied existence. The situation of *that* doctrine is the same as it was before Central State Materialism was invented.

III

So much for the first difficulty that the belief in survival has to face. I now turn to the other, which has always seemed to me far more nearly intractable. This is the problem of identity. The philosophical problem of personal identity is the problem of determining what it is that justifies the ascription of identity through time to a changing person, or, more simply, what it is that makes a person at a later time one and the same as a person at some earlier time. One common view is that identity of persons depends upon the identity of the bodies they have. An equally common, and generally opposing, view, is that identity of persons depends on mental factors, particularly memories. In daily life it is clear that we use both of these criteria to settle actual problems of identification. The philosophical problems arise when we start to ask which of these standards has priority. It is in connection with this question that philosophers have invented dozens of deliberately perplexing puzzle-stories, the purpose of which is to test our intuitions and see what we would be inclined to say if the ordinary criteria of identity were to clash. For example, what would we say in the face of the situation that John Locke imagined,[10] in which a man who looks in all respects like a cobbler wakes up one morning with all the apparent memories and attitudes of a prince, and at the same time a man who looks in all respects like the prince wakes up with all the apparent memories and attitudes of the cobbler? To say that each person is the person he physically seems to be is to give preference to the criterion of bodily identity, whereas to say that each is the person he *claims* to be is to give preference to the criterion of memory.

The way we are inclined to resolve this dispute is obviously relevant to our estimate of the belief in survival. At any rate it is obvious that if we decide that bodily identity is a necessary condition of personal identity, we must reject as absurd the belief that we survive death disembodied, since in the absence of a body no disembodied spirit could be identified as the same as any pre-mortem person. In addition, (and of great importance), if we decide that bodily identity is necessary for personal identity, we shall throw grave doubt upon the very notion of an incorporeal individual. It is not merely that we shall be unable to give any sense to the idea of identifying some supposed spirit with some previous embodied person; it is also going to be impossible for us to understand how a person without a body can sustain its own identity through time in the incorporeal state. To say that bodily identity is necessary for personal identity, then, is to throw doubt upon the intelligibility of the very idea of a *bodiless individual*; to suggest that there may be no sense to the suggestion that it is such an individual that perceives this or does that.

The standard argument in favour of the primacy of bodily identity, which goes back to Bishop Butler,[11] depends on saying that memory itself requires it. Our discourse about memory requires a distinction between true and false memories, or, more correctly, between real and apparent ones. Only the real ones guarantee identity. For this distinction to have application, it is essential not only that the events supposedly remembered did in fact happen, but that they happened *to the person "remembering" them. This* requirement cannot itself be met by an appeal to memory without blatant circularity. As Butler crisply expressed it, "consciousness of personal identity presupposes, and therefore cannot constitute, personal identity."[12] But if memory does not constitute it, something else must, and the natural candidate is the sameness of the body. In addition to this argument, I shall mention one other. In order even to wonder whether a person before us now is the same person as some person previously known to us in the past, we have to have before us now a clearly recognizable continuing individual, and have to have had before us in the past a clearly recognizable continuing individual. Such recognition seems clearly to imply, in the past and now, the physical continuance on which recognition depends. So even if it is in order (and in practice it undoubtedly often is) to accept people's claims to remember at their face value, without making independent physical checks of their identities, such checks must in principle be available for us to have, as we do have, the distinction between true claims to remember and false ones.

Such arguments seem to leave us with bodily identity as a necessary condition of personal identity in all cases. But in fact we are at least tempted to resolve dilemmas like those of the cobbler and the prince in a way that is inconsistent with this conclusion, and to say that it is the man who "remembers" the cobbler's experiences who is the cobbler, and the man who "remembers" the prince's experience who is the prince, so that they have *changed bodies*. In *SDE* I suggested that such a decision, though it does entail a change in our present conventions concerning self-identity, represents a reasonable change in the face of such imagined circumstances, especially if they started to happen frequently![13] But I added two provisos to this, which still seem to me to be necessary ones. (1) Although we could decide to say that the cobbler and the prince had changed bodies, we could also decide to stay with our present conventions and say instead that each had lost his memories of his own past, and mysteriously acquired a detailed retrocognitive access[14] to the past of the other. There is nothing in the story that *requires* the hypothesis of bodily exchange.

(2) The reason that the hypothesis of bodily exchange is an open option, however, is that a large part of the standard conditions for the ascription of identity are provided for: in particular, the previous histories of the cobbler and the prince are assumed to be known, the physical identifiability of the two present claimants is assumed to be possible, and the events they claim to remember really did happen to the bodies that they will both say (correctly or not) that they had when these events took place. The only anomaly is the fact that the body uttering the memory-claims is not, in either case, the body these claims "fit." What all this shows is that even though a puzzle-story of this kind can loosen our conceptual attachment to bodily identity as a condition of personal identity, this at most means that we must recognize the conceptual possibility that one and the same body may not always belong to one and the same person, that people might exchange bodies. What it does not show is that we have any understand-

ing of the suggestion that people might exist *without bodies at all*; that people who exchange bodies could exist independently of the bodies they exchange; or that what happens when bodily exchange occurs is that persons *come out of* one body and *go into* another. This is the suggestion that many have thought the puzzle-stories support, but they do not. So recognizing that bodily identity might, in certain circumstances, lose its primacy as a criterion of identity for persons, takes us no way toward showing that we can even understand the notion of a disembodied person.

IV

If we turn now to recent literature about the criteria for personal identity,I should like to pick out two areas of discussion for comment.

(1) The first is the literature that has taken its rise from the puzzling phenomena of brain bisection. It is always a relief to turn from the ponderous fantasies of philosophers to actual empirical examples, and in this instance the change offers us puzzles at least as bewildering as those philosophers can invent. I hasten to confess my own total incompetence in neurophysiology before my comments begin.[15]

As I understand the matter, clinical procedures designed to counter epileptic seizures have from time to time involved the severing of the higher connections between the two hemispheres of the brain. Patients treated in this way have been subjected to experimental tests in which information is projected into the hemispheres separately. The results have suggested that it is more natural to speak in these situations of there being two centres of consciousness, which normally collaborate but may function separately, than it is to speak of one conscious subject—since, for example, the left-hemisphere-controlled speech patterns will deny the presence of some object which the right-hemisphere-controlled left hand will try to grasp after it has been displayed in the right-hemisphere-controlled left visual field. For whatever reason, the fact that these dissociations have a clear physiological basis, has made the temptation to talk of more than one self inhabiting a single body seem even greater than in the purely psychological cases of dissociation, such as those of Eve or Sally Beauchamp, which were previously familiar.[16] What acts against too simple a resort to the language of multiple selves, however, is the apparently normal unity displayed by patients whose perceptual information is not artificially restricted—one and one seem to add up to one and not two, as it were.

I find such data baffling and worrying, as do others. The detailed exploration of the logical possibilities has hardly begun, and I could not pursue it here. But however radical the departures from commonsense that are forced on us by further data, it seems clear that even if we adopt the language of dual selves, each with its own hemisphere, we shall have gone no distance at all towards the conceptual recognition of personal disembodiment. Even putting aside the obvious fact that each alleged self has it own hemisphere, and that a brain-hemisphere is a physical object (or half of a physical object), the actions and perceptions of the selves that are identified are embodied and not disembodied actions. To agree to the possibility of two-selves-with-one-body in some cases, is not to countenance the possibility of one-self-with-no-body in any cases.

(2) The second set of recent discussions I must mention derive primarily from the work of Derek Parfit, which has largely transformed the discussion of self-identity in the last few years.[17] If I may hazard a brief comment on a very subtle and original set of theories, I would say that Parfit's primary objective is to question the *importance* of self-identity, and to contend that its apparent importance is due to the fact that it is intertwined in human thought with other relationships that *are* important. We live in a world in which identity seems to be a necessary condition of what Parfit calls psychological connectedness. Psychological connectedness is exemplified by the sort of direct awareness each of us has of his or her own past in memory, or the direct forward-looking concern that each of us has for his or her own future when we plan and look foward to our later activities. Now, as things are, I cannot be psychologically connected, backwards or forwards, with the thoughts or activities of anyone but myself. But psychological connectedness has an important feature which identity does not have: it admits of degrees. I can have a high degree of psychological connectedness with an earlier stage in my life, or a low degree. For a famous historical example of the former, think of St. Augustine, who was deeply involved in adult life with his childhood theft from the pear tree, which would hardly have been recalled, and certainly would not be an occasion for concern, for the majority of men. I can have a high or low degree of psychological connectedness with events in my distant future. Insurance salesmen do better out of people who do than out of people who do not. Yet identity does not admit of degrees. It is all-or-nothing; either I am the same person who robbed the pear tree all those years ago, or I am not.[18] There is another difference between them: identity is a one–one relationship, whereas connectedness need not be. Two present objects or persons cannot both be identical with one previous one, for it would follow from the suggestion that they were, that they were also identical with each other, which is absurd.

Now, as the world is now, connectedness also seems to be a one–one relationship; there is only one person (myself) with whose earlier or later stages I can be psychologically connected. But this does not seem to be a necessary truth, merely a brute fact about how the world is at present. It is not hard to imagine situations in which it did not obtain. If it were possible, for example, to perform brain transplants in such a manner that the two hemispheres of Smith's brain were placed separately in two different bodies, even though the two resultant persons could neither of them be identical with Smith, each would be psychologically connected with Smith, and we might even want to say that Smith had survived as both, though he was identical with neither.[19] So the coincidence between personal identity and psychological connectedness is *mere* coincidence. Parfit goes further; it is connectedness, not identity, that matters to us. (He draws the conclusion that the principle of self-interest—that I should be as concerned with remote stages of my future as with near ones, even though my psychological connectedness with them is much slighter—has nothing to recommend it.)

I think myself that the notion of psychological connectedness needs much more examination than it has yet had, but I cannot argue that here. The relevance of Parfit's position to the analysis of the notion of survival of death is considerable, and I shall return to it shortly. For the moment, I will comment only on how far, if at all, it bears on the possibility of disembodied existence. It does have an indirect bearing in this way: it helps us to see more clearly why we have such a strong temptation to settle puzzle-cases like Locke's story of the cobbler and the prince, in favor of memory. It is because the human concern for oneself is a concern for the one with whom one has psychological connectedness; and the connectedness in this story is between each person after the "transfer" and the person who "occupied" *the other* body before the transfer. If Parfit is right, we could decide to keep identity and connectedness together by saying that each person *is* the one he says he is; but if we choose to stay with our present conventions and say that it is the body that confers identity, then we must recognize that although neither person *is* the person he says he is, he does have to that person the only relationship that matters, viz. connectedness; for *mere* identity without connectedness is a purely formal characteristic which does not matter *in itself*.

So these considerations give us a deeper understanding of the strengths of the philosophical tradition deriving from Locke, which seeks to locate the identity of the person in psychological factors such as memory, rather than in the continuity of the body. But however

we estimate the degree to which they increase the plausibility of that
tradition, it is still obvious that they do nothing whatever to help
attach sense to the thesis that persons can exist disembodied. For the
persons between whom psychological connectedness obtains, still have
to be continuing and identifiable individuals. All that is in dispute
about them is the nature of their relationships to each other. And
nothing in the arguments I have considered suggests that this requirement can be met without presupposing that these individuals, who-
ever we decide they are, have human bodies. So although these arguments may weaken the doctrine that bodily identity is required for
personal identity, or may show that even if it is, this does not
matter as much as we thought (because identity itself does not matter
as much as we thought), they do nothing to show that persons could
exist without any bodies whatever.

V

I have so far discussed the problem of identity in connection with
the belief in disembodied survival. I turn now to the belief in bodily
resurrection. First, I rehearse briefly the position that I took, with
some hesitation, in *SDE*. It appears superficially that the condition
of bodily identity is met by this prediction, since it can be supposed that
what will appear at the time of the predicted Resurrection will be the
same body, revived, that belonged to the person who died. It can
also be supposed that the persons appearing at that time, will each
have all the appropriate apparent memories for the persons they will
say, in each case, that they are. But there is a traditional difficulty
about this.[20] It seems absurdly artificial, but will not easily go away.
Could not an objector suggest that what will appear, in each case, will
not be the very same person that died previously, but merely a replica
or simulacrum of him; for, since there is a time-gap between death
and resurrection, during which the original body may very well have
been destroyed altogether, the connecting link that would make it unambiguously the same person and *not* a replica, will have disappeared?
In the absence of such a link, it seems that the objector's position,
though not likely to be taken up by someone who is there, and certainly not a mandatory way of describing what has happened, is just
as correct a description, as far as our conventions go, as the traditional
one. What exactly is the difference between the prediction that God
will re-create us, and the prediction that God will create new beings
who are just like us?

It is, of course, easy enough to suppose additional circumstances that would rule out this tiresome ambiguity. If the body itself were preserved in every case, there would not be a gap between death and resurrection in which no bearer of identity persisted. When the early Christians rejected the Roman practice of cremation, and buried their bodies, it was surely because they expected that God would resurrect *these bodies*? But when this intermediate bearer of identity is absent, what would stand in its place? What does *not* seem to be available, is the continuance of a disembodied spirit between death and resurrection—at least, as our arguments have carried us so far. If no intermediate bearer of identity seems available, there seems just to be a gap; and to say that the resurrectees will *be* ourselves is to commit oneself to the decision that persons are not continuous, but in a certain way discontinuous, or gap-inclusive, entities—like the performance of a play that has a long interval in the middle of it. Well, why not say this? Why not, indeed? The only snag is not that one cannot decide this is how it will be, but that one does not *have* to decide this way; and a matter of the greatest moment seems to hinge, of all things, on a decision about linguistic conventions.

Some philosophical problems are deep and illuminating, and some merely exasperating, and this one seems to me to be in the latter category. But saying that does not make it evaporate, and I turn, with interest, to two recent comments.

(1) First, to Parfit once again.[21] He agrees that in the resurrection-story above, our identity is not unambiguously preserved. But psychological connectedness is, and this ought to satisfy us. Even if resurrection, thus described, is not survival, it is as good as survival. We ought to be as concerned for those future persons, whose futures we will presumably be affecting here and now, as if they would be unambiguously ourselves. Although this has much strength, I am inclined to respond by saying that an ambiguous situation is only "as good as" an unambiguous one if one's value-judgments are strictly Utilitarian; and the deity of the Judaeo-Christian tradition is manifestly not a Utilitarian. This can be seen readily enough if one reflects on the obvious question of moral responsibility: according punishment (or, for that matter, forgiveness) to someone who resembles me and is willing to assume responsibility for my actions is not morally equivalent to according it to me. By such a standard, identity does indeed matter.[22]

(2) Second, I wish to refer briefly to some arguments of Professor Robert Herbert.[23] One of his suggestions is that the supposed ambiguity can be resolved by reference to God's (declared) intentions. Suppose, he says, you see a painting by Andrew Wyeth, and decide it could either be a portrait of Robert Frost or of George C. Marshall.

What would decide the ambiguity, would be the information that
Wyeth intended to paint Frost. His intention is decisive, even if the
painting could be taken both ways in the absence of any knowledge of
it. Similarly, the divine intention to raise men again is sufficient to make
the act God performs under that intention into the re-creation of the
dead, even though someone unaware of that intention would be at
liberty to interpret it differently. This is simple and ingenious. I do not
know whether it works. It only works if we do not have to understand
God's intention as being that of raising the dead *rather than* creating a
new race of similar beings; for if we had to interpret God's intention in
that manner, we would need some independent characterization of
what the difference between the two is, and our original ambiguity
would reappear at another level. Since I do not know whether or not we
have to understand it this way, I can only leave this argument in the air.
I am more nearly persuaded by another, which goes as follows: the
suggestion that the resurrection situation is ambiguous, depends on
assuming that our concept of a person does not at present admit into it
the possibility of a person having a "gap" or stretch of nothingness in
his existence. It depends on assuming that to admit this would be to
make a change in our concept of a person that we could very well not
decide to make. But someone of (say) Christian persuasion already has
a less restrictive concept of a person than this; he already thinks of a
person as a gap-inclusive being, and, for someone who does this, the
resurrection-story is not ambiguous at all. The difficulty about this
argument is that it also seems merely to displace the problem to
another setting. If we accepted it, we would now be faced with a
situation in which a believer and a skeptic would each offer differing
interpretations of one and the same story, because they had differing
concepts of what a person is. The story itself would still not decide
between the two concepts they had. This, however, might be an
advance, since there might be independent reasons for preferring the
gap-inclusive understanding of what a person is, derived, for example,
from the Christian understanding of human nature as distinct from
some of its competitors.

VI

These have been very much reports and comments on arguments in
progress, arguments whose outcome is very much in doubt. I turn in
conclusion to what is, for me, most difficult of all: the attempt to relate
these discussions to the investigations of parapsychology. The idea of
survival is obviously relevant to some of these inquiries, but many of the

discussions I have mentioned may not seem to be. I will attempt to show how they could be, and how the data of parapsychology might, in turn, affect how one approached some of these philosophical issues. It will surprise no one if I confine my comments to the phenomena of mediumship.

The most natural way to explain these phenomena, even if it is a mistaken one, is to treat them at their face value and say they are due to communication from the dead. There are some strong arguments for holding that the alternatives to this imply intolerable complications.[24] But this explanation runs headlong into a fundamental conceptual difficulty. It seems that it requires us to postulate *disembodied* survival. Yet, this is the form of survival doctrine that is open to intractable objections. The doctrine of resurrection can be stated in ways that avoid it, but only if one insists that between death and resurrection there is a gap, and does not assert continuing intermediate activity. The survival explanation of mediumistic phenomena requires the postulation of continuing personal activity in the period in which (manifestly) the Resurrection has not yet taken place. Surely, therefore, we either have to insist on using the idea of disembodied personal survival, in spite of its difficulties, or we have to insist that explanations of mediumistic phenomena *must* be found among the alternatives to survival, whatever *their* difficulties.

Is this problem insoluble, or can some hints for its resolution be gleaned from recent contributions to the problems of personal identity? In suggesting one or two moderately positive lines of reflection, I must emphasize that I write tentatively, in a mood of perplexity, not confidence, but in the real hope that some way of softening this problem can be found.

Let us first recall that the suggestion that persons might be gap-inclusive entities seems at least logically possible (see V (2) above); and let us recall, also, that the apparent conceptual necessity for personal embodiment does not rule out talk of more than one self occupying a particular human body, either simultaneously or successively (see IV (1) above). Let us now put these two recollections together. Perhaps it is conceivable that there might be persons who do not merely have one gap in their histories, as my over-simple resurrection-story has it, but a series of them; and that some of these gaps are gaps between brief embodiments. One can perhaps talk this way about some pre-mortem cases; perhaps one body may be the embodiment of two alternating selves, with or without overlap.[25] After death, of course, the pre-mortem body would no longer be the embodiment of either, but other bodies might be. The suggestion I want to make now, however, is that a living human body that is the embodiment of one pre-mortem person might, under certain conditions (I have no detailed idea *what* conditions), serve also as a temporary embodiment for a postmortem self, or for several postmortem selves at different times. Sometimes the postmortem embodiment might preclude the embodiment of the person whose earthly body it was and sometimes not. I refer, of course, to the phenomena of ostensible possession.[26] It is sometimes assumed that the ostensible possession of the medium's body by another personality is a more difficult phenomenon to understand than those phenomena which suggest the medium is communicating with a separate disembodied spirit. I am suggesting that it is, on the contrary, somewhat easier to grasp, since one could think of it as a form of short-lived re-embodiment, a temporary interruption of the long gap which would otherwise only end (if it ever does) when the self in question got back its original body or (if one prefers this) was embodied in a body exactly similar to its pre-mortem one.

I must emphasize two things about this suggestion. First, I am still not suggesting that we have any understanding of the notion of an individual self, in distinction or separation from the bodies it "has"; rather the contrary. Second, I am not suggesting that there are gaps in a person's *existence*; that persons, after death, cease to exist and then start to exist again. I am suggesting, rather, that their existence might *include* gaps in the way in which symphonies include periods of silence. With these provisos, it seems just possible that our common standards of identity would not be intolerably violated, but merely stretched and bent, especially since the content of the mediumistic messages might preserve, at least, fragments of what most *matters* to us in those who have died (see V (2) above).

But, of course, only some mediumistic communications purport to be cases of possession. Others purport to be messages coming from spirits to sitters via the medium, without the medium's body being taken over by the spirit. To insist that such cases would be cases of possession seems to smack of intolerable legislation in favor of what is, in any case, a wildly speculative interpretation. But how can we accommodate the desired possibility of a continuing postmortem individual who acts on, or through, the medium's body, while having no longer a body of its own? I will try to offer some very hesitant suggestions, all of them philosophically very unattractive, in the hope that someone can make more of them than I feel able to at present. None of them even has the merit of originality.

Let us first get out of the way the Platonic-Cartesian suggestion that there is a spiritual substance which owns postmortem experiences, and is therefore also the locus of postmortem agency. Without some independent characterization of that substance (independent, that is, of the statement that it is *that which* thinks or perceives or acts), the doctrine has no content, and just amounts to an empty asseveration that our problem really does have an answer.

There is a little more hope in the suggestion that we should re-examine the assumption that the postmortem person, or self, has "no body of its own." Perhaps it does have one, but of a different sort. There are two possible versions of this hypothesis, which at any rate seem different from one another. The first is the hypothesis of immediate postmortem resurrection; the claim that at death a person acquires at once another physical body, one which is not in any part of our space, but from which it telepathically or psychokinetically communicates with us, or with the medium.[27] The difficulties this faces are (1) that it raises again the puzzles about identity versus replication, that the more conventional theory of resurrection raised; and (2) that it entails the postulation of other bodies in their own space which is not in Space, a suggestion that I find deeply bewildering. The second possible version of the hypothesis of postmortem embodiment, is the theory of the astral body. I take this to be a body which has some of the characteristics of ordinary bodies (e.g. visibility) but not others (e.g. solidity). It, at least, *can* occupy our space, although not in a way that precludes ordinary objects (such as ordinary bodies) from occupying the same portions of it. Such a theory looks like an attempt to have one's cake and eat it, but perhaps we have to try this feat from time to time. In general, however, it seems to me to come to much the same as the hypothesis of instant resurrection, except in one particular: it is, I understand, usually taken to include the suggestion that we have astral bodies here and now as well as ordinary ones, with the implied suggestion[28] that these are, at present, the bearers of our real identity. This suggestion, however, surely needs to have independent evidence for it here and now, before its advantages, if any, deserve assessment.

There is finally another, even more metaphysical, suggestion, which dispenses with the need to postulate a multitude of disembodied postmortem individuals. I have hinted at it before.[29] The difficulty about disembodied persons is that there is no characterization of the individual who is said to *have* the thought or to *do* the action ascribed. Without this characterization there is no sense available to the statement that a particular thought or action was had, or done, by one disembodied person rather than another. On the other hand, the temptation to talk of disembodied persons comes from the fact that we want to ascribe certain phenomena to thought or agency, and thoughts and actions cannot exist by themselves, unowned. Perhaps we could avoid the latter absurdity without postulating a plurality of bodiless selves, by postulating that there is *only one*—which would, therefore, not have to be distinguished from any others, even in thought. And, just as our physical remains will eventually merge into their physical environment, perhaps there are also psychical remains which no longer belong to the individuals who used to have them, but are in some way absorbed into the single all-embracing spirit which makes them intermittently available to us, perhaps as some reassurance of the eventual full re-emergence of the whole embodied individual from whom they derive. This might account for the fact that some of what becomes available in mediumistic communications is mixed and jumbled, whereas some of what becomes available is highly specific and apparently individuating.

This may well not only seem, but be, nonsense. I risk uttering it, nevertheless, because I am still not convinced that the apparently clearer notion of disembodied personal survival is not nonsense too. But I should be very happy indeed to be persuaded that it is not. Nothing would please me, philosophically and personally, more than to be shown that this near-universal notion, which the evidence of parapsychology so tantalizingly suggests may be true, makes better sense than these very murky alternatives. Failing this, however, I can only air both my suggestions and my perplexities, and look forward for help to the discussion.

REFERENCES

[1] Butler, Joseph, Dissertation "Of Personal Identity", appended to *The Analogy of Religion*, Everyman's Library, Dent, London, 1906, page 257.

[2] For a little more on this notion of unintelligibility, see page 10 *et seq.* of my *Survival and Disembodied Existence*, Routledge and Kegan Paul, London, 1970. Parts of this work, which I refer to at intervals throughout this paper, have recently been reproduced in an anthology edited by James M. O. Wheatley and Hoyt L. Edge, entitled *Philosophical Dimensions of Parapsychology*; Charles C Thomas, Springfield, Illinois, 1976, pages 308–329.

[3] Toughness of this particular point can, and often is, combined with reasonable open-mindedness about the evidence itself.

[4] See, for example, the essays (19 and 20) by Price and Ducasse in the Wheatley-Edge volume, and the essays by Price and Flew in my *Immortality*, Wadsworth, Belmont, California, 1973.

[5] See Oscar Cullmann, *Immortality of the Soul or Resurrection of the Dead?* Epworth, London, 1958, reprinted in *Immortality*.

[6] Obviously this assumes some limits on predictions of transformation.

[7] See the two essays by U. T. Place and J. J. C. Smart in V. C. Chappell's anthology *The Philosophy of Mind*, Prentice-Hall, Englewood Cliffs, N.J. 1962.

[8] For a recent, highly sophisticated, discussion of the difficulties of the notion of contingent identity, see Saul Kripke, "Identity and Necessity" in Milton K. Munitz (ed.), *Identity and Individuation*, New York University Press, 1971, pp. 135–164.

[9] I omit reference here to the fact that the same data appear to justify both interactionism and parallelism.

[10] See Chapter 27 of Book II of his *Essay Concerning Human Understanding*.

[11] See Butler, op. cit.; also Antony Flew, "Locke and the Problem of Personal Identity", *Philosophy*, Vol. 26, 1951; also Sydney Shoemaker, "Personal Identity and Memory", *Journal of Philosophy*, Vol. LVI, 1959. These essays, and others referred to here, can be found in the anthology *Personal Identity*, edited by John Perry, University of California Press, 1975.

[12] Butler, op. cit. page 258.

[13] For a vigorous critique of my arguments on this point in *SDE*, see Michael Durrant, "Penelhum on Persons as 'Gap-Inclusive' Entities", in *The Southern Journal of Philosophy*, Vol. XII, 1974. I offered a reply in the same issue.

[14] One cannot of course say "memory"; though *they* might.

[15] For some comments on this, see Thomas Nagel, "Brain Bisection and the Unity of Consciousness", *Synthese*, Vol. 22, 1971, reproduced in Perry. This essay also has a useful bibliography of the relevant literature.

[16] See Corbett, H. Thigpen and Hervey M. Cleckley, *The Three Faces of Eve*, Popular Library, New York, (undated) and Morton Prince, *The Dissociation of a Personality*, Longmans, Green, New York, 1906.

[17] See, primarily, his essay, "Personal Identity", *Philosophical Review* Vol. LXXX, 1971 (repr. Perry); also his essay "Later Selves and Moral Principles" in Alan Montefiore (ed.) *Philosophy and Personal Relations*, Routledge and Kegan Paul, London, 1973. Of considerable importance here also is Sydney Shoemaker's "Persons and Their Pasts", *American Philosophical Quarterly*, Vol. 7, 1970. I attempted some criticisms of Parfit in "The Importance of Self-Identity", *Journal of Philosophy* Vol. LXVIII, 1971, which also contains his response, "On 'The Importance of Self-Identity.'"

[18] The notion of psychological connectedness obviously has affinities with the popular notion of self-identity. This sort of self-identity, which is clearly not the sort under discussion here, does admit of degrees.

[19] The example is a travesty of one of Parfit's in "Personal Identity." Each "survivor" would not remember, but would do something *as good as* remembering, which only he and the other survivor could do. Parfit calls it, following Shoemaker, "q-remembering."

[20] It worried Aquinas, for example. See Chapters 80 and 81 of Book Four of the *Summa Contra Gentiles* (reproduced in *Immortality* in the translation by Charles J. O'Neil).

[21] See pages 689–90 of "On 'The Importance of Self-Identity.'"

[22] Connectedness would too, no doubt; but identity seems in this case a necessary condition of its relevance.

[23] Of the University of Oregon. His arguments are contained in a fine essay, "The General Resurrection," to appear in the future, I understand, in a volume of his papers on philosophy of religion.

[24] See the essay by H. H. Price "Mediumship and Human Survival" in Wheatley and Edge, and his essay "The Problem of Life After Death," in *Immortality*.

[25] Perhaps this is the way to talk about Eve White and Eve Black.

[26] See Price, op. cit. ref. 24; also the discussions of mediumistic phenomena in C. D. Broad's *Lectures on Psychical Research*, Routledge and Kegan Paul, London, 1962.

[27] Such a theory is in fact a theory of reincarnation rather than resurrection, since the person's original body still may continue, resurrection being his ultimate re-occupancy of it, or (if preferred) of its ultimate duplicate.

[28] See Antony Flew, "Is There a Case for Disembodied Survival?" in Wheatley and Edge, also "Survival," a symposium with H. D. Lewis, *Aristotelian Society Supplementary Volume XLIX*, 1975.

[29] See the final chapter of *SDE*.

DISCUSSION

BELOFF: I listened very intently to Professor Penelhum's address, to see what modifications he might have made since he first wrote that very intriguing little volume that he referred to. But it struck me that he was still in the grip of the same verificationalist fallacy, as I am bound to call it, which in my opinion, vitiated the arguments in the book and has also vitiated the great bulk of modern philosophical literature on personal identity. Now, what I mean by the verificationalist fallacy is the idea that no concept can be meaningful unless you can spell out the criteria by which you can verify the existence or occurrence of this concept. Now, verification is tremendously important in science; tremendously important to us parapsychologists, and, obviously, if we are engaged in investigating postmortem survival, we must have criteria for saying when we believe the communication comes from some surviving entity rather than just from the medium or her subconscious. But I would, for one (and I'm not alone in this), deny that the idea of survival or of any concept, requires that you are able to specify what criterion you are going to use to recognize the occurrence of such a thing. It seems to me, beyond any real shadow of doubt, and I don't think here I'm just misled by my intuitions, that I understand perfectly what it would be for me to have experiences when this body that you all see me in now has just simply dissolved. Now, it might be the devil of a job to recognize that it is John Beloff still having experiences of some kind, somewhere. That's your problem after my body is gone; but that such a concept is meaningful—it would take a long time to persuade me otherwise. I very much agree with the views expressed in H. D. Lewis' recent book *The Elusive Mind*. There he strikes a blow, as it were, against the idea that we have got to look for criteria for identity in the first place. If you can't find it in memory, then we switch to bodily identity or some combination of the two and juggle from one to the other. I think we ought to recognize that the concept itself is meaningful and then get down to the scientific business of saying what would be the most satisfactory evidence.

PENELHUM: This raises very big issues of philosophic methods and procedure. I agree that the verificationalist fallacy is a fallacy. At any rate, it is a dogma and I see no particular reason to believe the dogma. I did try, in the book, to avoid succumbing to it, although apparently you think I failed. I was trying to ask whether we had as clear an understanding as philosophers often think, of the notion of disembodied existence, and it seems to me that we do not. Not because we are not in a position to decide in a particular case whether or not a given individual exists disembodied. In the nature of such a suggestion, there would be no obvious observable evidence, of course. (Incidentally, it wouldn't be observable to disembodied beings, themselves, either.) It was not this that made me hesitate about saying the notion was intelligible. The claim was that I could not see what the *assertion* of the identity of a disembodied spirit would mean, in that I would not know what you mean when you say, "this particular experience belongs to disembodied spirit J.B., rather than disembodied spirit T.P." I do not know what that difference comes to when these are not physically distinct individuals. That is not quite the same difficulty, as that of deciding how one would, understanding it, decide which one it belonged to. I think I have a more elemental difficulty than the one you think I was addressing myself to.

FRENCH: Would you want to hold, or could we force you to the view, that all identities are necessarily so? Also, can you provide some strong reasons why the problem of the identity of persons is in kind different from any other kind of identity problem? That is, I wonder if the problem of personal identity is but a sub-class to the general problem of identity. Would you like to talk about how it is somehow different from problems of identity across the board?

PENELHUM: My concern on the subject of necessary contingent identity is this; it seems to me that the apparently new notion, or newly recognized notion, of contingent identity, has not been very clearly defined by philosophers. I am tempted to say "yes" to your question, but am not certain yet what the implications are. The retort which I raised in the paper was the result of failing to see any particular reason why the notion of contingent identity should not be so wide open as to admit everything that it commonly is assumed it prevents one from saying. On the matter of personal identity and other kinds of identity, I think there are special problems of personal identity because we are persons and seem to have special access ourselves to some of the key facts; and because although we may use criteria or standards for determining the identity of other kinds of beings, there are lots of arguments in the book suggesting that we do not use them in our own case, and this seems to make the case special. I am inclined to say in this case that there are some special problems. These would be, I would suppose, of a technical kind not necessarily relevant to this argument.

LESHAN: Since you referred to the problems raised by brain physiology, I'd like to mention that there is some new work in a new book out which has complicated the problems almost beyond recognition—far beyond the level you speak of. I wonder if you know the book by Wilder Penfield, called *The Mystery of the Mind?*

PENELHUM: Yes.

LESHAN: Penfield is an old line, hard core brain physiologist. He recently published a book which, I think, has tremendous importance for us in this entire field. What he points out, in a very lucid, readable way, is that fifty years of experiments designed on the assumption and to prove that the brain generates thought like a loom generates cloth, have all pointed in the opposite direction and pointed to the brain simply being an organ of liaison with mind and quite separate from it. The fact that he was forced to this conclusion against his will, and the clear lucidity with which he presents the sequence of experiments, I think raises the problems even further that brain physiology brings to this field.

PENELHEM: I am willing to recognize that the specialist's knowledge would, indeed, complicate the conceptual problems that interest philosophers, and complicate how we would respond to the evidence of parapsychologists also. Of course, if the evidence forces one to talk of the brain as a liaison with mind, this does raise the problems that are perplexing me here, namely the question of how one then goes on to talk about the mind if one thinks of it as distinct from body and how one individuates minds from one another—that would suggest it makes it all worse.

THAKUR: I agree that disembodied survival will definitely involve the failure of at least some of the identity criteria. My question is, what conclusion should we draw from this? Would you take that as proof of the impossibility of survival or merely as an indication of improbability?

PENELHUM: This kind of question raises, of course, the very fundamental issue of what you do in the face of philosophical perplexities of a conceptual sort. My hope would be that the difficulties I still find in the notion of disembodied survival, are like the difficulties about motion that Zeno's paradoxes raise: there is, in fact, an answer to them, but we don't know what it is. That would be very nice because then the natural and almost universal tendency to use the notion of disembodiment to deal with this information, is one that we could follow—at least in the reasonable hope that somebody would unscramble the difficulties. On the other hand, I don't think that all conceptual difficulties can be assumed to be like that. At the moment these look to me rather like those that surround the science fiction notion of time travel—the notion that one could step into a spaceship at five o'clock and go forward two thousand years and come out of it again at six o'clock. This is something that we can follow as we read a novel, yet on even slight analysis it's patently logically absurd. Now how you decide when a difficulty is of the former kind and when it is of the latter kind, I wish I knew.

THAKUR: The particular reason I think I phrased the question this way, was that it had a reference to one of your remarks towards the end, that personally you would like someone to be able to show that the idea of disembodied survival still somehow made sense. The reason I asked this question was that unless you're prepared to see the failure of identity criteria as proof of the impossibility of survival, you will have got what you are looking for to some extent. There may be still hope.

PENELHUM: You mean just because the evidence is accumulating?

THAKUR: And because the impossibility wouldn't have been shown.

SERVADIO: Personal identity is the capacity to say "I." The ego feeling. And as we all know, it depends on many circumstances. The first circumstance is to have object relations. That is, material objects or mental objects. Now this becomes reduced, disturbed or annihilated under certain conditions such as sleep, sensory deprivation, etc. A second one depends on age, disease, etc., which alter the ego feeling. Therefore, the capacity to say "I," if personal survival were true, should continue when all object relations cease to exist, and when all bodily supports of the capacity to say "I" have crumbled down. Now, is that possible? Some schools of thought, such as Yoga, for instance, say yes. Yoga describes, for instance, a state, the so-called seedless samadhi, in which one is supposed to preserve an ego feeling without any support from any object or inner image and also apart from any particular state of the organic body. If such were the case, survival would not be a "yes" or "no" proposition. It would be the result of deep-seated self-integration—that is, it would be a conquest and not something that has been given to all human beings as a gift from the gods.

PENELHUM: Firstly, I think we are probably using the notion of personal identity in different ways. When I have spoken of it, I have not been speaking of something which depends for its existence on the person who has it being aware of it. That is to say, when you speak of personal identity, you are speaking, I think, of what one might call an individual's consciousness of himself, or awareness of who he is. Now, it seems to me that a person, after certain kinds of breakdown, might very well lose this, but not for that reason cease to be the person he was. He would just not himself know who he was, and we would simply express this by saying, "that person has lost his sense of self-identity." Now it would seem to me, as far as life after death is concerned, that one of the possibilities might be that individuals might continue, but lose their sense of self-identity as you have described it, in which case the problems which I have raised would still apply. I think our notions of self-identity are not the same; we are not using the same notion of self-identity. I am trying to use the one which enables us to count people and distinguish the one from the other and not one which refers particularly to the integration of a person's personality. Secondly, you referred to "mystical states"; of course, a large number of these also involve those who have experienced them, saying they have experienced a negation or denial of self-identity, and they have insisted in consequence of this that the common belief in self-identity is in some sense a mistaken one. They don't all point in the direction that you say.

ROLL: The recent development of the discussion interests me very much. The remarks I intended were somewhat like those Dr. Servadio made, so let me just add this: I think that in trying to conceive of what might continue after death, it's very helpful to get a picture of what exists before death. And there it seems uncertain to what extent the notion of identity applies. Certainly, the facts of parapsychology suggest that people are connected with other people and with things in ways that we usually do not account for in our everyday experience, such that my memories might be recalled by somebody else. Well, in what sense then are they my memories? Of if my emotions might be experienced by somebody else, to what extent are they then mine? Together with these epistemological puzzles, there are the kind of existential puzzles that Dr. Servadio referred to when he mentioned people who had been undergoing various sorts of self-development, which resulted in the feeling of extension into what they previously experienced as their environments. I think that this is something that you were beginning to develop in the latter part of your paper and that's something that I think would be very interesting for us to try to continue developing, because it seems to go together with the facts of parapsychology, particularly the more recent studies of altered states where people seem to be somewhat different from what they are ordinarily.

PENELHUM: As far as the understanding of strange events in this life is concerned, we seem to presuppose a simple ability to distinguish one person from another, and we have to use this presupposition in order to describe the data which worry us, when one person seems to have memories that ought to belong to another, or when one person seems to have an experience we expect another to have. We can describe what makes these situations puzzling to us only if we make use of the ordinary simple distinction between one person and another. It is the nature of that ordinary distinction and the basis of it that concerns me, because only if that ordinary distinction and its ordinary basis can be assumed to some extent to continue can we understand predictions of separate personal existence in another realm. The suggestion that I made at the end of the paper, that post-mortem experiences might all belong to one rather than to many individuals, was made on the assumption that we did not have a situation in which we could distinguish one individual from another in the next world, and we could therefore talk about all the experiences as forming a unit and not have to ask which unit. In other words, the suggestion depends upon our being in a situation where we can no longer use the ordinary distinctions between one person and another. But in describing *this* world, I think we have to make use of them.

EDGE: I hesitate somewhat to make some comments here for a couple of reasons. One, as I indicated earlier, it came out in discussion, that I don't any longer consider myself a dualist. Secondly, in the latest issue of the *Journal* of the SPR, I have written some comments about your book and in the next issue there is going to be criticism of mine. I would like to get your reaction to one or two things. First, I think there's one line in your book that ought to go down as one of the all-time great sentences in the literature of philosophy, and that is, "Memory is parasitic and needs a body to feed on." In relation to that, is it possible for a clairvoyant to have a memory of a clairvoyant event, where the actual memory is not my being in Copenhagen and clairvoyantly seeing something that's happening in London, but in fact, my total consciousness and therefore my total memory being in London? In what sense then doesn't it seem more plausible to say this is one of those cases that would make it a bit questionable that memory needs a body to feed on? And in relation to that, could we make some sense of a disembodied person? A number of people, of course, in the out-of-body experience describe their being some sort of astral body or something like that. But I was surprised to find out that seemingly the majority of cases in the out-of-body experience were described as being, in fact, disembodied experiences. Would not this be some sort of phenomenological empirical help in describing what it's like to be disembodied?

PENELHUM: The only comment I think I can make is this: If in the out-of-body experiences a person seems to himself to be looking down on his own body, if that's what he gives as a description of his experience, that, we will say, is the experience that he had. But, of course, the person who had that experience, wherever his point of view was on which the visual field he described *seemed* to be based, his body was six feet underneath, and there always was a body during that period. In other words, the identification of the person is not shown not to depend on the body merely because one of the visual experiences of the person is, as it were, from a point of view distinct from the body. It's not logically absurd that each of us should see the world in which he or she moves as from a point of view three feet to the right of the nose. That's not what happens, but we can easily imagine a world in which that happened, and we still say, "the person was here, not there."

HAYNES: From what you last said, it may not be logically, but it is physiologically extremely unlikely that we should see with our normal bodily sensations six feet above our normal bodies, because the eye and the brain are not connected in the kind of way which makes this possible. But that was the least I wanted to say. The other was: what about the part played from youth to very old age by the body image, by the person's perception of his bodily feelings? This goes not only with a kind of sensory feeling of himself, but also with his memory. Thus, I knew a very old lady who had to go into a nursing home who, when asked, "How do you feel?" said, "I'm the same me as I was when I was four years old and had a new nurse and I knew I had to get along with that woman and I have to get along with this nursing home." But she had this extraordinary close sense of identity with the child of four and, though her body obviously had changed throughout, she had worn right through those many, many years. Was it not possible that after death the body image may persist as a kind of feeling of self-identity together with a memory?

PENELHUM: The role of a body image in one's sense of identity is of itself an argument in favor of thinking that the basis for personal identity may be physical. On the suggestion that the body image might persist when the body does not: during life the body image is a mode of the perception of the subject whose identity, I would suggest, depends upon the body of which it is an image. When the body of which it was an image is no longer there, it is no longer clear that the identity which the image previously represented, would be preserved.

LESHAN: Since this is a meeting of The Parapsychology Foundation, it may be apropos to end with a comment that Eileen Garrett once made on her struggles with this specific problem. A group of us were talking about what it would mean to talk to somebody who claimed to be disembodied, a spirit communicator, what kind of reality were we talking about, who were they and what were they? And finally she said it reminded her of a story she'd heard right after the war. The story concerned a group of twenty fighter planes going off on a special mission and in each plane the pilot was seated alone and was under complete radio silence, very strict orders. Suddenly over the airplane intercom, in an obviously disguised voice, one of the pilots hoarsely whispered, "Who d'at?" There was silence, and then another pilot whispered, "Who d'at who say who d'at?" A third pilot followed with "Who d'at who say who d'at who say who d'at?" At which point the commander lost his temper and said, "That's enough. I'll court-martial the next man who speaks." There was absolute silence, until another disguised voice said, "Who d'at?"

PARAPSYCHOLOGY IN SEARCH OF A PARADIGM

Shivesh C. Thakur

This paper, or rather a part of it, is an attempt to examine the present state of parapsychology as a science. This task can, of course, be undertaken from somewhat different points of view and with different criteria of assessment. What I have in mind is the application of the very important and illuminating concept of *paradigm* made famous by T. S. Kuhn.[1] The word "paradigm" has many distinct, though somewhat related uses, even within the work of Kuhn, not to mention its many different senses in, say, grammar or "ordinary" English. We will return to this primary, ordinary English, sense at a later stage in this paper. The Kuhnian sense in which the word has come to be widely understood, signifies the body of theory and methodology which provides the unifying basis for the practice of science at a particular time. A paradigm serves as the conceptual and methodological framework for scientists working in a particular field at a particular time. It not only determines the character and direction of research in the appropriate science, but, implicitly at least, even legislates as to what sort of entities or phenomena may or may not be said to exist. The natural question to ask in our present context would be whether parapsychology could be said to have a paradigm.

But before we tackle this question, perhaps another, more fundamental one, needs to be raised: Is parapsychology a science? For if it's not a science—nor likely to be one, as some no doubt would wish to add—then whether it has a paradigm becomes at best an idle question, at worst wrong-headed. While I am not unmindful of the considerations that could be brought up to deny the claim, let us, for the sake of the argument at least, accept that parapsychology is a science.

Even those who accept this claim unhesitatingly, however, will hardly wish to maintain that parapsychology is a "normal" science, i.e. one which operates within the framework of an established paradigm. The latter claim would, in my view, be so palpably false as to require no argument. This would still leave two possibilities to be considered.

Parapsychology could be said either to be in the "pre-paradigm" phase of development or, arguably, in a state of "crisis," awaiting a *paradigm-shift*—the state that heralds a scientific revolution. The relatively short time for which parapsychology has been in existence as a distinct field of research would seem to suggest, very strongly indeed, that it is still awaiting the emergence of its first full-scale paradigm. But since I wish to argue that there is a way of looking at parapsychological work which does not render the second alternative absurd, I intend to discuss both the possibilities in some detail.

Starting on a rather light note, there is one aspect of work in parapsychology today which may create the illusion that research in the area is already paradigm-based. According to Kuhn,[2] one symptom of the emergence of a paradigm in a particular science is that its practitioners no longer address their research reports to the generally educated public nor do they feel obligated to justify the use of each concept or principle introduced. This latter task is left to the writers of textbooks and the former, perhaps, to the "popularizers" of the field. Consequently, the research reports appear by and large in short articles in professional journals, and become increasingly more technical. This phenomenon, for whatever it's worth, can be said to be already occurring in parapsychology, even though books, other than texts and not necessarily collections of articles, are still being written—perhaps a few too many!

But such appearances notwithstanding, the state of what I shall call "theoretical anarchy" within contemporary parapsychology will hardly support the view that research within it is paradigm-based yet. At best, it seems to me, we have a collection of "mere facts," but perhaps not even that, since there are many, not necessarily outside parapsychology, who still challenge the factuality of one or more of the claims to important discovery. Even the Helmut Schmidt effects in PK experimentation,[3] technically, perhaps, the most sophisticated experiments in parapsychology, have not proved susceptible to systematic replication.[4] This is hardly surprising. Kuhn, quite correctly, says, "No natural history can be interpreted in the absence of at least some implicit body of intertwined theoretical and methodological belief that permits selection, evaluation, and criticism. *If that body of belief is not already implicit in the collection of facts—in which case more than mere facts are at hand—it must be externally supplied, perhaps by a current metaphysic, by another science, or by personal and historical accident.*"[5] (Italics mine.) In the absence of a well-integrated and coherent theory, implicit or explicit, reports on so-called facts as well as their refutations may simply be the products of individual commitments to incommensurate models, attitudes and idiosyncracies; and the line between fact and fiction will be hard to draw.

Parapsychology may not, strictly speaking, have the *schools* character-istic of the early stages of a science's development, but that there are many competing models, methods and metaphysical commitments operative in the field can hardly be disputed. How else could one account for the co-existence in the field of various "physical radiation" models for, say, telepathy and clairvoyance;[6] an account of psi phenomena in terms of the "hidden variables" of quantum mechanics;[7] the many different forms of "synchronicity" for the "explanation" (?) of ESP phenomena;[8] claims as to the phylogenetic origins of "psi" ability,[9] the multi-dimensional view of time rec-ommended for the explanation of precognition;[10] and the confident assertions of the demonstration by psi phenomena of the existence of the mind,[11] not to mention the existence of the soul required for survival and mediumistic communication? A measure of confusion reigning in the field—due largely, I think, to the lack of theoretical underpinning for its facts—is provided by the opening paragraph of John Beloff's review of *Philosophy and Psychical Research*, of which I am contributing editor. "It used to be taken for granted," says Beloff, "that, if the evidence for paranormal phenomena were valid, this could not but have far-reaching impli-cations for the entire structure of beliefs embedded in our science, philosophy and common sense. Controversy, therefore, centred upon the crucial question of validity. More recently, however, the view has been put forward that, even if the basic parapsychological evidence were to be accepted at face value, nothing would follow from it. At worst we should be left with a whole lot of anomalies that we should not know what to do with but no drastic revision of our existing outlook would be called for. If I may be permitted to coin a term," Beloff continues, "I would like to call this view 'Flewism' in honour of its most original and able exponent Flew. . . "[12]

Since Beloff evidently regards "Flewism" as some sort of infectious disease, I can only feel relieved that he does not directly consider me afflicted. But in defence of those fellow contributors to the volume who, in Beloff's opinion, have shown symptoms of acute Flewism, I must say that, given the fluid state of theorizing in parapsychology, Flewism cannot easily be shown to be inconsistent or unwarranted. Since parapsychology does not itself have a clear unambiguous view of what is or will be established or refuted by parapsychological phenomena, it is not entirely fair to accuse Flew, or any other philosopher of parapsychology, of "negativism," physicalism or general skepticism, even if the profession of these views were somehow shown to be undesirable.

The view that parapsychology is an "infant" science, very far yet from the development of a paradigm, is so eminently plausible that it may seem paradoxical, if not absurd, to suggest that it could, or should be seen as being in a state of crisis or of a "breakdown of normal scientific activity," so often the precursor of a paradigm-shift. Undoubtedly, the suggestion can only be made on a special interpretation, and we will come to that shortly. But let us first note that the *symptoms* characterizing the pre-paradigm phase of science are bound to be similar, in many ways, to those of the breakdown of a reigning paradigm. In the former state there is no generally accepted theory; in the latter there is a theory but it can no longer account for important sets of data: the scientific community has encountered genuinely recalcitrant facts, or *anomalies*, which demand a new paradigm. According to Kuhn, "The proliferation of competing articulations, the willingness to try anything, the expression of explicit discontent, the recourse to philosophy and to debate over fundamentals, all these are symptoms of a transition from normal to extraordinary research."[13] Practitioners of parapsychology should have no difficulty whatsoever in recognizing these symptoms either in their own work and feelings or in those of others in their larger community.

Central to the characterization of scientific activity as extraordinary or revolutionary is the concept of anomaly, the discovery of facts that stubbornly refuse to fit accepted theory. Now, it is possible, indeed quite plausible, to treat parapsychological phenomena as anomalies within the existing theoretical framework of the natural sciences, especially perhaps of physics, but possibly even of physiology and biology. The use of terms like "*para*psychology," "*paranormal* phenomena" and "*extrasensory* perception," lends credibility to this interpretation. Indeed, most of the fundamental terms of parapsychology proclaim, loudly enough, that in their initial articulation parapsychological phenomena were seen as anomalies, phenomena that should never have occurred if the natural scientific view of the world was correct. This interpretation may also explain why, as parapsychologists often complain, scientists tend to dismiss paranormal phenomena as absurd without examining the evidence for them. The dismissal occurs, not because scientists are dishonest or obtuse, but because, as scientists, they cannot accept these phenomena until a new paradigm incorporating present anomalies as normal facts has appeared. Not entertaining recalcitrant facts is a well-known feature of paradigm-based science; and the history of science abounds in examples. If the parapsychologist wishes to have his research findings accepted by the scientific community at large, he has to wait until the required paradigm-shift has occurred, either as a consequence of his own or someone else's work. At this stage, parapsychology does not seem to be making much progress towards creating the conditions that could bring about the paradigm-change, if that is what is required. Neither the appropriate kind of theory nor the methodology seem to me to be on the horizon.

The foregoing discussion may perhaps be taken as indicative of what one might call an identity-crisis for parapsychology, an uncertainty about its "self-image." It does not seem to have been able to decide whether it should fashion itself after, say, physics, the most developed of the natural sciences; psychology, its nearest kin in the social sciences; or perhaps, even after classics or history. An outsider reviewing research done in the field since its beginnings is bound to notice work characteristic of all three, if not of more, distinct disciplines. Rarely, if ever, does parapsychological research bear the marks of an independent and unique kind of inquiry. This can be interpreted as a basic indecision about paradigm in its ordinary English sense, i.e. a failure on the part of parapsychology to decide which, if any, of the existing disciplines, e.g. physics, biology, psychology, classics, should serve as the model or example of its own activity. Some of the more sophisticated, automated experiments in parapsychology, e.g. those of Helmut Scmidt and others, have the appearance of advanced experimental work in the developed natural sciences. But at the same time, work resembling that in *Phantasms of the Living*,[14] though on a less ambitious scale, which consists largely of comparison and classification of case histories—typical of research in history or classics—still appears in parapsychological journals and books. Not only its name, para*psychology*, but a great deal of its research since the pioneering days of Rhine and Soal have, perhaps consciously, been fashioned after psychology.

This should be neither surprising nor regrettable. After all, psychology set out to be the study of the mind, or psyche, and only later adopted the methodological goal of identifying mind with behavior, which has now become the dominant trend in contemporary psychology. Such methodological behaviorism, however, cannot take parapsychology very far. And this for two reasons. In the first place, the typical examples of parapsychological phenomena do not as a rule present much, if any, observable *behavior* which will set them apart as identifiable paranormal phenomena; always it's the *information* or effect produced that does so. Moreover, parapsychology, unlike psychology, seems to, and perhaps needs to, explicitly postulate non-dispositionally interpreted *abilities, powers* and *energies*, often expressed by terms such as "psychic power," "psiability" or "psychic energy." In this context, it may be interesting to note that R. Harré and P. F. Secord have recently argued that psychology—social psychology at any rate—needs to postulate real human powers, "liabilities" and natures for an adequate explanation of human social behavior.[15] If this argument wins the day, then, perhaps, psychology and parapsychology may find themselves working within a broadly similar, though not identical, framework.

This failure of parapsychology to develop its own unique identity could be said to spring largely from the contingency that it has not succeeded in developing, or adopting, a coherent theory of its own which will allow the treatment of its data as a normal (in the sense of expected) set of facts, rather than as anomalies within the existing paradigm(s) of other scientific disciplines. The message remains the same if parapsychology is seen as requiring a transition from infancy to adulthood as a science. The emergence of a full-fledged paradigm, insofar as it involves the appearance on the scene of a Newton or an Einstein, cannot be the object of conscious planning or preparation; that will have to await a historical accident. But pending such a development, and without prejudicing (as far as possible) its scientific status and aspirations, there is no reason why parapsychology should not adopt a metaphysical theory, if one were available or could be constructed. The history of science demonstrates that in its pre-paradigm as well as revolutionary stages, a science often operates within the framework of metaphysical theories which may later either be abandoned altogether or, unusually, transformed into scientific paradigms.

In what follows I shall, with not inconsiderable trepidation, attempt to outline a speculative-metaphysical theory, using various concepts from traditional Indian philosophy.[16] In saying that these are Indian philosophical concepts, it is not at all my intention to claim that they are in any sense exclusive to the Indian tradition. On the contrary, many of them have their counterparts in non-Indian religious philosophies, even though the terms used are often not easily inter-translatable across the different cultures. Consequently, it's unlikely that the proposed theory will appear altogether strange to any religious-philosophical tradition.

If parapsychological phenomena are genuine, then what they

demonstrate, above all, is the vastly greater complexity of both man and nature than what our common sense or science has yet given us reason to believe. Only with the explicit recognition of this complexity can we even begin to hope to accommodate psychic phenomena as warranted facts rather than absurd anomalies. This complexity has been a strong and recurrent theme of the earliest Upanishadic literature in India and has provided the backdrop for the speculation of many subsequent systems of metaphysics. The expression of this complexity, often in esoteric and mystical jargon, has taken many different forms. But the substantive theme seems to be that neither man nor nature is what it seems to be "at first sight."

The description of man, for example, as a complex of body and soul is regarded as correct, but only as an inadequate first step toward a true account of his reality. The self or soul (*ātman*), the ultimate essence of man, is hidden beneath many "layers" of not-self, just as the nucleus of the onion lies hidden behind its many layers of skin. The ordinary man may stay quite happy believing that he *is* his material body. But as he learns to be discerning and introspective, he would begin to experience some unease at this identification. Through a series of faltering, but increasingly more revealing steps, he may learn to identify himself, next, with his desires and impulses, then with his mental states, then again with his rationality, until, finally, he experiences himself as being identical with the ultimate ground of the universe (*Brahman*). In view of this identification, at different stages, with different entities or principles, man could be said either to *be* many different selves, or, more appropriately, to *have* different "bodies": (1) the material (*annamaya*), (2) the vital (*prāṇamaya*), (3) the mental (*manomaya*), (4) the rational (*vijñānamaya*) and, finally, (5) the "cosmic" (*Brahmamaya*). The specific details perhaps do not matter. What does matter is the belief in the Indian tradition that the realization by man of his essential non-materiality gradually frees him from the operations of the laws of matter.

Just as man has these many "levels" of selfhood, each succeeding level more "real" than the preceding, so the universe, or nature, has many different levels of reality too. These could be said to be: (1) nature with its manifold, as revealed to ordinary perception (*virāta*), or the world of commonsense; (2) the world as the manifestation of physical energy (*hiranyagarbha*), or the world of science; (3) the world as created by the causal energy of a personal God (*karana* or *īshvara*), or (perhaps) the world of religion; and, finally, (4) the eternal, impersonal ground of the universe (*Brahman*), the world of the mystic or the liberated.

This parallel between the increasingly subtle and more real aspects of man on the one hand and of nature on the other, both culminating in *Brahman*, suggests that in the final analysis man may be the world in microcosm. Any process of self-discovery, therefore, must at the same time lead not only to the increasingly fuller understanding of nature, but ultimately end in a state where knowing nature (as something external) can hardly be distinguished from the experience of identity with its ground. This is obviously referring to a state of mystic vision and I must not presume the competence to say much more about it. But the similarity with Spinoza's cognition *sub specie aeternitatis* and the *amor dei* as the inevitable product of this state, is too striking to be missed.

In what form and with what typical characteristics one would experience his self or indeed nature, will be determined by his *state* or *level* of consciousness or awareness. The Indian tradition speaks of at least four different states of consciousness, three of them empirical commonplaces and the fourth a metaphysical or transcendental construction on the first three. The first is the waking state which is "outwardly cognitive," "enjoying the gross" and is "common-to-all men."[17] The second, the dreaming state, is "inwardly cognitive" and enjoys the "exquisite, the brilliant"[18] etc. The third is the state of deep sleep, "enjoying bliss" and is just a "cognition mass"[19] i.e. "unified or undifferentiated" awareness. (It is, perhaps, because deep sleep is still characterized by this amorphous consciousness, that on waking we do not experience any significant breach in the continuity of our consciousness.) And, finally, there is the, hypothetical, transcendental state of consciousness (*turīya*) which presumably results in the experience of identity between the individual self (*ātman*) and the ground of the world (*Brahman*), but which is otherwise regarded as unique and indescribable.

The progression through the increasingly deeper levels of awareness, revealing the subtler and deeper levels of one's self as well as of nature and culminating in the experience of identity with *Brahman*, is believed to have the following consequence. The discovery by man that he is essentially non-physical gradually frees him from the "limiting conditions" of space, time and causality, principles which organize and govern matter alone. This freedom from limiting conditions can also be viewed, positively, as the attainment of various *powers (siddhis)*. Parapsychological phenomena such as ESP and PK, on this view, are instances of this power and, understandably therefore, *appear* as violations of the laws governing space, time and causality. *In principle*, anyone could acquire these powers, if he were to put in the required effort. In practice, however, it is considered unlikely that everyone will succeed, for the goal of "self-realization" is exceedingly hard to achieve. Yoga and other, similar, "practical" disciplines are believed to help in this process. One could say, without sounding too facetious, I hope, that these disciplines provide the "technology" for the discovery of deeper levels of the self and, coincidentally, for the attainment of the attendant powes. But the tradition insists that a true seeker is unlikely to be motivated by the attainment of these powers and equally unlikely, when he has attained them, to use them for self-aggrandizement or for any other selfish end.

This theory is metaphysical and it would be neither possible nor profitable to pretend otherwise. We set out, in the absence of a paradigm, to construct a theory which will allow paranormal phenomena to be viewed as normal and expected, rather than anomalies; and this I think it does. But a metaphysical theory which aspires to provide genuine explanations of empirical phenomena, must have *some* empirical consequences and must lend itself to empirical, preferably experimental, models. To what extent, if any, this theory does so, must ultimately be left to be judged by parapsychologists and scientists who are equipped to translate abstract ideas into empirical and experimental terms. I claim no competence whatsoever in this respect. But a few general remarks may not be out of place.

First of all, the belief in the Indian tradition is that the concepts employed in this theory are not altogether, perhaps not at all, speculative. They are regarded as the expression, howsoever inadequate, of the personal experiences of sages and seers of antiquity. Moreover, Yoga and the like have consistently been claimed in the tradition to be *practical*, as against, say, *Sāmkhya* and some other systems of philosophy, which are regarded as theoretical. Now there can be no obligation, *a priori*, to treat these claims as true. But, on the other hand, to treat them as false, without thorough examination, will be pedagogically wrong, especially when ideas resembling the above in some respects have come to form the basis of certain forms of contemporary "scientific" practice.

Psychoanalysis is founded on the idea of levels of personality; and if the Indian doctrine of levels of selfhood is metaphysical in character, it must share that characteristic with psychoanalysis. The differences may be those of degree and detail rather than of basic insight. Similarly, recent researches into "altered states of consciousness" induced by the use of drugs and the practice of meditative and other techniques, has lent some plausibility to the idea of levels, or discrete states, of consciousness. Charles Tart, who has done a significant amount of work in this area, has coined the term "discrete altered states of consciousness," "d-ASC" in short.[20] Likewise, the contrast between the commonsense and scientific views of the world has in recent years been sharpened to such a degree that the hypothesis of the discovery of an altogether new perspective need no longer sound altogether absurd. A great deal more research in these and other pertinent areas must, of course, take place before one would be in a position even to claim *general* plausibility for the theory outlined above. Until that happens, it would remain metaphysical but, hopefully, neither too abstruse nor absurd. It is true that the theory postulates a final state of awareness which culminates in the mystic vision of identity between the self and the ground of the universe. In the context of certain other sciences this itself, and perhaps for good reason, may put the theory out of court. But parapsychologists would be less than openminded if they did not entertain the possibility of other paranormal phenomena being on a continuum with mystic experience.

At this point, it may be useful to mention that a theory such as this may be more easily tested by developing what Tart calls a *state-specific science*.[21] If I understand him correctly, his suggestion is that if one wants to ascertain what happens, say, in a drug-induced state of consciousness and, more important, the validity of the claims made by people who have experienced this state, then one would need a science which is specifically designed to answer questions relating to the drug-induced state of consciousness. And, similarly, for other discrete states of consciousness. This would presumably involve creating a community of scientists who are willing and able to enter into drug-induced states, not just for the kicks—though, of course, this would be a bonus—but for the sake of making an objective study of the conditions, experiences, claims and after-effects of such states. The theoretical and practical problems involved in developing such a science must be quite considerable, and it may even be questionable whether such a study will ever amount to a science. In the context of drug-induced states, the idea seems to get off the ground because drugs can be administered as and when required. But since mystic states, for which presumably there would be a distinct state-specific science, are not known to be subject to voluntary induction nor at all easy to identify, it is extremely difficult to visualize how such a science could ever come into being. But since Tart is himself fully aware of the problems and perils involved, I will not here undertake any further criticism of his suggestion. All I would say is that perhaps the idea deserves careful investigation.

Viewed externally, scientific knowledge is, after all, nothing but the body of so-called facts and theories that a community of specialists has

208   *The Philosophy of Parapsychology*

agreed to accept. And if such a community can be created in relation to a particular discrete state of consciousness, then we would apparently have created a state-specific science for that state. Whether our theory is mere speculation or a correct account of reality will, then, have a simple test. In Kuhn's words "As in political revolutions, so in paradigm choice—there is no standard higher than the assent of the relevant community."[22]

REFERENCES

[1] Kuhn, T. S., *The Structure of Scientific Revolutions*, 2nd enlarged edn., London, 1975.
[2] *Ibid.*, p. 20.
[3] Schmidt, H., "PK Tests with a High-speed Random Number Generator," *Journal of Parapsychology*, 37, 2, 1973, pp. 105–118.
[4] Results of work done by H. Akbulut, a graduate student at the University of Surrey, under the joint supervision of Professor G. King, of Electronic & Electrical Engineering, and myself, have so far proved inconclusive.
[5] Kuhn, *op. cit.*, pp. 16–17.
[6] See Chapter 1 of *Philosophy and Psychical Research*, edited by S. C. Thakur, London, 1976.
[7] Walker, G. H., "Foundations of Paraphysical and Parapsychological Phenomena," in *Quantum Physics and Parapsychology*, Parapsychology Foundation, 1975.
[8] Jung, C. G., *Synchronicity*, London, 1972; also Koestler, A., *The Roots of Coincidence*, London, 1972.
[9–11] See *Philosophy and Psychical Research*, *op. cit.*, especially Chs. 1, 2 and 10.
[12] *Journal of the Society for Psychical Research*, Vol. 48, No. 768, 1976, p. 336.
[13] Kuhn, *op.cit.*, p. 91.
[14] Gurney, E., Myers, F. W. H. and Podmore, F., *Phantasms of the Living*, London, 1886.
[15] Harré, R. and Secord, P. F., *The Explanation of Social Behavior*, Oxford, 1972.
[16] The various concepts used in the outline occur over a wide area of traditional Indian philosophy. But for a relatively brief collation of these, see Chaudhuri, H., "Yoga Psychology," in *Transpersonal Psychologies*, edited by Charles T. Tart, London, 1975.
[17–19] Radhakrishnan, S. and Moore, Charles A., *A Sourcebook in Indian Philosophy*, Princeton, 1971, pp. 55–56.
[20–21] "Science, States of Consciousness, and Spiritual Experiences: The Need for State-Specific Sciences," in *Transpersonal Psychologies op. cit.*, pp. 11–58.
[22] Kuhn, *op. cit.*, p. 94.

DISCUSSION

STANFORD: Initially, hearing Dr. Thakur's remarks about paradigms might lead one to believe that there is a strong contradiction between the conclusions that he reaches in the initial part of his paper and my own. That may be more apparent than real, however, because of the considerations of the definitions of "paradigm," and because I believe that Dr. Thakur has been discussing in his paper the relations of parapsychology to what he calls "normal science," in terms of the relationship to the larger body of science. I don't understand the concept of paradigm, even in the Kuhnian sense, as necessarily implying that. I think Kuhn talks about paradigms within specific sciences. A paradigm is not necessarily an over-bridging kind of paradigm across all sciences, and thus I think that in another definitional sense compatible with Kuhn's, it could be argued that we have had a paradigm within parapsychology. However, hearing Dr. Thakur's remarks makes me want to modify the title of my paper to say "Have Parapsychologists Been Paradigmless in Psiland," because I think Dr. Thakur has been more strongly focussed on the current state of parapsychology, whereas I have been immersed for well over a decade in a different kind of parapsychology than I think we're seeing right now. I would reaffirm my own interpretation that within parapsychology we have seen something like a Kuhnian paradigm, but I certainly wouldn't dispute with Dr. Thakur and suggest that this paradigm has in any sense been one which could be assimilated into some kind of general concept of a normal science that bridges across all the sciences. I do want to say something else here with regard to the latter remarks in your paper. Why should parapsychologists adopt a metaphysical theory instead of a specifically scientific one? I have my own answers to that which might or might not concur with those of Dr. Thakur. I think that a metaphysical theory, if it's taken more or less in the sense that you have suggested, might have a psychological use, and that is helping us break out of some of our sets, which is certainly something that we need if we don't come to take the metaphysical perspective too seriously. Also, I have noted elsewhere that out of some of these traditions come some specific suggestions that could lead to specific parapsychological research, and I think these are useful for us to study. One final comment; you are advocating state-specific science, and I would want to take strong issue with that as a way to proceed in parapsychology or in any other scientific area. While I'm in sympathy, I think, with the purposes behind such a formulation, I can't help but feel that such state-specific science leads to a kind of solipsism, because it says that we can determine when persons are in the same state by the fact that we'll see emergent agreements and laws, and this is where you get your state-specific science. But it's obvious that you have to have an external criterion for being in a state, otherwise somebody will come along and disagree and say you're not in the same state. Well, we're all, perhaps, in a similar state of consciousness now, but we certainly wouldn't all agree about what is lawful or meaningful as we've seen some examples in this conference. So I think there is a serious problem in the state-specific science concept, in that it can lead to solipsism unless it's further refined.

THAKUR: I'm delighted to note the first conversion to my cause, especially because you have offered to change the title of your paper. It is true, that I have deliberately taken a rather large metaphysical theory to use as a unifying set of concepts which, hopefully, will allow us to get after some of what I might call "the rot" in other areas. Finally, and this is a more serious one, I share your misgivings about Charles Tart's idea of state-specific science, but I have said in my paper that he is, himself, fully aware of the problem and he talks about it at great length. I just didn't want to do the intellectually dishonest thing of ruling him out of court. There is some promise and all I have recommended is that the idea should be given serious consideration. So if it qualifies, perhaps there is something there.

BELOFF: I would like to go on record as a skeptic with regard to the Kuhnian concept of a paradigm. For that reason I rather regretted that Professor Thakur spent so much of his paper discussing what I consider to be essentially the idle question of whether parapsychology is or could become a normal science in the Kuhnian sense, instead of devoting much more time to what I consider a far more fascinating question, as to whether these insights into Indian philosophy could help to give us a perspective on parapsychology. Incidentally, although we have at this conference had three papers, as Professor Thakur pointed out, with "paradigm" in the title, I consider that only two of them concern paradigms in the Kuhnian sense. What Dr. Rex Stanford gave us was, I consider, simply a particular theoretical model and none the worse for that. In fact, much the better for it, but it was not what Kuhn understood by a paradigm. Now I think it's very important—you know the word "paradigm" is bandied about so much—it's terribly important to know what we are talking about, and I think it's very desirable to remember that in Kuhn's book which launched this concept (*The Structure of Scientific Revolutions*), he does not touch upon the social and psychological sciences. His concept is clearly inspired and fueled, I would say, by the idea of the revolution in physics which obviously was very prominent in his mind. He applies it also in the history of chemistry and a few other well established sciences in the physical area. And there has been an enormous amount of controversy, of a rather tedious kind, as to whether psychology has ever acquired a paradigm, whether behaviorism was a paradigm, and so on. None of this debate, it seems to me, led anywhere and I think it would be far better to simply skip this whole approach and ask more important questions.

THAKUR: I'm entirely in agreement with what you say. The reason I talked at any length about paradigms at all was more out of defensiveness than anything. I thought that if I were going to go to a conferenece of parapsychologists and tell them that they haven't got a paradigm or a "super theory." they probably would be offended, so I was trying to put some flesh on my charge. But it is quite true that it is the second part which is the more interesting job, and I would love to do some more elaborating of this perhaps on a subsequent occasion. It is a huge area and I don't think I could do it justice in one paper, so probably some time in the future I may come back with a bit more.

MAUSKOPF: Maybe because I'm an historian rather than a philosopher or a psychologist or a parapsychologist, I see use and interest in talking about paradigms. I would disagree with Dr. Beloff here. But I would agree with him and with Rex Stanford in what I understood to be at least implicit in their comments, that the use of paradigms has perhaps been coarsened in the papers here. Reified is perhaps a better word. There is an entity, a paradigm which every science worth its salt must possess and at some time, t_1, it doesn't have it and at some time, t_2, it does have it, and parapsychology is still in t_1 time and ought to be moving towards t_2. Now, in our own studies of the history of parapsychology, my colleagues and I, in fact, try to use the paradigmatic concept in more flexible ways, in line, I think, with what Dr. Beloff suggested about paradigms if they exist in the social and the behavioral sciences. Specifically, we see, and we think we can justify parapsychology at least as having passed through a partially paradigmatic stage—paradigmatic both in terms of its theory and method, and also in terms of its institutional structure. I'm referring to the period of the 1930s and 1940s following the publication of Rhine's book *Extrasensory Perception.* Now I think that book and the subsequent work in America and England, in fact, did lay down most of the components of a paradigm that Kuhn is talking about,and it's a rich and complex concept. There were specific methods focused on; there were specific problems considered to be the important ones; others that were considered to be ruled out, and there was even the sketch—and this is, I think, where the paradigmatic concept in full blown form doesn't apply—there was a sketch of a theory. A sketch which strikes me in many ways as similar to yours. That is, it was basically a nonmaterialistic sketch of a theory which strongly asserted that parapsychological phenomena evaded the laws of physics as they were then known; evaded normal temporal and spatial requirements, etc., and I think Rhine in *Extrasensory Perception* and his followers hoped that this sketch would be articulated in the way I gather you're hoping your sketch, an Orientally-derived theory, will be articulated. Now as it has transpired, it wasn't articulated, it didn't continue to move on. I think the reasons it wasn't articulated had as much to do with social and institutional factors as they did with philosophical and metaphysical ones and even methodological ones.

THAKUR: I wasn't intending to get involved in comments on the social sciences at all. I was trying to avoid it, but since the subject has been brought up a second time, I would say very briefly, that, as far as I'm concerned, I don't believe the social sciences, psychology and sociology for instance, have a paradigm. Now this is not damning in itself, but what is unsatisfactory is that neither of these disciplines seems to have a unified structure, so that a lot of work done is of a very *ad hoc* kind, and the least I expected to convey by way of a message was that parapsychology should not unthinkingly get into that state. On the second point, I note that Rhine's sketch wasn't articulated —it was somehow thrown out of court, in a way, which is very unceremonious. The social and institutional factors that you talked about and that made that situation occur, should include, I believe, an undue deference for so-called scientific objectivity that took over and that was a very important nineteenth century trademark. I think we know much more about science now; enough to get out of that particular mystique and therefore draw certain lessons from this. So maybe this sort of theory has a better chance than it had in the early years.

PENELHUM: I can't contribute anything at all helpful on the debate about what a paradigm is, but the discussion that has gone on with regard to this, has revived a certain misgiving that was with me as Dr. Thakur began. I seem to understand that a paradigm is something that belongs to a specific science, like physics or chemistry, and he says it doesn't belong to the social sciences as yet. I am beginning to wonder whether we have any right to take for granted that parapsychology is a specific science in that sense. It seems to me that it's quite possible that people of a certain type of mentality (conceptual elasticity, ability to accept facts that others wish to overlook) might band together to study all those things that nobody else will pay attention to, and these might turn out to be a very heterogeneous bundle of phenomena. The people who studied this heterogeneous bundle of phenomena might acquire a name, and this name might be "parapsychologists." It seems to me that we cannot take for granted that there is a theoretical unity among those phenomena, and their explanations, that seems to be taken for granted in your discussion of there being a paradigm for parapsychology. My second comment relates to your extremely interesting resort to Oriental, specifically Hindu, ideas to develop a theory—I'll stop talking about paradigms, if I may—a theory to provide a framework for the interpretation of parapsychological phenomena. I have an anxiety of a different kind here. I would take an explanatory theory to be something which would have to provide some way of integrating the phenomena, showing systematic interconnections between them. Now, if I understand the tradition that you lean upon here correctly, the fundamental perception on which it rests, which derives from mystical practice, is the perception of the unreality of many of those phenomena in relation to some ultimate reality. Now, I am very worried about the notion of explaining phenomena in terms of their ultimate unreality. It seems to me that if you try to do this, then the phenomena become conceptually parallel to those phenomena called miraculous in western theologies. That is to say, they are in essence things which show there is a higher reality than the ones that you are seeking to explain. (In connection with your suggestion that one might rope together those prepared to participate in certain types of drug-induced experiences in order to test the theory, it seems to me that if these experiences are parallel to mystical states (which, of course, is controversial) it would seem that what they would do would be merely to duplicate the perception of the unreality of the phenomena which are to be explained.) I worry about this as a mode of explanation. It seems to me that to interconnect phenomena systematically, predict one on the basis of the other, is quite a different enterprise from determining on the basis of the one that the other is unreal.

THAKUR: There's a great deal in that, and I am absolutely certain that in order to satisfactorily answer all those, I'll need a great deal more time than I have. In relation to the first part of your general comments, that it is not that I am saying parapsychology should have a paradigm in the sense that the physical sciences have, the drift of my argument is that that's not what one should be after, because when I come down to propose the theory, I'm specifically talking about a speculative-metaphysical theory, not a paradigm. If you allow me to put it this way: physics, chemistry and these natural sciences may be said to have a paradigm in the sense that they have a theory as well as a methodology. The social sciences, I believe, neither have a distinctive methodology nor a theory which will unify the data in the way it should be done in a properly objective systematic study. Learning from their experience, as it were, parapsychology should at least be avoiding this absence of a theory altogether, a theory which might give us the unifying framework. Hence, I propose a meta-physical theory.

About the unreality of things at a certain stage, this is one of the beliefs that happens to be ascribed to Indian thinking in general, but that's a complete misrepresentation. There are many very different systems of Indian philosophy, and only one of them goes in that direction, and the concepts that I have used are derived from very many different systems. So it's not as though it is built into this theory that the universe be viewed as being essentially unreal, certainly I'm not for it. Now, if this still happens, I don't know whether I would like to pre-judge this possibility. Remember, I have talked about many different levels. On most of these levels there should be no question of the world being in any sense unreal, but perhaps at the mystical, the highest plane, as you say, this is conceivable and if that happens, well, that's the way it is. I would hate to say anything more than that.

FRENCH: What interests me is that, given the suggested metaphysics, as I understand it, the notions of space and time and causality are at best instrumental at a certain level of awareness, and yet it seems to me those notions are essential, as we understand it, to explanation. I'm wondering if the explanation, at the level of awareness that you're considering, might be that what the parapsychologist is interested in would then become redundant or totally unnecessary. I'm also wondering if your view of a paradigm isn't indeed the ordinary notion and that what we have here isn't a scientific paradigm that might arise from the metaphysics you suggest, but something like a religious paradigm or even better still, a community interest of some kind. Beyond that, I'm wondering if you haven't done something that parapsychologists have been wanting to do for some time, and that is turn the worm, as it were, on the sciences. If we adopt the metaphysics you suggest, then don't we have the same kind of things to say in criticism of the standard sciences that they have been saying all along about parapsychology? Doesn't their work become less significant and the work of the parapsychologist more significant if we adopt your view? Is it not true, that scientific knowledge becomes specific for a state that, given the metaphysics, is of a lower level or grade than the state of interest to parapsychologists?

THAKUR: I do want to make a distinction between explanation by cause and explanation by reason. Now, it is true that the physical sciences largely do what is called explaining by causes, and therefore, of course, space/time and causation are important. But there is another kind of explanation—explanation by reasons. I would have thought that at the particular level I'm talking about, at a higher level, if you like, the explanation of those phenomena will be in terms of reasons rather than causes. Now whether, in fact, the adoption of my sort of theory would imply that the sciences, as it were, become less prior, I'm not sure. But if that happens, I don't think it would worry me in the least, because it is a feeling I have, that the sciences have probably misled themselves a little and certainly have misled us a little, and a check of some sort, whether in terms of a theory or anything else, probably couldn't do much harm.

GRUBER: I want to add a remark on Dr. Thakur's interpretation of a paradigm, somewhat referring to what John Beloff and Seymour Mauskopf pointed out. I think that Dr. Thakur said that a theory and a methodology are required for parapsychologists shifting from pre-paradigmatic science to paradigmatic science. But in Kuhn's sense paradigms also exist without any theory. I think this is pointed out in Kuhn's remarks in "Reflections on my Critics." He says that any scientific community has had a paradigm whether or not it has pro-vided a theory involved in this paradigm. Compare, for example, systematic botany and zoology under Linnaeus, or Rhine's scientific program which started with what Margaret Masterman called an arti-fact paradigm.

THAKUR: Well, I don't know that I will, in Kuhnian terms, anyway, be particularly sympathetic to accepting that a paradigm can simply and only involve a methodology without a theory. I have a feeling that, in fact, biology up to Linnaeus is regarded as a pre-paradigm science just for that reason, so I don't feel that I would quite agree with your suggestion. What I'm after is, really, the emphasis on the community. There are, as Penelhum pointed out earlier, certain sorts of phenomena requiring investigation; certain sorts of people who like investigating those. Now if they had a theory which gave them an over-view of what they are doing and why they are doing what they are doing, it will be a good thing. That's all I'm after. I don't think it would be a particularly interesting exercise for me to look for any-thing more or try to mime or mimic anything else, whether it's physics, biology, or what have you.

PARAPSYCHOLOGY AND THE AMERICAN PSYCHOLOGISTS: A STUDY OF SCIENTIFIC AMBIVALENCE

Seymour H. Mauskopf
AND
Michael R. McVaugh

The history of science is replete with cases of new scientific fields or specialties coming into existence, often accompanied by radical conceptual or methodological innovation, and finding a berth in established scientific activity. There are also the cases of old scientific interests being dropped from serious scientific consideration as "wrong" and outmoded or, worse, superstitious. Experimental chemistry and mathematical mechanics in the 17th- and 18th-centuries, experimental psychology in the late 19th are examples of the first set of cases, Aristotelian physics, alchemy and astrology of the second. Psychical research/parapsychology provides a unique intermediate example. This field has not yet really succeeded in finding acceptance into the mainstream of science, yet it has persisted in maintaining connections with science, claims to scientific attention, and its own dream of eventual incorporation into organized science. In order to examine the complex relation between parapsychology and more established science, I shall discuss the history of parapsychology's interaction with academic American psychology down to 1940, focusing on the reactions and attitudes of the psychologists to this would-be specialty of their own field.*

In his monograph *Extra-Sensory Perception* (1934), J. B. Rhine de-

*The material for this paper is largely taken from a book on the history of experimental psychical research and parapsychology which I am writing in collaboration with Professor Michael R. McVaugh of the Department of History, University of North Carolina. In particular, Professor McVaugh deserves the credit for the material of the second half of this paper, though I have reworked it somewhat (and therefore accept the responsibility for any misinterpretation or error of fact). We wish to thank Dr. J. B. Rhine for permission to use and cite material from his papers. Much of the research for this paper was done under NSF grants GS-39680/1.

fended the denotation of his subject as "parapsychology" by arguing that it was "beside" psychology—i.e., that psychology was the science most closely related to parapsychology.[1] It was particularly appropriate that this point be made by an American in the major *experimental* study of psychic ability. For there had long been a relation between academic psychology and psychical research.

This relation was never a broad one; it was only occasionally close; and moreover, it was usually acerbic. Yet nothing quite like it existed elsewhere, and the course of psychical research and parapsychology in the United States has been indelibly colored by it. It went back some fifty years prior to the appearance of *Extra-Sensory Perception*, and was to reach something of a climax in the decade after this monograph appeared.

Psychical research became systematically organized in the U.S. at just the time when academic psychology was coming into focus as a field distinct from philosophy, medicine, and psychiatry. In 1884, the American Society for Psychical Research was born. The Society's early membership reflected the interest (or, I might say, the concern) of some of the founders of American psychology. One of its first Vice-Presidents was the great rival to William James as founder of American psychology, G. Stanley Hall. Active members included James himself, Joseph Jastrow (the first Ph.D. in American psychology and Hall's own student), Morton Prince of Harvard, and the psychologically-interested philosophers, Charles Peirce and Josiah Royce.

By 1900, American psychology had grown into an established and visible scientific field, with major emphasis in experimental psychology. There were flourishing graduate programs in psychology here at Harvard, Johns Hopkins, Cornell and Chicago, with departments at many other universities and colleges.

Organized psychical research in America had not been nearly so successful. The original ASPR disbanded and was absorbed by the London SPR in 1890, not to be revived in the U.S. until 1907. That the ASPR went under so rapidly was partly due to the fact that American psychical research suffered a lack of sympathetic intelligentsia to support it (in comparison with European countries). There was hardly anyone in the U.S. *ca* 1900 of the intellectual eminence of an Oliver Lodge, a Lord Rayleigh, or an A. J. Balfour in England, or a Charles Richet in France, to support psychical research. Hardly anyone, but not quite no one. For the psychologist William James, the most eminent of American psychologists, was highly sympathetic towards the study of psychic phenomena and carried out important studies himself.[2] And the other psychologists who belonged to the original ASPR, most notably Jastrow and G. Stanley Hall, were, if not sympathetic, certainly concerned about psychical research. By this, I mean that they were skeptical and often scathingly critical of the field, but they were obviously intrigued by it. They were willing to be associated with psychical research societies and they took the research seriously enough to subject it to elaborate rebuttal.

As academic, experimental psychologists, their position (Hall and Jastrow) was that psychical research could only become a legitimate research subject insofar as it accepted the strategy, outlook, and professionalism of the experimental psychologist. As Jastrow put it in 1900: "If the problems of Psychical Research, or that portion of the problems in which the investigation seems profitable, are ever to be illuminated and exhibited in an intelligible form, it will only come about when they are investigated by the same methods and in the same spirit as are active psychological problems, when they are studied in connection with and as a part of other general problems of normal and abnormal Psychology. Whether this is done under the auspices of a society or in the psychological laboratories of universities is, of course, a detail of no importance. It is important, however, what the trend and the spirit, and the method and the purpose of the investigation may be; and it is equally important, what may be the training, and the capabilities, and the resources, and the originality and the scholarship of the investigator."[3] However, it must be admitted that there was a joker in the psychologist's attitude: Jastrow's and others' insistence on psychological training for the psychical researcher barely veiled a generally negative *a prior* attitude towards the existence of psychic phenomena and entities. Hence built into their attitude was a basic circularity nearly impossible to break. While they insisted on the rigor of experimental psychology to "test" psychical phenomena, they were sufficiently skeptical so as to be quite sure that such test could only yield negative results.

This complex of attitudes towards psychical research—and, it must be pointed out, the seriousness with which it was viewed—was clearly illustrated by the review G. Stanley Hall published of the first six volumes of the *Proceedings* of the SPR and of Gurney, Myers & Podmore's *Phantasms of the Living*, in 1887, in the first volume of his *American Journal of Psychology*.[4] Hall's review is surely one of the longest and most elaborate critiques psychical research has ever received from a psychologist. The first part of this review was given over to criticism of experimental techniques and here he was scathing: the English experimenters had omitted crucial details of their set-ups, had provided incomplete protocols, and had in general shown remarkable naiveté concerning the possibility of fraud and hyperaesthesia. Moreover, to the experimental psychologist, it would have been important to record the details of *mistaken* guesses for the patterns they might reveal concerning the sensory modality closest to the "psychic" transfer. For example, consistent confusion of "9" and "5" in number guessing might well suggest that the means of communication resembled auditory transfer of information. None of this had been done. Hall's point in all of this was to emphasize what he considered to be the unprofessional and casual procedures of the English investigators.

But what if rigorous and competent methods were used? To Hall, they could only play a destructive role. For he was convinced that telepathy (the subject of his review) did not exist. The reason for his conviction seemed to stem in part from his scorn for the spiritualist associations of psychical research. But more specifically, telepathy seemed to undercut the psycho-physiological basis of mental activity. Telepathy, he argued, was in conflict with the law of "isolated conductivity," whereby sensory signals passing along one nerve fiber did not jump to another no matter how close they were. Hall asked rhetorically of telepathy: "Is it likely that a neural state should jump from one brain to another, through a great interval, when intense stimuli on one nerve cannot affect another in the closest contact with it?" Given not merely the difficulty of a possible neurological mechanism for telepathy but indeed its inconceivability (at least as far as late 19th-century neurology and physiology were concerned), even the use of statistical evidence favoring telepathy did not impress Hall.

Similar refutations of the possible existence of telepathy were leveled by other psychologists. Hugo Münsterberg at Harvard, for example, argued that the purported existence of psychic phenomena threatened to undercut the entire program of psychology (and the other sciences) to construct a public, objective mechanical world-view, and, as a result: "We reject every claimed feat in which the psychological fact were without a physical substratum, as in the case of departed spirits and those in which psychical facts influenced one another without physical intermediation, as in telepathy."[5] For good measure, Jastrow injected another theme into the chorus of objections to psychical research: the professional one. By its prominence in the public mind and its popular association with psychology, psychical research gave a false—and damaging—public image to experimental psychology: "The right appreciation of scientific aims and ideals by the intelligent and influential public has come to be almost indispensable to the favorable advancement of science. Psychology can less afford than many another science to dispense with this helpful influence; and no science can remain unaffected by persistent misinterpretation of its true end and aims. If Psychical Research is to continue in its present temper, it becomes essential to have it clearly understood just how far its purposes and spirit are, and how much farther they are not, in accord with the purposes and the spirit of Psychology. The optimistic psychologist anticipates the day when he will no longer be regarded, either in high life or in low life, as a collector of ghost stories or an investigator of mediums."[6]

Thus, serious though they may have been about psychical research, the majority of American psychologists at the turn of the century could hardly be called "encouraging" in their attitude to it. To be sure, there was the major exception of William James. James' attitude towards psychical research was almost the mirror-image of Hall's and Jastrow's. Unlike them, he was open-minded to the possibility of supernormal psychic phenomena and even to the spiritualist hypothesis. His subtle, complex, holistic psychology made him much more conducive to tolerance on these matters than almost all of his colleagues. James participated actively and enthusiastically in the work of the British and American SPR and he devoted much time and energy to studying and publicizing the psychic abilities of Mrs. Leonore Piper. By the same token, however, James did not make an issue of the necessity for psychical research to be a laboratory experimental science. He himself conducted no laboratory studies in psychical research and seemed content to base his conclusions on his personal investigations of mediums like Mrs. Piper or upon reports of his English colleagues.

But, by-and-large, the skepticism and suspicion in which psychical research was held by most American psychologists, was the dominant attitude. Insofar as they took it seriously, it was to debunk the field, not to do any positive research themselves, much less to teach it. This was brought out vividly in two surveys of the place occupied by psychical research in the American university system, one of 1898 and the other of 1917.[7] In the first survey, eleven psychologists were polled; in the second, twelve. In the first, only two psychologists gave any positive or substantive evidence of teaching about psychical research (H. Gale of Minnesota, the survey-taker, and William James); in the second survey, no one admitted to treating the subject in any but a most peripheral way. (James was dead by then.)

Yet the very existence of these surveys shows that, to some people, psychical research was considered naturally to have its home in the network of American psychology departments, if anywhere. And, by 1917, despite the negative response to the second survey, experimental psychical research had in fact found a precarious home in the psychology department at three major universities: Clark, Stanford, and Harvard. All three universities had been the recipients of special bequests for the furtherance of psychical research. The funds had been accepted with misgivings in all three cases, but at Stanford and Harvard research fellows in the psychology departments had been appointed: L. T. Troland at Harvard and J. E. Coover at Stanford.[8]

Troland was only appointed in 1916 and had time to carry out very limited experiments before America's entry into World War I disrupted his psychological laboratory. Coover had been appointed at Stanford in 1912. In the ensuing five years, he had had time to carry out what was certainly the most ambitious set of experiments in psychical research to that date. His results were published in a massive monograph by Stanford University in 1917; Troland's were published in the same year in a small, privately printed pamphlet.[9]

The research that both these men did—trained psychologists as they were—conformed closely with the attitudes towards psychical research dominant in psychology. It was carried out as experimental psychology, in the laboratory rather than the séance parlor. Test materials which were both manageable and measurable were used. Each man's work reflected aspects of experimental and theoretical approaches then current: Coover, for example, used the elaborate introspection techniques of Wundtian-Titchnerian psychology; Troland's principal theoretical idea was the reflex-arc concept, then so prevalent in functionalist and behaviorist psychology (although Troland was not a Behaviorist). Moreover, Troland introduced a thoroughgoing mechanized test situation, so as to promote exact reproducibility and "eliminate the personal equation of the researcher." Both made use of statistically analyzable data.

In one other respect, Troland and Coover conformed to the attitudes of their fellow psychologists: both were skeptical about psychic phenomena. If it goes too far to characterize them as *a prior* disbelievers in telepathy, it would also be a distortion to say that they expected to find anything in their data. Coover's conclusion to his massive testing program was: "That no trace of any objective thought-transference is found either as a capacity shared in a low degree by our normal reagents [subjects] in general [Richet's 'suggestion Mentale'] or as a capacity enjoyed in perceptible measure by any of the individual normal reagents."[10] A conclusion which J. B. Rhine, R. H. Thouless and Cyril Burt were later to criticize as not really warranted by the data. Troland, compiling very limited data (some 605 trials) was unable to conclude much of anything (he did note that his results were 1.5 times the standard deviation below chance). Neither man ever published any experimental sequels to his 1917 *opus* (although Coover remained Psychical Research Fellow at Stanford until 1937).

Nevertheless, psychical research had been carried out in psychology departments of two major universities, something unprecedented in any other country, and itself a reflection of the degree of seriousness with which the subject was taken by early American psychologists. Yet the concomitant skepticism and even hostility made the housing of psychical research in university psychology departments very precarious. 1917 could well have marked the end of academic psychical research in the U.S.

That it did not was due to the arrival at Harvard of a new Professor of Psychology in the fall of 1921: William McDougall. McDougall was then in his fiftieth year, a psychologist of international reputation. Moreover, he was highly sympathetic to psychical research; and indeed had been President of the London SPR in 1920. In part, this attitude was a reflection of his English background, where psychical research enjoyed much more sympathy from the academic elite than it did in the United States. In part, it reflected the Jamesian orientation of McDougall's own psychology. In part, it was connected with McDougall's own general anti-materialism, expressed in his belief in what he himself called psychic "animism" and in purposive behavior of the organism, as well as in psychic events and abilities.

Being the senior Professor of Psychology at Harvard, McDougall was in a position to do something for which there had been no opportunity in England—to revive psychical research there under the auspices of the special bequest of the Hodgson Fund that had supported Troland's work. In 1922, a young psychologist who had, in fact, assisted Troland back in 1917 and now was completing his Ph.D. at Columbia, was named Hodgson Fellow. This was Gardner Murphy. Unlike his predecessor Troland (as well as Coover and most American psychologists), Murphy not only took psychical research seriously, but was highly sympathetic to it. In this respect, he resembled both William James and McDougall. In his actual psychic research, Murphy's resemblance to James extends further, for Murphy never felt easy about using strict "laboratory" techniques, or using readily quantifiable materials to test for psychic abilities. Rather, he felt more at home with psychic incidents or psychic material which had rich emotional associations for his subjects.

Murphy was Hodgson Fellow from 1922–1925 (publishing none of his results). He was succeeded by G. H. Estabrooks from 1925–1926. With McDougall's removal from Harvard to Duke in 1927, subsidized psychical research at Harvard once again lapsed; Hodgson Fund money was not to be used again to support psychical research (parapsychology) until 1938.

But during McDougall's tenure at Harvard, psychical research received a wider academic exposure than at any previous time. Various graduate students assisted the Hodgson Fellows. Thus, Harry Helson who acted as Murphy's assistant, reminisces about how he and Murphy used to visit McDougall "to talk about our last séance with Margery or about some medium I had investigated or about the phenomena at our last table-tipping session in the laboratory."[11] Reference to "Margery" brings to mind the great psychic *cause célèbre* of these years: "Margery, the medium"—the wife of a Boston surgeon whose abilities were investigated under the auspices of *Scientific American* and on whose Investigation Committee sat McDougall and Murphy (as alternate). Not only did "Margery" receive national publicity; she also elicited considerable interest among the Harvard faculty and advanced students. The most notable psychologist to express curiosity (even taking part in sittings with her) was Edwin G. Boring, about whose interest in parapsychology we shall hear more presently.

One result of the focus of interest in psychical research at Harvard in the mid-1920's was the organization of a Symposium in November, 1926, at Clark University under the sponsorship of its psychology professor Carl Murchison. The papers of the meeting were published as the book, *The Case For and Against Psychical Belief.* McDougall's paper was a plea for university sponsorship of psychical research; Murphy's, a plea for experimental research.[12]

But despite this uptake of activity and curiosity, the thread of serious interest in psychical research on the part of academic psychologists was, in fact, a very thin one in the late 1920's. The reasons are not hard to discover. At best, the revival of the Hodgson Fellowship and the hubbub over "Margery" in the mid-1920's had been evanescent. None of the Hodgson Fellows had continued with serious psychical research; even Gardner Murphy, who was to return to active interest in the 1930's, had largely gone on to more orthodox projects after 1925. Coover was silent out in California. To the community of academic psychologists the results of the work at Stanford and Harvard could hardly have looked very exciting. Indeed, they were unlikely to have known of any of it except possibly Coover's, and his was the one study with a strongly negative conclusion.

Estabrooks, it is true, published an article on experimental telepathy centering on his own tests in *The North American Review.*[13] The article was a thoughtful one, but its overall tone was hardly encouraging. Estabrooks dwelt on the problem of fraud in psychical testing, citing an ingenious trick played on himself by two sophomores, presumably when he was carrying out his tests under the *aegis* of the Hodgson Fund. While he by no means ruled out his own experiments as possible evidence for telepathy, noting that he had obtained above-chance results and a curious pattern of decline in success as each experiment proceeded and which would have been difficult collectively to fabricate, he refused to endorse them either, because of the real possibility of fraud and incomplete safeguards against sensory cues. His conclusion reinforced the pessimism of the body of the article: "Thus, you see, telepathy is still as [sic] unanswered puzzle. Those cases which seem most striking are very hard indeed to refute. But proof in science is repeatability, and every time we attempt to repeat these experiments in the laboratory we have a dismal failure. Why? I do not know. Possibly because the whole thing is a mass of fraud, superstition and faulty observation. But also possibly because we cannot introduce violent emotion into laboratory technique. Which of these alternatives is correct we must leave to the future."

There was thus no reason for academic psychologists either to see in experimental research the potential for fruitful endeavor or a serious anomaly to be debunked. Even for a James, a G. Stanley Hall or a Jastrow, psychical research had been peripheral to their principal professional work back at the turn of the century. By the late 1920's, James and Hall were long since dead; Jastrow was quiet. Their intense reactions to psychical research, both pro and con, had been all but swamped by the silence and indifference of a new generation of psychologists who had research interests of their own to pursue. Academic experimental psychical research had all but died a second time, a mere decade after the first near fatality.

It would take nothing less than a spectacular claim of university-based research to rekindle interest (and opposition) among psychologists. This was provided, once again, under McDougall's auspices at Duke University, where he went in 1927 and in the work of J. B. Rhine. Beginning in 1930, Rhine conducted experimental tests with Duke students, the results of which were written up in monograph form by the fall of 1933 and published as *Extra-Sensory Perception* in April, 1934. The importance of Rhine's book was recognized in psychical research circles at once, although it was by no means received with unqualified approbation. Rhine had not only discovered spectacular test subjects, but had also brought together into synthesis many of the issues, approaches and conclusions of the earlier psychical research tradition.[14]

Rhine also had tried consciously to relate his work to experimental psychology, as his choice of the term "parapsychology," indicated. He gave considerable attention to the psychological aspects of the ESP test situation: the conditions of stress and relaxation, attention and abstraction, interests and boredom; the effect of stimulants and depressants, of the presence of outsiders or of change in the nature of the test. He systematically preceded his account of each major subject with a personality profile, intending thereby to suggest correlations between conscious or unconscious motivation and scoring. The very test material—the ESP cards (or "Zener cards" as they were originally called)—was designed by Rhine's colleague in the Duke psychology department, Karl Zener, with the idea of insuring greater uniformity of response from the subjects than playing cards could, as well as much greater computational ease. The strong emphasis on statistically-computable card guessing as the testing method for psychical ability was also part of the tradition of American academic psychical research.[14a]

Rhine's monograph certainly contained the ingredients to engage the community of academic psychologists. But the psychologists were at first relatively slow to react. In part, this had to do with Rhine's own professional relation to psychology. Rhine was not a trained psychologist. It was only after he had been at Duke a few years that he became a member of the Duke psychology department. Although he was a member of that department by the time *Extra-Sensory Perception* was published, he had as yet no professional credentials in that field and presumably few professional acquaintances outside the local university departments and those psychologists with whom he and his wife had come into contact during the year they had spent in auditing courses at Harvard before coming to Duke.

Moreover, *Extra-Sensory Perception* was published by a source not likely to be readily available to psychologists: the Boston SPR. As a result, there was little reaction from the psychologists to Rhine's monograph throughout the rest of 1934. The few responses that there were in that year—three in number—bear out this point. For two of them were from men with long involvements in psychical research: Joseph Jastrow (a very negative response[15]) and Gardner Murphy (an enthusiastic review in the *Journal of General Psychology*[16]). And even though the third respondent, R. R. Willoughby, had had no previous direct involvement in psychical research, he was at a university with at least marginal involvement (Clark University); indeed, Willoughby's own salary had been at first paid out of the psychical research fund there.[17]

Willoughby's attitude presaged what was going to be a general response of psychologists over the next two years. He was skeptical but interested enough to try seriously to grapple with the methodological problems of ESP research. His first tack was to probe the statistical assumptions and methods Rhine had employed, questioning Rhine's use of a theoretical normal distribution without an empirical check.[18] Added to this later, were criticisms of the experimental method as reported in *Extra-Sensory Perception*. Despite his search for weaknesses in Rhine's work, Willoughby was intrigued by it; he remained in active contact with Rhine, paid a visit to the Duke laboratory in April, 1935, and, in 1936, put an undergraduate of his on to testing for ESP.

By 1936, more psychologists had reacted to Rhine's work; the interest in psychical research which had lain dormant for so long in the academic psychological community was beginning to revive. Some of this interest was stirred up among young psychologists who had had connections with Duke and/or Stanford: R. C. Carpenter of Bard College, R. Wilfred George of Tarkio College and Eugene Adams at Colgate (philosophy) were examples. But for others, their attention was caught by the publicity that Rhine's work had received in the press and periodicals. Rhine's monograph had been picked up by a group of science writers. Some of these, like Waldemar Kaempffert of the *New York Times*, had had previous involvement with psychical research.[19] In addition, their synoptic view of science, necessitated by their work as science writers, made these men aware of the profoundly unsettling implications of the revolution which had taken place in physics in the 1920's, for the traditional materialism which had been the philosophical bulwark against the claims of psychical research. Largely through the activities of the science writers, Rhine's work was placed and kept before the public.

As a result of dissemination through personal contacts and through the newspapers and periodicals, Rhine had received inquiries about his work from at least a dozen psychologists by late 1936. Some of his correspondents carried out their own tests, occasionally with unsettlingly (to them) positive results.[20] Perhaps the most notable indication of the rising interest of psychologists in Rhine's work was an invitation to him from Edwin G. Boring of Harvard to speak to the Psychological Colloquium about his work. Boring had been seriously interested in (if skeptical about) psychical abilities and phenomena ever since he had come to Harvard in 1922. He had taken part in sittings with "Margery" and in connection with this, he had published an article in *Atlantic Monthly* in 1926 in which he had offered thoughtful if strong criticism of psychical research.[21] His main criticism, one which became something of a keynote of his, was that psychical research was sterile for scientific research in that it asserted *negative* propositions—that psychical phenomena and abilities were produced by no normal means. Yet, Boring was by no means unremittingly hostile or close-minded and in 1935 he was one of the psychologists who contacted Rhine about his work. Before and after Rhine's visit to Harvard, Boring and Rhine engaged in extensive epistolary discussions of the issues of parapsychology.

The visit took place on November 18, 1936. Rhine had some quite understandable trepidation about how he and his work would be received. But, in fact, he appears to have impressed his auditors with his thoroughgoing thoughtfulness, not only in handling all their objections but also raising (and answering) some they hadn't brought up.

By the start of 1937, then, parapsychology seemed at last on the verge of receiving some acceptance from the academic psychological community as a "normal" field of research. Significantly, Gardner Murphy at Columbia, who had been quietly supportive of Rhine's work, became more public, publishing a popular article in *The American Magazine* in November, 1936,[2] and making a request to Boring in the Spring of 1937 that the Hodgson Fund be reopened for use in psychical research.[23] It must be pointed out, however, how very difficult it is to gauge just how far the favorable change in attitude towards parapsychology had proceeded and exactly what it meant, due to the scanty and fragmentary nature of our evidence for these years. That the subject was discussed informally at professional meetings we know was true, but equally apparent is its absence from the professional correspondence between psychologists.[24] Those psychologists who did take up the testing for ESP did not advance beyond the attempt at replication to any of the more purely psychological issues Rhine had raised in his monograph; indeed, the parapsychologists themselves no longer had the striking success in finding good subjects that they had achieved in the early 1930's. It seems clear that to most psychologists, parapsychological research remained remote from their interests.

Yet no newly-developing sub-field attracts more than a small core of researchers at first. Parapsychology had clearly elicited serious and even sympathetic interest from a group of psychologists and showed many of the signs of building quietly into a sub-specialty of academic psychology. But, by the fall of 1937, there were ominous signs of impending confrontation. Before then, although Rhine had had his critics, such as Jastrow, they had kept their criticism private. Now, in October, 1937, the first published criticism by a professional psychologist, Chester E. Kellogg of McGill University, appeared in the semi-popular *The Scientific Monthly*.[25] This was followed by journal articles, book reviews, and denunciations and defences at professional meetings through the winter and spring of 1937–1938.

The cause of this series of outbursts against parapsychology lay, ironically, in the same source of much of the earlier interest: publicity. From 1934 to the end of 1936, the publicity parapsychology had received, although generous, had remained fairly constant in level and format, being mostly newspaper and magazine articles by science writers, newspapermen and occasionally Rhine himself. But in November and December 1936 there appeared two articles in *Harper's Magazine* by the chairman of the English Department of Columbia University, E. H. Wright.[26] The articles, well-written synopses of Rhine's work, in themselves added nothing new to the discussion of ESP. But they were by an academic in a journal widely read by academics and the well-educated generally, on the one hand; on the other, Wright was not a scientist and yet was discoursing on and evaluating a controversial matter of scientific, and particularly psychological, import. Wright's articles became the point of departure for Kellogg's *Scientific Monthly* attack.[27]

In 1937, publicity for parapsychology intensified and broadened out to include new forms. Weekly radio broadcasts by the Zenith Radio Corporation began September 5 and included both dramatizations and mass telepathy tests. In October, a popular book on parapsychology by Rhine, entitled *New Frontiers of the Mind*, was published and made a Book-of-the-Month Club selection. Also at about this time, the Zenith Corporation made ESP cards available on a commercial basis to the public.

One usually thinks of scientific controversy as being engendered by developments within science itself. This one, however, seems to have been largely brought about by extra-scientific factors. Indeed, when, in the midst of the controversy, an important new research development was published—the work in psychokinesis—it did not cause so much as a ripple of reaction from the psychologists. There is no question that some psychologists, who either had not previously given parapsychology much attention or who had thought it unnecessary to state their views, were stung into action by what they took to be unwarranted publicity for a field which, in their eyes, still had to establish its scientific credentials.[28]

But, however motivated and however emotional in tone, most of the critiques concentrated on the specific issues of ESP investigation. Not for these psychologists (in print, at least) were the broad philosophical questions which had exercised predecessors of theirs, like Münsterberg. One would be very hard pressed to identify the "school" of psychology to which any of the critics adhered from their published criticism of parapsychology. Issues of materialism vs. the anti-materialistic implications of parapsychology were certainly raised at this time, but by the science writers and the book reviewers, not by the psychologists.[29] The psychologists concentrated on statistical issues (particularly that having to do with statistical distribution) and methodological issues (adequate safeguards, the problem of recording errors, optional stopping, selection of data, etc.).[30]

The active opposition to parapsychology among psychologists was actually quite small, if vocal. What was the attitude of the professional psychological community generally to parapsychology in the wake of the publicity and controversy? Unlike the situation in 1936, we are in a position to give some answer to this—from questionnaires sent out to members of the American Psychological Association in February and in July, 1938, to ascertain just this.[31] The responses to the July questionnaire (which survive in the Rhine papers) show that the events of 1937 had by no means caused the profession generally to adopt a hostile posture towards parapsychology. 352 of the 603 full members of the A.P.A. replied. Regarding the existence of ESP, 5 accepted it as established, 26 admitted it as likely, and 128 as a remote possibility; 142 labelled it as "merely an unknown" and 51 ruled it out as impossible. As to its investigation, 89% agreed that this was legitimate scientific research and 76% accepted it as "within the province of academic psychology." Interestingly enough, there was practically no disparity in age between the mild-to-active espousers and the strong opponents of ESP. Where any differentiation lay was in professional activity: clinicians and abnormal psychologists tended to be sympathetic; experimentalists, critical.

The survey reflected the persistence of the ambivalence towards parapsychology which had characterized American psychology earlier in the century. Skeptical though most psychologists were of ESP, most could not bring themselves dogmatically to rule it out as an impossibility and they were also willing to see it treated seriously. If the publicity of Rhine's work in 1937 had highlighted the opposition within psychology to parapsychology, it had also brought out the felt need to examine the issue seriously. In order to do so, a symposium on parapsychology was arranged for the national A.P.A. meetings held in Columbus, Ohio in September, 1938. John Kennedy of Stanford and Harold Gulliksen of Chicago were the critics; Rhine and Murphy the principle defenders of parapsychology.

Not unexpectedly, confrontation more than dispassionate examination marked the session, even to the factionalized auditors. Yet, to many minds, parapsychology came out ahead from this session, the reasonableness of Rhine and Murphy contrasting with what looked to some psychologists as unscientific dogmatism on their opponents' part. Psychology and parapsychology had, for once, officially been brought nto contact at a national meeting.

In the ensuing developments, there were signs that the events of 1937–1938 actually enhanced the potential for parapsychology's winning a niche in psychology. In 1939, Rhine was voted Associate Membership in the A.P.A.; an Advisory Committee of A.P.A. members was established to vett and comment upon articles submitted to the *Journal of Parapsychology*. The parapsychologists, for their part, made efforts to respond to criticisms and suggestions of the psychologists. The Pratt-Woodruff paper of 1939, for example, had an unprecedented degree of detailed description of the experimental situation and design, eliciting from the Advisory Committee generous praise: "The members of the Committee have been impressed with the thoroughness with which the experimental work had been conducted and the report written up. From the standpoint of 'repeatability' the report is very satisfactory. The procedure has been described in complete detail. Every step is explicitly written up."[32] In the early summer of 1939, Rhine and his group wrote a large-scale updating of the 1934 monograph, this one quite consciously written with the academic psychologists in mind and containing elaborate expositions and rebuttals of the main criticisms which had been levelled against experimental parapsychology. Titled *Extra-Sensory Perception After Sixty Years*, the book was published in 1940 and was the climactic effort by the Duke group to "normalize" parapsychology within academic psychology.

By the end of the 1930's, then, there were promising indications for the future of parapsychology *vis-à-vis* academic psychology. But the process of normalization did not advance beyond the level reached in 1939–1940. It would be beyond the scope of this paper to account for what went wrong. But I shall hazard some general thoughts. First, it should be apparent that to view the reception of parapsychology by psychologists in the 1930's and even earlier in blanket terms as the refusal of orthodox science to entertain radical innovation would be a gross oversimplification. It is perhaps closer to the truth to say that this reception exemplified the difficulties any marginal area of research encounters in gaining recognition and support, aggravated by the aspects peculiar to parapsychology: its background association with spiritualism and the occult, its radical departure from accepted scientific values, and its perennial appeal to the non-scientifically trained public. Scientists had and continue to have mixed (and therefore, perhaps, all the more intense) feelings towards parapsychology, arising out of their own image of what science is and how it came to its present state. On the one hand, the spiritualist, occult and antimaterialistic context of psychical research and parapsychology are viewed by scientists as just those features of pre-modern belief that the Scientific Revolution and its aftermath succeeded in combatting and expunging from scientific consideration. On the other hand, there has always been an important component of scientific ideology since that very same Scientific Revolution, which has emphasized the virtue of open-mindedness towards radical innovation and the liability of dogmatism. Did not Galileo succeed by his daring? Was he not made to suffer because of the intransigence of his Aristotelian opponents?

There has always been a considerable degree of this ambivalence in the reaction of American psychologists to psychical research and parapsychology. In the post-1934 years, the component of open-mindedness began to come to the fore in the wake of Rhine's claims and, despite the reaction of some to the publicity of 1937–1938, continued to be present in the minds of most psychologists, as the 1938 surveys bear witness. But we must be careful to specify what this "open-mindedness" or "receptivity" towards parapsychology actually meant—and what it did not mean. Clearly, it meant willingness to allow Rhine's results and claims to receive serious consideration. But much less clearly did it mean that academic psychologists then or earlier were prepared to push the new field themselves: to do any sustained investigations, to encourage their own students to take up research in ESP, or to hire a parapsychologist for their department. As we have seen, there was a group of psychologists who did respond to Rhine's work in the mid-1930's, and there was a handful of young psychologists who elected to take up parapsychological research on something like a full-time basis. It is just possible that the *rapprochement* following the September, 1938, A. P. A. symposium might have led to a more significant advance of parapsychology into a branch of academic psychology. But from the first, research and career opportunities in parapsychology were severely restricted and most of the young psychologists who took up parapsychology in the 1930's left the field after only a few years each. And in any case, it would seem that events were overtaken by World War II and the ensuing disruption of academic life. Even Rhine's staff was cut to skeleton size. In 1946, parapsychology was forced to begin again the struggle for academic and professional acceptance.

REFERENCES

[1] Rhine, J. B., *Extra-Sensory Perception* (Boston: Boston Society for Psychical Research, 1934), p. 7.

[2] There were also the neurologists and psychotherapists, headed by Morton Prince and James Jackson Putnam, who were sympathetic to psychical research from its inception. I thank Ms. Molly Noonan for letting me read her as yet unfinished dissertation, "Psychic Research and the American Scientific Community, 1880–1890" which deals with the attitudes of psychologists and psychotherapists to psychical research in Chapter 5.

[3] Jastrow, J., *Fact and Fable in Psychology* (Boston: Houghton Mifflin Co., 1900), p. 54–55.

[4] Hall, G. Stanley, *American Journal of Psychology*, 1887, *1*: pp. 128–146.

[5] Munsterberg, H., "Psychology and Mysticism," *Atlantic Monthly*, 1899, *83*: p. 82.

[6] Jastrow, *Fact and Fable*, pp. 76–77.

[7] Gale, H., "Psychical Research in American Universities," *Proceedings of the Society for Psychical Research*, 1898, *13*: pp. 583–587; J. H. Hyslop, "Psychical Research in American Universities," *Journal of the American Society for Psychical Research*, 1917, *11*: pp. 444–458.

[8] Dommeyer, F. C., "Psychical Research at Stanford University," *Journal of Parapsychology*, 1975, *39*: pp. 173–205.

[9] Coover, J. E., *Experiments in Psychical Research* (Leland Stanford Junior University Publications, Psychical Research Monograph No. 1, 1917); L. T. Troland, *A Technique for the Experimental Study of Telepathy and Other Alleged Clairvoyant Processes* (Albany, N.Y., The Brandon Printing Co., 1917).

[10] Coover, *Experiments in Psychical Research*, p. 124.

[11] In his autobiographical account in E. G. Boring and G. Lindzey (eds.), *A History of Psychology in Autobiography* (Vol. 5) (N.Y.: Appleton-Century-Crofts, 1967), p. 201.

[12] McDougall, W., "Psychical Research as a University Study,"; Murphy, G., "Telepathy as an Experimental Problem," C. Murchison (ed.), *The Case For and Against Psychical Belief* (Worcester, Mass.: Clark University Press, 1927), pp. 149–162 and 265–278 respectively. There were also articles by Coover and Jastrow.

[13] Estabrooks, G. H., "The Enigma of Telepathy," *The North American Review*, 1929, *227*: pp. 201–211.

[14] McVaugh, M. R., and Mauskopf, S. H., "J. B. Rhine's 'Extra-Sensory Perception' and Its Background in Psychical Research," *Isis*, June, 1976.

[14a] In *Extra-Sensory Perception*, Rhine claimed for parapsychology a place "clearly within the field of Psychology and, of course, full into the midst of Experimental Psychology," p. 6. Of course, many of the psychological points, and the card-guessing technique, had also been important in the psychical research tradition.

[15] As reported by Rhine to Lydia Allison, May 21, 1934, Rhine Papers, Department of Manuscripts, Duke University.

[16] Murphy, G., "Extra-Sensory Perception. A Review," *Journal of General Psychology*, 1934, *11*: pp. 454–458.

[17] Willoughby had come to Clark in abnormal psychology. One of the complimentary copies of *Extra-Sensory Perception* had been sent by Walter Franklin Prince to Carl Murchison at Clark. Murchison had probably given it to his associate, R. S. Hunter who, in turn, had interested Willoughby. There is extensive correspondence between Willoughby and Rhine in the Rhine papers.

[18] E.g. Willoughby, R. R., "A Critique of Rhine's 'Extra-Sensory Perception,'" and C. E. Stuart, "In Reply to the Willoughby Critique," *Journal of Abnormal and Social Psychology*, 1935–36, 30: pp. 199–207 and 384–388 respectively.

[19] Kaempffert had been on the Board of Trustees of the *American Society for Psychical Research* in the 1920's.

[20] E.g. J. F. Brown of the University of Kansas.

[21] Boring, E. G., "The Paradox of Psychic Research," *Atlantic Monthly*, 1926, *137*: pp. 81–87, especially 84–85.

[22] Murphy, G., "Things I Can't Explain," *The American Magazine*, 1936, *122*, *no. 5* (Nov., 1936), pp. 40–41, 130–132.

[23] This request following on Rhine's visit to Harvard and successful by the end of the year.

[24] Which we have examined at the Archives of the History of American Psychology, University of Akron.

[25] Kellogg, C. E., "New Evidence(?) For Extra-Sensory Perception," *Scientific Monthly*, 1937, *45*: pp. 331–341.

[26] Wright, E. H., "The Case For Telepathy," and "The Nature of Telepathy," *Harper's Magazine*, 1936, *173*: pp. 575–586 and *174*: pp. 13–21 respectively.

[27] Kellogg made this clear on the first page of his *Scientific Monthly* article.

[28] This was certainly true of B. F. Skinner, who also exposed the commercially prepared ESP cards of the Zenith Corporation as being imperfectly manufactured.

[29] The science writers stressing the relation of the anti-materialistic implications of the new physics to parapsychology; the *literati* book reviewers, curiously enough, defending traditional materialism.

[30] Perhaps the most searching of these being the one by Dael Wolfle, "A Review of the Work of Extra-Sensory Perception," *American Journal of Psychiatry*, 1938, *94*: pp. 943–955 (with reply by Rhine, pp. 957–960.

[31] The results of both surveys were published in the *Journal of Parapsychology*: L. Warner and C. C. Clark, "A Survey of Psychological Opinion on E.S.P.," 1938, *2*: pp. 296–301, and J. C. Crumbaugh, "A Questionnaire Designed to Determine the Attitudes of Psychologists Toward the Field of Extra-Sensory Perception," pp. 302–307. The Warner and Clark survey was the July, 1938 survey whose original data is preserved in the Rhine papers.

[32] "Letters and Notes," *Journal of Parapsychology*, 1939, *3*: p. 246.

DISCUSSION

DOMMEYER: I'm sure that Dr. Mauskopf is aware of this, but it was of interest to me that Coover and the authorities at Stanford reacted in an antagonistic way to Rhine's successes. Coover had taken the stand, of course, against psychical research and yet here was Rhine and the Duke people having this success, so when Coover retired, and they were thinking of getting a replacement for him, there was great caution always about not taking in a Duke man to succeed him. They seemed to be very much afraid that if they had brought in a Duke man, there would have been successes recorded and this would have been very embarrassing to them. I don't know whether you care to comment about that, but it was an interesting phase of this history at Stanford University.

MAUSKOPF: I don't know anything about a fear that a Duke man might get successes. That I've never come across. I do know that Coover was very evasive and then antagonistic towards Rhine and any of Rhine's emissaries. I would say that Coover himself is perhaps the best exemplification of this dilemma that this ambivalence towards parapsychology presents. It's very difficult for me, and I gather for you as well, to really figure out exactly what was Coover's attitude and why did he stick with this.

DOMMEYER: Well, I think Coover's, at least, expressed view was that he didn't regard Rhine's work as scientific. That was one of the reasons he didn't want Duke people in. He said that Rhine had nothing that would correlate with these excesses over chance scoring that he had got and therefore that it was not a scientific endeavor at all—that the excesses over chance had been the result of hidden variables, etc. This was the kind of thing he believed. So he didn't want someone trained in Rhine's methods to come over and succeed him. And there is correspondence that indicates that they feared that, if the Rhine people got in there using these unscientific methods, they would get successes in their results. Of course, Charles Stewart came in '42 and did get successful results and then this was officially denied by the university later on.

FRENCH: I just wonder if some of the ambivalence that you've been talking about amongst the orthodox psychologists might be due to the fact that in the history of psychology itself during the period in question, the orthodox psychologists were themselves occupied with the defense of their own subject against attacks from the physical sciences, so that the inclusion of parapsychology might have, in their view, made them even more susceptible to the kinds of attacks they were trying to fend off.

MAUSKOPF: I think you're probably right. There is relatively very little concrete evidence, although almost on *a priori* grounds it makes sense and we thought of that. Perhaps the only thing in my paper that bears on it, is the rest of the quotation from Joseph Jastrow of which I only read a sentence. At the very beginning of organized academic psychology, he says specifically, "We musn't allow this association with psychical research to continue. We have to make our case to the relevant fund-giving organizations." He puts it in those terms, "we need support, and if people think we're ghost-hunters and medium watchers, they won't support us."

NICOL: Dr. Mauskopf made a comparison between the early British SPR and the early American SPR and pointed out that the SPR of London got support from many scientists and scholars, whereas it was something rather different in the ASPR. The actual facts, Dr. Mauskopf, are somewhat different. The SPR was founded predominantly by spiritualists. They managed to bring in Frederic Myers and Edmund Gurney, who in turn persuaded Henry Sidgwick to accept the Presidency. There were hardly any scientists or scholars in the SPR in its early days. Apart from the physicist William Barrett there were two minor figures named Coffin and FitzGerald, and one Fellow of the Royal Society, Walter Weldon; and all four were spiritualists.

MAUSKOPF: I don't think I made, and I certainly didn't mean to make, the distinction that there were simply eminent scientists. I could see why it seems that way because I named Lord Rayleigh, Oliver Lodge, etc., but it was more the general intellectual support of eminent intellectuals of a variety of different disciplines in England as compared to America, that I was referring to.

NICOL: Rayleigh was not an original member, nor was Lodge; they came in later. By contrast, the American SPR was distinguished by the large number of scientists and intellectuals in its Council and membership. Nevertheless, in a few years it collapsed. I don't think the absence of spiritualists or the presence of scientists was the explanation of its failure. The membership consisted largely of prosperous Bostonians living in large houses in the Back Bay. But they failed to provide the necessary funds, and so in 1890 the Society died. The British SPR took over its assets, such as they were, and created an American Branch of the British SPR. Thereafter Sidgwick and Myers subsidized it very privately.

On another matter, I don't think that Stanley Hall is deserving of our respect. William James had serious reservations about him, saying that though Hall was not a liar in any vulgar meaning of the term, he had a talent for mystification. I may add that he practised a talent for misleading his readers. Hall and his assistant Amy Tanner conducted a series of investigations of Mrs. Piper, that very respectable lady medium. In a book nominally written by Dr. Tanner, Hall claimed that their report contained a full account of what transpired at the séances. But we have only to notice the peculiar brevity of the séance reports to realize that some items are missing. Indeed, William James afterwards wrote to J. G. Piddington, in London, that the alleged spirit of Hodgson had accused Hall of murdering his wife—no doubt an exaggeration, though the lady did die tragically.

Concerning the so-called "Zener cards," Dr. Zener told my wife (who spent a dozen years at the Parapsychology Laboratory), that he had objected to the use of his name for the ESP cards, because he was only one of several people who suggested symbols. In view of Zener's objection, the Duke Laboratory writers thereafter referred to the cards only as "ESP cards."

Lastly, Dr. Rhine's *Extra-Sensory Perception* is marred by a crippling weakness. The book consists mainly of reports of ESP experiments. Now, the test of the validity of any scientific report is: Could we, on the information provided, repeat the experiments under the same conditions? Unhappily, as R. H. Thouless pointed out, the book rarely describes what the experimental conditions were. Therefore nobody can even attempt to repeat the experiments. We cannot judge whether the original experiments were sound or unsound. The book therefore falls by the wayside.

MAUSKOPF: I bow, certainly, to your superior detailed knowledge about the early period, especially. About Zener's invention of the ESP cards, that I would say is still a matter of obscurity and controversy. We've asked numerous people at Duke, and on the whole, colleagues of Rhine and Zener who were around in the early thirties, have supported the claim that Zener invented them. I must confess, I don't know precisely that Zener did, but the weight of the evidence at Duke, at least, is that he did invent them. The final thing I would say is that granting many of your points, I don't think that the main import of my argument is invalidated, namely, that these people were profoundly ambivalent in their attitude towards psychical research, and it is this degree of ambivalence that, as it were, allowed a little breach in the curtain of what otherwise might have been uniform opposition, to get parapsychology established precariously, and it's still precarious, in the American university system.

PSYCHISM AND CHANCE

Pierre Janin

In the present work, which I would like to be considered as a mere essay, my intention is to show how the known facts of parapsychology lead us to a working hypothesis which seems to offer new insights into nothing less than the essence of psychism or the essence of life. I am quite aware that this is an ambitious purpose and that when one comes to proposing all-embracing views, the risk is great of losing one's grip on reality and merely playing with the docile wax of purely theoretical speculation. My hypothesis, however, is both philosophical *and* experimental: philosophical because it implies a particular vision of the relationship between psychism and the physical world, and experimental not only because it is based on facts, but also and especially because it suggests concrete new lines for research. In both directions, the consequences may be far-reaching, but this, of course, will depend on whether or not the experimental findings follow expectation. Let us now tackle the problem without losing sight of this commitment to ultimate practical efficiency.

SOME CHARACTERISTICS OF PSI EFFECTS

In the abundant record of well controlled field and laboratory parapsychological research we regularly observe the following:

(1) experiments which are meant to demonstrate psi effects but where no effect actually occurs, or where something does occur but with largely unpredictable efficiency; and spontaneous cases which are scarce, and almost always unexpected. Considering now only the actual psi effects, we further observe:

(2) mere wishes which have unmistakable orientation effects on ongoing physical processes in the absence of all detectable means of influence, such as in PK experiments on rolling dice, for example;

(3) physical events which happen in overt violation of the laws of inertia and gravitation, such as when "causeless" moves of various objects occur in poltergeist disturbances, presumably linked with psy-

chological conflicts at an unconscious level in at least one of the concerned persons;

(4) subjective representations in one person which correctly reflect those of another person, in the absence of all possible sensory communication between them, as in spontaneous or experimental telepathic events. It was amply shown, however, that telepathic events can be accounted for in terms of either one or both of the next two types of psi effects, so that for simplicity's sake I shall not consider them separately in the rest of this work;

(5) subjective representations which correctly reflect objective data in the absence of all detectable sensory mediation, sometimes at very large distances and despite considerable material obstacles, such as in spontaneous or experimental clairvoyance;

(6) subjective representations which correctly reflect future objective events, such as in spontaneous or experimental precognition.

Summing up these first six characteristics of psi effects, we can say that psi effects are subject-object interactions which typically occur at rare and irregular intervals, and, quite unlike usual deterministic processes, occur independently from all known physical supports, and irrespective of the usual distance or time barriers.

But a full description of psi effects would not be complete without the following additional features:

(7) in laboratory PK results or in forced-choice ESP experiments, there is frequent evidence of time-dependent, reversed, or misplaced efficiency of psi transaction. By *time-dependent efficiency*, I mean an irregular rate of success of the subject throughout the experiment, which results in local or general position effects: decline or incline, U-curves, variance effects, etc. *Reversed efficiency* is psi-missing, where the outcome of the experiment is opposite to the subject's declared wish. *Misplaced efficiency* shows up when the subject for example systematically guesses one card ahead of that which is actually being presented—in other words, in displacement effects. These so-called "secondary" effects, position effects, psi-missing, displacement, are by no means the only ones that can occur, but merely those which were most often observed or looked for, until now at least. There is no theoretical limit to a systematic search which would aim at uncovering other, probably more intricate, secondary biases in experimental data. The important point here is that all the known secondary effects go along with strong suggestion that psychological factors in one or several participants may be responsible for such indirect or modified manifestations of psi: in position effects, the subject's oscillation between eagerness and fatigue; in psi-missing, the subject's under-

lying disbelief in psi phenomena at large; things are less clear perhaps in displacement effects, though they seem to be characteristic enough of some subjects at particular times, as was the case with Mrs. Stewart or with Shackleton in part of Soal's classical experiments. So the general implication here is that however disregarded, visibly or not, psychological factors regularly interfere with most laboratory psi tasks;

(8) the other additional feature is this: in many successful free-response ESP experiments and in many ESP spontaneous events as well, the "received" message does *not* convey the exact objective information contained in the target, but does convey one or several *meanings* attached to it, often through marked distortion or even complete substitution of information contents. One typical illustration of this may be given here, as the difference between information and meaning is essential and should be as clearly understood as possible. In the famous Biblical precognitive dream which warned ancient Egypt of seven oncoming years of abundance, to be then followed by seven years of drought, the years were actually not pictured as years but as fat or lean cows coming out of the Nile river. This may certainly be readily understood in terms of Egyptian life of those times, where the yearly flood of the Nile was the main determinant of the country's food supplies for the coming year. But reasoning like this amounts to saying that the target information—years of abundance and years of drought—was actually conveyed to the dreamer in the form of different, new information contents which simply had to be *meaningfully* related to the target. Thus, fat cows followed by lean cows *meant* plenty followed by shortage; cows regularly coming out of the river *meant* the yearly rhythm of the Nile's floods, etc. Clearly then the precognitive process in the dream was concerned with the meanings around the target information, *not* with that information as such, which nowhere shows up in the dream. Now, thoughtful examination of other spontaneous occurrences will show that this conclusion in fact holds for a great many cases; and further, that it is true not only in ESP but also in PK: in more than one poltergeist outbreak it is rather clear that the highly whimsical physical events are linked by an underlying meaningful purpose which each one of them expresses differently: demonstrating hostility to someone without having to feel responsible for it, for example.

These last two features—items (7) and (8)—which characterize psi effects in a more psychological perspective than the first six, may be summed up as follows: psi phenomena, when confined to limited targets, typically may be interfered with by psychological traits in the participants, and, when freely occurring, typically convey meanings, not information as such. Both features, of course, are unknown in ordinary deterministic processes. These certainly do not depend on the observer's personality, mood or expectations, nor are they able to create *meaningful* information contents by themselves. Only a living individual can appreciate whether a given relationship is meaningful or not. A deterministic device such as a computer, for example, can certainly transform the incoming information content "fat cows on a river bank" into an outcoming content "years of abundance." This would not mean, however, that it is sensitive to the meaningful relationship which leads from the former to the latter, but only that it was rigidly programmed to do that particular task; certainly that would not render it able to give the new correct meaning of the same incoming information in another, quite different psi occurrence where it might possibly be offered.

In conclusion and to sum up the above considerations it can be said that psi effects present five main characteristics, of which the last four at least are distinctively non-deterministic, and which any fully comprehensive explanatory model must account for: (1) they are relatively scarce and unpredictable; (2) they occur in the absence of all known physical supports; (3) they are not limited by the usual time-space constraints; (4) they often are interfered with by psychological factors; (5) they convey meanings rather than information.

SOME CHARACTERISTICS OF PSYCHISM

I shall take the word "psychism" to designate that which conscious individuals generally perceive as being their inner—and not necessarily fully conscious—source of feelings, thoughts, imaginary representations, wishes, wills, memories, fears, interests, etc. These may be called "psychical contents" or "psychical activities." The word "psychological" is understood as referring to isolated and permanent enough psychical tendencies rather than to the total inner activity as such. Also, it must be clear that "psychical" does not have here the limiting sense of "pertaining to psychics or to psychic powers" —as in "psychical research"—but the most general sense of "pertaining to psychism." Note that "subjectivity" would be close to "psychism," but somewhat narrower, as it does not seem to allow for unconscious data. Also, there is no real objection to attributing psychism to animals, although whatever evidence may be produced in favor of the hypothesis necessarily is of a more indirect nature than with human beings.

Psychism characteristically tends to materialize its contents, or at least part of them, through bodily expression or action. As a matter of fact, the existence of psychism—at least outside the observer himself—is essentially inferred from such concrete manifestations as speech, mimicry, or material action. But even these are not proofs of psychical activity: a robot with a loudspeaker saying "I am sad," would not really be sad; so, from a strictly physical point of view, an alleged psychical content as such is a void notion, or at best a risky bet. In fact, current scientific philosophy rests on the mostly implicit materialistic assumption that reality is that which can be described in terms of physical objects or processes, and consequently that psychical contents and psychism as such may not be granted the status of real data, precisely because they cannot be so described. Logically, then, anything psychical tends to be considered as the mere epiphenomenon of an underlying purely objective and deterministic interaction which alone is "real," presumably one of the numerous physiological processes that are going on in the human body and especially in the brain.

Now, once again, deterministic interactions typically have a physical support, are regularly replicable, occur within precise time and space limitations, and are insensitive to whatever meanings they may be loaded with from the witnesses' standpoint. They process information, not meanings. We must then ask: to what extent does psychical activity actually bear the mark of the deterministic process which supposedly underlies it? Although brain activity, of course, does have a physical support, it is difficult to tell whether psychical activity *as such* has one, as it certainly cannot be equated to brain activity. Now, is it replicable, that is, do we have exactly the same feelings, or emotions, or memories when the circumstances are exactly the same? Here, too, it is rather difficult to answer, because circumstances never seem to be exactly the same in the psychical realm. The picture is clearer, however, as concerns the two other points: about time and space localization, we readily observe that although each psychically active subject necessarily is located somewhere in space and time, *what* he is feeling, or being impressed by, or imagining may actually be located *anywhere* in space or time: past, present, future, close or remote, physically accessible or not; or even, so it seems, in several time-space places at the same time; it may also—and this perhaps is the most frequent case—be rather difficult to localize at all. Thus, even if we remark that, in the particular case of ordinary perception and in concrete reasoning on present physical objects, psychical activity neatly complies with the usual time-space regulations, we must admit

that generally speaking it does *not* appear to be bound by such constraints. Now, as far as the meaning-vs.-information question is concerned, we remark this: efficient, rational reasoning operates much
like a computer, in that it typically processes information without
adding anything new to the initial data. We all more or less successfully learnt to do that in mathematics. But the very fact that we had
to learn it, clearly enough indicates that psychical activity in general
does not inherently comply with the rules of logical reasoning. Rather,
it constantly tends to create new information, or at least to draw information from other sources, and to add to or mix with or even
entirely substitute it for the original contents in the subject's psychism;
and that adding, mixing or substituting occurs between contents which
are in one way or another *meaningfully* related for the subject. A handful of cherries, for example, may make you remember cherry-picking
parties in the family orchard, from where you go to cherry blossoms
in the spring, which in turn make you think of flowers in general,
etc. Clearly, each one of these successive information contents features
elements which cannot be found in the others, and their association
mainly rests on a common underlying meaning, something like the
feeling that you have of the generosity of the vegetal realm. In a
depressed subject on the contrary the cherries might recall spoilt
fruit he saw in the market the same morning, hence various feelings
of waste or frustration, which will in turn bring a money problem back
to his mind, and so on. Quite obviously then, trying to explain psychical
processes merely in terms of information contents and information
processing would be utterly inadequate: the meaning in the information is the main factor, not the information itself.

Two points can be made here. The first one is that psychical activity as such definitely does *not* bear the mark of an assumedly
underlying deterministic process. Rather, it appears to develop
regardless of the usual rules of deterministic interactions, as it essentially is time-space independent and concerned with meanings, not
information. Also, we readily remark—and this is the second point
—that these two features of psychism were also mentioned in the
previous section among the five main characteristics of psi effects.
This evidently points to some close relationship between psi and
psychism, which seems to mean that the search for a theoretical model
for psi events implies tackling also *the general problem of the nature of
psychism*. That things are actually so will clearly appear in the coming
section.

THE PSYCHOPHYSICAL PROBLEM

If it is clear now that psychism may not reasonably be considered
as a by-product of material processes, what is the exact nature of its

relationship to materiality? I suggest consideration of the following steps in reasoning:

(1) From the standpoint of objective experience the physical world is an irreducible datum and exists in its own right. Physical objects, as such, are unequivocally located in time and space and physical processes are information-conservative in the sense that they do not yield information which was not implied from the start in the initial data. At first sight, the whole spectrum of our experience of reality may be considered as resulting from one type or another of physical effect: different states of matter, particles, fields, etc. At one end of this spectrum of physical realities, life and psychism may appear— and this is the materialistic view—as the products of those particular physical arrangements or processes which are called the body, the nervous system, the senses, the physiological activity in the brain, etc. Yet, as we earlier saw, some, at least, of the characteristics of psychical activity are most difficult, if not impossible to account for in a purely physical perspective.

(2) Indeed, and now from the quite symmetrical standpoint of subjective experience, psychism too is an irreducible datum and exists in its own right. Psychical activity, as such, is in terms of meanings and for that reason features the constant creation of information, and it is not clearly localized in time and space. At first sight, the whole spectrum of our experience of reality could be considered as emanating from one mode or another of psychical activity: will, imagination, memory, etc. At one end of this spectrum of psychical realities, the material world may appear—and this was maintained by idealistic philosophy and especially its solipsistic variant—as the product of this particular psychical activity which is called perception. But here, again, we come up against the fact that some essential characteristics of physical processes are definitely not those of psychical activity in general.

(3) Now, since neither the basic experience of psychical life, nor that of the physical world can be denied, a comprehensive view necessarily must allow for both. Does this mean, however, that we should accept the Cartesian dualistic hypothesis of two independent substances: mind on the one hand, matter on the other hand? This would seem difficult to maintain, in view of the fact that no pure psychical activity was ever decisively proved to exist in the absence of a physical body, and that, conversely, a purely physical system would have no existence at all in the absence of at least one person—one psychism—to look at it or even only imagine it. In other words, to adopt the dualistic view would be to overlook the fact that mind and matter *never* are experienced separately. This fact is quite obvious in ordinary life, where the physical world constantly impinges on

psychical life through sensations and perceptions, while psychism continuously projects itself into the physical world, which it tends to modify or interfere with through speech, mimicry, or material action. The most reasonable stand in such a situation seems to grant *equal and symmetrical status* to psychical life and the physical world, and to admit that the body is the meeting point where both originate, or, in other words, where psychophysical interactions take place.

(4) This view has a number of consequences. The first one is straightforward: unlikely purely *physical* interactions, *psycho*physical interactions, as we just defined them, will necessarily be concerned with meanings. Such is indeed the case for all our perceptions and all our actions: even in their simplest form, our perceptions already are an interpretation of whatever physical reality triggers them. Red is not in nature; it is *our* interpretation of a specific electromagnetic wavelength, and our actions obviously interfere with the existing information contents in the physical world around us. The second consequence is double: first, from the standpoint of its information content and physical efficiency, a bodily-mediated psychophysical interaction necessarily is limited to the body's sensorimotor possibilities. Indeed, we do not perceive more than a given range of electromagnetic radiations or sound vibrations; and on the motor side, a given individual cannot develop more than his own maximum amount of physical skill or strength. And second, the localization in time and space of any bodily-mediated interaction necessarily is that of the physical body; it is a fact that all my perceptions are here and now, like my body, and that so are all my physical actions.

This being stated, a further and important consequence ensues. Assuming that any psychophysical interaction should happen to bypass the body's physiological equipment—namely the sensorimotor channels—then its load of meanings would no longer have to comply with bodily constraints as far as sensory ranges, skill or strength limitations, and being present in time and space are concerned. Consequently, the physical term of such a hypothetical interaction might very well be (1) off the normal sensory ranges—X-rays might be "seen" or ultra-sounds "heard," (2) unattainable by ordinary bodily action—heavy objects might be easily "handled" and intricate material tasks correctly "performed," or (3) located elsewhere in time and/or in space—past, future or remote events or objects might be "perceived" or "acted upon."

Of course, what we are speaking about here is not merely hypothetical, it actually exists and is called psi phenomena. It does happen that remote objects or events are perceived, through clairvoyance, or acted upon, through psychokinesis; that future or past events are precognized or retrocognized; and that difficult or even seemingly impossible tasks are nevertheless performed by poltergeists. Does it also happen that X-rays or ultra-sounds, for example, are directly perceived? Even if evidence could be found for this, however, it might not be easy to decide whether to invoke ordinary, though unusual, sensory abilities, or genuinely paranormal factors. This, perhaps, is why classical parapsychology does not seem to have dwelled much on the question. Let us also note, as a last remark here, that, in the present perspective, psychokinesis on *past* events does not appear less likely—all commonsense objections being put aside—than ordinary PK on present events, and that, precisely, two researchers recently obtained independent positive results in retroactive PK experiments (Janin 1975, Schmidt 1976).

Back, now, to the status of psi events. It appears that we can adopt the following definition: *psi events are normal psychophysical interactions, essentially similar to those which sensorimotor channels usually convey, but which in fact bypass these channels and thus escape the corresponding limitations.* It can be easily understood now that, in such interactions, the absence of all sensorimotor "centering" in time and space may accordingly allow for more diversified, intricate or interwoven psychical contents to manifest than in ordinary interactions which are linearly laid out in time and unequivocally localized in space. Hence, the typically meaning-concerned character of spontaneous psi phenomena as compared to ordinary perception or action; hence, also, the frequent interference of parasitic contents (such as those due to personality factors) in experiments where the psi task is deliberately confined to targets which are almost devoid of meaning—namely, in classical laboratory PK and in forced-choice ESP research.

A final and important consequence stems from our granting equal and symmetrical status to psychical activity and to physical objects or processes. In such a perspective it is self-contradictory to expect that a psychophysical interaction should be physically mediated, since it precisely constitutes *the original bond* at the ends of which a physical pole and a *non*-physical pole emerge. In other words— and this accounts for one more characteristic of psi effects—the question of the physical support of psychophysical interaction *is inherently irrelevant.*

Note that this last assertion holds for all psychophysical interactions in general, whether occurring through the body's sensorimotor channels, as most of the time in daily life, or outside these channels, as in psi effects. The fact that only psi effects and not the sensorimotor events are usually felt to be question-raising, as far as the problem of the physical support is concerned, merely reflects the most widespread and deep-rooted opinion according to which ultimate reality, psychism included, is physical in essence. I certainly shall not pretend that the view I advocate instead is easy to accept or immediately answers all questions. What I do say, though, is that it is sounder to reason in terms of a single enigma in all psychophysical interactions—that is, in the whole of our experienced interchange with reality, with or without use of the bodily machinery —than to postulate that reality is but physical and, thus, to see no problem in that part of our experience which is bodily-mediated, but to be then faced in the other part, namely psi events, with a hopelessly intricate conundrum. Between a cosmic enigma and a riddle in a ghetto I prefer the cosmic enigma, because only at the level of that which is both universal and contradictory can we hope to find really general working models. Let us recall here that relativistic physics rests on a basic principle which acknowledges constant velocity for light in all systems of reference—an enigma by all daily life standards—or that wave mechanics acknowledges constant wave-particle association—an enigma from the standpoint of the common-sense basic difference between radiating energy and material bodies. These examples show us the way; because it appears that we may never ultimately succeed in reducing our experience of reality to terms of either psychism only or physical processes only, and because psychophysical interactions obviously exist, we have to acknowledge that a basic unity underlies the apparent duality or contradiction between psychical life and the physical world and warrants their permanent interplay, or in other words, that *reality is psychophysical in essence*.

This is nothing else than a possible basis for the solution to the age-old but still unsolved mind-matter problem. I am, naturally, aware that if the postulate should be proved reliable, the consequences would potentially be incalculable both for philosophy and for science, and I do not want to try to list them here even tentatively. Also, I believe that it could and should be expressed in various other ways and that more fundamental reflexion is needed for that. What I would simply like to do in the rest of this work is to show how we can immediately draw on it, first for shedding further light on what is not yet clear in psi phenomena, and then for suggesting new paths to experimentation.

THE DAEMON IN THE DIE

In the above section, four of the five main characteristics of psi effects were accounted for, namely lack of physical support, time-space independence, concern with meanings, and proneness to being interfered with by psychological parasites. Thus, only the relative scarcity and unpredictability of psi still have to be dealt with; this will be one of the objectives of the present section.

The simplest limb motion when we decide to move, the quasi-immediate translation of mere representations into speech sounds, the ready deciphering of printed words into meanings, etc., are psychophysical interactions; so are psi effects. But what a difference between them! What an incredibly efficient psychophysical "machine" the human body appears to be, when one considers the ridiculously low and whimsical performances of the classical subject + die setting in PK trials, or even the more impressive, yet notoriously sporadic events produced by poltergeists! Certainly, scarcity and unpredictability do not apply to the psychophysical interactions between a subject and his own sensorimotor system. How can we account for that?

Such a huge discrepancy between two kinds of effects when the basic phenomenon is held to be the same must be meaningful, and I shall try to show how, using an apologue. Imagine a reduced-size, more or less human-like daemon sleeping inside a hollow die. Each time the die is being cast, the daemon instantaneously awakes and must decide which of the six faces shall be upward when the die comes to rest. Let us further assume that he is endowed with perfect or at least very good PK and ESP abilities: through ESP directed at the utilizers of the die he knows what face or faces are being wished for if any, and this may or may not influence his final decision. Then, through PK on the motion of the still rolling die, he very efficiently succeeds in enforcing that decision. Then he goes to sleep again.

Now for the human utilizer such a daemon-operated die is perfectly equivalent to a normal die, because (1) the daemon's unpredictable decisions account for the die's behavior in ordinary use, where it is a mere source of random events, and (2) in a PK setting, introducing the daemon amounts to relieving the utilizer from his direct responsibility in the actually obtained results and transferring it, unchanged, to the daemon. Where the subject tried, knowingly or not, to exert PK on the die and more or less succeeded, it is now the daemon who chooses to more or less comply with the subject's wish and exerts PK to bring about what he finally freely decided.

The interest of the apologue precisely lies in this sharing of responsibilities. In the classical situation, the subject was alone with his die, while in the daemon-in-the-die situation he has a partner, a vis-à-vis, a companion. In the former situation, the subject's drive was to achieve a good solitary performance by exerting a "force," it was something like an athletic feat; whereas in the latter situation the accent no longer lays on force, but on the psychological factor, on dialogue: if the experiment turns out well, it means that for some reason the daemon decided to favor the subject's wish, for example, because he found he liked him, or because the subject succeeded in convincing him to do so. Now, if the experiment fails, in the solitary performance perspective all we can say is that the "psychic force" was not correctly applied; but as nobody can tell anything about this assumed "force" nor about how it should be correctly applied, nothing is learnt from the failure. Pushing in the dark on the wrong button doesn't tell anything as to *why* it was not the good one. In the daemon-in-the-die perspective, on the contrary, a failure of the experiment does tell something. It indicates that the subject did not please the daemon, or that no fruitful dialogue took place with him. Now, this *is* something to be pondered over by the thoughtful subject. Bettering one's general attitude, and one's aptitude to dialogue, is definitely possible. And, finally, just as scarcity and relative unpredictability of psi events have to remain basically unexplained in the classical subject + die setting, so they appear to be well enough accounted for when the die becomes daemon-inhabited. PK phenomena usually are scarce and relatively unpredictable, not just because things are so, but just to the extent that subjects in general rarely and irregularly happen to have the right inner attitude; that which is needed for at least some positive contact with the daemon.

Such a conclusion, it should be remarked, is consistent with the results of rather a large body of experimental work, mostly classical already, by various authors. It was regularly observed that such factors as one would, from the present perspective, expect to generally enhance communication and dialogue were more psi-conducive than the opposite factors with unfavorable conclusions. Let us quote the following: (1) a positive attitude toward psi, as opposed to a negative one: see in Palmer (1971) a good review of the research by Schmeidler and her followers on the sheep-goat effect. (2) The attractive character of the psi task, as opposed to its lack of attractiveness: see for example Freeman (1969) or Rao (1962). (3) A positive affective relationship, as opposed to a negative one, between the various participants in the psi test: see Anderson and White's classical classroom studies (1958), and also Fisk and West (1956), Rice and Townsend (1962), for example. (4) Extraversion, (5) low neuroticism, (6) expansiveness, as opposed to introversion, high neuroticism compressiveness: for a systematic study see Kanthamani and Rao (1971, 1972). (7) Various states of relaxation or hypnosis: see the works of

Casler, Braud, Honorton and others, the references of which can be found in (1976).

The objection that these studies were in fact mainly ESP, not PK research is a minor one here, as our daemon-in-the-die could easily be made into a daemon-in-the-cards—or, in whatever target is being used—with the same essential shift of accent as in the PK setting, from the idea of a particular "psychic force" in the subject to that of a particular subject-daemon relationship. I may therefore, consider that the experimental findings mentioned here support the general idea that success in psi experiments (whether ESP or PK) is a matter of readiness, in the subject, for direct or experimenter-mediated communication and exchange with his targets.

Yet, if some light is now shed on the possible reason why experimental psi effects are weak, namely because on the whole the needed "dialogue" is difficult to establish, it is still quite obscure why the efficiency of the mind-matter interaction within our bodies, or the allegoric PK powers of the daemon on his die, is so enormously greater and more reliable. Examples are available, however, of intermediate cases which may suggest an answer. It is generally thought that raising an arm at will is straightforward enough; certainly if it is *your* arm at your will. But what about somebody else's arm at your will? Imagine a stranger standing by your side in the bus or on the train. You decide to try a mind-matter interaction experiment on him, and silently wish him to raise his arm; this is the classical "psychic force" model of PK trial. Statistically speaking, though, and even if you do have some PK "powers," it is rather improbable that you would succeed. Remembering, then, the daemon apologue you realize that here, the daemon-in-his-die actually *is* this man-in-his-body, a "daemon" of a quite familiar kind to whom you can even physically speak, so that the conditions for an efficient dialogue are most favorable. So you speak to the man and tell him to raise his arm. But, as he does not know you and is not likely to immediately understand what your intentions are, he probably will not raise his arm, at least not right away. Now, of course, you may also have an inviting smile and a subtly imperious tone of voice, and the man himself may be naturally trustful, easily impressed by strangers or prone to joking, and so do what you asked him. Your experiment would then be a success. Such a situation, I would say, would be fairly similar to the subject-target relationship in any classical ESP or PK experiment. It is a temporary deal, where you succeed if you are good enough at public relations; hence, the utility of being at least momentarily positively concerned, outgoing, relaxed, etc., as was earlier noted.

But your story with the stranger-in-his-body can also be told in another way. The above type of instant relationship would presumably not prove to be very long-lasting. You couldn't reasonably expect a stranger to raise his arm upon request without any further explanation each time you would meet him on the bus or elsewhere; so did many initial successes in psi research inexorably taper off after a while. Things might be different, though, if the experiment took place in the context of a more gradually established, more personal, constantly renewed dialogue between you and the man about your purposes, his participation, your common interest in the success of the experiment, the general psychophysical problem, etc. After a sufficient time, you might finally induce him into a long, tight and fruitful cooperation with you, with probably many more regularly successful psychophysical interactions between you and him than mere arm-raising episodes. Note, that for arriving at such a result, if your having at least some positive interest in your undertaking still appears to be required, yet your being a tense introvert must not necessarily turn out to be an unfavorable factor.

So we come now to the second teaching in our apologue. The difference between a weak and irregular psi effect and a highly efficient in-the-body psychophysical interaction appears to be that between a rapid, superficial encounter and a progressively, patiently built companionship or complicity. And here again the roundabout way with the apologue brings us back to sheer reality. As we may readily realize or recall, the smallest will-controlled bodily motion or the commonest meaning which speech or print conveys to us actually is the result of those particular kinds of patiently built psychism-body complicities which we call learning processes.

It may be argued here that quite a few laboratory experiments in parapsychology have actually been so arranged as to allow for at least some learning in the subjects. I am referring here not only to Honorton's specially designed feedback research (1970, 1971), or to Tart's reflection and experiments (1966, 1975), but more generally to all procedures which simply let the subject know whether he is being successful or not. Indeed, in terms of our basic subject + die experimental setting, can some learning not take place as soon as the subject is aware of what face comes up in each throw? Allegorically speaking, isn't there some sort of a dialogue with the daemon-in-the-die as soon as each throw conveys the daemon's answer to the subject's wish? Yes, in a way, but obviously it is a very gross dialogue as the daemon has only six different "words" for physically expressing whatever he may actually think; so that the subject is left with mere conjectures as to what the daemon means when, say, he answers 3, then 2, then 6 to a wish for fives. Things are radically different, though, in the stranger-in-his-body variant of the apologue. Besides the actual raising of his arm, the range of the man's possible answers to your arm-raising request *is virtually infinite*, and, with a few exceptions, each one of them can be felt as bearing some close or remote, positive or negative, yet meaningful relationship to your project. And *this is precisely why* a fruitful dialogue could take place between you and him.

If we now transpose this in terms of experimental parapsychology, we come to the following conclusion: for establishing the patiently built subject-target companionship or complicity which alone can bring about regularly efficient psychophysical interactions, it is required that a sensitive enough practical criterion of his progress should be offered to the subject, just as in the supposed arm-raising-oriented dialogue with the stranger; in other words, it is required that *an extremely wide range of versatile and overlapping meanings* (from the standpoint of the subject's wish) *should be allowed for in the available behaviors or contents of the target.* It readily appears here how far the classical forced-choice targets lie from this standard. Cards of various types (ESP cards, clock cards, etc), coins, dice, balls or other moving objects, all convey narrow ranges of poorly varied and weakly overlapping or non-overlapping meanings. Things might have been different in free-response ESP tests with complex meaning-laden targets, for example all those in the early psychical research, but also those in Ullman and Krippner's dream studies or similar research. But as far as I can see, these experiments were definitely not so designed as to induce the subjects into entering the patient trial-and-error learning process which alone could have resulted in increased hit scores. Now, if classical parapsychology has fallen short of opening the way to the much longed-for regularly successful psi experiment, what could such an experiment possibly be?

DIALOGUE WITH CHANCE

Imagine a small self-powered vehicle which moves at random, for example, following a broken line, the straight segments of which are random both as to length and as to orientation (type-1 path), or following a curved line with a randomly varying curvature radius (type-2 path). If recorded on paper with a tracing pen attached to the vehicle, the paths could be something like this:

Type-1 Path   Type-2 Path

Such a randomly moving device could be called a *tychoscope*, from the Greek roots in *tycho*: chance, fate, and *scope*: to see, to look at; because it enables one to "see chance" either in the above form of its recorded path—which can be called a *tychogram*—or in the form of its actual instantaneous motion. A few tychoscopes with type-1 path were built by the author; they are cylindrical devices with the approximate size of a drinking glass.

The range of the possible behaviors of a tychoscope is very large: assuming a type-1 path, at the local level—the "words" of its "language" —each new direction may make any angle from 0 to 360 degrees with the preceding one, and the lengths of the straight segments in the successive directions are random within a wide enough range about their mean value. At a more synthetic level—the "sentences" of the tychoscope's "language"—the variety of the possible paths between one point and another is virtually infinite. Also, each local move of the device is a more or less direct and important contribution to its final displacement; in other words, from the standpoint of a PK subject who would try to obtain a specified type of displacement. General direction, distance, shape of path, etc., each one of the many possible behaviors of the tychoscope, would in its own way be meaningfully related to the task at hand.

It is clear enough that such characteristics meet with the earlier defined requirements for the type of target to be used in the yet-to-be-done fully successful psi experiment. A tychoscope *is* a PK target with a wide range of behaviors with versatile and overlapping meanings. So, building up the close companionship which is needed to finally obtain such results as may be expected may begin right now; the most important piece of hardware is available. One just has to let the tychoscope run on the table or on the floor, with whatever limits for local or maximum displacement and whatever settings for speed and other internal variables may be felt most favorable, then start "asking" it to behave in a specified way, see how it actually responds, modify the request accordingly, etc. Tychogram records may be used if detailed path analysis appears to be called for. Once again, though, let us not expect rapid results. It takes time to tame a horse, or a bird, or to learn to speak a foreign language, or to teach something to a child, and not everybody is equally successful at doing it; yet techniques exist for that, whereas in the "taming" of a tychoscope everything has to be invented and nobody ever did it.

Let us, finally, come to the fundamental question which arises in the context of tychoscope experimentation. *What* exactly is a tychoscope? A physical device which was so designed as to behave randomly, that is, in an unpredictable way, but which is expected to behave more and more predictably—at least up to a certain point—as the "dialogue" with the subject goes on and its motion more and more clearly reflects whatever meaningful contents the subject is trying to convey through this dialogue. So, because it may react to psychical contents as such, a tychoscope appears to be more than a mere physical object in the ordinary sense; rather, it is *a psychophysical "something."* Note, that although this conclusion is clearest in the case of a tychoscope, it would also hold for all other sources of chance events: rolling dice, flipping coins, rolling balls on rough surfaces, random number generators in operation, and also, ultimately, for all quantum particles in ordinary inanimate matter at the moments when they interact, since at that level, too, chance can be influenced by PK. The whole physical realm, of course, is potentially concerned by this last reflection; this is not surprising, though, in the light of the earlier stated general postulate that reality is psychophysical in essence. As concerns now the living realm, to the extent that a tychoscope is a psychophysical "thing" it obviously has something in common with living bodies, which we may recall are basically psychophysical. A tychoscope then, or any other source of random events, may to some extent be paralleled to a psychism-inhabited body. This was already tacitly implied by the way we spoke of "taming" it like an animal. Do we have, then, to conclude that it is actually psychism-inhabited itself? In this perspective we would, more generally, have to envisage that randomness in behavior might be *the* essential criterion of psychism or of life, so that the main difference between an ordinary living being and an inanimate physical object, in which myriads of elementary particle encounters with random outcomes permanently occur, would be that chance shows up at the macroscopic level in the former, and does not in the latter. Ordinary sources of random events such as dice, coins, etc., where chance operates only in special conditions (upon their being thrown, tossed . . .), would then have to be considered as endowed with intermittent psychism.

If there was at least some truth in the above reflections, a novel path would appear to be open to research; that of *the experimental study of psychism; and of life on quasi-living (or really living?) man-made models*. The tychoscope is the simplest example of such models, but all of them will, like the tychoscope, be built with mere mechanical parts and electronic components. There probably existed a forerunner to this venture; in so far as the alchemists' *homunculus*, a small creature which occupied an important place in the alchemical enterprise, was conceived of as artificially made yet endowed with life, it should be considered as a tychoscope's ancestor. In fact and more generally, the idea of creating life at will, with one's own hands and outside woman's womb, thus closing in on the essential enigma of life's meaning and man's status in the universe and perhaps mastering it, was probably already implied in the very first flash of human consciousness. So, if tychoscope taming succeeded, thereby demonstrating a basic connivance between living psychism on the one hand, and chance physical events on the other hand, it would open the way to an at last concrete approach to one of the world's oldest questions. It is thus perhaps not unreasonable to hope that along such new experimental lines as were defined here, through his dialogue with the Sphinx of chance the thoughtful researcher might be offered some far-reaching answers.

REFERENCES

[1] Anderson, Margaret and White, Rhea., A survey of work on ESP and teacher-pupil attitudes. *Journal of Parapsychology* 22, 4, december 1958, 246–268.

[2] Fisk, G. W., and West, D. J., ESP and mood: report of a "mass" experiment. *Journal Soc. Psych. Res.* 38, 689, september 1956, 320–329.

[3] Freeman, John A., The psi-differential effect in a precognition test. *Journal of Parapsychology* 33, 3, september 1969, 206–212.

[4] Honorton, Charles, Effects of feedback on discrimination between correct and incorrect ESP responses. *Journal Am. Soc. Psych. Res.* 64, 4, october 1970, 404–410.

[5] Honorton, Charles, Effects of feedback on discrimination between correct and incorrect ESP responses: a replication study. *Journal Am. Soc. Psych. Res.* 65, 2, april 1971, 155–161.

[6] Janin, P., Psychocinèse dans le passé? Une expérience exploratoire. *Revue métapsychique* 21–22, 1975, 71–96.

[7] Kanthamani, B. K., and Rao, K. R., Personality characteristics of ESP subjects: *Journal of Parapsychology:* I. Primary personality characteristics and ESP. 35, 3, sept. 1971, 189–207. III. Extraversion and ESP. 36, 3, sept. 1972, 198–212. IV. Neuroticism and ESP. 37, 1, march 1973, 37–50. V. Graphic expansiveness and ESP. 37, 2, june 1973, 119–129.

[8] Palmer, John, Scoring in ESP tests as a function of belief in ESP. Part I: the sheep-goat effect. *Journal Am. Soc. Psych. Res.* 65, 4, october 1971, 373–408.

[9] Rao, K. Ramakrishna, The preferential effect in ESP. *Journal of Parapsychology* 26, 4, december 1962, 252–259.

[10] Rice, George E., and Townsend, Joyce, Agent-percipient relationships and GESP performance. *Journal of Parapsychology* 26, 3, sept. 1962, 211–217.

[11] Rogo, D. Scott, Research on psi-conducive states: some complicating factors. *Journal of Parapsychology* 40, 1, march 1976, 34–45.

[12] Schmidt, Helmut, PK effects on prerecorded targets. *Journal Am. Soc. Psych. Res.* 70, 3, july 1976, 267–292.

[13] Tart, Charles T., Card guessing tests: learning paradigm or extinction paradigm? *Journal Am. Soc. Psych. Res.* 60, 1, january 1966, 46–55.

[14] Tart, Charles T., The application of learning theory to ESP performance. *Parapsychological Monographs* n°15. New York, Parapsychology Foundation, 1975. 149 pp.

DISCUSSION

STANFORD: I want specifically to compliment you on what I think is one of the most ingenious and potentially useful of the feedback modes for possible PK effects. I certainly would like to know whether these are commercially available, because I would think they would have some excellent applications and psychological appeal in the laboratory, particularly with children and with a lot of adults if they're anything like me.

JANIN: Well, to build one like this takes me two weeks at least and there is about $80 worth of components in it, so a tychoscope ends up being quite expensive. If you are ready to buy one, I'll gladly build it for you. I must say however, that I do not consider this model of a tychoscope to be perfect as far as mechanical and electronic behavior is concerned: it still needs some improvement. If you decided to buy one, I would ask you to give me a few more months to get the next model ready.

BELOFF: I must confess I found your paper extraordinarily difficult and I don't claim as yet to be able to understand it, but perhaps you could help me if you could clarify your position on one particular aspect. In talking of psychophysical interactions you seem at first to be committed to a dualist position, but you reject any kind of Cartesian or categorical dualism on the grounds that we never have independent evidence for both mind and matter. Now, it certainly can be argued, as Dr. Penelhum argued yesterday, that we don't have such independent evidence of minds existing apart from bodies, unless we take survival evidence more literally; but the question of matter existing apart from mind—this surprises me very much. I mean, are you committed to an idealist position? Do you believe that matter is just a construct of mind? Or do you admit, as I would want to do, that the universe existed long before there were any observers there to describe it?

JANIN: I really think that there can never be any proof that the universe existed before anyone thought of it or looked at it. Of course, this sounds like an idealist position, but I don't think it is, and I don't see how you can avoid it.

PENELHUM: I have difficulty with your daemon theory, which may merely show I don't understand it fully. You, I think, are suggesting that we should understand psychokinesis on the model of telepathic persuasion, so that in the case of PK, what is taking place is similar to what would take place if I walked up to you and telepathically persuaded you to raise your arm. Now, if that is your theory, then it seems to me you have to assume that we fully understand or have no problem about the relationships between *my* mind and *my* body, because, if your theory is correct, then it explains why *his* arm goes up by saying that *I* persuade the daemon *in him* to lift it. It explains why the die falls as I will by saying that I somehow persuade the daemon on the die to make it come down in that way. Now, you cannot also say that when I raise my own arm I persuade the daemon in *my* body to raise it or there will then be two spirits in my body—mine and the daemon who controls the movement of my limbs. Therefore, in order for your theory to work, you have to assume that the relationship between each person's psyche and his own body is unproblematic. Is that an acceptable consequence for you?

JANIN: I think that the relationship between your psychism and your own body or my psychism and my own body is problematic in the beginning. So, when you say that you would have to assume that there are two spirits in the same body, well, I would rather agree. It does happen that some people do not control their bodily motions.

MATTUCK: I would like to say, first, that I found this a very fascinating talk and I agree that randomness is extremely fundamental. I think it is *the* fundamental thing to look at in trying to understand psi phenomena. The reason why I feel this way is that one of the big problems in psychokinesis is the fact that the energies of the moving PK objects—for example, in a Kulagina-type phenomenon—are much too large to be accounted for by any sort of known radiations from the mind transmitted to the object. No electrostatic field or electromagnetic field or acoustic field from the mind can account for the energy of the PK object. Randomness helps us here, since we can visualize that what the mind is doing is to make use of the energies already present in the environment in the form of random fluctuations or noise. Now, with regard to the daemon and the dialogue with the daemon, I feel that these ideas can be put into terms which are more satisfying to physicists. Firstly, you don't have to put a daemon into that die, because the die is going to move in a random way as a result of thermal fluctuations. Secondly, the dialogue, I feel should be phrased in terms of information, an information field which comes from the mind, and is present at the object. These two things—randomness, which you call the daemon, and the information field, which you call the dialogue—can be expressed in completely quantitative terms, so you can actually do calculations to show that at least some of the phenomena that Kulagina produced can be accounted for on the basis of a simple picture involving mind, thermal fluctuations in matter, and the amount of information that mind is able to process. Why is it that the mind seems to be able to control its own brain better than it can control these glasses of mineral water on the table? Well, I think some of the observations of William Roll have shown that in the poltergeist phenomena, the number of phenomena taking place decreases rapidly with distance. Hence you might say simply that the information field is most dense inside the cranium of the person himself, so he's best able to convey information to control the random behavior of the electrons and atoms and molecules in his own brain. So you get the most effective type of psychokinesis in the brain itself. As far as the outer information field is concerned, it's much lower in intensity. This means the amount of information you're able to convey to the environment is much smaller, so you'd expect that you would get considerably smaller effects. So I think that there is a quantitative way of expressing these things which you expressed qualitatively.

JANIN: When I speak of dialogue, and in reference to what I said in my paper, I mean a dialogue where *meanings* are exchanged, not information. So I do not think I can accept, at least in my perspective, your idea of an information field.

HILL: The first thing Janin mentioned was the role of the observer in the experiment. Of course, this is deeply involved in the dualist hypothesis which has been bandied back and forth for the last three days, and I think this is a very important point, because, of course, there is no experiment which can be performed where there is not an observer at some point or another. Mr. Janin has done experiments on retro-PK where the role of the observer at a *future time* perhaps could be important, and there's a lot more we can say about that. In fact, Walker's latest formulation in the so-called "Pandora's Box Experiment" says that the only way you can guarantee no effect in a PK experiment is if neither the subject nor the experimenter nor any other person is ever informed of the results, and of course, in that case you can't detect the results, so it seems to be an inviolable hypothesis. We also think that the effect of the observers is in the experimenter's effect and this sort of effect is cropping up in my own work now, and I think that a lot more thinking needs to be done about possible ways that an observer can enter into a system. Now, one of the ways you mentioned was the daemon. I assume you're referring to the Maxwell daemon now. I'm sure you're also aware that the original problem with the Maxwell daemon was that it violated the laws of thermodynamics because it used energy. Now, as Dr. Mattuck has mentioned a few times, we have another formulation of the Copenhagen interpretation of quantum mechanics, where we think the daemon draws energy from the noise energy in the environment so I would like you to clarify a little bit what you mean by the daemon and where he gets his energy.

JANIN: My daemon is a completely allegorical creature. I do not have to look for where he gets his energy from. What I ultimately mean is that in order to control by PK a material object outside your body, you just have to be in a good psychological relationship to that object, and this is what I wanted to illustrate with the daemon idea—nothing else.

ROLL: It's true that poltergeist disturbances involve meaning in the way you said, but it also seems that these forms of PK, if indeed they are the same as dice and other laboratory PK phenomena, conform in a striking way to known energetic processes. Now, in general, I think it's very useful in trying to reach an understanding of psi phenomena to explore them where they exist at their most striking, and poltergeist phenomena certainly are striking in more ways than one. What is your opinion about the tendency for poltergeist phenomena to attenuate with distance from the apparent agent, and related effect such as the tendency for light objects to move short distances.

JANIN: I might answer that these tendencies are only illustrations of what the subject himself believes, consciously or not. The subject would find it very strange, and also the observer would find it very strange, if things moved three miles away rather than in the close vicinity of the subject so as a rule it doesn't happen. However unusual they may be, poltergeist events can not be meaningless.

ROLL: As a rule, poltergeist agents are entirely unaware of their involvement in these occurrences. It's often only when the parapsychologist enters on the scene that a relationship is found between the phenomena and a particular person. Do you think that this creates any difficulties?

JANIN: I would say that the poltergeist agent is not unaware. There are various reasons to believe that he is unconsciously very much aware of what is happening.

A PHILOSOPHICAL ANALYSIS OF TELEPATHY

ROLF EJVEGAARD

In this paper I intend, from a philosophical point of view, to discuss the concept of telepathy. I begin by ostensively defining what telepathy is. The ostensive part consists of three case-studies taken from the female paragnost Ms. Eva Hellström's paranormal diary. A brief presentation of Ms. Hellström and her remarkable casebook follows. After that, I touch upon the question of whether telepathy can be considered a form of knowledge and a form of perception. Finally, I take up some theories of telepathy. A summary concludes the paper.

It is necessary from the beginning to point out the fact that the concept of telepathy does not seem to have been treated extensively by philosophers or in philosophical discussions. The concept of precognition, on the other hand, has in this respect been much more considered. This may arise from the fact that precognition is, from a *prima facie* philosophical point of view, a more challenging concept than telepathy.

In order not to disappoint the reader, it is my duty to state here that I do not come up with any new explanations of telepathy. This paper may be seen more as a summary of some of the most important philosophical ideas concerning telepathy that so far have been put forward. Of course, in a short paper like this, the summarizing can neither be extensive nor complete.

Three actual cases of telepathy provide the grounds for an ostensive definition of the notion of telepathy. One advantage among several of an ostensive definition is that everyone has to form his own personal opinion or concept of the defined matter. Thus, the ostensive definition may be false from one person's view, in the sense that what one person defines as a telepathic event will perhaps not be accepted by another. Hence a disagreement may arise in this matter between the reader and me. This enables the reader to continue the analysis after I have stopped.

CASE 1

Background

Eva Hellström, a housewife with four children, married to Bo Hellström, Doctor of Technology and Professor of Hydraulics at the Royal Institute of Technology, Stockholm, Sweden, had on a number of occasions suggestive paranormal experiences of different kinds. She was a good friend to Jan (pseudonym), a professional man much younger than herself and unmarried. Among the experiences were several telepathic ones.

From the Diary

On July 6, 1950, Ms. Eva Hellström wrote the following:
"I was at Skodsborg in Denmark recuperating. I had written an ordinary letter to Jan, ended it about nine p.m., and was planning to go to bed. However, I started to feel an anxiety which gradually became a terrible agony and I got the impression it concerned Jan. At last, at 9.30 p.m., I ordered an express telephone call to Stockholm, but at 9.40 I was informed that there was no answer. I had never before ordered a telephone call to him when I was out traveling. After taking a sleeping pill, I calmed down gradually and fell asleep. The next morning Jan telephoned me and said that something very personal had happened to him which had been horrible and that he had during the evening and night been crying out to me, wishing that I had been there to help him."

Affirmation

This entry in the diary of Eva Hellström is verified by Greta Norrlin and Britta Warbert.

Eva's Comments

On February 15, 1961, Eva noted the following:
"That was the first summer (1950) I knew Jan. I had not then grasped what a terrible psychic contact had been established between us. It was with great hesitation I phoned Stockholm. I had the feeling I was making myself ridiculous but an inner force drove me to act. Such events were repeated over a period of years and nearly destroyed my nerves as Jan was a manic-depressive and hysterical man."

Comments

This alleged telepathic experience took place between Skodsborg in Denmark and Stockholm in Sweden, a distance of about 650 kilometers. Eva was making preparations to retire but was fully awake. Her paranormal experiences, especially her precognitions, usually occurred in a very relaxed mood; for example, when she took an afternoon rest or, when she was falling asleep, or in the process of awakening.

CASE 2

Background

Professor Bo Hellström was a very well known scientist and therefore a consultant for several governments. Eva had the opportunity of accompanying him on many of his journeys. A good amount of her paranormal experiences took place during these travels abroad. It was on a return trip from Egypt that Eva decided to stop in Rome to visit Jan, who had moved his practice from Sweden to Italy. After the stopover in Rome, Eva was planning a week or two in London before returning to Sweden.

From the Diary

On February 23, 1951, Eva entered the following:
"On the way from Cairo to London, Jan and I met for a couple of days in Rome. There was a peacefulness and happiness about everything. We spent a delightful time together making visits to the Catacombs, for example, and so on.
"One morning I awoke early about six o'clock. I could not go back to sleep. I lay thinking about the time when Jan was ill and I nursed him and some other factors in connection with that time. I lay there truly again suffering through the difficulties in connection with the disease. At last, at eight o'clock, I dressed in my morning-gown and walked toward his room, which was situated far off in another corridor. On my way I met a maid who handed me a note from Jan. It read: 'Won't you come in to me now? No. 32. Have thrown up and been ill.'
"Jan had last evening after we parted written some letters and gone out to mail them. He fell for the temptation of going into a small bar and having something to eat. The food probably was not fresh causing him to be ill almost all night."

Affirmation

This entry in the diary is verified by Britta Warbert.

On the original, and saved, note with the text: "Won't you come . . ." Jan immediately, after Eva entered his room and saw his condition, signed his full name and dated it: the 23rd of February 1951 at 8:25 a.m.

Comments

This alleged telepathy with certainty took place during the early morning and perhaps sometime during the night. Eva had been fast asleep and the anxiety may have caused her to awaken much earlier than she was used to or had planned to, although she had no recollection of a dream or worry. During the next two hours she was completely awake and had the feeling that something was wrong with Jan. She wanted to go to him as soon as possible but did not think it appropriate until eight o'clock. There had been no reason for her to believe that something was wrong with Jan, especially since they had spent the entire preceding day together and he had felt extremely well, and, this was still the case when they parted in the evening. Apparently, Jan had felt so well after he returned to his room that he sat down to write some letters. He even felt well enough to go for a short stroll in order to mail those letters. If he had felt nauseated he certainly would not have had something to eat at that late hour.

Can a natural explanation be found of this event? Maybe Jan, without being aware of it, was gradually becoming ill during the afternoon and evening. Eva, at the same time, more or less unconsciously, was getting sensory cues about Jan's condition.

Perhaps Jan's on-coming illness caused him to feel a hunger sensation and the desire to look for something to eat. That the food brought about his illness is thus a rationalization made afterwards.

An explanation of this sort is rather complicated. Among other things it involves theories of advanced sensory cues, of the effect of the sickness on behavior (also on the hunger sensations), of Eva's ability to unconsciously draw the right conclusions from the cues, and of the disregarding of what importance the letter-writing could have had on Jan's decision to take a walk.

CASE 3

Background

Swedish engineering companies were in many ways involved in the regulation of the Nile and the dam constructions. A Swedish company was responsible for the preservation of some priceless treasures of art. Among these were a couple of immense statues and cliff temples which had to be moved away from the area that was to be flooded. Professor Bo Hellström made several sojourns in Egypt as hydraulic consultant. One of the major dams he was involved in was the Sadd El Aali. Bo Hellström suffered from allergic reactions and on all his travels he was constantly subjected to substances triggering off mild to severe attacks.

Some other persons mentioned in this case are: Ms. Horsell, Secretary of the British Society for Psychical Research; Gabriel Marcel, famous Existentialist philosopher who took a great interest in parapsychology; Lennart and Bosse, two of Eva's sons; and Lillan, Lennart's wife.

From the Diary

In October, 1955, Eva Hellström wrote the following:

"Bo and I had been in Egypt at Sadd El Aali since the beginning of October (October 5). We had agreed that if he felt well when we returned home from Egypt I would be allowed an eight to ten day's vacation in London on my way home in order to visit old friends and old, dear places. We flew to Rome where we spent the night. Bo felt fine, accompanied me in the morning to the airport where I, at dawn, took off for London. One hour later he was to fly to Stockholm.

"After a flight of four and a half hours I was in London. As soon as I had registered at the hotel, I went to arrange for my driver's license in order to rent a car during my stay.

"Sometime in the afternoon, after lunch, I began feeling anxious. It grew worse. I had the feeling that I must return home and that it was wrong of me to be in London.

"At tea-time I visited the S.P.R. and had tea with Ms. Horsell, Dr. Soal, and Ms. Goldney. Ms. Horsell told me that the Frenchman Marcel was going to give a 'Myers' Memorial Lecture' in ten days and she hoped that I would be able to stay and attend it, something I very much wanted to do.

"However, my anxiety grew worse. The following day, on Tuesday, I went to S.A.S. and booked a flight home at first possible occasion. On Wednesday I flew home without even ringing home to inquire. At the airport I was met by Lennart and Lillan. They told me that Bo had fallen ill on the flight from Rome and was home in bed with a fever of 39 degrees centigrade. He had bronchopneumonia. Our maid, Ms. Eriksson, was hospitalized after an operation and had left the apartment in a mess. It was lucky I flew home. When my telegram had arrived on Tuesday informing of my coming home on Wednesday, Bo said to Bosse: 'You will see that mother has sensed that I am ill.' He was so happy to receive my telegram."

Affirmation

This entry in the diary is verified by Britta Warbert.

The entire statement (and the correctness of its content) is verified by Bo Hellström.

The telegram from London to Stockholm reads as follows:

    L 80 LONDON 10 18 1015
    HELLSTROM SVEAVAGEN 77 STKM
    —ARRIVING WARM SVEAVAGEN WEDNESDAY SK502
    SK502

Stamp of arrival: Stockholm, Skeppsbron 18 OKT 1955

Eva's Comments

In August 1961 Eva added the following:

"I never sensed that my husband was ill. I experienced only strong uneasiness and felt it wrong to be in London and a necessity to return home. I have been alone in London both before and after this event and have never felt any worry. And last September I went alone to the USA without uneasiness and everything went fine. I have only once since that occasion felt uneasiness and anxiety—see the case of October 25, 1957."

Comments

The word "warm" in the telegram is a misunderstanding, perhaps of the word "home".

This supposed telepathy took place over a very great distance between England and Sweden. It happened, as so many of Eva's paranormal experiences, while on a journey. The feeling of anxiety started when she was clearly awake and went on for a long time, i.e. several days, and did not stop until she arrived home.

This is one of many examples of telepathic experiences she has had with her husband.

Comments on All Cases

In Eva's telepathic experiences (not only the three taken up here) the sender of the communication is always a new friend or relative;

one who has a strong desire and an urgent need to share the existing problem or trouble with Eva.

The distance between sender and receiver seems to be irrelevant for the establishing of the contact. In Case 2 the distance is short; Eva and Jan being in the same building. The longest distance is the one in Case 3 showing telepathy between England and Sweden. Bo fell ill on the plane over Germany but Eva had no feeling of agony until afternoon when Bo had arrived home. It was also then that Bo realized he could not cope with his illness alone and would be unable to manage the home with the maid hospitalized. Bo was in fact so ill that he soon after was sent to the Red Cross Hospital.

It could be argued that the telepathic message in Case 3 is somewhat more vague than in the other two cases. In Case 3, Eva is not clear who the sender is, but in the first two cases she knows that it is Jan. One could speculate that the distance makes the difference.

On the other hand, two facts contradict such a conclusion. There is also a great difference in vagueness. It has not been established who the sender is in Case 3. Apart from Bo, it may have been Lennart, his wife or Bosse. It may also have been a combination of two or more senders.

In all cases Eva has a strong feeling of conviction that something is wrong. It is striking that this feeling in Case 3 is so strong that she returns to Stockholm without first checking the prevailing conditions at home.

EVA HELLSTRÖM AND HER DIARY

Eva Hellström was born in September, 1898. She was only ten when her mother, a concert singer, died. Her father, a Doctor of Geology, Mineralogy, and Petrography, also a member of the Swedish Parliament representing the Social Democrats, tended to his home and six children with the help of three maids.

Eva was 19 when she married Bo Hellström. Outside the duties at home—raising four children with a husband often out traveling kept her very busy—her greatest interests were music and since 1945 parapsychology. Paragnosts often seem to be musically inclined and Eva enjoyed playing the piano.

In 1947 she found the S.S.P.R. (The Swedish Society for Psychical Research) and was until recently its secretary and is at present its Honorary Secretary.

In 1949, she began to note in her diary dreams and visions that she thought had a precognitive significance. She soon started to make other parapsychological notes, e.g. telepathy experiences, three of which are included in this paper. Her last documented case (although she has had other experiences after a pause lasting some years) is from 1964 and all together there are 239 cases.

How many of these cases belong to each category (precognition, telepathy, etc.) is impossible for me to say today. First of all, it has to be established, to the fullest degree possible, which cases may be called genuinely paranormal. After that a thorough investigation of the entire material can provide more definite statistics of the cases. Hopefully, I will be able to carry out this analysis in the near future. It is mostly in connection with travels that Eva has reported paranormal experiences. All the ostensive cases in this paper took place on journeys.

Concerning precognitive cases it is very important that the entries of the diary have been verified by persons at hand. It is not so important to have telepathy cases verified, at least not when the entries are affirmed after the sender has been contacted. Under the heading "Affirmation" I take up signatures and other material confirming the cases.

Of course, what she has written in her diary are very short notes, and she had no thoughts about them being published. She did not, and no one can demand it, describe in detail her visions and feelings. It is also very difficult to give an accurate account of feelings in a natural language—the words miss or are vague. In Cases 1 and 3 Eva talks about anxiety and agony, not very precise terms when picturing the complicated feeling she was experiencing at those times.

TELEPATHY AS KNOWLEDGE AND PERCEPTION

What is telepathy? As seen from the cases presented here, telepathy is a form of communication. Feelings or the like are "transmitted" from one person, the "sender", to another, the "receiver." The perception of these messages seems to occur without help from the ordinary senses of hearing, seeing, etc. These feelings are associated with other ideas or arouse the memory of past events, as when Eva experienced the past illness of Jan. Thus, in telepathic situations, more or less vague messages are "passed" from one person to another. In Case 3, Eva was not sure why she was needed in Stockholm. Hence, telepathy appears as more of an activity for the parts of the brain where emotions are generated than the parts which command the speech abilities. Maybe telepathy is mainly connected with right hemispheric activities of the brain.

The Greek term "telepathy" is accurate, literally meaning "to feel at a distance." Cf. e.g. the word "sympathy" meaning "feeling together" or "the same feeling" and the word "pathetic." The prefix "tele," e.g. in "television," means "far off" or "remote."

The cases given are sporadic (often called "spontaneous"). Besides the sporadic cases we may talk about experimentally found telepathy. The question can be raised whether the latter ever proves the occurrence of telepathy. It is designed to exclude the likelihood of chance. The experimental work, based on statistical means, says what telepathy is *not*, not what it *is*.

Chance excluded among the explanations, the researcher goes on making the experiments more and more sophisticated, excluding one normal explanation after the other until he is not able to continue any longer. The result then is that telepathy is something paranormal, meaning that it cannot be explained within the framework of "old, established sciences."

Sporadic telepathy shows that "transmitted" messages are emotionally charged. It can, therefore, be questioned if paragnosts can perform to the best of their abilities in telepathy experiments using Zener cards or other kinds of simple, emotionally very poor material.

It could also be argued that we take notice only of the emotionally charged telepathic events. This would mean that telepathy as a phenomenon is more common than we are inclined to believe. There are certain elements necessary to constitute telepathy. I wish to point them out. Telepathy occurs between living organisms, as in our cases between two human beings. The sensation of telepathy is only within one person, as in our cases, Eva. The sender is totally unaware of telepathy in action, although he may more or less wish it to happen, as in Case 1. Telepathy is never a two-way communication. If it appears so, it is really two one-way sendings. That is to say, if both persons experience telepathy at the same time it is a mutual telepathy, which can be divided up into two separate events where the sender and receiver in the first event takes on the roles of receiver and sender in the second event. There is never any way of "knowing" telepathy is taking place.

Telepathy is a mental act which is not a direct perception of events surrounding the person. The feeling is often, and this is the fact in our cases, accompanied by another feeling (or maybe it should be said that the telepathy includes the feeling) of direction indicating from whom or in what area the feeling comes. Without this feeling of direction it is, from a scientific point of view, very difficult to separate telepathic events from, for instance, general anxiety. Without such a strong feeling of direction, Eva in Case 3 would not, without checking if it was substantiated, have returned to Stockholm. The feeling of direction is usually also the incentive that spurs a person to take down some notes of the supposed telepathy and even perhaps have them signed by someone, before it is actually established that it really was a question of something we call telepathy.

Perhaps some ostensive instances of telepathy have been judged as misses because of a misinterpreted feeling of direction. The receiver believes he was in mental contact with a certain sender but in reality (at least hypothetically, for the sake of reasoning) he was in mental contact with quite another sender.

Telepathy takes place between persons who know each other. Often, as in our cases, the persons are attached to each other. It seems likely that the more emotionally involved two persons are with each other the easier it is to establish a telepathic contact between them. It can, therefore, be questioned if optimum conditions ever can be obtained in an experimental situation where the paragnosts are more or less randomly picked.

More conditions of telepathy could be stated, but this is all I want to say at this point. Some of the problems hinted at here will be analyzed further on in this paper. In connection with this, I wish to point out that, from a philosophical angle, sporadic cases and experiments must be tested and placed within a logical structure. If this is neglected, experimentation and the collection of sporadic cases will degenerate into an aimless conglomeration of meaningless and uninterpretable facts. It is imperative, therefore, that, alongside empirical research, theory building is carried on.

Summarizing this section, we can say that telepathy is at the borderline of what we call knowledge and that this vague kind of knowledge is obtained in other ways than through known perceptors.

THEORIES OF TELEPATHY

Telepathy as a phenomenon can be, and has been, explained in different ways, but, as far as I understand, no satisfactory explanation has yet been given. There are a number of theories and I will here briefly give an account of some of them.

I will treat them in the following manner. First, I distinguish between religious and non-religious theories. The latter ones I divide up into paranormal and normal. Among the first ones I mention clairvoyance and psychokinesis (PK). Here I could have taken up telepathy as an example, meaning that telepathy is not explicable in other terms. Doing this, however, would certainly look like begging the question.

The normal theories, in accordance with old philosophical traditions, are divided up into physical and mental ones. It could be argued

that mental and religious theories, both being non-physical, are related, but the differences are, from a scientific point of view, more
important. In the religious theories, the spiritual part is postulated,
but in the mental theories it is up for investigation whether there is a
spiritual part. Furthermore, the religious theories take for granted
that the spiritual part may exist completely independent of any physical matter. That this may be the case is highly doubted in the mental
theories. In this latter respect the mental theories have something in
common with the physical ones. As an example of a mental theory, I
expand a little on the association theory of telepathy, mainly because
it is, in many respects, compatible with modern psychology.

RELIGIOUS THEORIES

Religious theories explain telepathy by postulating a supreme being,
demons, or surviving spirits which act as informers to paragnosts or
mediums. God or surviving spirits are not investigated or explained.
They are a matter of faith. Either you believe in God or you do not.
This way of reasoning is not scientific but religious. In this respect,
Spiritualism is a kind of religion.

Postulating spirits that carry information from one mind to another
is in a way avoiding analysis of the nature of telepathy. Explaining
extrasensory perception as interactions with spirits, has the same
character as explaining ordinary perception as interactions with spirits.
Doing the latter, one sets aside the whole of the psychology of perception, not to say all branches of psychology.

What I now say, and this has to be emphasized, does not mean the
exclusion from a philosophical point of view that telepathy is caused
by spirits or the like. It only means that I have limited my analysis to
theories compatible with theory building in well established sciences,
notably psychology, and which, from a scientific point of view, look
fruitful. There is nothing in our illustrating cases of telepathy that
supports a religious theory.

PARANORMAL THEORIES

Turning from religious theories, I will direct the rest of this part of
the paper to non-religious ones, consisting of paranormal and normal
theories. However, depending on how they are viewed, paranormal
theories in one way may be considered non-scientific and hence related
to religious theories. I will come back to this aspect at the end of
this section.

Explaining telepathy as a *clairvoyant* perception of another person's neural processes means that only the receiver is active. There is no sender. Hypothetically the "sender" may in every possible way be against tapping knowledge from his mind and yet can do nothing about it. Thus, in this theory, there is no difference between extrasensory perceptive knowledge of a lost necklace behind the back seat of a far off cab and extrasensory perception of the brain of a human being. There are, however, other differences that are essential. Knowing the position of a necklace (or a brain) is one thing; knowing how to read the nerve activities and from them deduce thoughts (pictures, sounds, feelings) is quite another.

How could one, by examining a living brain, see or understand what mental activities are going on inside the brain? Furthermore, is a mental activity really synonymous with a physical brain activity? Nothing in our illustrative cases indicates this theory to be true.

Explaining telepathy as a *PK-activity* means, again, that the sender-receiver theory has to be abandoned. In a clairvoyant theory of telepathy, there is an activity picking up information from other minds. In the PK-theory of telepathy there is an activity delivering information to other minds—the reverse situation from the clairvoyant theory.

But, again, we see that the analogy is not as simple as could be believed at first sight. It is one thing to cause the hand of a compass to spin around on its axis, and quite another to influence the very complicated nervous system within a human being to such an extent that the person "hears" or "sees" intended messages.

On a conscious level, this theory is incompatible with our cases, where our senders are unaware of any sending process. In Case 1, the sender seems to try to get in contact with Eva and in the other two cases this may be the fact, at least on an unconscious level. Although there is nothing to substantiate it, one could, of course, presume that a telepathic communication of PK-type is carried out unconsciously. If this is so in our cases, is impossible to tell from the facts we now know.

Instead of having Eva as the acted upon person we could, for the sake of reasoning, figure Eva as the activating person changing the brain activities of Jan and Bo. If this assumption is adopted, one also has to admit to the consequence that Eva caused the illness within Jan and Bo, something I consider extremely unlikely.

A criticism common to all explanations based on paranormal theories is that they cast no light on the problem. One scarcely comes to a greater understanding of a phenomenon by using a notion which is unclear. In this respect the paranormal theories can be compared to the religious ones where the problem is shoved one step backward.

To do this may be considered non-scientific. But this is not the whole truth. If one paranormal phenomenon is explained as an example of another paranormal phenomenon, matters are simplified, two difficult problems being reduced to one. If once, then, in the future a satisfactory explanation of clairvoyance is put forth, then automatically the problem of telepathy will be solved. Explaining one paranormal phenomenon by another can be seen as a step towards a unified paranormal theory explaining all paranormal phenomena.

ENERGY TRANSMISSION THEORIES

I now leave the paranormal theories and turn to the normal ones. Normal in this context means that telepathy is explicable within the framework of an established science. The standpoint in normal theories is that everything that happens must be normal and hence telepathy will sooner or later be removed from the paranormal realm.

One often used way of explaining telepathy is to see it as an energy transmission process. Such an explanation can in its details be formulated in many different ways. Although I do not say that this is the correct way of describing telepathy, it has, as the reader surely has noticed, influenced my language and I have throughout the paper adopted some of the terms in this theory. The theory can be pictured, in a simple diagram, in the following way. Sender → Means of Sending → Medium → Means of Receiving → Receiver.

The advantage of this theory is its resemblance to such well-known phenomena as television, where one has a sender, a receiver and some kind of waves acting as a medium. Also a code system is employed whereby sounds and pictures are translated into electrical impulses producing waves leaving the sender and reaching the television set. The waves are then decoded into sounds and pictures.

The energy transmission theory of telepathy then runs as follows. There are two human beings, one sender and one receiver. Their brains are in one way or other functioning as a sender apparatus and a receiver apparatus. Some kind of waves are leaving the sender and reaching the receiver. A very sophisticated sort of code system must be involved. A person understanding the transmission system used for television would find no difficulty in a *prima facie* understanding of a similar telepathy system. However, a further analysis shows difficulties in every point, adding up to the conclusion that this theory, at the standpoint of science today, must be rejected.

Science has so far found no trace of a sender apparatus or of a receiver apparatus within the human organism. No wave system as a medium has been traced. Telepathy even has been reported when the receiver or the sender have been placed in a Faraday cage, which is constructed to exclude all known forms of waves. There may be some other kind of radiation and "waves" than the ones science so far has discovered.

What sort of code can it be a question of? The "picture" is translated into a "language of the medium" and then after reaching the receiver, it is translated back to the "picture language." Since no medium has been detected it is impossible to have an idea of what the code looks like. What kind of energy is used? The only energy known of, so far, in the nervous system is a chemical-electric one. The electric waves of the brain can be measured and shown, for instance, on electroencephalograph charts. Perhaps energy can leave the nervous system and this may be what is captured in Kirlian photography. This photographed radiation, however, only seems to extend or be present a centimeter or two along the external parts of the body.

How good a transmission of this kind one gets is, among other things, dependent on how well the outside interferences from different sources are kept out. Since we have traced neither apparatuses nor waves involved, we know nothing of how this sending can be interfered with. We can see from our three cases that if the energy transmission theory holds, then strong disturbances have taken place. There is really nothing in our illustrative cases that indicates the energy transmission theory as the right one.

THE ASSOCIATION THEORY OF TELEPATHY

To avoid the difficulties embedded in religious, energy transmission, PK explanations, and so forth, one has to put forward a theory which does not depend on senders, receivers, media, coding, and energy. There are several such non-mediumistic theories resembling each other. Here I will give an account of the one called the association theory of telepathy.

William James at the beginning of the century advanced the theory of the common (often called "collective") unconscious, the basis for the association theory of telepathy. According to James, all single and individual conscious minds are linked together by a common universal mind which each individual mind, in a conscious state, is unaware of. The individual conscious minds are like islands in an archipelago. Rising above the water, each island has its own characteristic features. Under the water, they are all linked together by the sea bottom. In the same way, James argues, all individual minds are in connection with each other through a common, but for us, unconscious mental entity.

I will here, in a simplified manner, discuss the association theory of telepathy as it has been developed by Whately Carington. This theory tries to explain the paranormal communication as a non-physical one. Ideas are non-physical. The idea in one person's mind is, according to this theory, in an abstract way transplanted into the mind of another person. This presupposes that the sender and the receiver know the code system or have an apparatus that can deal with it, and that they know the language (English).

Now, what kind of code system is used in telepathy? Is telepathy between two persons not speaking the same language impossible? Why does the receiver pick up just one specific thought of the sender, rather than many other thoughts that passed though his mind? As a matter of fact, the sender continuously has brain activity. Why does the receiver pick up the sender's thoughts rather than those of other people? In what ways may telepathic communication be distorted or interfered with?

All these questions can be avoided by the association theory of telepathy. A common unconscious mind is presupposed in this theory. Instead of the simple Sender (S)—Receiver (R) formula, S → R, the association theory gives a more complicated formula: S: A(X, Y). This reads: S has an association of X,Y; X and Y being two thoughts, ideas or "pictures."

Let us take an example. S sees Elizabeth (X) walking along a street and immediately thinks of Andy (Y) since Elizabeth and Andy otherwise always seem to be together. This is the same as to say that S associates Andy with Elizabeth or vice versa. Now, the association A(X, Y) is transferred from the conscious mind of S to the common unconcious. Suppose then that R thinks of Elizabeth: R:X. From the common unconscious, X draws Y and thus R gets the same idea as S: R: A(X, Y). The procedure can be illustrated thus:

S: A(X, Y)	conscious level
(X, Y)	unconscious level
R: X at tl, A(X, Y) at t2	conscious level

First S: A(X, Y) occurs, then R: A(X, Y). If we have no claims of will, intention, or the like, this may then be considered as a kind of communication.

What brings R to think of X? It may be a sheer coincidence, but it is usually possible to come up with a more specific explanation. First of all, R must in one way or other know X. Second, he must come to think of X. If this is the case, then it is very likely that R knows Y. Maybe R is planning to contact X for some reason or another.

Let us take another example, our third case. Eva is traveling. Her husband is at home ill in bed. From one mind to the common unconscious the picture of Bo sweating and suffering is emitted. Eva thinks of home and receives via the common unconscious the association of the critical situation there.

Do all associations in the common unconscious rise to a conscious state? No, the "extrasensory perception" is like ordinary perception —it is selective. As a matter of fact, only a small percentage of all the information that hits us (vision, sound, feeling, taste, etc.) is allowed to enter into the conscious level of the mind. If every piece of information striking us is presented simultaneously and equally strongly in our conscious mind, then there would be total chaos and any form of constructive thinking would be impossible. The same kind of chaos would occur if all the billions and billions of associations in the common unconscious would have an equal chance to flow into the minds of human beings.

We are, to some extent, able to study the laws of perception and the laws of association formation. This is a task for psychologists and will not be taken up here. I will here only remind the reader of the laws of emotionality, of vividness, of repetition, of recency, of need, and of wishfulness.

Let us take the law of repetition as an example from psychology and apply it to parapsychology and the theory of association.

S1: A(X, Y)	S11: A(X, Z)
S2: A(X, Y)	S12: A(X, Z)
.	.
.	.
.	.
S10: A(X, Y)	S50: A(X, Z)
adds up to	adds up to
A(X, Y)10	A(X, Z)40

R_{t1}: X then gives R_{t2}: A(X,Z) and not A(X,Y), since this latter association is less frequent than the first one, *mutatis mutandis*.

Provided the association theory of telepathy is correct, the knowledge from psychology then can also be used in parapsychology. We can make another analogy between extrasensory perception and ordinary perception. In both cases the perception may be imperfect, distorted, sometimes even "false." (Take, as an example of the latter, hallucinations.) The ability to perceive is inherited, but the actual act of what we perceive is mainly learned. We train perception every day. As a rule, we never train extrasensory perception. How poor must not our extrasensory perception be compared to our ordinary perception. Also, ordinary kinds of conversation are trained daily. Conversation is difficult, many misunderstandings occur. Communication through telepathy is never trained. How much more confusing must not our extrasensory conversation be compared to our ordinary conversation. One advantage of the association theory is that it can be applied not only to telepathy but to most paranormal phenomena.

A big question raised by this theory concerns the matter and nature of the common unconscious. In psychology, the unconscious is an accepted and much used notion. Psychologists, however, usually refer to this notion as an individual entity, located together with the conscious in the nervous system of individual persons. Where is the common unconscious located? If it is divided in parts distributed to every human being, then the association theory begs the question. What kind of communication is there when one idea (association) goes from one part of the common unconscious to another part? The association theory was built up in order to avoid that problem.

I want to add two points here. It is true that William James' theory of a common unconscious located outside of individuals, was integrated in his philosophy of psychology and hence was applicable not only to the explanation of paranormal phenomena, but also to many kinds of normal behavior. This kind of a common unconscious had also been adopted by depth psychologists, notably C. G. Jung.

What is consciousness? This concept is certainly not fully clear. Here, I think, it is enough to point out that consciousness and unconsciousness are no kinds of matter. The question as to where the conscious and the unconscious are located might be irrelevant. Materia must fill a certain room or space. Non-materia cannot be measured in length, width, or thickness.

Non-materia, however, such as thoughts, dreams, hallucinations, etc. seems indirectly to have a position in space and in one way or another is connected to materia as brains, nervous systems, etc. What kind of connection this can be is an old philosophical problem, frequently referred to as the Cartesian dilemma. This spot of connection, it seems—and this is the way Descartes saw it—must be located in a special place which can be pointed out. The only problem is to find it. Other than a common unconscious mind, some psychologists (for example, Gustave Le Bon and William McDougall) have developed the idea of a group mind which is something more than the individual parts (minds) it consists of. When the group mind is active, all the individuals in the group are thinking, feeling, or acting alike. This group mind can be compared to the common unconscious mind, although they are clearly separate notions.

SUMMARY AND CONCLUSIONS

When analyzing telepathy, I begin by giving an ostensive definition, consisting of three examples taken from the case-book of Ms. Eva Hellström. Telepathy can be considered a kind of knowledge concerning living beings other than the paragnost involved. Paranormal knowledge of things is called clairvoyance. Certainly there are borderline difficulties between telepathy and clairvoyance, but these problems are not considered in this paper. Since the telepathic knowledge originates in other beings than the paragnost, we term telepathy a sort of communication. For the sake of convenience, but not as a result of analysis, we call the paragnost a receiver and the source of knowledge a sender.

The sender may be, and usually seems to be, unaware of the communication taking place. Even if the sender in one way or other tries to communicate telepathically, he has no way of telling if he is being successful during the actual sending. Theoretically, it is possible for telepathy to be a two-way transmission. This means that the persons involved are both senders and receivers. The two-way telepathic communication does not alter what I have already said. The knowledge in question is mostly of an unprecise nature. Why this is so, is impossible to say today, but this fact, among others, makes it troublesome to study telepathy. The most difficult hindrance is that paranormal abilities cannot be demonstrated at will.

Since ordinary communication involves sensory perception, we presume that this also must be so in paranormal experiences. This perception however, as it is very special and its details unknown, is termed extrasensorial. Neither sender organs nor receptors have been detected.

In order to understand telepathy a number of theories have been developed. I divide them up into categories and describe them in a general way. The religious theories, including the spiritualistic ones, are avoiding the problems. The paranormal theories, are intrinsic ones and give no explanation at all. An example from ethics will illustrate what I mean. Giving the notion "good" intrinsic explanation, is the same as saying "good" means "good" and cannot be interpreted in other terms. Explaining "good" in terms of "liked by everyone," "giving acceptable results," "something searched for," and so forth, is then called a "naturalistic fallacy." G. E. Moore develops this in his book *Principia Ethica*.

Thus, saying that a paranormal ability is something paranormal, is the same as saying that one either accepts that paranormal events happen or that they are impossible. This way of reasoning comes close to the religious way of reasoning, the main difference being that in paranormal theories one directly accepts the phenomena in question, while in the religious theories one accepts some factors behind the phenomena.

It should be noted that intrinsic theories are used in all sciences. Above I gave an example from ethics. An example from physics would be to explain magnetism as magnetism without being able to tell why a magnet attracts iron objects. There is a psychological reason based on acquaintance for accepting an intrinsic definition of telepathy. This has been developed by Bertrand Russell, who made a distinction between knowledge by aquaintance and knowledge by description. (See his book *The Problems of Philosophy*.)

Most parapsychologists seem to strive after a normal explanation of the paranormal. To do so sounds like a contradiction, but must be interpreted so that a paranormal event only is paranormal in the way of speaking until it can be analyzed in normal terms. This means that all paranormal phenomena in reality are normal.

The energy transmission theories try to fit telepathy into the framework of mechanics. This is bound to be unsuccessful, because telepathy involves purely non-physical entities such as thoughts, mental pictures, feelings, and the like. No physical instruments, energy or code systems have been found to participate in telepathy. The energy transmission theories, therefore, have not seemingly advanced parapsychology as a science one single step.

It remains to explain telepathy as a purely mental activity. As an example, in order to approach the problem in this way, I have taken up the association theory of telepathy. This theory makes an analogy between ordinary association creation and telepathy. Since ordinary associations only take place in a person's mind, this theory has to postulate a sort of general mind outside individuals. The procedure reminds one of the procedure in the religious theories. The existence of such a general, universal mind connected to all single, individual minds cannot be tested. The common unconscious is fed by individual minds. If all individual minds cease to exist, then the common unconscious also ceases to exist. No method for either verifying or falsifying the theory has been put forward.

Common to all the theories taken up in this paper are the metaphysical aspects they contain. None gives an acceptable answer to the question of what telepathy is. When it comes to theory-building, parapsychology still has a long way to go.

REFERENCES

[1] Beloff, J., "On Trying to Make Sense of the Paranormal." *Proceedings of the Society for Psychical Research*, 56, 1976, pp. 173–195.

[2] Broad, C. D., "Dr. S. G. Soal's forskning i telepati och framtidsförnimmelse." *Meddelande från Sällskapet för parapsykologisk forskning*, No. 1, 1950.

[3] Broad, C. D., "A Reply to my Critics." In P. A. Schilpp (editor), *The Philosophy of C. D. Broad*. Tudor Publishing Company: New York, 1959.

[4] Broad, C. D., "Dreaming, and Some of its Implications." Presidential address, 1959. *Proceedings of the Society for Psychical Research*, 52, 1959, pp. 53–78.

[5] Broad, C. D., "Tre föredrag." *Meddelande från Sällskapet för parapsykologisk forskning*, No. 8, 1962, pp. 3–17.

[6] Broad, C. D., *Lectures on Psychical Research*. Routledge & Kegan Paul: London, 1967.

[7] Carington, W., *Telepathy. An Outline of its Facts, Theory, and Implications*. Methuen: London, 1945.

[8] Carington, W., *Matter, Mind, and Meaning*. Yale University Press: New Haven, 1949.

[9] Ducasse, C. J., "Broad on the Relevance of Psychical Research to Philosophy." In P. A. Schilpp (editor), *The Philosophy of C. D. Broad*. Tudor Publishing Company: New York, 1959.

[10] Ejvegaard, R., "Some Remarks on Precognition." *European Journal of Parapsychology*, Vol. 1, No. 2, 1976, pp. 17–35.

[11] Hellström, E., "Intervju med Eva Hellström." *Sökaren*, No. 7, 1972, pp. 6–7, 24.

[12] Jung, C. G., *The Structure and Dynamics of the Psyche*. Pantheon: New York, 1960.

[13] Krippner, S., "Telepathy." In Edgar D. Mitchell (editor), *Psychic Exploration*. Putnam: New York, 1974, pp. 112–131.

[14] LeShan, L., *Toward a General Theory of the Paranormal*. Parapsychological monographs, Parapsychology Foundation: New York, 1969.

[15] Mundle, C. W. K., "The Explanation of ESP." In J. R. Smythies (editor), *Science and ESP*. Routledge & Kegan Paul: London, 1967, pp. 197–207.

[16] Price, H. H., "Some Philosophical Questions about Telepathy and Clairvoyance. *Philosophy*, 15, No. 3, 1940, pp. 363–374.

[17] Rhine, L. E., *Hidden Channels of the Mind*. Sloane: New York, 1961.

[18] Rhine, L. E., *ESP in Life and Lab: Tracing Hidden Channels*. Macmillan: New York, 1967.

[19] Schwarz, B. E., "Built-in Controls and Postulates for the Telepathic Event." *Corrective Psychiatry and Journal of Social Therapy*, 12, No. 2, 1966, pp. 64–82.

[20] Sinclair, U., *Mental Radio. Does it Work and How?* Werner Laurie: London, 1951.

[21] Smythies, J. R., "Is ESP Possible?" In J. R. Smythies (editor), *Science and ESP*. Routledge & Kegan Paul: London, 1967, pp. 1–14.

[22] Stevenson, I., *Telepathic Impressions, a Review and Report of 35 New Cases*. University of Virginia Press: Charlottesville, 1960.

[23] Sudre, R., *Traité de Parapsychologie*. Editions Payot: Paris, 1956.

[24] Ullman, M., "An Experimental Study of the Telepathic Dream." *Corrective Psychiatry and Journal of Social Therapy*, 12, No. 2, 1966, pp. 115–139.

[25] Ullman, M., "An experimental Approach to Dreams and Telepathy. Methodology and Preliminary Findings." *Archives of General Psychiatry*, 14, 1966, pp. 605–613.

DISCUSSION

STANFORD: I much appreciate the careful analysis you have given the telepathy problem, but I find myself puzzled and I think in some disagreement on one particular point. What it comes down to really, I suppose, is a matter of factuality. And this concerns your reason for rejection of the so-called PK theory of telepathy. You said in this connection, that a crucial objection was the problem of affecting the proper brain cells in order to make this possible, and, indeed, you gave a similar comment with regard to a clairvoyant interpretation. Now, it seems to me that this kind of comment reflects either a lack of familiarity, or a disagreement with a rather common opinion of parapsychology nowadays that psi processes seem to exhibit a goal-directed character. In PK theory or PK work specifically, which is most germane to your consideration here, the PK theory of telepathy, we haven't found any evidence of the decline of the PK effect with complexity of the task or with ignorance of known aspects of it. We also have pretty good evidence for PK upon complex biological processes, and it seems to me that this isn't a very far step from being able to suppose that it can influence brain processes.

EJVEGAARD: There is not much to say about that. I could agree with you, but I do also say that there is probably a difference, as in the example I used here, in doing something very simple, in moving something in a very simple way, or doing everything that you have to do to create thoughts in another person. Now, of course, it's very difficult to discuss this problem, since we know nothing about what's going on. We can only leave it at that, I think.

HILL: Well, first I want to thank you for presenting some of this unpublished data from Mrs. Hellstrom's diary, and I hope you and she will be able to go ahead with your plans for publishing in book form more of this very interesting material. Regarding the physicalist theory of telepathy, you said there were no wave carriers which could conceivably allow energy or information to pass from one person to another. Well, I'm afraid I can't agree with this at all. In fact, ELF and VLF waves are a very probable carrier for certain types of information transfer, especially over long distances, because these travel completely around the earth with almost no attenuation. It is, unfortunately, true that these ELF and VLF waves go right through a Faraday cage, and people who work with these things realize that it's impossible to shield out electromagnetic waves over all frequencies simultaneously. At the Parascience Conference in London last year, I tried to explode the myth which many parapsychologists have, that the electromagnetic hypothesis has been experimentally rejected. I showed that in several key experiments, including Vasiliev's experiments, which are often quoted as final proof, there were serious methodological errors and that it could be by no means considered the final word on whether or not telepathy can be carried by electromagnetic waves. I'm not claiming that we have all the answers in an electromagnetic model. In fact, there are a lot of problems, for instance, how you focus these extremely long wave lengths to get very detailed information, but I don't think you can reject it as easily as you have done in your paper.

EJVEGAARD: I said in my paper that there may be some other kinds of radiation and waves than the ones science has so far discovered. And, of course, it's open to speculation as to what kinds of means there can be behind this, but we haven't pinpointed anything of that kind as yet, as far as I know.

NICOL: Sir J. J. Thompson, the discoverer of the electron, who was a vice-president of the SPR, postulated in his memoirs his belief that there were two kinds of telepathy, one near and one distant, and that they were quite different things. Unfortunately, he didn't develop the idea. I merely throw it in here to see if anyone else can develop it, now or later. Like our speaker, I dug fairly deeply into theories of the nature of telepathy, from the rather uncertain ones of Augustine of Hippo 1500 years ago, right up to H. H. Price, Carington, and others. I would say this: that we know no more of the nature of telepathy than Augustine of Hippo knew in about A.D. 400. Our ignorance is devastating. As for various electromagnetic theories, they were postulated by Crookes in about 1896, and were eventually rejected. But I wonder what kind of electromagnetism would pass a spontaneous experience say from England to Australia and what would be the strength of the message when it arrived?

EJVEGAARD: I have to agree with what Mr. Nicol says here. Democritus very early put forward a theory of telepathy. He wrote a book on this subject about 400 B.C., which is lost now, but we have some quotations from other authors about it.

BENDER: Well, in the beginning of your paper you seemed to have laid special stress on the formulation that in telepathy and telepathic communication, "messages were passed from one person to another person," and (these are your words) you took up the same formulation in saying that there are "two separate events, sender and percipient." I don't think that this model's pattern is sufficient to cover all the experiences we have with telepathy. The experiments we were doing in the Freiburg Institute show that often it seems that telepathic communication stems from a sort of bi-personality, that what you call a sender and a percipient are not separate entities, but the telepathic communication brings them together and forms a sort of bi-personality, so that you can't distinguish between the sender and the percipient. Well, this stems from a close analysis of the material obtained where the contents of what you call a sender and the contents of the percipient just amalgamate. That complicates, for example, the effect of what you call the percipient amalgamate with complexes of the senders, and form a new unity. So, we prefer, in certain cases, just to describe this as a personality that has temporarily been formed, which seems to make obvious that telepathic communication may occur in a sort of psychic field. Some of you know, perhaps, that for twenty-three years, we were conducting a precognitive experiment with an actress, Mrs. Christina Mylius, a lady who has very marked paranormal capacities. She came, two years ago, to the Freiburg Institute, and I proposed an experiment with her which had nothing to do with parapsychology. An experiment with suggested dreams, ordered dreams. I gave her an envelope with a suggestion as follows: "I've won the big prize in a lottery." She had to open it before going to sleep, just to reflect upon it and report to me the dream of the night. Well, she came in in the morning and said, "I dreamt, but unfortunately not conforming to your suggestion. I've been dreaming that I was in Freiburg, where I actually am, [she was formerly in the Freiburg Theatre as an actress] and was looking for the house of a friend of mine and I had a feeling in the dream it was a musician. I went in the direction of the Black Forest, found the villa, rang the bell, and a young man opened, fair-haired with dark glasses and it was very strange to find that man here." She awakened depressed and flabbergasted, noted the dream and reported it to me. Now, that had nothing to do with the suggestion, but in the evening, accompanied, fortunately, by one of the collaborators, she went to a Freiburg theater to see an actress with whom she had been on friendly terms when she was in Freiburg years ago. They met after the show in a restaurant, and people told her that this actress has a new friend, a young one, and this new friend dropped in—the fair-haired boy with dark glasses she had seen in her dream. And it turned out that he was the son of the musician and, in the meantime, which she didn't know, the musician died. It was Count X. And now the point of the story is this: they began to talk about dreams and the young man said, "Well, I don't dream very often but this night I had such an extraordinary dream. I dreamt that I won a big prize in the lottery." And that's a pattern, a model which recurs rather often, and certainly not by mere chance. It's a psychic field, and if you analyze it profoundly, you'll find emotional motivations which led to this.

EJVEGAARD: Insofar as you say that the sender/receiver theory is not fully acceptable and that it's more in the language I used, I agree with you.

HAYNES: I wanted to bring out a general point which has emerged more and more clearly throughout the papers, and that is, that some of us are interested in the technology of psi and not always interested in its place in nature. It seems to me that if you investigate the one, you have also to bear the other in mind. It is the same distinction that Dr. Janin made this morning between information and meaning. It seems to me that even if the new radiomagnetic waves which have hardly yet been found—I think you said they were called ELF waves—are indeed operative through Faraday cages and over long distances, that is very interesting, but how do we know that we are going to react to their stimulus in terms of meaning, images of the reality they are supposed to carry? If you have television waves, you have an apparatus already constructed to produce the images which they are concerned with. In our brains, we don't know that we have any such apparatus, except as concerns the immediate senses. We have no means of transforming a stimulus into a picture, except in the senses. I once heard a conversation in which it was put to a philosopher that it's extraordinarily mysterious that we receive electrical stimuli and turn them into images, sounds, sense and all the rest of it. He said it wasn't very peculiar, because he didn't like anything to be mysterious. But it is mysterious, and what is even more mysterious is that waves should transform themselves through telepathy into meaningful images. They're not just like Morse code.

PARAPSYCHOLOGY AND THE "ULTIMATE REALITY"

EMILIO SERVADIO

When we use the expression "The Philosophy of . . . " we usually mean that from the discoveries and the achievements of a science, we can obtain or suggest conclusions and views that go beyond purely scientific ascertainments or constructions. For instance, many biological discoveries have encouraged some scientific writers to expound a "philosophy of biology"—be it the behavioristic philosophy of Professor Skinner, or the dualistic philosophy of Arthur Koestler.

In a previous paper, I reached the following judgment in regard to a "philosophy of parapsychology": i.e., that its contribution to our culture "is recognizable, above all, in the better knowledge it enables us to acquire of man's psychological and physiological nature or, in other words, of the human personality." Nowadays, this conclusion seems to me sorely inadequate. In fact, it is not very different from what could be said after reviewing the most recent data and findings of psychology, physiology, or even psychoanalysis. My present-day inferences are much wider. I really think that parapsychology, in spite of its limitations, can give us some reason to adopt an enlarged view of the ultimate essence of man, and of the universe.

In another paper, a more recent one, I have tried to show that in different degrees, the subjects of those investigations that we call "parapsychological" seem to bypass somehow (even if they are unaware of it) our usual ways of thinking and perceiving, and to partake of a world of "immediate thought." This world, I pointed out, "can be reached by obtaining a more or less pronounced reduction (or abolition, in extreme cases) of our usual, conscious, individualized awareness. . ." Therefore, mediumistic or similar states could be considered as more or less enlarged psychological areas, pertaining mainly to a different kind of thinking. This would be the precondition, for a medium, to show abilities such as bypassing the spatial or temporal limits of individualized thought, and also the way of considering, feeling, and disposing of "matter," i.e., of apparently "inanimate" pieces of reality, so closely connected with our customary, subject-versus-object distinction, typical of our usual state of mind. I know only too well that the views expounded this far are brushed off, or even considered with some contempt, by the supporters of an alleged "new trend" in our discipline. I will attempt presently to examine and to summarize the whole issue.

The "new trend" I have mentioned aims at tracing back all possible psi-γ or psi-κ phenomena to marginal, hypothetical, or not yet discovered *physical* energies. It was according to such a main trend that, in the Second International Congress of Psychotronics, held in Monte Carlo from June 30 to July 4, 1975, the very term "parapsychology" was hardly used, or was vaguely frowned upon. Psychotronics, in the concept of many of its supporters, was to be the only legitimate approach to those phenomena that several researchers and men of learning (obviously considered "old hat") persist in calling "parapsychological." The definition of psychotronics, as it was suggested by a restricted "Scientific Committee," was *per se* very eloquent. "Psychotronics," it was declared, "is a science which, in an interdisciplinary fashion, studies fields of interaction between people and their environment (internal and external) and the energetic processes involved. Psychotronics recognizes that matter, energy and consciousness are interconnected in a way which contributes to new understandings of the energetic capabilities of the human beings, life processes and matter in general."

It can be easily observed that in the above quoted definition, total emphasis has been put on "matter" and "energy." Although something formally pertaining to psychological disciplines has been preserved in the general term "psychotronics," terms like psychological, paraphysychological etc. have been carefully avoided. In the definition, one finds indeed the term "consciousness", but in a fashion that seems to imply the exclusive existence of *conscious* processes and mechanisms. Apparently, for those who accept the aforesaid definition, mental processes that are not conscious do not exist. In fact, a staunch supporter of this "new trend" openly declared during the Congress that "unconscious" is simply "that, to which no attention is being paid." All modern discoveries regarding the human unconscious, its processes, its laws, etc., were thus flatly denied.

It is widely known, by now, that in some countries, and especially in the Soviet Union, quite a few parapsychological terms have been deleted from what could be called the official, scientific dictionary. For example, one is not supposed to speak or to write about *telepathy*. The approved term is "bio-communication." What is still called psychokinesis by many parapsychologists is related to "bio-energetics," and so forth.

In my opinion, it would be a great mistake to think that all that has been reported so far boils down to a simple question of terminology. This can indeed be said of several changes that have occurred in the "labels" that parapsychologists have used for many decades—starting, as we all know, from the very term "parapsychology," which right now has the majority of the votes, whereas the British have adopted long ago, and still seem to prefer, "psychical research," and the French go on using "métapsychique." I am definitely convinced that behind the difference in terms there exists a fundamental difference of *philosophical* premises. To put it in very clear-cut, uncomplimentary words: it is my view that the subject-matter of our investigations is nowadays considered under two completely different philosophical angles; one is non-exclusive, but mainly non-materialistic, the other one is an angle whereby all nonmaterialistic views on *anything*, including our field of research, are unscientific, and to be condemned. The consequences of this philosophical clash are not yet completely visible for one major reason, that I shall try to describe in philosophical terms.

In spite of all that has been contended by a wide range of philosophers and thinkers (I shall mention some of them in a subsequent part of this paper), it has to be admitted that *empirically speaking*, we usually feel that we are moving in a reality-system where there are causes and effects, where time runs in one direction, where space has three dimensions, where if one applies a certain known stimulus one can expect a certain response, etc. This is why an idealist and a materialist can agree about devising or using innumerable technical instruments, from a pair of scissors to a jet-plane. This is why in many realms of science and technology there can be an understanding and a cooperation between people having a completely different philosophical background, say, between a convinced atheist and a devout Catholic. A well known example of the possibility of such cooperation is the "Bureau Médical" of Lourdes, where medical doctors of different creeds (or having no creed whatsoever) can examine and discuss the same case of a purported process of illness and recovery.

Things seem to change considerably, however, when one deals with problems that have an almost immediate reverberation on "ultimate realities," i.e., with problems whereby the very essence of man, nature, the universe, etc., can be viewed, nay, *have* to be viewed, according to this or that philosophical conviction. A person who abides by the conviction that nothing transcendental can be *proven* on a non-transcendental level will not be able to collaborate in a purported "experiment," devised with the declared aim of demonstrating survival. A non-religious medical man at the "Bureau" of Lourdes would refuse to discuss with a religious colleague whether a sudden, medically incomprehensible case of recovery could be the consequence of a miraculous intervention of the Virgin Mary, whereas he would certainly agree to examine with his colleague the anamnesis and the X-ray photos pertaining to the case.

Let us now see how this kind of what might be called a "mutual non-understanding" could be applied to our subject matter. I will take into consideration that most studied and best-known phenomenon: telepathy.

It is hardly necessary to mention that many attempts have been made to "explain" telepathic occurrences, and that many hypotheses regarding the phenomenon have been suggested, but I shall consider two main "models" only. One I would call the "communication" model, implying the transmission of "something" (waves, particles, neutrinos, bio-energetic radiations, or some other element) from "transmitter" A to "receiver" B. The other might be called the "communion" model, implying that in telepathy, nothing "physical" is "transmitted"; that there is a nonphysical field, or denominator (more or less corresponding to the "collective unconscious" in the Jungian sense) which unites all human beings—perhaps simply all that lives; and that in those cases where this union, even for a second, becomes actual, A and B can cease to feel as if they were utterly separated, and can "merge into each other psychologically, to go then immediately back to their previous, empirical separation, which is what we usually perceive in our everyday experience.

In the Western world, the first kind of approach to telepathic phenomena (assuming the "communication" hypothesis) is still pursued by some researchers, in spite of the difficulties and contradications it presents, and that were openly acknowledged by many investigators (including the Russian physiologist, L. L. Vasiliev). But the second idea—although it may seem rather abstract and far-fetched to some— has a full right of citizenship, can be openly declared, and has been expounded and sustained in many ways by many prominent philosophers and parapsychologists. Could we say the same of those people who can think only in terms of bio-communication, and who have adopted the materialistic philosophy as the only valid one? Certainly not. For them, any such approach is unscientific, idealistic, etc., and has to be repelled. If they were asked to cooperate in a series of experiments, aimed at giving some support to the "communion" hypothesis of telepathy, they would certainly refuse.

It seems to me that we have thus reached an unavoidable consequence, i.e., that parapsychologists can no longer ignore or forget the philosophical background to which they finally have to trace back their work—even if it is admitted that much of this work is not strictly or directly dependent on one's philosophical assumptions (let me remind you of what was said of the Lourdes Medical Bureau and of its variegated members). In fact, I think that this Conference is the right place where a man of science, who has studied parapsychological phenomena for a long period of time, can freely express his philosophical convictions. Starting from this statement, I shall now proceed to express my own personal views.

In the very beginning of this paper, I put forward two bold assumptions: first, that there are in nature two different kinds of thinking of basically opposite essence; second, that some individuals (in particular, those who are considered apt to show evidence of psi phenomena) partake, if only partially and momentarily, of a universal, unconscious, timeless, spaceless thought, representing the inner face of nature. Let us now see if and how these hypotheses can be substantiated.

A whole range of thinkers and philosophers (in the West, particularly, Plotinus, Roger Bacon, Pascal, Schopenhauer, Schelling, and to a certain extent also Bergson) have contended that beyond the boundaries of empirical reality, there exists a quite different, transcendental reality (the *Noumenon* according to Kant, the *Wille* according to Schopenhauer). A similar view has been maintained all along by mystics and seers, especially by people like Ruysbroeck, Eckhartshausen, Marsilius Ficinus, Swedenborg, Robert Fludd and many others in the West; Lao-Tze, Milarepa, Shankara, Ramakrishna, Ramana and several others in the East. Many poets and writers have expressed this same basic idea—of a limited and empirical *versus* a total, eternal Reality—in some of their works; let me only mention Dante, Blake, Hölderlin, Novalis, Balzac, Whitman, Tennyson, Carpenter, Rimbaud, Nerval, and, in modern times, Maurice Maeterlinck, André Breton, and Aldous Huxley.

Could it be that all the aforesaid people were victims of delusions, wishful thinking, or day-dreaming? Hardly! For some of them, by the way, the realization of an Absolute Being has been a shattering, almost terrifying experience, which they probably would have avoided if possible. Allow me to recall a few words written by Charles G. Finney; " . . . I literally bellowed out of the unutterable gushings of my heart.

These waves came over me, and over me, and over me, one after the other, until I recollect I cried out, 'I shall die if these waves continue to pass over me'. . . " Horace Traubel writes: "What is this flood, overcoming body and sense? I feel the walls of my skull crack, the barriers part, the sun-flood enter. . . " Yet, they, too, arrived at the same conclusion as those who had experienced only bliss and joy and ecstasy in their perception of Total Awareness (or Cosmic Consciousness, as Richard M. Bucke prefers to call it).

On the other side of the coin, it has often been pointed out that the "rules and regulations" which pertain to parapsychological phenomena, and to those people concerned with demonstrating these phenomena, are fundamentally different from those of our usual psychological understanding. In fact, they are no less different from those found at the time of "beyond the looking glass" of Alice in Wonderland, in comparison with those that Alice acknowledges and is submitted to at the beginning and end of her "adventures." This basic difference has been beautifully described and emphasized by Lawrence LeShan in some well known books and essays.

This characteristic of psi phenomena, and of the psi-γ or psi-κ "ways of functioning" of those people who are instrumental in bringing them about, is one of the causes of the resistance that parapsychology still encounters in many academic circles. It is also the cause of the consistent difficulties we meet when we try to squeeeze such phenomena into the same containers, and to put them under the same laws, as we admit and use in other scientific fields. Some time ago, I tried to give some examples of this, apparently blatant "irrationality" of several parapsychological contentions. Psychology tells us, for instance, that a "communication" takes place under certain conditions, and with the use of signs, or signals, that in one way or other are emitted, and received, by the sense organs. Parapsychology tells us that in telepathy, there can be a communication or a communion between two or more people separate from any known sign, signal, or channel. Physics tells us that a physical effect (e.g. the movement of a solid object) can be obtained if a certain physical stimulus is applied. Parapsychology tells us that man's thoughts can *directly* exert an influence over a solid object, without any known physical link between the two. No wonder that so many people should have rejected similar contentions, and that many others should think that such contradictions to what science tells us are surely due either to errors, or to fantasy, misapprehension, fraud, conjuring, and so forth.

Parapsychology, in my considered opinion, has given us ample evidence in favor of some basic views about man and reality, which had been put forward for centuries by speculative thought (religious, philosophical, etc.), but had never been adequately substantiated. Parapsychology has shown that the empirical, customary, everyday reality as it impinges on our sense-organs or our instruments of obeservation is only one facet of a total reality, and that some people are sometimes able to live and act (for different lengths of time) beyond the limits of that facet. This is more or less the view that has been expounded and preached by those Easten traditions which purport that the world in which we live is only phenomenal, delusional, a world of *Maya*; that beyond this world of appearance and necessity there is a world of Truth and Power; that deep down from the apparent multiplicity, Unity can be reached and realized.

Starting from this point, several further considerations can be made. The first that comes to mind is whether the aforesaid philosophical inferences from the parapsychological findings should reduce or invalidate the importance of parapsychological research and experimentation, or that of the scientific approach altogether. The answer to this question is an emphatic "No!" First of all, parapsychology can give us plenty of information about the mechanisms of the human mind, the processes at work in interpersonal relations, our usual ways of dealing with "objects," and so on. Moreover, let us not forget that even those people who can show indications of the existence of a transcendental world are human beings—even if they are called Milarepa or Aurobindo or Saint Francis or any of the contemporary great seers or mediums. These people have bodies, they have thought-processes, they have emotions. Several years ago, at a Conference sponsored by the Parapsychology Foundation, somebody asked a ·Dominican Father if God could not provoke a state of bliss in a saint by temporarily modifying the biochemical conditions of his brain-cells. The Father replied "Why certainly!" without winking an eyelid. I doubt whether a parapsychologist will ever be able to perform a blood examination of a holy man during a mystical rapture; but I maintain that this would be a most legimate, interesting, and informative experiment. In a similar, but more practical vein, several observations have been made, using EEG, on yogis and inspired people while they were meditating or praying. Once more, I say that this is a good, scientific, truly parapsychological approach. But obviously, if such an approach can be agreed upon with regard to holy people and their "phenomena," I think that we can safely go our own parapsychological way when we study mediums, clairvoyants, or just ordinary people!

Some other important questions can now be raised. One is, whether our parapsychological tools are apt to fill the gap that exists between our ordinary way of apprehending reality and the awareness of an Ultimate Reality. The second is, whether there might be other possible ways of filling such a gap if the answer to the first question should be in the negative.

In fact, such an answer *has* to be in the negative, for very simple methodological reasons. No *scientific* approach, method or experiment can ever give us certainties of a transcendental order (hence the *a priori* futility of all attempts aimed at "demonstrating," in a scientific fashion, the reality of survival, reincarnation, or the existence of God). Parapsychology purports to be, *has* to be, a scientific discipline. Therefore, as I have tried to show, it can and does give us plenty of "pointers" towards the necessity of admitting an Absolute Reality beyond our usual, limited reality; but it cannot give us any *proof* of this, and will never be able to do so "because of the contradiction that does not permit of it," as Dante would have said.

The second question appears then even more cogent; but it is obvious that an answer to it can only be a tentative one, and one that requires that we abandon our usual, logical way of thinking. There are indeed several methods or techniques whereby a person can hope to get a direct—if only fleeting—awareness of the Ultimate Reality. In a recently published paper, I have tried to describe the characteristics of three of them, namely: mediumship, mysticism, and initiation. In short, my contentions have been the following:

(1) Usually, a medium does not bother to "prepare" himself for his performances through any particular "exercise" (physical or mental as the case may be). He "abandons" himself to "something," loses contact with his customary level of consciousness, and is not able to foresee what will happen to him, or to have a clear awareness of the "different reality" which he enters. Descriptions of such a reality by trance mediums have therefore always been vague, and very often contradictory.

(2) The attitude of the religious mystic is very different. The mystic believes in a superior order of things, in God, in Life eternal. He continuously tries to purify his inner being. When he goes into different states of consciousness, he knows that this is bound to take him nearer to God, and toward the supreme beatitude of Paradise. His mystical experiences are therefore quite different from those of the ordinary medium, and different also—beyond some superficial resemblances—are the paranormal events that may accompany them. The mystic always maintains that the Creator and the created world are substantially different, and that no spiritual achievement will ever make one and the same thing of the Supreme Maker and his creatures.

(3) An initiate usually admits knowing that every human being is a spark of an Absolute Fire, and that people in general feel different because they are "ignorant" in a philosophical sense. Initiation techniques (from Yoga or Zazen to transcendental meditation, psychedelic methods with or without drugs, and a whole series of other rites or exercises) are certain to actualize the aforesaid virtual essence and to obtain the cessation of all distinctions between the individual and the universal Self, the re-absorption of all apparent realities into one, of the delusional multiplicity into an unique and only Truth.

It is obviously beyond the scope of this presentation to go further. I think I have sufficiently developed my main assumptions, clearly stating what, to me, a "philosophy of parapsychology" can actually mean. It means very much indeed. As a scientific discipline, parapsychology cannot give us the explanation of the universe, but it certainly can give us plenty of help in our search for such an explanation, within the limits of our human possibilities.

DISCUSSION

PENELHUM: I would like to begin by expressing my appreciation for the combination of depth and clarity in your presentation. I would like to follow this by a question designed to make sure that I fully follow the implications of the view you put forward. I was very interested in the early part of your address, when you drew a comparison between the two groups of parapsychologists whom you distinguished and the medical men at Lourdes, who approached the special phenomena they were investigating there in apparently different ways. It's a striking feature of our culture that people who differ as totally as this in their general understanding of our world, can nevertheless cooperate in detail in scientific and other investigations, and I take it, in the case of Lourdes, one would express this by saying they disagree deeply on the question of whether or not there is—excuse the expression—a supernatural factor. All of them operate with a distinction between the supernatural and the natural, and they merely disagree as to whether the supernatural *exists* or not, so they can agree totally about what the natural is like, and this is why they can combine medically. Now I've always thought, myself, that one of the major interests of parapsychology is the fact that this neat separation of the natural and the supernatural is constantly being challenged by the things which parapsychologists discover. Now, am I right in thinking that in your view the two groups of parapsychologists that you distinguish, differ in the following way: that one group wishes to treat the investigations of parapsychology as uncovering wider and deeper understandings of the natural, but does not wish to accept the suggestion that these understandings point to anything beyond the natural, but the other group insists that they point beyond the natural; and that you associate yourself with the latter view? If that is correct, I'm extremely interested in your concluding remarks, which suggest not only that the investigation of parapsychological phenomena will continue to be rigorously scientific, but also that there can be no conclusive philosophical demonstration of what I might loosely call the supernatural implications of them. have I summarized your view correctly?

SERVADIO: Yes, you have. What I tried to express was an apprehension. That is, whereas I am quite prepared to perform an experiment with a person whose ideas I know to be materialistic, as I am not a materialist, I fear that if I, as a non-materialist, should plan, for instance, to demonstrate that telepathy could be indicative of a collective unconscious, an experienced materialistic parapsychologist would say, "I am not prepared to perform such an experiment because the aim you have in mind, or the idea or the frame of reference you have in mind is unscientific, so I cannot agree to collaborate with you in such an experiment." This is my apprehension.

STANFORD: It's easy for me, thinking at one level, to see how a transcendentalist view (to use a very general term) allows us to feel comfortable with the concept of knowledge outside of the reach of the senses, and that immediately makes us comfortable also when we hear about psychics who seem to have experienced a so-called mystical, transcendental experience such as apparently Mrs. Garrett had, but this kind of view is one I want to ask some questions about. One is, we see plenty of instances of psi interchange in which there doesn't seem to exist in the person experiencing the psi interchange any of this mystical or transcendental world view, and I wonder how that accords with the viewpoint that there is such a transcendental reality that underlies these phenomena. The second and, I think, closely related point is this: if you adopt that viewpoint, I'm wondering where that would take us in our research. It can, I admit, make us feel comfortable about the phenomena, but where does it take us? How does it lead us beyond our present position in research? Does it have payoffs in terms of what we're going to do tomorrow when we go back into the laboratory?

SERVADIO: As I've tried to show in my paper, descriptions of mystics in the East or the West or even some mediums from totally different cultures, seem to have many things in common, so while I don't say this is a proof that what they say corresponds to this transcendental view of reality, it certainly strikes one as significant, as meaningful. It's not by chance that something that Milarepa said a few centuries ago corresponds to what a European seer or perhaps Mrs. Garrett could have said during one of her trances. This is the first point. The second point I tried to maintain in a communication to the Edinburgh Parapsychological Association Convention was that perhaps certain difficulties between researchers and parapsychologists in our parapsychological research could be reduced; it can be meditation, it can be trying to know our depths a little more, and, of course, we have means that are known to everybody such as the value of psychoanalysis and things like that. But there are also other techniques, you have mentioned at least three or four of them, and I really think that this kind of descent into ourselves, as Sir John Woodroffe suggested many years ago, would be instrumental in making our work a little easier.

FRENCH: Currently philosophers of the physical sciences don't generally think of themselves as telling scientists how to proceed or what assumptions they are to make, but as explicating or analyzing what is done by those scientists. You leave me with the impression that philosophers of parapsychology ought to take a more direct role in setting the bounds, shall we say, of assumption in methodology for the discipline.

SERVADIO: I'm not of the opinion that any scientist should imagine himself as a good microscope or something that cannot be discussed. I think that every scientist would do well to examine himself a little bit. We know that the history of science is full of cases in which scientists made "mistakes," gave a push to some experiment to make it work out, or have behaved in the scientific field they were working in, in a way which indicated that they certainly had something in their inner structure that was not functioning as it should have been. Now, if this is true in general, I think that it is even more true in our particular field, where we face very subtle and delicate interpersonal relations, such as observations of Gertrude Schmeidler about "sheep" and "goats," and the importance of participation of the observer in the observed field.

ROLL: I think one of the ways our field is unique and distinct from other sciences, is that our primary instruments are ourselves, and I suspect that we're really going to be moving when we regard ourselves as subjects for investigations along with our so-called subjects. In connection with another point you made, I wonder what you think about Dr. LeShan's discovery of the rather striking similarity between the statements of mystics and the statements by people who take the other route, who explore outwards, that is, contemporary physicists.

SERVADIO: It is said in Yoga that from a certain point onwards there is no more distinction between inner and outer reality. Now I have wondered if some physicist, perhaps unawares, has not found the same thing. I think that when Heisenberg, in 1926, found the principle of indeterminacy, that is, the presence of the observer as being part and parcel of the total field of things that we're observing and of the observer himself, he reached something that the seers of all the ages in India had reached two or three thousand years ago.

ANGOFF: With Dr. Servadio's paper, we have come to the end of the formal presentations of this conference. The proceedings will be published and the Foundation will keep this book in print indefinitely along with others in the series. The Foundation is grateful to all of you who have contributed to these meetings.

BENDER: I may be the senior member of this symposium, and without having been delegated by you, I feel that I want to express the warmest thanks for this excellent symposium to the Parapsychology Foundation—to its President, Mrs. Eileen Coly and her colleagues who have organized it. It was an interesting and encouraging symposium, and for the elder people, it was a wonderful opportunity to meet with younger ones and to establish a contact which might help to find new ways for parapsychology. In this moment, I remember that some weeks ago I received an invitation for a discussion in Paris on Gabriel Marcel's work which bore the title, "Presence Gabriel Marcel." And I would like to end this conference by naming it for the late founder and president of Parapsychology Foundation: "Presence Eileen Garrett."